D1086616

Cast Out

This series of publications on Africa, Latin America, Southeast Asia, and Global and Comparative Studies is designed to present significant research, translation, and opinion to area specialists and to a wide community of persons interested in world affairs. The editor seeks manuscripts of quality on any subject and can usually make a decision regarding publication within three months of receipt of the original work. Production methods generally permit a work to appear within one year of acceptance. The editor works closely with authors to produce a high-quality book. The series appears in a paperback format and is distributed worldwide. For more information, contact the executive editor at Ohio University Press, 19 Circle Drive, The Ridges, Athens, Ohio 45701.

Executive editor: Gillian Berchowitz
AREA CONSULTANTS
Africa: Diane M. Ciekawy
Latin America: Brad Jokisch, Patrick Barr-Melej, and Rafael Obregon
Southeast Asia: William H. Frederick

The Ohio University Research in International Studies series is published for the Center for International Studies by Ohio University Press. The views expressed in individual volumes are those of the authors and should not be considered to represent the policies or beliefs of the Center for International Studies, Ohio University Press, or Ohio University.

Cast Out

VAGRANCY AND HOMELESSNESS IN
GLOBAL AND HISTORICAL PERSPECTIVE

Edited by

A. L. Beier and Paul Ocobock

Ohio University Research in International Studies
Global and Comparative Studies Series No. 8
Ohio University Press
Athens

© 2008 by the
Center for International Studies
Ohio University
www.ohioswallow.com

All rights reserved

To obtain permission to quote, reprint, or otherwise reproduce or distribute material
from Ohio University Press publications, please contact our rights and permissions
department at (740) 593-1154 or (740) 593-4536 (fax).

18 17 16 15 14 13 12 11 10 09 08   5 4 3 2 1

Printed in the United States of America
The books in the Ohio University Research in International Studies Series are printed
on acid-free paper ⊗ ™

Library of Congress Cataloging-in-Publication Data
Cast out : vagrancy and homelessness in global and historical perspective / edited by
A. L. Beier and Paul Ocobock. — 1st ed.
    p. cm. — (Ohio University research in international studies. Global and comparative
studies series ; no. 8)
    Includes bibliographical references and index.
    ISBN 978-0-89680-262-9 (pbk. : alk. paper)
    1. Homelessness. 2. Vagrancy. 3. Poverty. I. Beier, A. L. II. Ocobock, Paul R. (Paul
Robert), 1980–
    HV4480.C37 2008
    362.5—dc22
                                                                        2008027559

Contents

Acknowledgments

First and foremost we thank the History Department at Princeton University for hosting the conference from which many of these papers were drawn. The conference was generously funded by the History Department as well as the Shelby Cullom Davis Center for Historical Studies and the Princeton Institute for International and Regional Studies. For their support in meeting royalty costs for the book's cover, we thank the Department of History and the College of Arts and Sciences of Illinois State University and Ohio University Press. We also extend our gratitude to the contributors of this volume, who have been a pleasure to work with and have brought so many intriguing studies into a shared and sustained conversation. Finally, thanks to Gillian Berchowitz and the editors of Ohio University Press for their constant patience and help.

Introduction

Vagrancy and Homelessness in Global and Historical Perspective

Paul Ocobock

VAGRANTS, VAGABONDS, TRAMPS, beggars, bums, mendicants, idlers, indigents, itinerants, the underclass, and the homeless—all these names and legal categories seek to describe poor, unemployed, and highly mobile people—people who form the focal point of this collection of essays. Vagrancy laws are unique; while most crimes are defined by actions, vagrancy laws make no specific action or inaction illegal. Rather the laws are based on personal condition, state of being, and social and economic status.[1] Individuals merely need to exhibit the characteristics or stereotypes of vagrants for authorities to make an arrest.[2] Thus, vagrancy can mean and be many different things to many people, and therein lies its legal importance as a broad, overarching mechanism to control and punish a selective group of people.

Yet what are these qualities that arouse the suspicion of police and transform people into vagrants? Through history, those so labeled and arrested for vagrancy have often been poor, young, able-bodied, unemployed, rootless, and homeless.[3] Yet it has been the seeming voluntary unemployment and mobility of people for which vagrancy laws have been designed.[4] In general, the primary aim of vagrancy laws has been to establish control over idle individuals who could labor but choose not to and rootless, roofless persons seemingly unfettered by traditional domestic life and free to travel outside the surveillance of the state. Over time, particularly in the twentieth century, vagrancy became a catchall category favored for a "procedural laxity" that allowed the state to convict a "motley assortment of human troubles" and circumvent "the rigidity imposed by real or imagined defects in criminal law and procedure."[5] As the geography and heterogeneity of punishable social ills increased, more and more fell under the classification of vagrancy.

As a result, explaining what vagrancy means, who vagrants are, and why they attract the ire of the state, is fraught with difficulty. As this collection of essays attests, vagrants can be peasant farmers, literate ex-soldiers, famine victims, former slaves, beggars, political agitators, newsboys, migrant laborers, street people, squatters, and in some cases, those the state and the upper classes feared had breached social norms. Yet, the complicated nature of vagrancy and its connections to human labor, mobility, behavior, and status have made it a useful historical tool to scholars. Historians have used the concept of vagrancy to examine a vast array of processes, including the development and impact of the market economy, migration of labor, construction of modern states and imperial structures, formation of subcultures among the poor, rapidity of urbanization, and responses to poverty through charity, welfare, or prosecution. Since the 1960s, when the first historical work was conducted on vagrancy, the topic has remained divided by region and time period. Most histories of vagrancy have focused on European and American experiences from the medieval period to the twentieth century; after all vagrancy is a European invention. Even recent scholarship on vagrancy in Latin America, Africa, and the Middle East has focused on periods in which European notions of poverty and vagrancy law have been adopted through the imposition or influence of European law. In many ways, this collection of essays cannot escape the European experience. However, over half the chapters focus on regions outside Europe, and in each instance the authors seek to explore the ways in which vagrancy diverged from its European counterpart once introduced to the wider world. Furthermore, the collection attempts to bridge some of the geographic, temporal, and disciplinary divides that have discouraged a global history of vagrancy and homelessness. The purpose of juxtaposing these works is not to expose a uniformity of vagrancy's form and function among nations and across centuries, but rather to explore the development of vagrancy (or lack thereof) as a common response to managing poverty, labor, and social norms, and how this strategy changed over time and adapted to regional peculiarities.

The contributions in this collection straddle seven centuries, five continents, and several academic disciplines. They delve deeper into the struggle of societies to understand and alleviate chronic poverty, whether through private charity, criminalization, institutionalization, or compulsory labor. Some chapters illustrate the power of vagrancy laws as coercive engines in punishment and exploitation; others highlight the utter failure of vagrancy policies at the hands of human agency, state incapacity, and persistent personal charity. Several of the chapters envision vagrancy as a lifestyle, by choice and circumstance, in which people define themselves by both opposing and appropriating cultural norms. The authors offer fresh perspectives on old historiographical debates or new research in fields that have yet to fully investigate vagrancy and homelessness.

Poverty and Charity in a World without Vagrancy

Most histories of vagrancy set the stage in fourteenth-century England, as the Black Death ravaged the population, both rich and poor. Scholars have found this to be the most appropriate place to mark the origins of the term *vagrancy* and the laws that followed. However, poverty was not born amid the horror of the plague, and earlier societies had their own arrangements to cope with it. In some cases, the paths into poverty and responses to it did not take on the same form as they did in fourteenth-century England; in others they formed the precursors to Europe's religious charity and the struggle to determine those worthy of it.

The Greeks of the classical period made a distinction between a poor person (*penes*) and a beggar (*ptochos,* "one who crouches and cowers"). The poor were generally considered small landowners with just enough means to survive but who could not partake in the leisure of the city-state. In Rome, beggars, or the landless and wage earning, were described by Cicero as "'*dordem urbis et faecem*,' the poverty stricken scum of the city," who should be "drained off to the colonies."[6] Despite such colorful language, begging and destitution did not represent a serious social problem in the minds of Greek and Roman city leaders; the unemployed were merely lazy. The charity of the wealthy was given out of civic pride to their beloved cities or out of pity to their wealthy neighbors who had fallen on hard times. According to A. R. Hands, the truly poor had to seek salvation by their efforts, but options were few. They could obtain plots of land if they were willing to leave the city-states for the colonies or join the ranks of mercenary soldiers, as thousands did in the fourth century.[7]

In the late Roman Empire, the rise of the Christian church transformed these earlier notions of charity into concern for the well-being of the poor. Charity, or "love of the poor," by Christians and Jews, was a new departure from the classic Greek and Roman periods. This change in outlook occurred not only because of rapid demographic growth and increasing migration of the poor to cities, but because the leaders and the rank and file of the church made room for the poor in their lives. In the late Roman Empire, the church redefined the poor to include the very beggars and destitute the classical Greeks and Romans had excluded. The pity that was reserved for unfortunate citizens in Greece was refocused on the hungry, huddled masses standing outside city gates. Moreover, the poor were not associated, as they would one day be in early modern Europe, with bandits, rogues, and barbarians of the hinterland. It was the duty of the church to spend its wealth, through its representative, the bishop, on alleviating the suffering of the poor.[8] This compassion for the poor was bound to the belief that God was the supreme giver to those who believed, and likewise, that the rich man should emulate this relationship with his poorest neighbors. Over the course of the late Roman Empire, church leaders rose to prominence in their role of caretakers to the faithful as well as the poor, establishing a form of charity that would influence European society and politics for centuries to come.[9]

As in Christian and Jewish communities, religion played an integral role in poverty alleviation in the Muslim world. In the Middle East, Islamic and pre-Islamic Arab culture wove together to form an enduring tradition of private charity. Before and during the medieval Islamic period, gift giving by the wealthy to the poor was the primary means of poor relief and redistribution of wealth, as it was in many parts of sub-Saharan Africa.[10] Muslims had a religious and often legal duty to give alms to the poor. Muslim theologians stressed that poverty brought spirituality into closer focus. Dervishes among Sufi Muslims pushed this philosophy further by living in absolute poverty as a testament to their religious fervor.[11] Yet, not all poor were treated equally by the benevolence of the state and the wealthy. From the eleventh to the thirteenth centuries, immigration placed a strain on the elites of Middle Eastern towns, and foreign paupers were given the lowest priority on the scale of public charity. To be entitled to relief, foreigners had to seek out locals to vouch for them.[12] In both Mamluk Egypt and the early modern Ottoman Empire, private, personal charity existed side by side with some public forms of poor relief. Endowments made by elite Egyptians and Ottomans to promote their piety and prestige financed many institutions aimed at aiding the poor. Soup kitchens, medical facilities, and lodging were paid for through these endowments and were often built on the grounds of imperial palaces.[13] Some attempts were made to control public begging and urban migration, but these policies largely failed. Poor relief and the control of those who were known as vagrants in Europe remained part of public and private forms of charity in the Middle East.

Poverty in Africa before its colonization by Europe was fueled by a dearth of labor on a land-rich continent. Iliffe has argued that the African experience was the opposite of the process that took place in an overcrowded and enclosed English countryside. Kinship networks within and among families developed as a means to avoid labor shortages.[14] When areas grew overcrowded, access to land promoted outward migration and the establishment of new homesteads.[15] Of course, the African frontier was no boundless paradise. For those Africans who did fall into poverty, environmental factors such as drought and disease forced families into extreme poverty. African empires, states, and ethnic groups continually struggled with one another over resources, resulting in death, displacement, and the disintegration of families. Yet kinship networks and the availability of land often spared many impoverished Africans from the itinerancy and begging that their compatriots in Europe endured.

Labor, Poverty, and Vagrancy in Medieval and Early Modern Worlds

William Chambliss, one of the first social scientists to explore the historical origins of vagrancy laws, traced them back to fourteenth-century England, where the Black Death had decimated the supply of labor and increased demand and wages. As the landed elite refused to or could not meet the wage demands of their laborers, farmers fled the estates in search of work elsewhere. According to Chambliss, the 1349 law was an attempt to halt the mobility of laborers and force them to accept lower wages.[16] A year later, similar legislation was adopted in France.[17] In chapter 1 of this volume, A. L. Beier explores the role of vagrancy legislation and compulsory labor in managing the labor markets of medieval and early modern England. He argues that before 1500 vagrancy and labor regulations sought to control wages and meet labor demand in a market suffering from severe plague-induced shortages. After 1500, as the labor market shifted to one of surplus, the primary functions of vagrancy laws became labor discipline and social control. Thus vagrancy and labor laws were at the forefront of an early class struggle in England as civil and ecclesiastical authorities, merchants, and landowning elites were confronted with a growing number of mobile, unskilled, and unemployed poor.

Historians have compiled a long list of factors that played a role in the increasing concern about poverty in early modern Europe, including population growth, declining wages, rising costs of living, disease, famine, and military conflict. While poor migrants begged for survival, civil and ecclesiastic authorities worried about disorder and the subversive potential of the poor.[18] Returning soldiers were trained in violence, street performers attracted crowds, beggars spread disease, and hawkers infringed on guild regulations.[19] Humanists like J. L. Vives desired "a world of order, moderation, and piety" through education and hard work.[20] Europe's literati also had a hand in fostering a fear of the poor. Throughout the sixteenth and seventeenth centuries literature on vagrancy boomed in which authors described vagrants as a seething mass of criminals lurking beneath the social order, ready to thrust society into anarchy.[21] In chapter 2, Linda Woodbridge examines how returning soldiers-turned-vagrants were some of the most demonized figures in early modern literature. Yet some genres like theater were sympathetic to the plight of homeless ex-soldiers. Over time, these veteran vagabonds became literate, published work, and exposed the government's neglect and the injustice of their poverty. While vagrants and the poor were reviled and demonized in much of the popular press of the sixteenth and seventeenth centuries, Woodbridge reminds her audience that the poor, too, had a voice.

Demobilized soldiers filled the ranks of Europe's poor, but others shared in their poverty. Most people labeled as vagrants were single young men who traveled long distances alone or in small groups. Women, children, the elderly, and large families were only a small portion of those labeled as vagrants. This would remain a characteristic of vagrancy for centuries to come. For early modern England, Beier explains that demographic change had an influential impact on the number of youths in poverty. The majority of the population was under the age of twenty-one and young people were forced to leave home and seek employment when their families dissolved or they were cast out for bastardy, familial conflict, or extreme poverty.[22] Vagrants also traveled long distances. While there existed networks of regional and seasonal travel by which the traveling poor moved between local towns, festivals, and areas with employment opportunities, much of the movement of vagrants must be described as long-distance migration, often over a hundred miles.[23] Moreover, vagrancy was predominantly an urban phenomenon.[24] Cities in England and France strained to contain the massive influx of rural migrants who, when they arrived in the city, could find no work and no accommodation. Housing in early modern European towns was a precious commodity, and often the poor slept together in crammed, rented rooms in alehouses and other private lodgings.[25]

The rising levels of extreme poverty and migration began to strain preexisting forms of poor relief.[26] In medieval Europe, as in the late Roman Empire, poverty had been closely associated with Christian theology. The poor were a necessary part of social life and performed a significant role in the ability of the wealthy to perform good works and earn salvation.[27] Yet, the clergy and wealthy believed they could no longer manage the hundreds of people begging for charity, and over the course of the sixteenth century a dramatic shift occurred in the management of the poor. State authorities began to assume responsibility for poor relief, and vagrancy laws were adapted not simply to manipulate the labor market but to control the movement and behavior of the poor. Civil and religious authorities began categorizing the poor, distinguishing between the deserving and undeserving as well as local and foreign paupers. Orphans, widows, the physically and mentally disabled, and the aged qualified for state and ecclesiastical assistance; yet the able-bodied poor—vagrants, who allegedly chose idle lives—were given work or punishment. A whole new vocabulary of poverty was developed, as were a series of enhanced vagrancy laws and institutions to manage the behavior of unworthy paupers.

In England, sixteenth-century vagrancy acts and the Poor Law of 1601 had a profound impact on the state. The English judicial system underwent significant changes to meet the demands of arrest and removal of the poor. New methods of classifying criminals and vagrants as well as courtroom procedures such as trial by jury and oral testimony came into practice. Martial law was occasionally used to round up the idle and unemployed.[28] According to Beier, perhaps the most influential change came with the expansion of punishments for vagrancy and other crimes of poverty. Vagrants who refused work could be branded with a V, enslaved, and, in the most extreme cases, executed. However, the most common punishment was corporal punishment in combination with repatriation to one's parish, where relief was distributed or compulsory employment was found.[29] Other popular forms of punishment were impressment into military service and transportation to overseas colonies.

Some of the most dramatic forms of state intervention in the lives of the poor were the hospitals and bridewells that sprang up throughout Europe. In cities like Strasbourg, Basel, and Ypres new systems of poor relief outlawed begging, constructed hospitals to care for the worthy poor, and tried to correct the behavior of undeserving vagrants. In Lyon, the Aumône-Générale was developed in the 1530s to redistribute wealth to the deserving poor. House-to-house visits by officers were used to gather information on the poor, tickets were issued to the poor to control the length and amount of aid to be given, and deaths were recorded to ensure relief was discontinued. In 1553 the infamous Bridewell Hospital was created in London for the reform of beggars and vagrants through discipline and hard work. In the rest of Europe, institutions like the Dutch *Tuchthuis* and *Spunhuis*, French *dépôts de mendicité*, and German *Zuchthäuser* institutionalized the undeserving poor to punish their idleness and compel them to work while seeking to relieve the worthy indigent from their suffering.[30] In the midst of the Reformation and Counter-Reformation, the state and ecclesiastical authorities of Europe had reengineered poverty from a state of holiness and reverence to one of disease and disorder managed through a blend of charity and repression.

The Eighteenth Century and the Great Confinement

By the end of the seventeenth century, European efforts to relieve poverty and compel the idle to work still confronted large numbers of paupers; and economic crises, bad harvests, and warfare remained just a few of the principle drivers of impoverishment. Government officials and wealthy elites continued to panic, producing vivid accounts of wandering, criminal hordes terrorizing the respectable classes. It was believed that great bands of vagabonds pillaged the northern French countryside and that England was awash with Irish and Scottish indigents.[31] Vagrants became increasingly connected to organized crime and violence and were viewed by contemporary writers as a dangerous and subversive subculture thriving in the slums of Europe's cities.[32] In response, European states increasingly relied on institutionalization and incarceration. In France, the state sought new repressive means of controlling the poor such as urban police sweeps, mass arrests and convictions, expanded facilities to punish vagrants, and new schemes to prevent criminality.[33]

Two separate schemes were developed in France: *ateliers de charité* for the relief of the able-bodied poor willing to work and dépôts de mendicité for the incarceration and punishment of vagrants. The ancien régime understood that most vagrants were poor, migrating farmers searching for work. The ateliers de charité were designed to prevent this group from slipping into vagrancy and criminality by offering them employment partially paid by the state and inculcating in them a sense of labor discipline.[34] Those poor laborers who joined the schemes were organized into teams often made up of entire families, given supplies like shovels and wheelbarrows, and paid according to the amount work they did. By the time of the French Revolution, ateliers de charité were the preferred form of relief among poor rural laborers during winter months and temporarily unemployed industrial workers.[35] For vagrants and the intransigent idlers, dépôts de mendicité were developed in 1764 as places of internment, much like England's bridewells. According to Hufton, in 1773, 13,899 of the 71,760 vagrants placed in dépôts died while incarcerated. In the city of Vannes, the mortality rate of vagrants was 28 percent.[36]

Such horrific conditions led many, including Voltaire and Montesquieu, to decry the confinement of the poor and to call for employment opportunities, not prison cells, to be made available to all paupers.[37] In addition, the ability of the French state to arrest beggars and the poor living on the streets was severely constrained. In towns of five thousand inhabitants, the police numbered fewer than four, except in larger towns like Paris and Rouen.[38] Even the successful ateliers de charité could not eliminate extreme poverty in French cities and mass migration in the countryside.[39] Indeed other European countries were finding their experimentation with confinement difficult to maintain. In Spain the Bourbons worked to expand the power of the state and brought poor relief under greater state control by constructing workhouses known as *juntas de caridad*. Many Catholic clergy embraced the Bourbon reforms and opened their own workhouses, arguing that religious instruction could save the poor from the sin of vagrancy.[40] Yet financial shortcomings stunted the expansion of the policy, and the Bourbons were forced to ask the church for donations to keep workhouses operating. In addition, the Spanish public condemned the workhouses as prisons and undermined Bourbon efforts by continuing privately to give alms to beggars.[41] Around the same time and across the Mediterranean, Ottoman subjects also continued to rely on private, individual charity and the endowments of the imperial family and wealthy elites. Between handouts, hospitals, and soup kitchens, poor relief remained a personal experience between the beneficent elite and gracious poor. Ottoman officials took few actions against the begging and traveling poor except during periods of crisis.[42]

In England officials struggled with the desire to experiment with systematic incarceration and continued to rely on their unique brand of poor relief and wide-ranging vagrancy laws. The 1662 Settlement and Removal Act had determined that any visitors, traveling laborers, or beggars had to be returned to their home parishes. Once home, their parishes were required to punish or find labor for vagrants and provide relief for the truly needy. The act was decried as turning local communities into prisons and overburdening parishes with the financial and logistical costs of poor relief. As Sidney and Beatrice Webb have argued, English vagrancy laws and the Poor Law had transformed poor relief into a system of rewards by which bounty hunters, private contractors, and corrupt officials preyed on the innocent for personal enrichment. Moreover, the laws had been reduced to simply passing vagrants from parish to parish with local communities paying the bill.[43] In light of these abuses and failures, officials called for greater systematic incarceration to buttress the Poor Law and give added bite to vagrancy laws.

However, magistrates resisted these demands, and where the Webbs saw failure, other scholars have seen some success. Nicholas Rogers argues that magistrates witnessed firsthand a variety of poor persons passing through their courts and wanted to maintain their wide discretionary power. In their eyes, not every vagrant belonged in bridewells, and the passing system allowed the down-and-out to find some relief in the parishes.[44] However, this does not imply that vagrancy laws had lost their punitive and repressive nature. Vagrancy laws continued to compel laborers to work and prevent them from engaging in trades that threatened merchants and industrialists. Poor young men were swept up from the bridewells and city streets and impressed into military service. Commentators of the time argued that, though tyrannical, impressment kept the streets clear and transformed undesirable men into "the most industrious People, and even becoming the very nerves of our State."[45] Indeed some vagrants pressed into military service became part of the very apparatus seeking to repress them, and as the poor became the building blocks of nations, so too would they provide the foundations for empires. The expansion of European economic interests and overseas territories had profound implications for the uses of vagrancy laws and the indigenous peoples who would come to be known as vagabonds.

Vagrancy, Slavery, and Empire

In 1622, John Donne, dean of St. Paul's Cathedral, exalted the plantations of Virginia because they provided "Not only a spleen, to drain the ill humours of the body, but a liver to breed good blood; already the employment breeds mariners; already the place gives essays, nay freights of merchantable commodities; already it is a mark for the envy, and for the ambition of our enemies."[46] For Donne, the imperial frontier offered Europe a "safety-valve" to banish its poor and criminal and an opportunity to transform vagrants into productive building blocks of empire.[47]

England and Portugal developed some of the earliest and most systematized schemes for transporting vagrants abroad. In Portugal criminals, vagrants, orphans, and women of ill repute were rounded up, sentenced to exile, and transported to colonies like Brazil and Goa. Their destinations were determined by which colonies suffered from shortages of labor. Known as *degradados*, many went on to play pivotal roles in their adopted colonies. Thieves became soldiers, prostitutes became wives, and orphans became apprenticed artisans.[48] In the reign of James I, English adult and child vagrants were shipped to the struggling colony of Virginia. Young people were a particular target for transportation—ideal recruits for businesspersons and government alike. The Virginia Company, in desperate need of labor, encouraged the recruitment and forced transport of young people. With slavery years from taking root, young people were well suited for apprenticeship and indentured servitude. Planters and artisans gained an abundant source of laborers, whose transportation would be paid for by the government and to whom they had no contractual obligation. And the government had a seemingly endless pit into which it could pour those overcrowding its jails and houses of correction.[49] Aldermen were instructed to round up street children and orphans, recruit willing youths, and convince poor parents to give up their children. Beginning in 1619, seventy-five vagrant boys and twenty-four "wenches" were rounded up, collected at Bridewell Hospital, and sent to Virginia. In the following year the Virginia Company requested several more groups of vagrant youths.[50] Throughout the eighteenth century, 18 percent of emigrants across the Atlantic were between the ages of fifteen and nineteen and a further 11 percent under fifteen.[51] Most children were handed over to merchants and ship commanders and taken to the Caribbean, to islands like Jamaica and Barbados, while some were passed along to artisans or sugar growers.[52]

Not all European vagrants living overseas were considered productive or desirable, and vagrancy laws were established in the colonies to expel or control the growing numbers of failed entrepreneurs and adventurers who had found little fortune in the frontier. According to Sabine MacCormick, Spanish vagrants in Peru represented a wholly different problem than those in Spain. Spanish colonists complained that Spanish vagrants harassed and menaced Indian communities, but because of their Spanish heritage little could be done to stop them. Instead, charity had to be forthcoming in the form of free housing and food.[53] In the British Empire, vagrancy laws were quickly employed to rid port cities of drunken, idle, disorderly Europeans. In cities like Calcutta and Zanzibar, European vagrants were an affront to colonial sensibilities and a public display of European weakness that had to remain hidden.[54] Administrators also feared that vagrant Europeans aggravated local communities and fomented conflict, or that their idleness influenced groups whose labor was increasingly vital to the maintenance of empire.

The role of vagrancy in Europe's overseas territories was not limited to transporting and deporting European paupers; the laws were also used to shape the labor discipline and social order of indigenous communities. As miners in Peru and South Africa as well as farmers in Brazil and Kenya required more access to labor than the free market could provide, a whole host of laws, of which one was vagrancy, was used to control laborers who demanded higher wages, migrated to other areas, or chose not to exchange their labor for wages. Relying on free labor was especially perilous in slave economies increasingly under attack from abolitionists. As emancipation came to areas of Africa, the Indian Ocean, and Latin America, landowners and authorities feared economic collapse when free persons fled their former masters. Vagrancy laws were deployed in Cape Colony in the early nineteenth century as well as in Sudan, northern Nigeria, and francophone West Africa in the early twentieth century for precisely this reason. In each instance, vagrancy laws forced any non-Europeans deemed wandering or idle by authorities to labor on private companies or government projects.[55] In Cape Colony, the proposed Vagrancy Act of 1834 faced vociferous opposition from the Anti-Slavery Society as well as the African population, which mobilized to prevent the measure from being passed. In chapter 5, Richard Allen explores the ways in which colonial Mauritius typifies how vagrancy maintained imbalanced labor relations and how laboring communities resisted colonial authority during slavery's slow death.

Vagrancy laws also had a role in colonies where no slave economies existed but where rich natural resources like silver, diamonds, and fertile soils were found. In early colonial Peru the conquest of the Incan state, the collapse of its redistributive economy, and large-scale death from disease created levels of poverty and dislocation unparalleled to that seen in Europe at the time.[56] The establishment of silver mines at Potosí in the mid-sixteenth century drove the Spanish to compel indigenous communities to work at the mines. However, Incans quickly used migration, especially urban migration, to escape the dangerous work at Potosí and to seek more lucrative opportunities.

These migrants, known as *forasteros*, became in some ways the Peruvian equivalent of European vagrants. Throughout the seventeenth century colonial authorities tried in vain to eliminate forasteros by moving families into prefabricated settlements known as *reducciones*.[57] Several centuries later, as Andrew Burton and Paul Ocobock argue in chapter 10, British officials tried to mobilize African labor in similar ways. The authors examine the alienation of some African communities in Kenya from their land to make way for European settlement and the use of vagrancy to deflect Africans from migrating to towns and compel them to work on European agricultural estates and government projects.[58] In colonies like Peru and Kenya, among others, the need for vagrancy arose when Europeans, making new homes for themselves, contributed to the dislocation and homelessness of indigenous communities.

As Europeans built their estates, expanded their marketplaces, and planned their public squares, indigenous communities were left homeless and were pushed into the peripheries of urban and commercial life. The literature on vagrancy in imperial settings has, in general, focused on urban spaces, where anxious colonizers came into closest contact with poverty and marginalization. In the small, isolated communities of colonial New England, fear of the moral hazards of strangers and the burden of poor relief led many communities to banish the traveling poor. While the ever-expanding western frontier of eighteenth-century America offered the poor a property outlet, the eighteenth century also witnessed a rise in the number of poor due to the French-Indian War and King Philip's War, continual conflict with Native Americans, and destitution of former indentured servants.[59] In response, settlements and towns turned to English vagrancy laws to keep the poor from overwhelming community resources.

In larger communities and in more developed and racially diverse colonies, urban spaces acquired deep social hierarchies. In colonial Mexico City, Gabriel Haslip-Viera has argued that crime and punishment under eighteenth-century Bourbon rule were made to serve the social hierarchy of colonial society. Arrest, incarceration, and institutionalization controlled the unemployed, rooted them in their poverty, and preserved the social boundaries between the elite, middling class, and poor.[60] Other colonial historians such as Silvia Arrom have argued that policies of incarceration and reform in Mexico City did little to discipline the poor or alleviate their suffering. The city's poorhouse aimed to round up the idle, poor, and disorderly from the streets; yet, the state was unable to effectively differentiate between *vago y viciosos*—able-bodied vagrants capable of work—and beggars worthy of charity.[61] Over time, confusion over policy, state incapacity to sort accurately the increasing numbers of urban poor, and financial constraints transformed the poorhouse from a mechanism of social and racial order into a place of safety for Hispanic women and children. The poorhouse of Mexico City was certainly no Foucauldian "total regime."[62]

In the cities of colonial Africa, especially those with a large European emigrant community, the element of race was more explicit. In colonies like Namibia and South Africa, scholars have shown that vagrancy laws were aimed at preserving segregation. European settlers held deep-seated anxieties over the uncontrolled migration and poverty of Africans, especially single, young men. Fears of "black peril" or the sexual abuse of white women at the hands of African men often underpinned the use of vagrancy-related roundups.[63] Vagrancy laws served as a "massive local anesthetic" to sedate the worst psychological and economic insecurities of European settlers.[64] Yet vagrancy was not solely designed to placate settler fears or buttress segregation; rather, colonial officials believed it was one of a few strategies to combat the breakdown of law and order. In chapter 10, Burton and Ocobock argue that in British East Africa, vagrancy laws were seen by the administration as one of the few means to curb African crime, ease urbanization, and maintain African social order. As the authors contend, vagrancy was a way officials could slow what they believed was the detribalization of African communities. "Tribes" were crucial to the structure of the colonial apparatus, and so colonial officials arrested and returned single young men and women to their rural areas and families in a vain attempt to secure traditional forms of discipline and values. Yet, like Arrom's characterization of Mexico City, the hopes of colonial officials in British East Africa were dashed by constant financial and logistical constraints.

As transformative as colonialism was in Africa, Asia, and Latin America, it was often hounded by profound incapacity. In a nod to the limits of colonial military, economic, and political might, the British designed their colonial administration, known as indirect rule, around fiscal conservatism, or empire on the cheap. In chapter 4, David Arnold illustrates the marginal role played by the East India Company, and later the British state, in the relief of poverty in colonial India. Arnold argues that poor relief following intense famines in eighteenth-century India remained in the hands of private Indian philanthropists. British colonial administrations in India were little concerned with the welfare of their most desperate subjects. While vagrancy laws could be cut from European legal texts and pasted into colonial legislation, their application often diverged dramatically in colonial contexts. While the maintenance of unequal labor relations and law and order remained the core characteristics of vagrancy laws, virulent racism, financial and logistical shortcomings, colonial notions of indigenous social structures, and genuine lack of interest in relieving the suffering of indigent subjects altered the nature of vagrancy in empires.

The limitations of the colonial enterprise and its ability to effectively dictate labor policy and social norms also had implications for societies that won hard-fought freedom from imperial powers. Thomas Holloway and Robert Gordon describe the struggle newly formed states endure with their colonial legacies. While Holloway and Gordon come from different disciplines—history and anthropology, respectively—they both examine how newly formed states relied on vagrancy laws left over from the colonial period to reinforce their grip on society. In chapter 6, Holloway, on nineteenth-century Rio de Janeiro, demonstrates the constant struggle of police and magistrates to meet the demands of an urban elite clamoring for clean streets, the expectations of the modern bureaucratic state, and the long traditions of Christian charity. In chapter 12, Gordon describes the ways in which an independent Papua New Guinea endures its colonial legacies. He discusses the government's constant threat of reviving that country's vagrancy laws and exposes the ineffectiveness of the postcolonial state. He argues that Papua New Guinea was plagued by a "ceremonial state"; one inherited from colonial rule and merely over-laid onto a series of social structures that competed with and para-sitized the power of the government. Ultimately, officials in Papua New Guinea had little actual authority and were equipped only with the means of appearing in control. The imperial legacy lingers on in many nations, some nearly a half-century old, and the use or threat of vagrancy laws have been discovered as useful tools by a new genera-tion of political leaders.

Tramp Armies, New Poor Laws, and Labor Colonies in the Nineteenth Century

As colonial administrations set about using vagrancy laws to control imperial subjects and newly independent states struggled with this heritage, the nineteenth and twentieth centuries brought significant changes to the nature of vagabondage and the use of vagrancy laws in Europe, the United States, and other regions of the globe. In the United States vagrancy laws in the colonial period have been por-trayed as a means for small, isolated communities to shield them-selves from the moral decay of the homeless and the burden of poor relief. The rhetoric of the evil vagrant lingered on well into the nine-teenth century. In 1839 the mayor of St. Louis stated that vagrancy laws were used to "lessen the intemperance evil amongst us."[65] Yet, authorities in St. Louis, like their counterparts in other rapidly devel-oping cities, had to curb their rhetoric. Rapidly urbanizing and in-dustrializing cities depended on the migration, labor, and investment of mobile Americans. In St. Louis vagrancy laws were altered to focus on suspicious persons rather than the unemployed and poor. Indeed, as the nineteenth century progressed vagrancy laws were directed at professional criminals and crimes against property and businesses. When the economy was booming, anyone who threatened the safety and pocketbooks of the city's entrepreneurs were harshly dealt with. Yet in times of economic hardship, the poor and idle were again rounded up.[66] In many ways the war against poverty and itinerancy in Ameri-can cities like St. Louis shared many characteristics with the rest of the world. War, economic crisis, and demographic change compelled authorities to oscillate between periods of repression and indifference. As levels of crime and unemployment soared in nineteenth-century American cities, punishments under vagrancy laws grew harsher. The literature on American homelessness in the nineteenth century, as Toby Higbie illustrates in chapter 9, provides some unique and remarkable insights into the lives of the poor and destitute. The end of the Civil War and the depression of 1873–79 created a massive population of demobilized soldiers and out-of-work laborers. In Pennsylvania, Massachusetts, and Illinois, two-thirds of vagrants were veterans.[67] This massive, dispossessed population of men became commonly known as tramps and hobos. Before the Civil War, a tramp had been a long, tiresome walk or journey.[68] As applied to a person, *tramp* was certainly an accurate term, as American vagrants covered more ground in the search for employment than most of their global counterparts. The major expansion of transportation systems such as railroads and canals in the nineteenth century opened up the American West. American laborers could now travel across great swaths of the countryside in search of work, and levels of urban crowding and vagrancy arrests soared. Between 1874 and 1878 vagrancy arrests in New York City grew by 50 percent and overnight lodging in Philadelphia police stations increased fourfold. The railroads dispersed the unemployed and poor to areas that until the 1870s had little experience with poor relief. Throughout the period, farmers, local townsmen, and the police battled bands of vagrants in Pennsylvania cities like Harrisburg, Altoona, and Fulton.[69]

As the freedom of labor increased, so too did the number of those ready to exploit it. Although the railroads and unparalleled itinerancy made vagrancy a national obsession, vagrants also provided entrepreneurs in the frontier with a cheap supply of labor. As Monkkonen argues, a "symbiotic relationship" between cities and railroads developed. Railroads delivered laborers to the cities of the American West, where employers could find labor for their farms and businesses. The police aided employers by housing tramps during the working seasons and arresting them for vagrancy in the off-season to placate the fears of local townsfolk.[70] Cities like Omaha, Minneapolis, and San

Francisco were known as main stems, where migrant workers, fresh off the train, could socialize with their fellow travelers, find cheap food and housing, learn about possible employment opportunities, and find further transport. By World War I, San Francisco was housing forty thousand tramps at night, and Chicago was known to have housed even more.[71] By taking advantage of new forms of transportation and urban hubs, the vagrants of the nineteenth century crisscrossed the American landscape from New York to Chicago to Omaha to San Francisco, some even traveling as far as Europe and the Philippines.[72]

Who made up these incredibly mobile tramp armies, as they were known by contemporaries? The literature is surprisingly detailed. The majority of these traveling laborers were, like most of those charged with vagrancy, single young men. According to John C. Schneider, they ranged between the ages of twenty and forty, were unmarried, mostly of European descent, and between 22 and 55 percent were born outside the United States, mainly in Britain and Canada.[73] Tramp life was a distinctively white, male, and often homoerotic realm. Tramps were not generally welcoming of female and African American wanderers. Women represented a radical departure from hobo social norms, which were, in turn, opposed to domestic life and the influence of women in the household. To tramps, females were vagrants and criminals, an abomination of true hobo life.[74] As much as male tramps despised their female counterparts, mainstream society did not take kindly to wandering women either. Female vagrants represented the breakdown of the traditional household and loosening of sexual mores. These women were seen as unredeemable and left to ride the rails on their own terms. However, young single females arriving in cities looking for work and housing were considered salvageable as long as they quickly found a partner, married, and started a family.[75]

In addition to the gendered nature of vagrancy in the United States, there existed a racial element as well. In Virginia, vagrancy was primarily used to control disorderly former servants trying to purchase land. During the antebellum period vagrancy was brought to bear on returning runaway slaves to their masters.[76] In the postbellum South, the Black Codes and vagrancy laws were used to force freed slaves into contracts, as had been done in other slave economies transitioning to the free labor market. Yet, Amy Dru Stanley argues that throughout the 1860s and 1870s these increasingly harsh laws were part of a broader concern among Americans that begging and vagrancy were eroding free labor. Scientific philanthropists railed against indiscriminate almsgiving, arguing that it created a system of dependency and doomed the free labor market.[77] By criminalizing vagrancy and begging, placing the poor in workhouses, and putting them to hard and unpleasant work charity reformers believed they could inculcate a desire to work for pay under contract. According to Dru Stanley, "the vagrancy laws held beggars strictly to the rule of exchange, transforming charity into a punitive bargain."[78]

As determined as some authorities may have been to discipline migrant laborers, the underclass of nineteenth-century America proved itself willing and able to resist such discipline from above. In 1877 a nationwide strike occurred for which tramps were blamed. During the strike over one hundred thousand workers walked off the job, effectively shutting down St. Louis, Chicago, and Pittsburgh.[79] As Higbie argues in chapter 9, the Industrial Workers of the World and other labor organizations drew heavily from tramp communities, and former hobos were some of the most prolific agitators for labor reforms. Higbie's chapter also illustrates how countless tramps put their travels to paper and had a hand in shaping public perception and a romantic, literary form of vagrancy. Yet, tramps were not simply a force of opposition against industry. As Vince DiGirolamo argues in chapter 8, the young newsboys of New York City, often viewed as juvenile vagrants, were part of complicated and reciprocal relationships with some of the most powerful companies in nineteenth-century America: the media. The relationship was by no means equal, but the newspapers and vagrant youths of New York and other cities sustained and reinforced one another.

In Europe and parts of the Middle East, the nineteenth century was a time for reflecting on past failures to "solve" the problem of poverty by undertaking serious reforms. The result, as Timothy Smith argues for late-nineteenth-century France, was a blending of assistance and repression more intrusive than the century before. In Britain authorities were certain that the Poor Law had become a dismal failure. The number of vagrants had increased after the Napoleonic Wars and the depression of 1815–20, and the parish relief system lacked uniformity and had reached unparalleled costs. In 1818 the total poor rate reached a height of £7,870,801 and the percentage of paupers peaked at 13.2.[80] The presumed failure of the Poor Law and vagrancy laws reinforced a growing concern with not only the destitute but underclass Britons more generally. Concern often turned to vigilantism. Mendicity societies, or perhaps more appropriately antivagrancy posses, took matters into their own hands, making civilian arrests and registering vagrants for the authorities.[81] In chapter 3, Beier's close reading of Henry Mayhew's work reveals a near obsession among English elites that vagrants and the underclass were connected to a dangerous criminal underworld. As illustrated by the writing of Mayhew, it was believed that the jargon spoken among the poor was in fact a common language used to facilitate crime. Beier argues that this language was by no means uniform to the entire poor population of London, but it provided a potent symbol of the troubling growth of poverty and crime in Britain. Concern whipped up by writers like Mayhew and the failure of the Poor Law and vagrancy laws sparked a series of Parliamentary inquiries into simplifying and reforming the vagrancy and settlement laws. In addition, the reform-minded Robert Peel became Home Secretary in 1822 and set about creating the Metropolitan Police Force and passing a new Vagrancy Act in 1824 and Poor Law in 1834.[82] One of the chief aims of the 1824 act was to reduce the cost of repatriation among parishes and criminalize sleeping out, effectively making homelessness an act of vagrancy.[83] Under the 1834 Poor Law, parishes were merged into unions to standardize relief among the "deserving" and casual wards were created to give vagrants temporary, overnight shelter. Casual wards were a response to the continued refusal of workhouse authorities of admitting vagrants and petty criminals. Designed as shelters, the wards quickly adopted a punitive structure. To deter sleeping out in the open, the wards would force vagrants who had used them overnight to spend their day laboring on government projects. Unsanitary conditions, hard labor, and abuse by authorities kept many homeless people out on the streets.[84]

In France the Napoleonic Wars and extreme rural poverty created a mass exodus of the poor from the countryside to French cities. According to Smith, what seemed like middle-class hysteria in the late nineteenth century was in fact a reality: the cities of France were awash in beggars, paupers, and desperate criminals. Between 1872 and 1911 the population in the Rhône increased by 246,000, mainly from rural migration from the Massif Central. Meanwhile, in Paris, between one third and one-half of all arrests fell under vagrancy laws.[85] The response of the administration was in many ways similar to those in the eighteenth century. Schemes for assistance were developed for the deserving poor, while vagrants and undesirable paupers were prosecuted. At the turn of the century, tens of thousands of people were removed from the assistance rolls because they were believed to be undeserving of poor relief. This national obsession with denying poor relief to vagrants stemmed from a new scientific vision of vagabondage. The behavior of the idle poor was increasingly seen as the result of a deviant psychology that could be passed down from generation to generation. It was part of popular urban degeneration theories that had gained currency throughout Europe at the time. Armed with social Darwinism, many scholarly writers came to believe that the urban poor were a danger to social order and weakened domestic households. It was in the street that young men and women met: "With bad companions, [they] find a delight in spectacles like that of a man being dragged to gaol or of a drunken quarrel, which can only degrade their character, and encounter nothing but what fosters and appeals to their animal nature."[86]

Writers like Charles Masterman believed the child of the city became as unnatural and uncontrollable as his environment. The urban lifestyle did not produce the modern man; rather "civilisation works its miracles, and civilised man is turned back almost into a savage."[87] And vagrants in fin-de-siècle France were treated as such. In 1902 alone, 9,978 vagrants were transported to colonial, overseas prisons. In addition, the Republicans borrowed the dépôts de mendicité from the ancien régime, and vagrants could be imprisoned for three to six months or placed under state surveillance for up to ten years.[88]

European states also turned to labor colonies in the nineteenth century. In 1818 the Netherlands began to experiment with labor colonies as a way of confining and disciplining vagrants. Other European countries, like Switzerland and Belgium, followed suit. Belgium developed a colony at Merxplas, where in 1928 six hundred men were employed in workshops with a further one hundred in farming. They were divided between the old and infirm, the young, and the immoral, including homosexuals and the mentally ill. All were to be incarcerated for three to seven years.[89] Perhaps the largest and most expansive labor colony of them all was Siberia, where tsarist and, later, Soviet authorities banished and incarcerated millions of paupers, undesirables, and political dissenters. In chapter 7, Andrew Gentes explores the development of laws against *brodiazhestvo*, vagabondage in Russia, and the extents to which the tsarist regime went to rid the streets of St. Petersburg and other cities of the idle poor. Gentes views Siberian exile and tsarist policies as modern, disciplinarian processes, much in the spirit of what Michel Foucault described in France.

Indeed the nineteenth century was a period of growing state intervention in the lives of the poor outside Europe. In the Middle East the Ottoman Empire and Egyptian state were experimenting with a greater state role in poor relief. Under the khedive in Cairo, a small bureaucracy began to depersonalize charity. Poor relief began to involve bureaucrats like police officers, poorhouse employees, and medical officers rather than private philanthropists. Over time the Dabitiyya, the central police station, became the space where those in need could ask for assistance and those deemed vagrants were brought for deportation.[90] According to Ferdan Ergut, following the fall of the Ottoman Empire and rise of constitutionalism under the Committee of Union and Progress in 1908, the Ottomans also began to experiment with an expanded state role in the lives of the poor. Following many of the reforms made in France, the Ottomans began to adopt a series of categories to weed out the deserving from the undeserving. Punishment for vagrants included exile to remote cities like Baghdad and corporal punishment.[91] In regions where begging and homelessness were once managed through private charity, the state ultimately assumed the mantle of poor relief.

World Wars and Welfare States in the Twentieth Century

The twentieth century, with its world wars and rise of welfare-oriented states, had a profound impact on the nature of vagrancy and homelessness.[92] In Europe and the United States governments and employers moved away from the compulsory labor of the idle and violent repression of the homeless. Instead they encouraged the development of a sedentary and permanent workforce and a blending of state and nonstate welfare schemes. After World War I, American industrialists promoted welfare capitalism as a means to control labor discipline. Pensions, vacations, insurance, loans, and stock options became part of a new system of disciplining labor.[93] Mechanization of industry also had an impact on the demand for unskilled labor. The combine alone disrupted the work of one hundred fifty thousand Great Plains harvesters, just as the automobile altered migration patterns and the state's ability to round up tramps. While the Great Depression sank millions of Americans into curbing destitution, sympathy for the down-and-out grew, and Roosevelt's Federal Transient Scheme aimed to link local, state, federal and nongovernmental services to provide shelter, health care, and food to the American people.[94] During World War II the draft and wartime economy radically reduced the unemployed population in Europe and the United States. After the war, the problem of returning soldiers slipping into vagrancy was addressed by legislation like the American G.I. Bill, which ensured most demobilized soldiers and their families received housing. Technical training, employment opportunities, and suburban life seemed to have killed the tramp.[95]

Perhaps more important were changing perceptions of the poor and personal freedoms. At the turn of the century, intellectuals like T. H. Green and Henry Sidgwick concluded that poverty was the root of vagrancy rather than a genetic predisposition to laziness.[96] Moreover, throughout the 1950s and 1960s, numerous cases before state and federal courts began to question the constitutionality of vagrancy laws.[97] In 1972 the issue reached the U.S. Supreme Court, in the case of *Papachristou v. City of Jacksonville*. One of the cases included in the suit involved the arrest of Margaret Papachristou and Betty Calloway (both white women) and Eugene Eddie Melton and Leonard Johnson (both black men), who were riding in Papachristou's car after having dinner at a diner owned by Johnson's family. According to police, the four were arrested when they pulled over on the side of the road outside a used-car lot, which had been burgled several times. All four of the occupants of the car were charged with vagrancy, specifically "prowling by auto." The other cases involved African American young men who were charged with vagrancy for loitering on the street and being suspected of thievery. In a 7-to-0 decision, the Supreme Court ruled that the Jacksonville Vagrancy Ordinance was too vague for citizens to understand what sorts of conduct were illegal. It also criminalized innocent behavior and invested too much power in the hands of authorities.[98] Vagrancy laws like the one employed by the city of Jacksonville were suddenly invalidated in the United States.

Yet not all states abandoned the notion that beggars and vagrants could be institutionalized and reformed. As Aminda Smith argues in chapter 11, the Communist regime in China tried unsuccessfully to reeducate beggars in the 1950s. What was meant as a strategy to transform petty criminals into dedicated, nation-building peasants often slipped into the realm of fantasy and farce. In many ways, the reeducation centers of Communist China were as unsuccessful as Europe's vagrancy laws in colonial Africa, policies that are still used by African states to this day.

Yet even as welfare programs expanded in the later half of the twentieth century, and focused on the eradication of poverty and reform of the idle poor, homelessness has not disappeared from the public view or imagination. Poverty has been increasingly ghettoized and hidden from view in urban centers, while the wealthy have retreated behind suburban, gated communities protected by private security firms. Signs of failure, those homeless who remain in public, are considered unredeemable and even resistant to poor relief. Yet, the last chapter of this volume makes a striking argument against views that vagrants and the homeless are resistant or even hostile to work discipline or "traditional" cultural norms. Abby Margolis's work on the homeless of Tokyo's Ueno Park vividly illustrates that sleeping out is a way of life, but not necessarily one in opposition to the world around it. Rather, the homeless of Ueno Park maintain and appropriate conventional Japanese social norms, even so far as to have their own prejudices against other homeless communities.

In 2005 33,227 people were arrested for vagrancy in the United States, representing only 0.2 percent of the over 14 million arrests made that year.[99] This figure underscores that while vagrancy laws, and even the term *vagrant*, have lost currency in the later decades of the twentieth century, the destitute continue to live on the street and scratch an existence out of charity and petty crime. Fear of the disorderly and criminal potential of the homeless persists, too, as does the effort by governments the world over to arrest, discipline, institutionalize, reeducate, or reform their most marginalized citizens. As long as there is, in some, a desperate need to escape poverty and willingness to wander, and, in others, a desire for safety and orderliness, there will be vagrancy laws and vagrants to prosecute.

Notes

Special thanks must be extended to Robert Tignor, whose support made possible the conference from which some of these papers were derived and who greatly improved this introduction. I also thank Kevin Dumouchelle, John-Paul Ghobrial, Jennifer Johnson, and Elena Schneider for their help and friendship. Finally, thanks to A. L. Beier, who agreed to help me with this project and has been a constant source of encouragement.
    1. Forrest W. Lacey, "Vagrancy and Other Crimes of Personal Condition," *Harvard Law Review* 66, no. 7 (1953): 1203–66.
    2. Gary V. Dubin and Richard B. Robinson, "The Vagrancy Concept Reconsidered: Problems and Abuses of Status Criminality," *New York University Law Review* 37 (January 1962): 111, 114.
    3. A. L. Beier, *Masterless Men: The Vagrancy Problem in England, 1560–1640* (London: Methuen, 1985), xxii.

4. Lacey, "Vagrancy," 1209.

5. Caleb Foote, "Vagrancy-Type Law and Its Administration," *University of Pennsylvania Law Review* 104, no. 5 (1956): 631, 649.

6. A. R. Hands, *Charities and Social Aid in Greece and Rome* (Ithaca, NY: Cornell University Press, 1968), 64.

7. Ibid., 63–64, 74–75.

8. Peter Brown, *Poverty and Leadership in the Later Roman Empire* (Hanover, NH: University Press of New England, 2002), 5–8, 10, 12–13, 26.

9. Ibid., 79, 87.

10. Michael Bonner, "Poverty and Charity in the Rise of Islam," in *Poverty and Charity in Middle Eastern Contexts*, ed. Michael Bonner, Mine Ener, and Amy Singer (Albany: SUNY Press, 2003), 25.

11. Adam Sabra, *Poverty and Charity in Medieval Islam* (Cambridge: Cambridge University Press, 2006), 22–27.

12. Mark Cohen, "The Foreign Jewish Poor in Medieval Egypt," in Bonner, Ener, and Singer, *Poverty and Charity*, 61, 64.

13. Sabra, *Poverty and Charity*, 69; Miri Shefer, "Charity and Hospitality: Hospitals in the Ottoman Empire in the Early Modern Period," in Bonner, Ener, and Singer, *Poverty and Charity*, 121, 126–27.

14. John Iliffe, *The African Poor* (Cambridge: Cambridge University Press, 1987), 5–7.

15. See Igor Kopytoff, *The African Frontier* (Bloomington: Indiana University Press, 1987).

16. William J. Chambliss, "A Sociological Analysis of the Law of Vagrancy," *Social Problems* 12, no. 1 (1965): 69.

17. Emanuel Chill, "Religion and Mendicity in Seventeenth-Century France," *International Review of Social History* 7 (1962): 400.

18. Beier, *Masterless Men*, 28; Robert Jutte, *Poverty and Deviance in Early Modern Europe* (Cambridge: Cambridge University Press, 1994), 27–30; John Pound, *Poverty and Vagrancy in Tudor England* (London: Longman, 1971), 4–8; Paul A. Slack, "Vagrants and Vagrancy in England, 1598–1664," *Economic History Review* 27, no. 3 (1974): 374; Natalie Zemon-Davis, *Society and Culture in Early Modern France: Eight Essays* (Stanford: Stanford University Press, 1975), 21–23, 26.

19. Slack, "Vagrants and Vagrancy," 104–5.

20. H. C. M. Michielse, "Policing the Poor: J. L. Vives and the Sixteenth-Century Origins of Modern Social Administration," *Social Service Review* 64 (March 1990): 2, 4, 8; Pound, *Poverty and Vagrancy*, 36; Zemon-Davis, *Society and Culture*, 28–29.

21. See Craig Dionne and Steve Mentz, eds., *Rogues and Early Modern English Culture* (Ann Arbor: University of Michigan Press, 2004); Linda

Woodbridge, *Vagrancy, Homelessness, and English Renaissance Literature* (Urbana: University of Illinois Press, 2001).

22. Beier, *Masterless Men*, 54.

23. Ibid., 10, 29–31, 38–39; Slack, "Vagrants and Vagrancy," 365–68.

24. See Jonathan Barry, ed., *The Tudor and Stuart Town: A Reader in English Urban History, 1530–1688* (London: Longman, 1990).

25. Jutte, *Poverty and Deviance*, 64–66. See also Peter Clark, *The English Alehouse: A Social History, 1200–1830* (London: Longman, 1983); Patricia Fumerton, "Not Home: Alehouses, Ballads, and the Vagrant Husband in Early Modern England," *Journal of Medieval and Early Modern Studies* 32, no. 3 (2002): 493–518.

26. For the management of poverty in late antiquity, see Peter Brown, *Poverty and Leadership in the Later Roman Empire* (Hanover, NH: University Press of New England, 2002); A. R. Hands, *Charities and Social Aid in Greece and Rome* (Ithaca, NY: Cornell University Press, 1968).

27. Beier, *Masterless Men*, 4; Jutte, *Poverty and Deviance*, 194–99. On charity see Brian Pullan, *Poverty and Charity: Europe, Italy and Venice, 1400–1700* (Brookfield, VT: Variorum, 1994). The seminal work on the redefinition of medieval concepts of poverty is Hans Baron, "Franciscan Poverty and Civic Wealth as Factors in the Rise of Humanistic Thought," *Speculum* 13, no. 3 (1938): 1–37.

28. Beier, *Masterless Men*, 152–53, 156 58.

29. Ibid., 158–64; C. S. L. Davies, "Slavery and Protector Somerset: The Vagrancy Act of 1547," *Economic History Review* 19, no. 3 (1966): 533 38; Pound, *Poverty and Vagrancy*, 39–41.

30. Chill, "Religion and Mendicity," 403; Jutte, *Poverty and Deviance*, 173–76; Zemon-Davis, *Society and Culture*, 39–41; A. L. Beier, "Foucault Redux?: The Role of Humanism, Protestantism, and an Urban Elite in Creating Bridewell, 1500–1560," in *Crime, Gender, and Sexuality in Criminal Prosecutions*, ed. Louis A. Knafla, Criminal Justice History 17 (London: Greenwood, 2002), 33–60; Pieter Spierenburg, *The Prison Experience: Disciplinary Institutions and Their Inmates in Early Modern Europe* (New Brunswick, NJ: Rutgers University Press, 1991).

31. Olwen Hufton, *The Poor of Eighteenth-Century France, 1750–1789* (Oxford: Clarendon, 1974), 124–25.

32. Olwen Hufton, "Begging, Vagrancy, Vagabondage and the Law: An Aspect of the Problem of Poverty in Eighteenth-Century France," *European Studies Review* 2, no. 2 (1972): 106–7. See also Hal Gladfelder, *Criminality and Narrative in Eighteenth-Century England: Beyond the Law* (Baltimore, MD: Johns Hopkins University Press, 2001).

33. See Robert M. Schwartz, *Policing the Poor in Eighteenth-Century France* (Chapel Hill: University of North Carolina Press, 1988); Stuart Woolf, *The Poor in Western Europe in the Eighteenth and Nineteenth Centuries* (London: Methuen, 1986).

34. William Olejniczak, "Working the Body of the Poor: The *Atelier de Charité* in Late Eighteenth-Century France," *Journal of Social History* 24, no. 1 (1990): 89–91; Hufton, *Poor of Eighteenth-Century France*, 18.

35. Olejniczak, "Body of the Poor," 96–98, 100; Hufton, *Poor of Eighteenth-Century France*, 126–27.

36. Hufton, *Poor of Eighteenth-Century France*, 225–37.

37. William J. Callahan, "The Problem of Confinement: An Aspect of Poor Relief in Eighteenth-Century Spain," *Hispanic American Historical Review* 51, no. 1 (1971): 24.

38. Hufton, "Begging, Vagrancy," 111, 113.

39. Hufton, *Poor of Eighteenth-Century France*, 193.

40. Callahan, "Confinement," 5–11.

41. Ibid., 13–14, 22.

42. Eyal Ginio, "Living on the Margins of Charity: Coping with Poverty in an Ottoman Provincial City," in Bonner, Ener, and Singer, *Poverty and Charity*, 170, 174.

43. Sidney Webb and Beatrice Webb, *English Local Government* (London: Longmans, 1927), ch. 6.

44. Nicholas Rogers, "Policing the Poor in Eighteenth-Century London: The Vagrancy Laws and Their Administration," *Histoire sociale* 24 (May 1991): 137.

45. See Philonauta, *The Sailor's Happiness* (London: n.p., 1751), 19–20, as quoted in Nicholas Rogers, "Vagrancy, Impressment and the Regulation of Labour in Eighteenth-Century Britain," *Slavery and Abolition* 15, no. 2 (1994): 108.

46. John Donne, "Sermon CLVI Preached to the Virginia Company," as quoted in *Children and Youth in America: A Documentary History*, vol. 1, *1600–1865*, ed. Robert H. Bremner (Cambridge, MA: Harvard University Press, 1970), 8.

47. Beier, *Masterless Men*, 150.

48. Timothy Coates, *Convicts and Orphans: Forced and State-Sponsored Colonizers in the Portuguese Empire, 1550–1755* (Stanford, CA: Stanford University Press, 2001), 78–79, 116.

49. Peter Wilson Coldham, *Emigrants in Chains: A Social History of Forced Emigration to the Americas, 1607–1776* (Phoenix Mill, Gloucestershire: Alan Sutton, 1992), 43.

50. Robert C. Johnson, "The Transportation of Vagrant Children from London to Virginia, 1618–1622," in *Early Stuart Studies,* ed. Howard S. Reinmuth Jr. (Minneapolis: University of Minnesota Press, 1970), 140, 146–47; see also Barry M. Coldrey, "'A Place to Which Idle Vagrants May Be Sent': The First Phase of Child Migration during the Seventeenth and Eighteenth Centuries," *Children and Society* 13, no. 1 (1999): 32–47.

51. Bernard Bailyn, *Voyagers to the West: A Passage in the Peopling of America on the Eve of the Revolution* (New York: Knopf, 1986), 128, 138.

52. See Peter Wilson Coldham, *Child Apprentices in America, from Christ's Hospital, London, 1617–1778* (Baltimore, MD: Genealogical Pub. Co., 1990).

53. Sabine McCormack, "Social Conscience and Social Practice: Poverty and Vagrancy in Spain and Early Colonial Peru," in *Home and Homelessness in the Medieval and Renaissance World,* ed. Nicholas Howe (Notre Dame, IN: University of Notre Dame Press, 2004), 99–100.

54. David Arnold, "European Orphans and Vagrants in India in the Nineteenth Century," *Journal of Imperial and Commonwealth History* 7, no. 2 (1979): 104–27. For Zanzibar, see ch. 10 of this volume.

55. For Cape Colony, see Elizabeth Elbourne, "Freedom at Issue: Vagrancy Legislation and the Meaning of Freedom in Britain and Cape Colony in 1799–1842," *Slavery and Abolition* 15, no. 2 (1994): 114–50; Robert Ross, "'Rather mental than physical': Emancipations and the Cape Economy," in *Breaking the Chains: Slavery and Its Legacy in the Nineteenth-Century Cape Colony,* ed. Nigel Worden and Clifton Crais (Johannesburg: Witwatersrand University Press, 1994), 145–68. For Sudan, see Ahmad Alawad Sikainga, *Slaves into Workers: Emancipation and Labor in Colonial Sudan* (Austin: University of Texas Press, 1996). For Northern Nigeria, see Paul Lovejoy and Jan Hogendorn, *Slow Death for Slavery: The Course of Abolition in Northern Nigeria* (Cambridge: Cambridge University Press, 1993), 84–87. For francophone West Africa and the use of vagrancy in a similar way, see Martin Klein, *Slavery and Colonial Rule in French West Africa* (Cambridge: Cambridge University Press, 1998).

56. McCormack, "Social Conscience," 108.

57. Ann M, Wrightman, *Indigenous Migration and Social Change* (Durham, NC: Duke University Press, 1990), 3–4, 12–13, 41, 48–50, 68.

58. East India Company officials also used labor and vagrancy laws to wrest control of the labor market from Smith's invisible hand in eighteenth-century Madras. See Ravi Ahuja, "The Origins of Colonial Labour Policy in Late Eighteenth-Century Madras," *International Review of Social History* 44, no. 2 (1999): 159–95.

59. Douglas Lamar Jones, "The Strolling Poor: Transiency in Eighteenth-Century Massachusetts," in *Walking to Work: Tramps in America, 1790–1935*, ed. Eric Monkkonen (Lincoln: University of Nebraska Press, 1984); Ken Kusmer, *Down and Out, On the Road: The Homeless in American History* (Oxford: Oxford University Press, 2006), 18; Jeffrey S. Adler, "A Historical Analysis of the Law of Vagrancy," *Criminology* 27, no. 2 (1989): 214.

60. Gabriel Haslip-Viera, *Crime and Punishment in Late Colonial Mexico City, 1692–1810* (Albuquerque: University of New Mexico Press, 1999), 77, 105–8, 128.

61. Silvia Marina Arrom, *Containing the Poor: The Mexico City Poor House, 1774–1875* (Durham, NC: Duke University Press, 2000), 21.

62. Ibid., 76, 86–87, 283–84.

63. See Jeremy Martens, "Polygamy, Sexual Danger and the Creation of Vagrancy Legislation in Colonial Natal," *Journal of Imperial and Commonwealth History* 31, no. 3 (2003): 24–45.

64. Robert J. Gordon, "Vagrancy, Law and 'Shadow Knowledge': Internal Pacification, 1915–1939," in *Namibia under South African Rule: Mobility and Containment, 1915–46*, ed. Patricia Hayes et al. (Oxford: James Currey, 1998).

65. Jeffrey S. Adler, "Vagging the Demons and Scoundrels: Vagrancy and the Growth of St. Louis, 1830–1861," *Journal of Urban History* 13, no. 1 (1986): 7.

667. Ibid., 9–11.

67. Kusmer, *Down and Out*, 37–39.

68. Todd DePastino, *Citizen Hobo: How a Century of Homelessness Shaped America* (Chicago: University of Chicago Press, 2005), 5.

69. Ibid., 42.

70. Monkkonen, *Walking to Work*, 9, 11.

71. DePastino, *Citizen Hobo*, 72.

72. See Frank Tobias Higbie, *Indispensable Outcasts: Hobo Workers and Community in the American Midwest, 1880–1930* (Urbana: University of Illinois Press, 2003).

73. John C. Schneider, "Tramping Workers, 1890–1920: A Sub-Cultural View," in Monkkonen, *Walking to Work*, 215–16.

74. Lynn Wener, "Sisters of the Road: Women Transients and Tramps," in Monkkonen, *Walking to Work*, 173.

75. Ibid., 171–72, 178.

76. Kusmer, *Down and Out*, 17, 68.

77. Amy Dru Stanley, *From Bondage to Contract: Wage Labor, Marriage, and the Market in the Age of Slave Emancipation* (Cambridge: Cambridge University Press, 1998), 99–100, 109–10.

78. Ibid., 134–35.

79. DePastino, *Citizen Hobo,* 23–24.

80. Webb and Webb, *English Local Government,* 1037–38.

81. Robert Humphries, *No Fixed Abode: A History of Responses to the Roofless and Rootless in Britain* (London: Macmillan, 1999), 18.

82. Lionel Rose, *Rogues and Vagabonds: Vagrant Underworld in Britain, 1815–1985* (London: Routledge, 1988), 2–3.

83. Ibid., 16–18; Robert Humphries, *No Fixed Abode: A History of Responses to the Roofless and Rootless in Britain* (London: Macmillan, 1999), 83.

84. Rose, *Rogues and Vagabonds,* 80, 104–5; Humphries. *No Fixed Abode,* 94.

85. Timothy Smith, "Assistance and Repression: Rural Exodus, Vagabondage and Social Crisis in France, 1880–1914," *Journal of Social History* 32, no. 4 (1999): 821–25.

86. Charles Masterman, *The Heart of the Empire: Discussions of Problems of Modern City Life in England* (London: T. Fisher Unwin, 1901; repr., New York: Barnes and Noble, 1973), 125.

87. Alex de Tocqueville, commenting on Manchester during a five week visit to Britain; quoted in Asa Briggs, *Victorian Cities* (London: Odhams Press, 1963), 68.

88. Smith, "Assistance and Repression," 826–27, 835–36.

89. John L. Gillin, "Vagrancy and Begging," *American Journal of Sociology* 35 (November 1929): 430–32. Labor colonies were also used in late-nineteenth-century Pernambuco, Brazil. Several labor colonies were conveniently situated next to large sugar estates; even schools for orphan and vagrant children were part of sugar production. The children's Escola Industrial Frei Caneca turned out five thousand kilograms of high-quality sugar each year as well as the facilities to produce rum. Martha K. Huggins, *From Slavery to Vagrancy: Crime and Social Control in the Third World* (New Brunswick, NJ: Rutgers University Press, 1985), 72, 75.

90. Mine Ener, "The Charity of the Khedive," in Bonner, Ener, and Singer, *Poverty and Charity,* 186, 189. For a more detailed discussion see, Ener, *Managing Egypt's Poor and the Politics of Benevolence, 1800–1952* (Princeton, NJ: Princeton University Press, 2003).

91. Ferdan Ergut, "Policing the Poor in the Late Ottoman Empire," *Middle Eastern Studies* 38, no. 2 (2002): 156–57, 162.

92. Humphries, *No Fixed Abode,* 137–38.

93. DePastino, *Citizen Hobo,* 183, Monkkonen, *Walking to Work,* 2–3.

94. Kusmer, *Down and Out,* 210–13.

95. DePastino, *Citizen Hobo,* 224.

96. Humphries, *No Fixed Abode,* 110–11.

97. For more detail on these cases and their influence, see Robin Yeamans, "Constitutional Attacks on Vagrancy Laws," *Stanford Law Review* 20, no. 4 (1968): 782–93.

98. For the Supreme Court's decision and Justice Douglas's opinion on the case see *Papachristou v. City of Jacksonville*, 405 U.S. 156 (1972); also see Robert C. Ellickson, "Controlling Chronic Misconduct in City Spaces: Of Panhandling, Skid Rows, and Public-Space Zoning," *Yale Law Journal* 105, no. 5 (1996): 1210–11.

99. Federal Bureau of Investigation, "Crime in the United States, 2005," table 29, http://www.fbi.gov/ucr/05cius/data/table_29.html.

1

"A New Serfdom"

Labor Laws, Vagrancy Statutes, and Labor Discipline in England, 1350-1800

A. L. Beier

> Rustics you were, and rustics you are.
> And in bondage you shall remain,
> not as of old, but incomparably harsher.
>
> —*Richard II to the men of Essex, at Waltham, June 1381*

AS MANY ESSAYS in this collection attest, the origins and objects of vagrancy legislation are complex, but arguably a central principle in most laws is the obligation to labor. Two of the five chief characteristics of alleged vagrants in early modern England—being able-bodied and out of work—assumed there was a duty to work.[1] Yet vagrancy laws were not the sole, nor the earliest, articulations of compulsory labor. In the fourteenth and fifteenth centuries, England's parliament passed labor laws requiring service at the same time that it sought to regulate vagrancy, and the two bodies of legislation continued to coexist and intersect in subsequent centuries. As Margaret Davies presciently observed, there was an "integral connection . . . between regulation of the service contract and the perpetual fear of the menace of vagrancy."[2] This chapter seeks to document that link through an overview of labor and vagrancy laws, through examples of their enforcement, and of resistance to the principle of compulsory labor.

Late medieval and early modern England evinced remarkable energy and continuity in the passing of legislation mandating obligatory work for those without independent means. English governments also demonstrated extraordinary creativity in devising institutions to enforce the will of Parliament in this arena. In the fourteenth and fifteenth centuries, like many European states hit by the Black Death, England passed labor laws requiring the able-bodied to work at regulated wages, including—for the first time—free laborers. And there is considerable evidence that these laws were enforced. After 1500, although demographic conditions improved, governments enacted numerous vagrancy acts as well as labor laws, the main thrust of which was still to compel people to engage in regular employment, which continued to be the law of the land into the nineteenth century. The early modern English authorities also deployed a host of institutions to police mobile and displaced labor, or "vagrants." These included parish officials, justices of the peace, the bridewell, the workhouse, domestic service, "service in husbandry," apprenticeship schemes, and (many involuntary) transfers to overseas colonies. It might seem paradoxical that England, the first country to espouse free-market economics and to industrialize, should contemporaneously be maintaining a system of unfree labor, but such was apparently the case into the nineteenth century.[3]

The persistence of these policies over several centuries raises questions about the motives behind them and prompts one to question the power of changing economic and demographic conditions in influencing those policies. One of the key historical discussions of recent times is the debate begun by Robert Brenner's attack on neo-Malthusian interpretations of the rise of capitalism in the West. In a nutshell, Brenner questioned whether demographic fluctuations and their economic and social effects should be assigned pride of place in causal explanations of capitalism. The neo-Malthusian view was that population growth and decline were the key variables. When the population rose, so did prices and farm profits, but with negative results for the incomes of the masses and for trade and industry. Contrariwise, when the population declined or was stagnant, prices and farm profits were lower, and the majority gained through higher real wages. Instead of this neo-Malthusian explanation of changes, Brenner proposed a Marxist one that emphasized class conflict.[4] I contend that Brenner was correct to question the determinative power of demographic forces in late medieval and early modern English social relations. Whether or not class conflict was the key remains open to discussion, but where labor policy was concerned there seems good reason to doubt the power of demographic changes. This is because the duty to labor was first devised in conditions of labor shortage but was maintained in legislation after that deficiency no longer held after 1500.[5]

Because of its relevance to these theoretical discussions, the subject of compulsory labor merits greater attention than it has hitherto received. In general, labor and its regulation have not been high on the agenda of recent generations of economic and social historians. Admittedly, in 1956 D. C. Coleman published a seminal paper on labor in the early modern economy, and there have been valuable recent studies of farm laborers, servants in husbandry, and the laboring poor. But, passing references aside, none of these studies paid much attention to state control of labor, and they hardly mentioned the subject of forced labor.[6] It was an earlier generation of historians who in the first half of the twentieth century took an interest in labor regulation; above all, B. H. Putnam, R. H. Tawney, and R. K. Kelsall.[7] But since the latter published a study of wage assessments in 1938, the subject has until recently largely languished. By comparison, studies of apprenticeship and indentured servitude in the colonies have seen somewhat greater progress.[8]

Forced labor can be considered in three parts: late medieval labor laws, sixteenth-century labor and vagrancy legislation, and the regulation of labor under the Old Poor Law from the sixteenth through the eighteenth centuries. The argument here is that, while the reasons for compulsory labor changed in the period, there was underlying continuity in government adherence to the principle. In the fourteenth and fifteenth centuries policies mainly sought to secure an adequate supply of cheap labor, while from the sixteenth through the eighteenth centuries the emphasis shifted to a concern with labor discipline. Before 1500 the policy was to force people to work and control their wages, because of severe, long-term labor shortages caused by recurrent epidemics of plague. But from the late fifteenth century the direction of policy shifted to broader, more varied policies aimed at enforcing compulsory labor, but also controlling labor's position in the social order. This was not only because the economic and demographic situation changed after 1500—from shortage to overabundance in the labor supply, from high wages to low, and from prosperity to hardship for laborers—but also because the authorities engaged in deeper analyses of vagrancy and concepts of social disorder. The result was that elements of a "command economy" persisted in regard to labor. The master-servant relationship continued to be important, including systems of hierarchy (those with means were not obliged to labor), forced labor, and ethical obligations involving mutual aid. Here in the midst of an increasingly mercantile economy was a labor system in which sellers and buyers were not "on a level." Why, John Hicks pungently queried, "should one be master and one servant? The master-servant relation does not fit."[9] In the circumstances, economic and demographic explanations are insufficient, and one must also consider the social and political concerns of those passing the legislation.

Late Medieval Labor Legislation

An attempt at centralized control of labor occurred in the second half of the fourteenth century, beginning with the Ordinance of Laborers (1349) and the Statute of Laborers (1351).[10] The action resulted, of course, from the shortage of labor following the first wave of the Black Death, but also involved a redefinition of the obligation to labor. In the process the legislation laid down new principles. The main provisions were, first, that work was compulsory for a large segment of the population; second, that conditions of service, particularly the length of contract, were regulated; third, that wage levels were to be controlled. The ordinance stipulated that all persons without independent means from land or a trade, whether male or female, unfree or free, and under sixty years old, could be compelled to work. Refusing was a crime and could result in imprisonment, which was also true for anyone leaving employment before the completion of a contract.[11] The Statute of 1351 specified that laborers were required to serve for a full year, not by the day.[12] As to wages, the ordinance required that they be set at the level of 1346 "or common years thereabouts," but the statute, complaining that laborers still were demanding double or treble the preplague levels, laid down specific rates of pay for different tasks.[13] Such provisions were reenacted and elaborated on over the next hundred years, resulting in eight separate sets of regulations from 1349 to 1445.[14]

The links with vagrancy legislation were sometimes explicit, for the new labor laws were also directed against able-bodied beggars. The Ordinance of 1349 stipulated that alms should be refused any beggar who was able to work, while the Statute of Laborers of 1351 prescribed "punishment and imprisonment of their bodies."[15] The Statute of Cambridge (1388) made able-bodied beggars liable to a spell in the stocks, and an act of 1445 directed that no one was to be excused service by the year "upon pain to be justified as a vagabond."[16] The Year Books included cases in which the link between vagabondage and compulsory labor was spelled out. An employer and plaintiff claimed the right to demand the labor of an alleged vagrant, who in turn asserted that he was already employed by the day. The judge ruled that the defendant should work his day and then be liable to serve the plaintiff by the year. In another case the plaintiff was a laborer, who claimed he was falsely imprisoned by an employer, who then riposted that the laborer was a vagrant, whose service he had demanded and put him in stocks as punishment. The laborer claimed that he possessed a house, two acres of land, goods, ten cows, and five sheep, worth in all £20, presumably arguing that he had sufficient wealth to be excused service.[17]

Sir William Holdsworth, the pioneering historian of English law, was ambivalent about the wider significance of this legislation. On the one hand he thought that it replaced the customary status of unfree labor with that of free contract labor. On the other he was aware that the relation of master and servant, while contractual in character, led, like marriage, to "a status of a peculiar kind." This was because contracts with free workers still included "such of the incidents of the status of villeinage as could be usefully adapted to the new situation" of the mid-fourteenth century. Holdsworth further discussed what many subsequent observers have missed—that the obligation to labor now applied to the free laborer lacking independent means of support. Henceforth the laborer had "a position of his own in society; and that position must be regulated by law for the good of the community. He must work, and he must work at reasonable rates."[18] What Holdsworth missed was that disputes over labor contracts predated the legislation of 1349 and 1351. Elaine Clark discovered cases in borough and manorial courts beginning in the 1250s in which breaches of covenant were alleged and adjudicated, including departures without master's agreement, expulsions by masters, and the procuring of labor by neighbors. These cases did not, it seems, involve refusals of compulsory service, but these offenses did increase dramatically from the 1360s.[19] Over the long term, Alan Harding found, the tendency in the law courts between the Statute of Winchester of 1285 and the commissions of the peace of 1380 was to create "a new serfdom."[20]

The late medieval and early modern laws covered a host of workers who without much question accounted for the single largest group in the labor force. In reality, there was a bewilderingly wide range of workers regulated by the laws, which ultimately included apprentices as well as servants and who can be lumped together under the rubric dependent workers, that is, persons who lived usually lived in with masters and mistresses and who received the bulk of their wage in kind in the form of room and board, pocket money, and even clothing. These dependent workers made up possibly as much as 40 percent of the population with occupations and statuses listed in seventeenth-century villages and between 50 and 66 percent of urban employees.[21] Yet the category of dependent worker masks a great variety of statuses and work lives. London apprentices, as is well known, could be sons of wealthy gentlemen, while domestic servants could come from backgrounds of great hardship. Frequently the documentation is too imprecise to identify who was who. The term *servant* included a huge variety of people, from domestics to "servants in husbandry." In the late medieval period *servant* was a broad label that covered masters' descriptions of apprentices, even parents' of their children, employees of corporate bodies such as boroughs, and anyone who contracted with someone to work for a stated time period.[22] More specifically, servants included anyone who covenanted to work in an "art," or trade, for a year. These included urban jobs as well as agricultural ones; servants in husbandry as well as in "huswifry" and the traditional apprentices to a craft.[23]

It is certain that living-in workers were significant in number in England since before the labor laws were passed. They were the famuli on demesne farms of the manorial system.[24] In the poll taxes of Richard II's reign at Kempsford, Gloucestershire, one visit by collectors listed 30 out of 118 taxpayers as servants, or 25 percent of the total. In a second visit to Kempsford another 39 servants were discovered, and it is thought they were underrepresented in these documents by as much as 50 to 100 percent. In East Anglia between 1380 and 1381 it was determined that 50 to 70 percent of males in villages were designated as either servants or laborers. Although the latter were not necessarily dependent workers and themselves were sometimes employers of labor, such high numbers suggest large numbers of servants under their supervision.[25] From the sixteenth to the nineteenth century the numbers continued to be significant. In censuses of one hundred English communities between 1574 and 1821 servants accounted for 13.4 percent of the total population. The share of households that included them was 28.5 percent.[26] Locally, they could account for a large share of the labor force. In the military census of 1522 in Exeter, of 308 listings of men's status or occupation, 217 (71 percent) were stated to be servants. Exeter may have had exceptionally high numbers of servants because of its large clerical establishment.[27] More representative of the numbers of servants in the countryside was the census for Gloucestershire in 1607, which found that servants made up 16.6 percent of the male working population aged between twenty and sixty.[28] But the numbers could go higher depending on the nature of the local economy. At Penshurst, in the pastoral Weald of Kent, around 1700, servants were just 7 percent of the occupations, whereas on the substantial arable holdings around Ash next Sandwich, in 1705 they accounted for 43.5 percent of occupations.[29] In the 1851 census for London, servants were the single largest occupational group, numbering in all 168,000, with laborers a distant second at 50,000.[30] There can be little doubt that servants were a significant part of the overall population and the workforce and that they remained so for a long time.

It is likely that the labor laws covered domestic servants as well as servants in husbandry and working in crafts. Breaches of contract remained numerous right down to 1875: between 1858 and 1875 there were ten thousand prosecutions of workers a year in England and Wales. Increasingly, however, violations of the compulsion to labor clauses came under the poor laws.[31] It is interesting to ponder the long-term consequences of such legislation. Did they create a culture of labor discipline that predated industrialization? Is it significant that clocks also first began in the fourteenth century to be put up in European churches and market towns? By the sixteenth it is thought most English parishes had erected a clock.[32] Or, rather than a cultural explanation, did the state's threat of the whip and the stocks constitute sufficient menaces, so that nonworkers over the centuries internalized the obligation to labor? How considerable were attempts at resistance to the laws, and how significant were they in fostering a disciplined workforce compared to market forces and the Protestant work ethic?

The late medieval labor laws were certainly an ambitious attempt at forced labor, but were they really enforced? Did they have any long-term effects? Answering these questions is complicated by the difficulty of disentangling secular demographic and economic changes from the impact of state action. Wages did not rise much between 1349 and 1375 and maintained their pre-1348 ratio to food prices,[33] but was this because the labor laws curbed increases? Or was there possibly a reserve supply of labor in the economy, which filled the gaps left by plague victims until further visitations hit in the 1360s and 1370s? Further, might residual social deference on the part of laborers toward lords and employers explain the slow reaction of wage levels to the new market conditions?[34] Yet there is good reason to think that the laws were effectively enforced and that they limited wage increases, at least in the short term. Reserves of labor and deference seem insufficient to explain the low wage levels that existed until the final quarter of the fourteenth century. With population losses of 30 to 40 percent during the initial epidemic, one might have expected a sharp rise in wages, which did not happen. In addition, if reserves of labor and deference were in evidence between 1349 and 1375, why was Parliament so strident about the aggressive resistance of workers on the issue of wages?[35]

There is little doubt that great efforts were made to implement the legislation. One authority observes that labor regulation was possibly "the most zealously enforced ordinance in medieval English history."[36] The effort lasted for over a century, and all aspects of the legislation were to some degree implemented. Over a third of the seventy-seven parliaments held between 1351 and 1430 passed labor laws, and further legislation was approved in the 1440s and 1490s. These were not simple reissues of previous statutes; they were "debated and modified"; parliaments also received significant numbers of petitions calling for the revision and enforcement of laws.[37] The most commonly prosecuted offenses involved the law on "excessive wages," which Christopher Dyer and Simon Penn estimate "was broken each year by hundreds of thousands of workers" in the 1350s.[38] But refusals to work were also significant, accounting for 12 percent of the labor presentments heard by justices of the peace between 1361 and 1396.[39] Justices were more reluctant to follow up allegations of breach of contract, because these were complicated and time consuming, but the numbers of such cases were not insignificant, with 299 known prosecutions between 1349 and 1359 alone.[40]

The unpopularity of the laws also suggests they had some impact. Even clerics voiced their doubts: in 1356 a hermit and a vicar in Hertfordshire were taken to court "for contemptuous public talk about the statute and ordinance: they claimed that no laws should stop artisans and laborers from earning as much as they could get."[41] Harding thinks that the ambiguous status in the legislation of clerics and of the "more substantial rebels" may have prompted them to join the resistance in 1381.[42] The populace, in particular, hated the legislation and the local justices who enforced it. The justices' activities are cited as "one of the most important causes of the revolts of 1381." It can be no coincidence that the rebellion was strongest in southeastern England, where the most thorough implementation of the labor laws had occurred.[43] When the rebels confronted Richard II at Mile End, one of their complaints was that they wanted contracts "freely agreed," which was very likely a negative reference to the compulsory labor clauses of the Statute of Laborers. His infamous response threatening them with worse conditions than traditional bondage provides the epigraph to this chapter.[44] The popular hatred of the legislation persisted beyond 1400 and cropped up in Cade's Rebellion of 1450, when the rebels castigated the Statute of Laborers, reenacted in 1445, for fixing maximum wages and limiting labor mobility.[45] The continued unpopularity of the laws probably reflected continued efforts to implement them after the 1350s, when, where records survive, "a few hundred offenders in each county" were prosecuted each year.[46] As late as the 1420s, in a Worcestershire justice of the peace's collection of precedents, one-fifth of the total (sixteen of seventy-eight) of documented offenses were against the Statute of Laborers. Putnam found that evidence of enforcement was abundant through the late fifteenth century.[47]

How innovative were late medieval English labor regulations? They certainly had precedents both in town and country. Urban authorities had imposed wage rates before 1349 and continued to do so afterward.[48] Some villages had bylaws that made harvest work compulsory, controlled migration during the harvest, and set wage rates for reapers.[49] It is tempting, given such precedents, to minimize the novelty of the labor laws, but that would be misleading. It is worth reiterating that this legislation attempted to regulate a type of person who was previously unfettered by restrictions on their work and movements—the free laborer. According to Putnam, before 1349 no court had placed restrictions on his freedom, whether in town or country, "or on his right to be an idle vagrant if he chose," as long as he did not break a contract.[50] Harding concluded that the labor laws constituted "a much more general social obligation than villeinage" because they gave landlords a "new public jurisdiction which allowed them to enforce service far more general than the obligations of villein tenure."

Ironically, one method of resistance was to claim villein status.[51] That Parliament sought to abridge the liberties of persons who were previously free goes a long way to explaining the widespread, persistent hostility to the laws and the frequent violations prosecuted in local courts. All in all, the argument that the labor laws constituted England's first national social policy is highly persuasive. These policies included "constructive" elements, such as an implied right to poor relief in the Statute of Cambridge of 1388, but also more coercive controls over dress and food, gaming, and potential conspiracies as well as labor. There was even possibly a new moral ethic in national legislation and local enforcement, which, in line with the laws, disapproved of idleness and treated offenders as vagrants.[52]

Early Modern Labor Laws

In the sixteenth and seventeenth centuries the labor laws continued in force and were actually further developed. But while the old rules continued, new labor legislation, often linked to vagrancy laws, was passed that shifted the emphasis from guaranteeing a labor supply to creating a more disciplined labor force. Ultimately these policies resulted in new institutions and programs, including the bridewell and the Tudor poor laws, which had the advantage over the medieval legislation of covering a larger population than just able-bodied laborers and of deploying a greater variety of devices to discipline labor.

The so-called Statute of Artificers of 1563 was the most thorough piece of legislation governing labor in early modern England. The full title of the law, An Act touching diverse orders for Artificers, Laborers, Servants of Husbandry, and Apprentices, while verbose, better describes its complex, sometimes contradictory, contents. The act codified labor regulations governing a host of workers, and many of its rules continued in force until the nineteenth century. It reaffirmed the principle of compulsory labor, establishing in clause 5 the obligation of all persons between the ages of twelve and sixty, with some exceptions, to work in agriculture by the year. In addition, clause 17 specified that females between twelve and forty could be directed to work by the year, week, or day. Clause 18 stipulated that qualified household-ers were to receive as apprentices in husbandry those between ten and eighteen, who were to serve to the age of twenty-one or twenty-four. More generally, clause 28 provided that justices were to compel the unemployed to be apprenticed to work in husbandry for anyone with the means to take them. Provisions were also passed governing work discipline that were similar to those laid down in 1495 and 1515.[53]

The compulsory service clauses of the Statute of Artificers contin-ued to be endorsed for two and a half centuries and were often directly linked to vagrancy law. In clause 8 anyone who left service without a testimonial letter from a previous employer was to be imprisoned for twenty-one days, after which, if no letter was forthcoming, he or she was to be whipped as a vagabond.[54] Legally, it became an established principle to associate labor violations with vagrancy, which is seen in both legal theories and in the handbooks written for justices of the peace. Sir Thomas Smith, a leading civil lawyer of the Elizabethan pe-riod, maintained that any person out of service, including both men and women, married and unmarried males, was compelled to serve a master or be punished as a vagrant. This litigation was one of the "chief charges" of justices of the peace, he wrote.[55] In the 1765 edition of his *Commentaries,* Blackstone repeated the age regulations of the Statute of Artificers, indicating that all persons in the relevant cate-gories, "not having visible livelihood, are compellable by two justices to go out to service, for the promotion of honest industry."[56] Michael Dalton's *The Countrey Justice* (1618), a handbook for justices that went through many editions, repeated the main provisions of the act of 1563, adding that a justice was empowered to "command vagrant per-sons to prison, if they will not serve."[57] Later manuals for justices similarly specified, right down to 1830, that the compulsory labor clauses of the 1563 act still pertained, and they indicated that vagrancy charges could be brought against offenders. In 1710 the anonymous author of a guidebook for justices, overseers of the poor, and church-wardens cited the 1563 act that servants leaving service early were to be prosecuted as vagrants. As late as 1823 White and Henson, while deeming many clauses of the act to be "obsolete," still maintained that someone without a testimonial was legally a vagrant.[58]

Vagrancy legislation of the early modern period also stipulated statutory, coerced labor. The infamous Slavery Act of 1547 provided that vagrants aged from age five to twelve could be apprenticed for terms of years—for males to age twenty-four and females to twenty—and that their masters could sell their labor.[59] This act was repealed in 1549, but similar provisions were passed in 1572 and remained in force for several centuries. The 1572 act mandated that the children of beggars aged from five to fourteen could be taken into service "by any subject of this realm of honest calling" until the age of twenty-four for males and eighteen for females.[60] Kussmaul treated the labor and vagrancy laws as distinct, but in practice they are difficult to separate. The Vagrancy Act of 1572 actually cited the Statute of Laborers as its authority for prosecuting children who fled masters and mistresses and those who might entice them to leave.[61] When prosecutions occurred, it is usually impossible to determine under which statute the charge was brought. In any case, the unemployed were also subject to vagrancy laws dating back to the fourteenth century.

Forced labor was certainly implemented in the early modern period. Instances in which the able-bodied unemployed were placed in service crop up in local records, particularly after the Act of 1572.[62] The usual procedure was for justices at quarter sessions to commit an offender to serve a gentleman or tradesman. Such cases, as well as refusals to take up work, particularly at harvest time, appear in local court records from the 1560s to the 1660s.[63] On occasion there were blanket refusals to work involving several offenders. After Ket's Rebellion was suppressed in Norwich in 1549, a number of young servants rejected their labor obligations.[64] At Devizes in 1559 the legal authority of the Statute of Laborers was invoked, and all day laborers of the borough were ordered to appear at the town cross to be hired from Michaelmas to Candlemas. Similar actions were ordered in the same period in Buckinghamshire, Caernarvonshire, and in the towns of Doncaster and Worcester. Buckinghamshire actually set up Governors of Laborers in every town, who were to require a year's service (as opposed to day labor) and to check mobility into crafts from agricultural trades. The governors were also supposed to force husbandmen and servants to wear only "mean clothes," which justices of the peace were to enforce by ensuring that tailors made no "fancy clothes" for laborers![65]

Similar complaints of refusals to work or the rejection of year-long contracts crop up at quarter sessions in the seventeenth century. Sometimes the accused even refused to take up harvest work. In 1610 three single males of Cayton in the North Riding of Yorkshire were presented to justices "for denying to work amongst their neighbors in harvest, and for departing forth of the liberty for greater wages."[66] In Wiltshire in 1612 the authorities at Tinhead complained that single men refused to work in husbandry, and there were many such complaints in the period.[67] In Hertfordshire in 1649 the inhabitants of Ashwell petitioned the bench about persons "of loose carriage, going of stout body and strong to labor, who have agreed not to work with the said inhabitants in harvest but upon excessive wages" and were also allegedly gleaning illegally.[68] Two Mountgrace men described as vagrants refused to work at all, it was reported to Thirsk Sessions in the North Riding in 1651.[69]

If people declined to labor, they were threatened with vagrancy charges; on some occasions convicted vagrants were given the option to take on work, which some did. At Exeter in 1560 George Webb, a runaway servant and alleged vagrant, was declared "content to serve," while two years later one Walter Capp, described as "pretending to the art of tooth-drawing and surgery" but having no dwelling place, agreed to "convenant" with a local barber for a year.[70] At Sussex Assizes in 1573 a number of convicted vagrants were placed in service as a penalty. William Calpstake, indicted as a vagrant rogue at Doncaster in 1577, was taken into service by a local man, "by which means he [Calpstake] escaped punishment."[71] There were many similar cases in the national search campaign for vagrants between 1569 and 1572, at Essex Quarter Sessions in the 1570s, and at Warwick in the 1580s.[72] We usually lack much detail about the circumstances of these offenders, but in 1657 a Rotherham master's report provides a little more than usual. John Jackson of Howell was accused of being "a lusty young man under the age of 30 years, able of body, [who] refused to work this harvest time, though he has nothing to maintain him but his labor and is lately departed from his master." No reason was given for Jackson's departure, and he was ordered to accept the wages ordered at Easter Sessions. If he refused, he was to be sent to a house of correction.[73]

Even though mandated by law, employers were not always willing to take on extra hands. This is certainly the impression gained from reactions to official efforts to "apprentice" the young along the lines stipulated by the Vagrancy Act of 1572. The Book of Orders of 1630, which attempted to energize the poor-law system, had as one of its objects the "binding out of apprentices, the setting to work of poor children," and over the next decade county justices proceeded to place people in service. At least 3,238 youngsters under age eighteen, two-thirds of them males, were found employment under this project in the 1630s.[74] But such programs enjoyed limited success. In James I's reign Hertfordshire assizes heard that fifteen hundred poor children were apprenticed but that most had left their masters and returned home to live in idleness. Similar complaints cropped up in response to Charles I's efforts. For example, Wiltshire authorities reported in 1633 that it was a "a troublesome and difficult business" because the wealthiest tradesmen resisted taking children whom they described as "untrusty and thievish and therefore dangerous for them to keep." Justices alleged that some pauper parents resisted parting with their children.[75]

Another form of labor control and discipline was the annual statutory assessment of wages established by the act of 1563, which required that yearly and daily wage rates be set "respecting the plenty or scarcity of the time." Anyone paying over the maximum was liable to ten days imprisonment and a fine of £5; those receiving the excess, twenty-one days in jail.[76] This procedure was widely followed from the 1560s to the early 1800s, yielding 1,452 assessments for England and Wales. The numbers increased steadily from the decade of the 1560s, when 35 survive, on to 67 in the 1620s, 97 in the 1650s, and anywhere between 70 and 93 per decade until the 1740s, when they tailed off sharply.[77] Although identical assessments were often reissued, actual rates of pay closely approximated the statutory ones in the sixteenth and seventeenth centuries. Of course, violations occurred, and sometimes they were prosecuted. But wage rates in farm accounts kept from 1614 to 1704 were very close to local assessments.[78]

As a form of labor coercion and discipline, the annual assessment of wages was partially successful, and here the neo-Malthusian model may have some validity. The policy was especially effective as long as labor was abundant and cheap, which was true for much of the period from 1500 to 1650. But once population growth slackened and then dipped in the later seventeenth century, officially assessed wages and those actually paid began to diverge.[79] The "statute sessions" that set wages and coerced labor into service and apprenticeship went into decline at the same time. "Hiring fairs" took their place in the eighteenth century, where masters and servants bargained openly, which both parties came to prefer, for a variety of reasons, to the old sessions.[80] The law increasingly confined the assessment process to agricultural workers on one-year contracts, continuing enclosure and displacement of owner-occupiers produced a sufficient supply of wage labor, and the new class of entrepreneurs opposed wage controls because they limited their freedom of action.[81]

It is striking, however, given demographic and economic conditions between 1500 and 1650, how considerable efforts were to enforce compulsory labor. Given the near doubling of the population—from 2.7 million in 1541 to 5.3 million in 1656—one might have expected labor control to be minimal.[82] There were, it is true, short-term shortages of workers after epidemics such as that of the late 1550s. But the long-term picture was quite different from the late Middle Ages, and after 1540 there were frequent complaints of the excess of population, rising levels of hardship for the poor, and conflicts over economic resources associated with expanding pastoral farming, the woolen industry and its exports. What changed and maintained a preoccupation with labor, however, was a rising concern about social disorder.

Tudor labor legislation was not limited in purpose to the coercion of labor; discipline was also the aim. The chronology of disciplinary efforts belies the impact of putative models of a Protestant work ethic. An act of Parliament of 1495 "for Servants' Wages," in revising the statute of 1445, restated the principles of compulsory labor but also struck a new chord concerning labor discipline. It complained that workers "retained to work and serve, waste much part of the day and deserve not their wages; some time in late coming unto their work;

early departing therefrom; long sitting at their breakfast, at their dinner and noon meat; and long time of sleeping at afternoon, to the loss and hurt of such persons as the said artificers and laborers be retained with in service."[83] The law's solution was that laborers would come to work by five in the morning between mid-March and mid-September; would have a half hour for breakfast and an hour and a half for midday dinner; and work until seven or eight at night. From September to March they would labor from sunrise to sunset; they were to be allowed naps only between mid-May and mid-August (presumably because daytime hours were at their longest). Laborers who were remiss would have the appropriate amount docked from their wages.[84] The same law required that no laborer was to quit employment until his work was actually finished. This concern with the work process and labor discipline was largely absent in previous legislation. The act of 1445, for example, stated that servants in husbandry who were completing their terms must give notice and "make covenant" with a new master, but it said nothing about their duties as such.[85]

That labor discipline had little to do with confessional issues is shown by a set of orders from the king and queen and from the Council of the North to Yorkshire justices of the peace in the reign of Mary I. In a wide-ranging document entitled "Certain Articles Devised by the Lord President and Council in the North Parts to be Put in Execution by the Justices of Peace," which was preoccupied with public order and included provisions about heresy and rebellions, a number of clauses focused on the compulsion to labor. Perhaps following the ancient Roman practice of censors, the first article in the document called for the appointment of "overseers" in every parish, who were to call before them all the inhabitants to determine "what every of them have to occupy for maintenance or supportation of themselves and their families, either in husbandry or craft, or by other labor or industry, and what provision they make for setting to work themselves, their wives, children and families." If the overseers found any man who "uses no trade whereby he may attain his living in truth or to set his wife, children and families to work," they were to provide the family with flax, hemp, or wool to work and "to see them occupied continually therein, or to put them to such other occupation or necessary labor as every of them shall best be apt to take and use." "Continual" application according to one's "aptness" sounds very modern. If any refused to follow this "gentle admonition," their names were to be given to the justices "to be used by imprisonment, whipping or otherwise by the laws and statutes appointed for idle and loddering [loitering] persons."[86] Although issued in the reign of the Catholic Mary, it is hard to see how a Protestant could have been more positive about a work ethic.

It should by now be apparent that sixteenth-century labor legislation sought not only to discipline laborers' work but also to control their position in the social order. The aim was to put a brake on geographical, occupational, and social mobility by keeping labor on the land and away from employment in the volatile cloth industry. The Statute of Artificers of 1563 mandated that a seven-year apprenticeship was required of all existing trades throughout England and Wales. This was an extension to the countryside of a rule previously limited to incorporated towns. Further, the law stated that urban masters could take as apprentices only those who were not employed in husbandry and were not the sons of laborers. In corporate towns their fathers had to be worth 40s. a year in landed income, or £3 a year in noncorporate towns, and no one was to be taught cloth making unless his father had £3 a year freehold income. Twenty-four occupations, many of them building trades, were excluded from these regulations. Here was a comprehensive attempt to impose occupational and social status on English society.[87]

Moreover, the foregoing social restrictions were modest in comparison with some that William Cecil proposed in 1559 and that were sent to Parliament for consideration. Cecil called for the revival of the Slavery Act of 1547, as well as the labor legislation of Richard II's reign. What is more, he even proposed to limit upward social mobility in the middling ranks of society, which is ironic considering Cecil's own modest beginnings. Except in towns, husbandmen, yeomen, and artificers were not allowed to purchase more than £5 worth of land. No merchant was to buy more than £50 worth of inheritance, with the exception of London aldermen and sheriffs, who could purchase £200. No one was permitted to become an apprentice unless his father had a 40s. freehold or to apprentice to a merchant unless his father had a £10 freehold. The inclusion of labor regulations along with so-cial controls clearly indicates the existence of a broader social agenda in the legislation of the 1560s.[88]

It would be misleading, of course, to conclude that these rules were comprehensively enforced. In reality, the system of yearly con-tracts, combined with adverse conditions for wage earning between 1500 and 1650, meant that labor mobility remained high and hard to control. Just the same, the seven-year term was widely enforced in rural England between 1563 and 1642, mainly through private prose-cutions, but whatever the agency the effect was the same. If the seven-year term was in effect, then it probably did have some impact on geographic, occupational, and social mobility.[89]

Labor Discipline under the Old Poor Law

Like the Tudor labor laws, the poor laws took medieval policies sev-eral steps further in respect of labor regulation. The English poor laws were a remarkably wide-ranging body of legislation, which covered children, adults, the unemployed, the disabled, the criminal poor or "vagabonds," and their relief, punishment, *and* employment. There is insufficient space here to explore the whole range of poor law provi-sions, but two subjects related to labor deserve examination: early modern provisions for forced labor; and how the system developed up to the eve of the New Poor Law of 1834.

Early modern governments devoted considerable energies to dis-ciplining the labor force. Their chief concern was with disorder, a problem they linked with the laboring classes, whom they saw as a "Many-Headed Monster."[90] The need for disciplining these groups was consistent with social conditions after 1500. Long-term unemploy-ment and long-distance subsistence migration were the byproducts of economic changes, and the authorities attempted to police the vic-tims through the poor laws. Unemployment among the able-bodied was identified with "idleness" and "sloth," and state poor relief was refused to such persons. Migrants without fixed abodes were liable to prosecution as vagrants.[91]

Legislation on vagrants and the poor sought to discipline labor in many different ways. The vagrancy laws specifically stated that certain occupations were illegal or were subject to various forms of licensing. They included peddlers, tinkers, soldiers, sailors, actors, musicians, itinerant healers, students, clerics, and magicians. In reality, however, the lower elements of the workforce—apprentices, servants, laborers, and journeymen—were also strongly represented among convicted vagabonds.[92] Forced labor continued to be the solution for the illegally employed and the "masterless." The most dramatic instances of this approach involved the employment of the poor in public works and prison workhouses. Many such plans concerned the criminal poor and how to make them better, more profitable citizens. The first such scheme was a plan of the 1530s to employ vagrants in constructing roads, harbors, and fortifications. It was never implemented, but the principle of "setting the poor on work" henceforth became a regular feature of English legislation concerning the poor. The idea reflected new theological positions on poverty, which criticized all kinds of voluntary destitution as well as humanists' belief in the possibility of reforming criminals.[93]

But the best-known experiment involving forced labor was Bridewell, founded in London in 1553 and thereafter widely replicated throughout England and overseas as the house of correction. Inmates, usually vagrants or prostitutes, received corporal punishment by whipping and imprisonment, but in addition significant numbers—about one hundred at any one time in London's case—were put to work beating hemp, making nails, and carding wool. After a statute mandated the creation of county houses of correction in 1576, their numbers proliferated. Between 1600 and 1630 one new county bridewell was founded, on average, every year; from 1630 to 1690 the rate was one every four years; and from 1690 to 1720, seventeen new foundations occurred.[94] These institutions took in a wide range of offenders, but significant numbers represented violations of labor regulations. In the Chelmsford house between 1620 and 1680, 52.4 percent of 846 inmates might be included under this rubric: 23.5 percent for vagrancy, 18.3 percent for "disorderly lives," 6.0 percent for being "masterless" and living out of service, and 4.6 percent for being a disorderly or runaway servant.[95] Judging by some later Gloucestershire evidence, bridewells continued to police the laboring classes for another century: between 1790 and 1810, 20 percent of cases involved breaches of contact of service; 15.8 percent, vagrancy; and 5 percent, offenses in woolen manufacturing.[96]

Bridewells were not the only institutions in which forced labor was the norm. From the early seventeenth century a movement developed to create special workhouses in which the able-bodied but noncriminal poor were employed. The thinking was that they would be removed from the deleterious atmosphere of houses of correction, which would also lighten the burden of poor rates on communities by helping support themselves and their families. Thus, too, young children might be protected from the evil influences they sometimes encountered at home. Entrance into such institutions was sometimes voluntary, sometimes not. The usual "choice" appears to have been to enter or to lose one's entitlement to relief.[97] The workhouse system became the law of the land in 1723, and thereafter hundreds were created: by 1732 perhaps seven hundred were in existence.[98]

The development of workhouses was a reflection of the long-established distinction, at the core of the labor and poor laws, between those able and unable to work. This legislation usually specified that the able-bodied were not to receive relief and were expected to labor. The principle extended beyond the creation of bridewells and workhouses. As one authority has observed, "the poor law was a system of employment as well as relief."[99] Under the Old Poor Law, parish officials used a variety of devices to get people to work rather than burden the parish. Means testing began as early as the 1570s: family members considered "fit" for work were denied relief, which was a powerful incentive to finding other means of support.[100] The legislation also, as we know, provided for poor children to be apprenticed, and indentured service in overseas colonies was an extension of this system. To these variants of forced labor, the eighteenth century added the parish's provision of work to paupers in their homes and their farming out to local employers on a "roundsman," or labor rate, basis.[101]

It is impossible to measure how far such measures forced people into work, deterred violations against the vagrancy and labor laws, and fostered a culture of work discipline, but their impact should not be underestimated. As one recent writer has observed, the influence of the poor laws was possibly enormous, "intruding as it did into most aspects of parish life, in a manner never since replicated on a comparable basis."[102] Perhaps in adopting such indirect, multifaceted strategies of coercion, the early modern state was more effective than the medieval legislation in regulating the labor force and fostering labor discipline. It is a serious gap in our scholarship, therefore, that in the recent flowering of social history the subject of compulsory labor has been largely ignored.[103] Even some Marxist historians have skipped over the implications of the application of compulsion to previously free workers beginning in the mid-fourteenth century, which might be considered England's version of the "second serfdom" that the landed classes of eastern Europe were imposing around the same time, only in the English experience it was wage labor that was mandated.[104] The final word, then, must belong to sociologists Philip Corrigan and Derek Sayer, who in 1985 acutely pointed to the influence of the labor and vagrancy laws. Specifically, they observed how the statutory control of labor was asserted in the Middle Ages and that Marxists (including Marx himself) had long considered the Old Poor Law to have been instrumental "in terms of structuring of the labor market, habituating the poor and dispossessed to wage labor."[105] If in this period England took the first steps toward a condition of economic "modernity," which political and neoclassical economists often associate with free markets, it is paradoxical (although historically and practically understandable) that it did so drawing on a disciplined labor force that had been compelled to labor.

Notes

The phrase "a new serfdom" is from Alan Harding, "The Revolt against the Justices," in *The English Rising of 1381*, ed. R. H. Hilton and T. H. Aston (Cambridge: Cambridge University Press, 1984), 187.

Epigraph by Richard II quoted and translated by Chris Given-Wilson, "Service, Serfdom, and English Labour Legislation, 1350–1500, in *Concepts and Patterns of Service in the Later Middle Ages*, ed. Anne Curry and Elizabeth Matthew (Woodbridge: Boydell, 2000), 21.

1. A. L. Beier, *Masterless Men: The Vagrancy Problem in England, 1560–1640* (London: Methuen, 1985), 4.

2. M. G. Davies, *The Enforcement of English Apprenticeship, 1563–1642* (Cambridge, MA: Harvard University Press, 1956), 195.

3. Robert J. Steinfeld, *The Invention of Free Labor: The Employment Relation in English and American Law and Culture, 1350–1870* (Chapel Hill: University of North Carolina Press), intro., esp. 1–7. I wish to thank my colleague Richard J. Soderlund for this reference.

4. Robert Brenner, "Agrarian Class Structure and Economic Development in Pre-Industrial Europe," in *The Brenner Debate*, ed. T. H. Aston and C. H. E. Philpin (Cambridge: Cambridge University Press, 1985), 13, 46.

5. For more extended discussion of these debates, see John Hatcher and Mark Bailey, *Modelling the Middle Ages: The History and Theory of England's Economic Development* (Oxford: Oxford University Press, 2001), 63.

6. D. C. Coleman, "Labour in the English Economy of the Seventeenth Century," *Economic History Review*, n.s., 8, no. 3 (1956): 280–95; A. M. Everitt, "Farm Labourers," in *The Agrarian History of England and Wales*, vol. 4, *1500–1640*, ed. Joan Thirsk (Cambridge: Cambridge University Press, 1967); Ann Kussmaul, *Servants in Husbandry in Early Modern England* (Cambridge: Cambridge University Press, 1981); K. D. M. Snell, *Annals of the Labouring Poor: Social Change and Agrarian England, 1660–1900* (Cambridge: Cambridge University Press, 1985).

7. B. H. Putnam, *The Enforcement of the Statutes of Labourers during the First Decade after the Black Death, 1349–1359* (New York: Columbia University, 1908); R. H. Tawney, "The Assessment of Wages in England by the Justices of the Peace," in Tawney and R. K. Kelsall, *Wage Regulation under the Statute of Artificers*, ed. W. E. Minchinton (1938; Newton Abbot: David and Charles, 1972). The paucity of recent work tends to belie Minchinton's reference to "the debate since 1938" (p. 21). See also Maurice Dobb, *Studies in the Development of Capitalism*, rev. ed. (London: Routledge and Kegan Paul, 1963), 231–33. For only partial exceptions, see D. Woodward, "The Background to the Statute of Artificers: The Genesis of Labor Policy, 1558–1563," *Economic History Review*, n.s., 33, no. 1 (1980): 32–44. Cf. Paul Griffiths, *Youth and Authority: Formative Experiences in England, 1560–1640* (Oxford: Clarendon, 1996), 356.

8. Abbot E. Smith, *Colonists in Bondage: White Servitude and Convict Labor in America, 1607–1776* (Chapel Hill: University of North Carolina Press, 1947); Davies, *Enforcement*.

9. John Hicks, *A Theory of Economic History* (Oxford: Oxford University Press, 1969), 122.

10. E. Clark, "Medieval Labor Law and English Local Courts," *American Journal of Legal History* 27, no. 4 (1983); L. R. Poos, "The Social Context of Statute of Labourers Enforcement," *Law and History Review* 1, no. 1 (1983): 27–52.

11. Putnam, *Enforcement*, 179–80. For a convenient summary of the ordinance, see Poos, "Social Context," 29; see also Alan Harding, "The Revolt against the Justices," in *The English Rising of 1381*, ed. R. H. Hilton and T. H. Aston (Cambridge: Cambridge University Press, 1984), 185.

12. Great Britain, *Rotuli Parliamentorum ut et petitiones et placita in Parliaments*, 6 vols. (London: n.p., 1783), 2:234.

13. Ibid., 2:233–34.

14. C. Dyer, *Standards of Living in the Later Middle Ages* (Cambridge: Cambridge University Press, 1989), 232.

15. Clark, "Medieval Labor Law," 349; Great Britain, *Rotuli Parliamentorum*, 2:233.

16. Steinfeld, *Free Labor*, 35–36; Great Britain, *Rotuli Parliamentorum*, 2:338–39, 586.

17. Cited in Steinfeld, *Free Labor*, 36–37.

18. W. S. Holdsworth, *A History of English Law*, ed. F. Pollock and F. W. Maitland, 2nd ed. (London: Methuen, 1968), 2:461–65.

19. Clark, "Medieval Labor Law," 334–6.

20. Harding, "Revolt," 187.

21. Charles Phythian-Adams, *Desolation of a City: Coventry and the Urban Crisis of the Late Middle Ages* (Cambridge: Cambridge University Press, 1979), 204; Peter Laslett, *Household and Family in Past Time* (Cambridge: Cambridge University Press, 1972), 151–58; Ann Kussmaul, *Servants in Husbandry in Early Modern England* (Cambridge: Cambridge University Press, 1981), ch. 2.

22. Clark, "Medieval Labor Law," 337.

23. Ibid., 337–38.

24. M. M. Postan, *The Famulus: The Estate Laborer in the Twelfth and the Thirteenth Centuries*, Economic History Review, suppl. 2 (Cambridge: Cambridge University Press, 1954), 1–5.

25. R. H. Hilton, *The English Peasantry in the Later Middle Ages* (Oxford: Clarendon, 1975), 31–32. For laborers as employers, see Dyer, *Making a Living*, 283, who gives examples of laborers as subcontractors.

26. Laslett, *Household and Family*, 219.

27. Margery M. Rowe, ed., *Tudor Exeter: Tax Assessments, 1489–1595, Including the Military Survey, 1522*, Devon and Cornwall Record Society, n.s., 22 (Exeter: Record Society, 1977), 7–33.

28. A. J. Tawney and R. H. Tawney, "An Occupational Census of the Seventeenth Century," *Economic History Review* 5, no. 1 (1934): 47.

29. C. W. Chalklin, *Seventeenth-Century Kent: A Social and Economic History* (London: Longmans, 1965), 246–47.

30. Gertrude Himmelfarb, *The Idea of Poverty: England in the Early Industrial Age* (New York: Vintage Books, 1985), 347.

31. Daphne Simon, "Master and Servant," in *Democracy and the Labour Movement*, ed. John Saville (London: Lawrence and Wishart, 1954), 160, 195–96, 198.

32. E. P. Thompson, "Time, Work-Discipline and Industrial Capitalism," in *Customs in Common: Studies in Traditional Popular Culture* (New York: New Press, 1993), 353, 361.

33. Maurice Keen, *English Society in the Later Middle Ages, 1348–1500* (London: Penguin, 1990), 34.

34. Dyer, *Standards of Living*, 218–19; cf. Nigel R. Goose, "Wage Labor on a Kentish Manor: Meopham, 1307–75," *Archaeologia cantiana* 92 (1976): 217.

35. See Great Britain, *Rotuli Parliamentorum*, 2:233–34.

36. E. B. Fryde, "Peasant Rebellion and Peasant Discontents," in *Agrarian History of England and Wales*, vol. 3, *1348–1500*, ed. Edward Miller (Cambridge: Cambridge University Press, 1991), 755 (cf. note 37, below); Miri Rubin, *The Hollow Crown: A History of Britain in the Late Middle Ages* (New York: Penguin, 2005), 69, who observes that the Statute of Laborers "was usually ignored, but when expedient it was applied." Cf. Miri Rubin, "The Poor," in *Fifteenth-Century Attitudes: Perceptions of Society in Late Medieval England*, ed. Rosemary Horrox (Cambridge: Cambridge University Press, 1994), 175.

37. Chris Given-Wilson, "Service, Serfdom, and English Labour Legislation, 1350–1500," in *Concepts and Patterns of Service in the Later Middle Ages*, ed. Anne Curry and Elizabeth Matthew (Rochester, NY: Boydell, 2000), 21, 23–25.

38. C. Dyer and Simon A. C. Penn, "Wages and Earnings in Late Medieval England: Evidence from the Enforcement of the Labour Laws," *Economic History Review*, n.s., 43, no. 3 (1990): 359.

39. Fryde, "Peasant Rebellion," 756; Clark, "Medieval Labor Law," 338.

40. Fryde, "Peasant Rebellion," 756; the numbers are from Clark, "Medieval Labor Law," 338; also see Putnam, *Enforcement*, 179–81.

41. Rubin, *Hollow Crown*, 69.

42. Harding, "Revolt," 186 and n90.

43. Fryde, "Peasant Rebellion," 759–60.

44. Christopher Dyer, *Making a Living in the Middle Ages: The People of Britain, 850–1520* (New Haven, CT: Yale University Press, 2002), 289.

45. Ralph A. Griffiths, *The Reign of Henry VI* (London: Ernest Benn, 1981), 638.

46. Dyer and Penn, "Wages and Earnings," 359.

47. Bertha H. Putnam, *Early Treatises on the Practice of the Justices of the Peace in the Fifteenth and Sixteenth Centuries* (Oxford: Clarendon, 1924), 91–92; Ellen A. McArthur, "A Fifteenth-Century Assessment of Wages," *English Historical Review* 13. no 50 (1898): 299–302. Cf. Donald Woodward, *Men at Work: Laborers and Building Craftsmen in the Towns of Northern England, 1450–1750* (Cambridge: Cambridge University Press, 1995), 182n30.

48. Dyer, *Standards of Living*, 219.

49. Poos, "Social Context," 36.

50. Putnam, *Enforcement*, 157.

51. Harding, "Revolt," 186–87.

52. Given-Wilson, "Service, Serfdom," 29–30, 34–35. For examples of prosecution for vagrancy of those who refused to work, see Dyer and Penn, "Wages and Earnings," 366; R. B. Dobson, ed., *The Peasants' Revolt of 1381* (London: Macmillan, 1970), 72–74.

53. For the text of the 1563 act, see R. H. Tawney and Eileen Power, eds., *Tudor Economic Documents*, 3 vols. (London: Longmans, 1924); specific references here are to 1:339–42, 344–45, 348.

54. Ibid., 1:342.

55. Sir Thomas Smith, *De republica Anglorum*, ed. Mary Dewar (London, 1583; Cambridge: Cambridge University Press, 1982), 141.

56. William Blackstone, *Commentaries on the Laws of England*, 4 vols. (1765; Chicago: University of Chicago Press, 1979), 1:413.

57. Michael Dalton, *The Countrey Justice* (London: Society of Stationers, 1618; repr. Amsterdam: Walter J. Johnson, 1975), 63.

58. Samuel Carter, barrister at law, *Legal Provisions for the Poor, or a Treatise of the Common and Statute Laws Concerning the Poor* (London: Printed by John Nutt, assignee of Edward Sayer . . . For John Walthoe, 1710), ch. 12; George White and Gravenor Henson, *A Few Remarks on the State of the Laws at Present in Existence for Regulating Masters and Work-People* (London, 1823), 44–52, esp. secs. 7, 11. I am grateful to my colleague Dr. Soderlund for the opportunity to consult his notes on these sources.

59. *Statutes of the Realm* (London: Dawsons, 1963), IV, i, 6.

60. Ibid., IV, i, 595; cf. Kussmaul, *Servants in Husbandry,* 166–67.

61. *Statutes of the Realm,* IV, i, 595.

62. Ibid., IV, i, 6.

63. See the evidence cited in Kussmaul, *Servants in Husbandry,* 166–67; a number of other cases could be cited if space allowed.

64. Tawney and Power, *Tudor Economic Documents,* 1:48–49.

65. B. Howard Cunnington, *Some Annals of the Borough of Devizes, 1555–1791* (Devizes: G. Simpson, 1925), 41–42; Tawney and Power, *Tudor Economic Documents,* 1:335–37; Gwynedd Archives and Museum Service, Caernarfon Area Record Office, Quarter Sessions Rolls (no catalog nos.), 1560s and 1570s; Guildhall, View of Frankpledge, I, 1555–68 (A.6), 1–3 Elizabeth I; Doncaster Archives Department, vol. 4, Court Rolls, 3 Sept. 4 Elizabeth I.

66. J. C. Atkinson, ed., *Quarter Sessions Records,* (1884–92), 9 vols. (London: Printed for the North Riding Record Society), 1:202.

67. Wiltshire County Record Office, Quarter Sessions Rolls, Trinity 1612/142/ 144, Easter 1614/146, Easter 1621/191, 192–93, Easter 1625/158, Hilary 1626/150, Michaelmas 1626/139; B. Howard Cunnington, *Records of the County of Wilts* (Devizes: G. Simpson, 1932), 26, 33, 184.

68. W. J. Hardy and W. Le Hardy, eds., *Hertfordshire County Records* (Hertford: C. E. Longmore, Clerk of the Peace Office, 1905–39), 5:395.

69. Atkinson, *Quarter Sessions,* 5:71.

70. Exeter Act Book, 4:15, 163, 165.

71. J. S. Cockburn, ed., *Calendar of Assize Records, Sussex Indictments, Elizabeth I* (London: HM Stationery Office, 1975), 69; Doncaster Archives Department, Court Rolls, vol. 10 (vol. 3, 185, printed calendar).

72. National Archives (U.K.), SP 12/80/26, 12/80/44 V, 12/80/49; Essex Record Office, Q/SR 47/59, 65/2, 3, 72, 2, 2a; T. Kemp, ed., *The Book of John Fisher, 1580–1588* (Warwick: Henry T. Cooke, n.d.), 65–6, 99–100.

73. West Riding County Record Office, Quarter Sessions, 1657, fols. 253a–b. See also Anthony Fletcher, *Reform in the Provinces: the Government of Stuart England* (New Haven, CT: Yale University Press, 1986), 222–24.

74. *Orders and Directions together with a Commission for the Better Administration of Justice* . . . (London: Robert Barker, 1630), 18, G.1.a; National Archives (U.K.), SP 16/237–266, 447, 533–538.

75. J. S. Cockburn, ed., *Calendar of Assize Records, Hertfordshire Indictments, James I* (London: HM Stationery Office, 1975), 275; SP 16/250/10.

76. Tawney and Power, *Tudor Economic Documents,* 1:343.

77. Tawney and Kelsall, *Wage Regulation,* 20–21.

78. Kussmaul, *Servants in Husbandry*, 36.

79. Kelsall, *Wage Regulation* (1938 ed.), 27, 194.

80. Ibid., 61–62.

81. Ibid., 106–8.

82. R. S. Schofield and E. A. Wrigley, *The Population History of England, 1541–1871* (London: Edward Arnold, 1981), 208–9; A. L. Beier, "Poverty and Progress in Early Modern England," in *The First Modern Society*, ed. Beier, David Cannadine, and James M. Rosenheim (Cambridge: Cambridge University Press, 1989).

83. *Statutes of the Realm* (London, 1818; 1963 ed.), 2:586.

84. Ibid., 2:586–87.

85. Ibid., 2:337, 586 (clause 2).

86. *Historical Manuscripts Commission, Various Collections* (55B), 89–90.

87. Tawney and Power, *Tudor Economic Documents*, 1:345–7 (clauses 19–25).

88. Alfred E. Bland, Philip A. Brown, and R. H. Tawney, eds., *English Economic History: Select Documents* (London: G. Bell and Sons, 1914), 323–24.

89. Davies, *Enforcement*, 275–77.

90. Christopher Hill, "The Many-Headed Monster," in *Change and Continuity in Seventeenth-Century England* (London: Weidenfeld and Nicolson, 1974), ch. 8.

91. A. L. Beier, *Masterless Men: The Vagrancy Problem in England, 1560–1640* (London: Methuen, 1985); Pieter Spierenburg, *The Prison Experience: Disciplinary Institutions and Their Inmates in Early Modern Europe* (New Brunswick, NJ: Rutgers University Press, 1991).

92. Beier, *Masterless Men*, ch. 6, "Dangerous Trades."

93. Ibid., 149–50.

94. J. Innes, "Prisons for the Poor: English Bridewells, 1555–1800," in *Labour, Law, and Crime: An Historical Perspective*, ed. Francis Snyder and Douglas Hay (London: Tavistock, 1987), 77–78.

95. J. A. Sharpe, *Crime in Seventeenth-Century England: A County Study* (Cambridge: Cambridge University Press, 1983), 151.

96. Innes, "Prisons," 99, 105.

97. David Underdown, *Fire from Heaven: Life in an English Town in the Seventeenth Century* (London: HarperCollins, 1992), 109–13.

98. Paul Slack, *The English Poor Law, 1531–1782* (London: Macmillan, 1990), 40–2.

99. Snell, *Labouring Poor*, 106.

100. Beier, "Poverty and Progress," 209–10.

101. Snell, *Labouring Poor*, 106.

102. Ibid.

103. Otherwise excellent examples of this flowering are Keith Wright-son, *Earthly Necessities: Economic Lives in Early Modern Britain* (New Haven, CT: Yale University Press, 2000); Steve Hindle, *The State and Social Change in Early Modern England, c. 1550–1640* (New York: St. Martin's, 2000).

104. For example, Perry Anderson, *Lineages of the Absolutist State* (New York: Verso, 1974); Aston and Philpin, *Brenner Debate*. A partial exception is R. H. Hilton, *Bond Men Made Free* (London: Temple Smith, 1973), 155, who noticed that "all smallholders were liable" to obligatory service. Maurice Dobb noted that "any able-bodied man or woman under sixty, whether of villein status or free, if he or she lacked independent means of support, could be compelled to accept work at the prescribed wage." Dobb, *Studies*, 231.

105. Philip Corrigan and Derek Sayer, *The Great Arch: English State Formation as Cultural Revolution* (Oxford: Blackwell, 1985), 67.

2

The Neglected Soldier as Vagrant, Revenger, Tyrant Slayer in Early Modern England

Linda Woodbridge

IN 1567, THOMAS HARMAN, an author of "rogue literature," adopted the posture of a proto-Homeland Security officer, warning the general public about vagrants. His particular orange alert dealt with panhandlers feigning disability. His compilation *A Caveat or Warning for Common Cursetors, Vulgarly Called Vagabonds* detailed the alleged "abominable, wicked and detestable behavior of all these rowsy, ragged rabblement of rakehells, that under the pretense of great misery, diseases and other innumerable calamities, which they feign through great hypocrisy, do win and gain great alms in all places where they wily wander." Harman classified twenty-four specialist categories of vagrant, including the bullying upright-man; the hooker, who hooks clothing and valuables through windows by night; the prigger of prancers, a horse thief; the counterfeit crank, a phony epileptic; the dummerer, a phony dumb man; the whipjack, who pretends to have suffered shipwreck; the demander for glimmer, who pretends her house has burned down; the bawdy-basket, autem-mort, walking mort, kinchin mort, doxy, and dell.[1] But the very first one he discussed was the ruffler, a vagrant claiming to be an ex-soldier, usually disabled. Like most vagrants of Harman's lurid imaginings, the ruffler was blessed with considerable histrionic talent, waxing aggressive or piteous depending on the situation: "With stout audacity he demandeth where he thinketh he may be bold, and circumspect enough, as he seeth cause to ask charity, ruefully and lamentably, that it would make a flinty hart to relent, and pity his miserable estate, how he hath been maimed and bruised in the wars, and peradventure some will shew you some outward wound, which he got at some drunken fray."[2] Harman preferred the aggressive stance to the tear-jerking wound display: highway robbery might be criminal, but at least it was manly.

In fact, Harman believed that a ruffler out begging was not only pretending to have war wounds but also pretending to have been a soldier, for a true soldier would be too proud to beg: "The hardiest soldiers . . . if they escape all hazards and return home again, if they be without relief of their friends, they will surely desperately rob and steal, or [else] shortly be hanged or miserably die in prison, for they be so much ashamed and disdain to beg or ask charity, that rather they will as desperately fight for to live and maintain themselves as manfully and valiantly they ventured themselves in the Prince's quarrel."[3] It is difficult to agree with this huffing, intolerant anecdotalist that impostors who allegedly feigned dumbness or epilepsy, to bilk ha'pennies out of passers-by, posed much of a threat to the social order. Yet the unemployed, disabled veteran of the period did pose a serious social problem. As A. L. Beier writes, "No occupational groups increased as much as sailors and soldiers among vagrants from 1560 to 1640."[4] Scholars of early modern poverty recognize demobilized, often disabled soldiers as a persistent, significant element of the destitute homeless, and disorder from hungry disbanded soldiers was feared with good reason. In 1589, for example, troops were called out and martial law imposed when hundreds of Sir Francis Drake's disbanded soldiers threatened the peace in London.[5]

As historians have shown, many Elizabethan soldiers were demobilized without pensions, compensation for injuries, or even full wages. As Beier observes, unemployed ex-soldiers seemed even more threatening than others classified as vagabonds because they often had weapons and knew how to use them.[6] Indeed, for John Awdeley, who wrote about vagrants a few years before Harman, it was the weapon that set rufflers apart from other vagrants: "A ruffler goeth with a weapon to seek service, saying he hath been a servitor in the wars, and beggeth for his relief."[7] Because of the weaponry they still carried, demobilized soldiers were feared through the seventeenth century, but over the course of a century after Harman wrote, this class of Elizabethan vagrant began to move from being part of the problem to being part of the solution.

The Neglected Soldier Onstage

Though rogue literature like Harman's or Awdeley's viciously caricatured demobilized soldiers, plays of the public theaters treated them with considerable sympathy. In *Edward II* (ca. 1592),[8] Christopher Marlowe quickly conveys the nastiness of Piers Gaveston by showing him cruelly rebuff a poverty-stricken demobilized soldier who asks him for a job, declaring himself "a soldier, that hath serv'd against the Scot." Gaveston snarls, "Why, there are hospitals for such as you: / I have no war, and therefore, sir, be gone." The departing veteran mutters a curse in Gaveston's general direction: "Farewell, and perish by a soldier's hand / That would'st reward them with an hospital!"[9] Playwrights of the period often depict veterans who are unemployed and in debt. In *The Honest Lawyer* (ca. 1615), by S. S., a veteran who cannot find work has to set up as a quack physician.[10] In Nathan Field and Philip Massinger's *The Fatal Dowry* (ca. 1619), a veteran languishing in debtor's prison commits suicide.[11] A character in William Shakespeare and John Fletcher's *Two Noble Kinsmen* (ca. 1613) laments the plight of the "unconsider'd soldier."[12] In John Webster's *The White Devil* (ca. 1612), Flamineo remarks that his chosen career—pandering for his sister—pays better than soldiering.[13] In John Fletcher's *The Honest Man's Fortune* (1613), a character vows always to aid "the poor neglected soldier."[14]

Plays are sensitive to the condition of soldiers on active duty. In Shakespeare's *Henry V* (1599), the king wanders incognito among his troops the night before the big battle, eavesdropping on their opinions of the war and himself. If he expected unconditional loyalty, what he gets from common soldiers is a flea in his ear. One soldier who just wants to go home wishes the king were at the battle all by himself; thus would "many poor men's lives [be] saved." Taken aback, the disguised king protests, "I dare say you love him not so ill to wish him here alone. . . . I could not die anywhere so contented as in the King's company, his cause being just and his quarrel honorable." To which a second soldier answers pointedly, "That's more than we know," and continues feelingly: "If the cause be not good, the King himself hath a heavy reckoning to make, when all those legs and arms and heads chopped off in a battle shall join together at the latter day, and cry all, 'We died at such a place'—some swearing, some crying for a surgeon, some upon their wives left poor behind them, some upon the debts they owe, some upon their children rawly left."[15] Philip Massinger's *The Duke of Milan* (ca. 1621) offers a soldier's-eye view of war. The men complain of their treatment by superiors and hope a besieged town will hold out rather than making terms—their only hope of getting paid lies in taking spoils. And anyway, they like taking revenge on the privileged classes of a sacked city, "choughs that every day may spend / A soldier's entertainment for a year / . . . . I have seen 'em stop / Their scornful noses first, then seem to swoon / At sight of a buff jerkin."[16] They predict that profit from the war will end up in "the emperor's coffers," while "the poor soldier" is "left / To starve, or fill up hospitals."[17] In both these plays, soldiers worry at least as much about their prospects after demobilization as about battle itself. In Shakespeare's *Henry V*, one soldier plans to become a beggar faking disability with phony war wounds—in short, a ruffler: "To England will I steal, and there I'll steal, / And patches will I get unto these cudgelled scars, / And swear I got them in the Gallia wars."[18]

Dramatists even evinced concern about the *emotional* health of veterans, dramatizing soldiers' difficulties reintegrating into civilian life. In Shakespeare's *Much Ado about Nothing* (ca. 1598), the returned soldier Claudio gets engaged, but volunteers to skip his honeymoon to accompany his commanding officer on an out-of-town errand. Ill suited to civilian life among women, Claudio is quick to believe a slander against his fiancée. In the same play, the soldier Benedick returns from war a confirmed woman hater, ranting against women and marriage, and has to be tricked into falling in love. The hero of

Shakespeare's *Othello* (ca. 1604), a general out of his depth in a civilian context, believes a slander against his wife partly because it comes from a fellow military man. In Francis Beaumont and John Fletcher's *The Captain* (ca. 1612), an officer just back from war is so uncomfortable with women that he cannot approach one unless he is either drunk or angry enough to rush into battle. When a woman tries to anger him enough to notice her by emptying a pisspot on his head from a balcony, he simply breaks all the windows in the street.[19]

Some plays show worthy commanders making sure their soldiers get paid: in Thomas Kyd's *The Spanish Tragedy* (ca. 1587), a king punctiliously resolves "to see our soldiers paid": "We will bestow on every soldier / Two ducats, and on every leader ten."[20] The playwright George Peele, whose father was a financial officer and author of the first original English-language manual of double-entry bookkeeping, includes a fiscally oriented scene in his play *Edward I* (ca. 1591). The king, returning from war, takes up a collection for the maintenance of his maimed soldiers; noblemen vie with each other in giving—three thousand pounds, five thousand pounds. The total pledged amounts to ten thousand pounds. The queen then contributes, modestly setting down only a zero; happily, the zero is in the right-hand column, turning ten thousand pounds into a hundred thousand.[21] Such a scene seems designed to inspire magnanimous gestures of gratitude toward the nation's soldiers. Other plays incite shame in the breasts of ungenerous audiences by staging the more typical scenario of veterans reduced to penury. In Henry Chettle and John Day's *The Blind Beggar of Bednal Green* (1600), creditors descend on a returning soldier who has been unable to draw his pay and therefore owes for expenses incurred while on active duty: he owes his victualler seven marks, his armorer twelve pounds, his carter twenty nobles. He settles up with them for all he has in ready money.[22]

Many soldiers whose good military service has been neglected like this turn bitter; and it is from these bitter veterans that Renaissance drama recruits many of its most forceful avengers. A son in Chettle's *The Tragedy of Hoffman, or A Revenge for a Father* (1602) sets out to avenge his father, a soldier who fought thirty battles for his country and then "for his merits he was named / A prescript outlaw for a little debt" (1.156).[23] The veteran Bosola in Webster's *Duchess of Malfi* (ca. 1614) seeks revenge on the world at large: "There are rewards for hawks, and dogs, . . . when they have done us service; but for a soldier, that hazards his limbs in a battle, nothing but a kind of geometry is his last supportation . . . to hang in a fair pair of slings, upon an honorable pair of crutches, from hospital to hospital."[24]

That so many abused soldiers get sympathetic treatment in the public theater, with its heterogeneous mix of social classes,[25] suggests public receptivity to the issue across a wide social spectrum. In an era of nascent English nationalism, public theaters staged many patriotic plays, and the soldier risking life and limb for his country was a popular figure. In Thomas Dekker's *The Shoemaker's Holiday* (1599), the newly married shoemaker Ralph Damport is stoic about being conscripted into a foreign war because it is his duty to support "his country's quarrel" and because he is urged to "fight for the honor of the Gentle Craft."[26] When he eventually comes home disabled and limping, his wife Jane, a regular shopkeeping Penelope, is being courted by a well-born suitor. The scene wherein "five or six shoemakers, all with cudgels, or such weapons," prepare to liberate Ralph's wife from the gallant's clutches on the disabled veteran's behalf[27] must have brought cheers from public theater audiences, of which London apprentices were always a conspicuous component.[28] Acting companies quickly found out what themes connected with audiences; that the underappreciated returning veteran appears repeatedly over many years suggests a groundswell of public sentiment on which real soldiers would eventually be able to draw.

Vagrancy, Vengeance, Resistance, Republicanism

If the neglected soldier was a popular stock figure in the drama of this time, the revenger was an even more ubiquitous character type, and the two appear fused into one surprisingly often. Neglected soldiers who turn revenger comprise a hinge between the motifs of vagrancy and vengeance. Although early modern England was not a feud culture, in the sense that Anglo-Saxon England and early modern Friuli in Italy were feud cultures, English Renaissance literature was preoccupied with vengeance. There were dozens of revenge tragedies; in fact most tragedies featured a vengeful figure, as did history plays, novellas, even comedies. Renaissance revenge plays are usually kept in a separate mental compartment from early modern resistance theory by such authors as John Ponet, Christopher Goodman, and George Buchanan, authors who justified the violent overthrow of monarchs who abuse subjects' rights. However, many literary revengers do act against political tyrants, and many revenge plays are contemporary with periods of resistance to unpopular monarchs. The social protest of Elizabethan drama's neglected soldiers usually takes the form of private revenge rather than open political resistance. But in real life, the out-of-work veteran victimized by society eventually did turn to political resistance. I want to link the politically activist English soldiers of the seventeenth century to the mistreated veterans of the sixteenth—those that the rogue literature called rufflers. But first a few words about republicanism.

At just the time that Elizabethans were dishing out very shabby treatment to veterans, humanists steeped in the republican ideas of ancient Rome were gingerly exploring the possibility of shifting England's political system gradually in the direction of a republic or at least a constitutional monarchy. As Markku Peltonen shows, humanist apologists for republicanism stressed civic duty, especially military service, a notion that contributed to the feeling that military service and civilian support for the troops were patriotic duties. Abhorring mercenaries, republicans set great store by a citizen militia. For republicans "the only way to have a good army, which looked to its own glory and to the good of the commonwealth instead of its own private pecuniary gain, [was] to arm the people."[29] At this point, the budding discourse of republicanism collided with contemporary hysteria over vagabonds: what looked to a republican like a responsible subject performing his civic duty in a citizen militia might well look to writers of rogue literature, such as Harman or Awdeley, like a vagrant with a gun.

In the sixteenth century most theory about republican armies, demobilized soldiers, and overhauls of the political system remained just words on paper, penned by armchair republicans like Thomas Starkey.

But in the seventeenth century the word became flesh. Mounting opposition to King Charles I found a focal point in Charles's powerful favorite, the Duke of Buckingham, with whom he hatched plans for unpopular wars that were even harder on soldiers than most early modern conflicts. As James Holstun claims, "Perhaps one third of the 50,000 men whom the king and Buckingham pressed into service between 1624 and 1628 died in battle, of wounds, or of disease."[30] The life story of one of the soldiers in these campaigns, John Felton, reads like a Jacobean revenge tragedy. Fathers were central figures for revengers, and Felton's father lost his position and died in debtors' prison, partly owing to the machinations of a close adviser to the king, whom Felton's brother even suspected of having poisoned their father, a scenario very Italianate and oozing with the ambience of revenge tragedy. His father's ruin forced Felton into the army, where his difficult and loyal service was eventually slighted by the Duke of Buckingham; he was owed a good deal of back pay. Like stage revengers and the drama's neglected soldiers, Felton was fired by a sense of personal injury at the hands of an abusive power figure, and like resistance theorists and republicans, he developed an ideologically sophisticated rationale for the violence he planned. He borrowed a copy of George Buchanan's antityrannical tract *Detection of the Doings of Mary Queen of Scots* and wrote a self-justifying letter containing republican aphorisms.[31] Then he assassinated the Duke of Buckingham. This piece of resistance met with fairly general delight in England, and was particularly popular with Felton's fellow soldiers, who asked the king to spare Felton's life.[32] Although Felton was executed, his action nudged the nation one step closer to the civil war that would eventually see the execution of the king, the abolition of monarchy, and the founding of a republic—a stunning revolution in which neglected, unrewarded soldiers were to play a central role.

The Civil War Era

During the English Civil War, after parliamentary armies had gained the upper hand over royalist forces and captured the king himself, many in Parliament got cold feet. It was radical elements in the army that pushed Parliament to put the king on trial and eventually execute him. The soldiers, flushed with victory and ready for serious participation in government, also pressed for a political voice.[33] In 1647 a manifesto entitled *The Case of the Army Truly Stated* called for biennial elections and universal manhood suffrage. In 1647–48 *An Agreement of the People* renewed the call for biennial elections, and the *Humble Petition* of September 11, 1648, with some forty thousand signatories, demanded religious toleration, no pressing for military service, equality before the law for all social classes, trial by jury, punishment proportionate to crimes, freedom from arbitrary prosecutions, and an end to imprisonment for debt.[34] Faced with such radical demands from the army ranks, revolutionary leaders began to show signs of being more interested in protecting property than in extending the franchise or overhauling the legal system. The soldiers, having tasted the heady brew of collective action, looked threatening, and Oliver Cromwell and other revolutionary leaders soon came up with a time-honored solution: divide and conquer—disband the army, turn them out without pensions or back pay, turn them into vagrants. As Beier and others have shown, the sixteenth-century vagrant typically traveled alone or with one or two others; but Harman and other sixteenth-century writers of rogue literature revealed, in their overheated fantasies of fraternities of vagabonds, that vagrants operating on their own were not anywhere near as frightening as the specter of dispossessed people working collectively. To Cromwell and his associates, a newly radicalized army must have seemed as threatening as a fraternity of vagabonds. A plan was immediately formed to demobilize many troops, break remaining troops into small, widely separated units and dispatch a goodly number of troops to a safe distance in Ireland. But this time the soldiers, rebuffed in their political efforts and suffering from arrears in pay, refused to be relegated to ruffler status. They stood their ground.

In *A Solemn Engagement of the Army* (1647), one of the central documents of this revolutionary era, members of the army refused demobilization, pledging not to allow themselves to be disbanded or divided until their demands were met.[35] In summer 1647 common soldiers defied their aristocratic officers; there were army mutinies in 1647 and 1649. One radical pamphlet, *The Poor Man's Advocate,* proposed in 1649 to use the proceeds from confiscated royalist estates to pay the army its arrears; like many others, this author advanced from advocacy of restitution to the soldiers to more radical progressive programs: confiscated royalist property could also relieve the poor and fund education.[36] Elected representatives of the soldiers ("we ... who have often seen the devouring sword of a raging enemy drawn forth against us, threatening destruction to us, and now see them vanquished") published *The Apology of the Common Soldiers* (1647), which saw the disbanding of the army and dispatch of its remnants to Ireland as "a mere cloak for some who have lately tasted of sovereignty, and being lifted beyond their ordinary sphere of servants, seek to become masters, and degenerate into tyrants."[37] "Many of our fellow soldiers that have been disbanded," the *Apology* reported bitterly, have been "imprisoned, indicted, and hanged, although without their efforts in the civil war, civilian legislators "could not have safely sat in the House of Parliament with their heads on."[38] The soldier authors sought redress of immediate (and familiar) grievances, demanding "that the wives and children of those that have been slain in the service, and maimed soldiers, may be provided for."[39] But those who signed themselves "your soldiers" went far beyond this as well: they demanded "an end to all tyranny and oppressions so that justice and equity, according to the law of this land, should ... [be] done to the people, and that the meanest subject should fully enjoy his right, liberty, and properties in all things."[40] Thomas Rainsborough, the highest-ranking officer in the parliamentary army to support the radical program, demanded to know "what we have fought for," seeing that the country was still saddled with "the old law of England ... which enslaves the people of England that they should be bound by laws in which they have no voice at all." Rainsborough was an early advocate of government by the consent of the governed. He argued, "The poorest he that is in England hath a life to live, as the greatest he; and ... every man that is to live under a government ought first by his own consent to put himself under that government; and ... the poorest man in England is not bound in a strict sense to that government that he hath not had a voice to put himself under."[41]

Soldiers in this era frequently campaigned for legal equality, striving to redress what was also a primary grievance of revenge-tragedy heroes: the unfairness of the law and its partiality to the propertied and educated classes. The 1649 *English Soldiers' Standard* charged, "We live under unknown laws, written in canting French, vexed and molested with a whole drove of corrupt judges, lawyers, jailers, and the like caterpillars of the commonwealth."[42] It is a satisfying irony that soldiers, who as disbanded rufflers were popularly believed to employ thieves' cant, turned the tables by charging that the law is written in "canting French."

Those who gave this movement its radical theory were not necessarily rank-and-file soldiers: for example, the theorist John Lilburne, jailed for denouncing members of Parliament who lived in comfort while foot soldiers fought and died for the parliamentary cause, was a lieutenant colonel. And resistance writing of this period had some nonmilitary models, in over a century of hard-hitting resistance literature, by such fiery religious dissidents as Ponet, Goodman, and Knox. But some radical documents *were* drawn up by the elected representatives of ordinary soldiers; for example, *The Apology of the Common Soldiers* (1647), which Alan Marshall calls "a key text in the radicalization of the parliamentary army."[43] And the rank and file also crucially contributed democratic practices, with decisions made by elected representatives, and a commitment to collective action and solidarity.

All this radicalism was fueled by a chafing sense of unrewarded service. These soldiers had risked their lives to win the war and overturn the monarchic government, and as a new form of government was coalescing, they were excluded from it. The soldier Edward Sexby demanded,

> Do you [not] think it were a sad and miserable condition that we have fought all this time for nothing? All here both great and small do think that we fought for something. . . . If this be the business, that an estate doth make men capable to choose those that shall represent them—it is no matter which way they get it, they are capa-

ble—I think there are many that have not estates that in honesty
have as much right in the freedom [of] their choice as any that have
great estates.[44]

The neglected soldier, so important a figure in the drama of the sixteenth and seventeenth centuries, was coming into his own politically,
and just as neglected soldiers in revenge plays assassinate tyrants, so
real-life neglected soldiers were committing determined acts of political resistance.

As the revolutionary party narrowed to one man, Oliver Cromwell,
who assumed quasi-monarchic powers as Protector, former soldiers
who had once resisted the king began resisting Cromwell. The
cashiered soldier Edward Sexby was involved in a plot to assassinate
Cromwell, and his famous apology for tyrannicide, *Killing No Murder* (1657), encourages England's army to rise up against Cromwell,
who had ignored its military sacrifices and betrayed its interests.[45]

Vagrancy and Soldiering, Urban and Rural

In London, a magnet for the unemployed, vagrants at many times
during the sixteenth and seventeenth centuries might easily find occupation as soldiers, and in turn become vagrants when armies were
demobilized. Beier writes, "Troops were always likely to become vagrants, because they were chiefly recruited from the poor and criminal
classes." The discontents of urban ex-soldiers acquired a special danger because of the denser concentration of demobilized soldiers in
the city, and because in London they were regularly exposed to other
rebellious practices—food riots, anti-immigrant libels posted on
walls, violent agitations against foreign workers.[46]

But in the mid-seventeenth-century civil war, soldiers of rural
background played a crucial role as well. As David Petegorsky argues,
peasants and agricultural laborers were one of the largest components
of the parliamentary army,[47] and had the army been disbanded and
cut adrift to take up the vagrant life of rufflers, they would have joined
many other unemployed agricultural workers. If demobilized soldiers
formed one perennial component of England's vagrants, unemployed

farm workers comprised another, all through the sixteenth and seventeenth centuries. Robert Jütte notes that "agricultural workers, casual labourers and textile artisans, and soldiers, sailors and servants and apprentices were predominant among the wayfaring poor of early modern Europe."[48] Farm laborers were vulnerable to being thrown into vagrancy because, as Paul Slack shows, "ten or twenty per cent of the [rural] population . . . hovered around the poverty line and . . . might fall below it when the harvest failed, when sickness hit the chief breadwinner, when employment opportunities for wives and children in rural industries contracted, or simply when there was a particularly bad winter."[49] In urban centers the proportion of the poor in the total population ranged from 5 percent to 25 percent in hard years in the early seventeenth century, but in some places these numbers underestimate the share of the real poor by listing only those deemed worthy of relief.[50] Writers of "rogue literature" heaped contempt on the rural unemployed as lazy and shiftless, or simply ignored them, despite their imposing numbers: Harman, for example, presents rural people mainly as dupes of clever rogues—the "conies" who are caught by cony catchers—rather than as themselves members of the vagrant category. Only one brief passage in his memorable anecdote about a shameless "doxy" gives away that she is a displaced agricultural worker.[51] But other writers faced the social problem more squarely. In about 1549, Sir Thomas Smith created a dialogue among five speakers—a farmer, a merchant, a knight, a craftsman, and a scholar—to discuss the nation's economic problems, especially inflation. The farmer complains that everything is so expensive that "by their daily labor [rural workers] are not able to live," and accuses the knight of raising rents on land; the knight rejoins that farmers have raised the price of commodities the knight buys, such as butter and corn.[52] Earlier in the century, Sir Thomas More's fictive character Raphael Hythlodaye made the following analysis of rural vagrants:

> They would be glad to work, but they can find no one who will hire them. There is no need for farm labor, in which they have been trained, when there is no land left to be plowed. . . . This enclosing

has had the effect of raising the price of grain in many places. . . . The price of raw wool has risen so much that poor people who used to make cloth are no longer able to buy it, and so great numbers are forced from work to idleness. . . . The wool trade . . . is concentrated in few hands . . . and these so rich, that the owners are never pressed to sell until they have a mind to, and that is only when they can get their price. . . . The high price of grain causes rich men to dismiss as many retainers as they can from their households; and what, I ask, can these men do, but rob or beg? And a man of courage is more likely to steal than to cringe.[53]

The whole era witnessed recurrent antienclosure riots and revolts. For example, during Ket's Rebellion in 1549, and during the Civil War in the mid-seventeenth century, bands of peasants attacked enclosures. In the 1640s the neglected veteran met the jobless agricultural worker in one memorable moment of cooperative resistance: St. George's Hill.

Ruffler and Digger

In the famine years between 1648 and 1650 a group of hungry commoners squatted on waste land at St. George's Hill in Surrey, cultivating crops to share and industriously issuing manifestos. In a letter of 1649, their leader Gerrard Winstanley informed Parliament of an agenda of economic communism: "The land of England is the land of our nativity, . . . and all of us, by the righteous law of our creation, ought to have food and raiment freely by our righteous laboring of the earth, without working for hire, or paying rent to one another"; a third of the kingdom is "waste and barren, and her children starve," but the earth is meant to be "a common treasury of livelihood to all."[54] Like the army radicals, Winstanley advocated universal manhood suffrage.[55] This movement, called the Diggers by posterity, spread to at least seven counties, and Winstanley (along with William Everard and others) spoke inclusively for "the common people of England."[56]

Like the land-liberating Ket's Rebellion a century earlier, the Diggers were crushed, but not without sowing more seeds of radical thought. On the class system, Diggers were eloquent: if aristocrats "can prove that the earth was made by Almighty God peculiarly for them, and not for others equal with them, then we have trespassed in digging upon their rights."[57] "Ye the great ones of the earth, the powers of this world, . . . your first estate was innocency and equality with your fellow creatures."[58] "In the beginning of time . . . not one word was spoken . . . that one branch of mankind should rule over another."[59] As landless vagrants flocked to St. George's Hill and other Diggers' sites to cultivate a plot of land, Diggers rewrote the Fall of Man as a plunge into a class system, into a "blindness of mind" that through greed "did set up one man to teach and rule over another"; then "the earth . . . was hedged into enclosures by the teachers and rulers, and the others were made servants and slaves; and the earth that is within this creation made a common storehouse for all is bought and sold and kept in the hands of a few, whereby the great Creator is mightily dishonored, as if he were a respecter of persons, delighting in the comfortable livelihood of some and rejoicing in the miserable poverty and straits of others. From the beginning it was not so."[60] For Diggers, an ideal society would be classless: "Take notice, that England is not a free people until the poor people that have no land have a free allowance to dig and labor the commons, and to live as comfortably as the landlords that live in their enclosures."[61]

Some of these radical Diggers were out-of-work farmhands. But one of them was a radical and now discharged soldier, and an aggressive one at that—William Everard was surely one of those whom Thomas Harman would have labeled a ruffler. Hailing from a poor provincial family, he identified himself as an ensign when signing a 1647 petition voicing the grievances of the parliamentary army. At the time of the petition, Everard was in prison awaiting court martial for plotting to kill the king. He was eventually cashiered from the army, and along with Gerrard Winstanley became one of first four unemployed men to take up digging at St. George's Hill; he and Winstanley remained leaders of the group, and coauthored or at least cosigned its manifestos.[62]

In the Digger movement of the mid-seventeenth century, then, two elements of mid-sixteenth-century vagrancy came together, rufflers and displaced rural laborers. Although the Digger movement was short-lived, it was, as Petegorsky maintains, "the one genuine proletarian ideology that the Civil War produced,"[63] and significantly, one of the midwives of this proletarian ideology, William Everard, was a neglected soldier—a ruffler. Perhaps his experience helped influence his collaborator Winstanley, who in his manifesto *The Law of Freedom* (1652) deploys a soldierly language to speak of radical change: "A monarchical army lifts up mountains, makes valleys, [that is], advances tyrants, and treads the oppressed in the barren lanes of poverty. But a commonwealth's army . . . levels the mountains to the valleys, pulls down the tyrant, and lifts up the oppressed."[64]

It is no accident that radicals in the parliamentary army agitating for what amounts to rule by the consent of the governed sound like the American founding fathers: one thinker with important influence on Jefferson and other framers of the Declaration of Independence was John Locke, son of an officer in the parliamentary army, who was "imbued with antimonarchy ideology at an early age."[65] The way forward lay through extralegal avenues. American founding fathers set forth their grievances against a tyrant and then engaged in armed revolt, violating British laws they had formerly felt obliged to obey. Soldiers in the parliamentary army set forth their grievances and then engaged in mutinies, refused to be disbanded, defied superiors, and heaped contempt on the legal system of their country. To rebel is one thing; to argue the *justness* of an extralegal act of rebellion is quite another. This big mental step is the military and political equivalent of a Kuhnian paradigm shift. In England it was those with no rights—exiled people and landless people hovering on the brink of vagrancy—who were able to take that step. I suggest that the disaffected soldiers of the seventeenth century found it possible to think outside the box, to break the frame of conventional political hierarchies and institutions, because for centuries they had regularly been expelled from the bosom of an established society, which used their services and then disowned them without recompense. They saw through the injustice of the law because they had unjustly been made outlaws.

A New World Order Delayed

In the long term, the radical ideas and practice of seventeenth-century soldiers took root and flourished. Many elements of their platform— universal manhood suffrage, an equitable legal system, prison reform, abolition of monopolies, adequate poor relief, a fair tax code—have become part of the agenda of modern progressive democracies. But in the short term, the army radicals lost. On November 15, 1647, army rebels confronted their own leadership head-on, in a mass military rendezvous in which radicals pressed for the adoption of *The Agreement of the People*. As the leadership held out for more a conservative political agenda a mutinous regiment launched into violence. As Holstun tells it,

> At this moment, with a charismatic and beloved rival leader in Thomas Rainsborough, a body of sympathetic troops drawn up, a published manifesto-constitution in *The Agreement* to provide an ideological rallying point, and the first blow struck, the Agitators [that is, the army's elected representatives] brought seventeenth-century England closer to a genuinely popular democratic revolution than ever before or after. But it didn't come close enough. Cromwell charged into the ranks with a drawn sword and demanded the regiment's submission.[66]

In this tense face-off, the army blinked. Soldiers from the mutinous regiment were court-martialed and one randomly chosen soldier was shot. The historical moment passed. Thirteen years later, the monarchy was restored. Why the army crumbled in this crisis can be endlessly debated. But a literary perspective can address at least one small corner of the puzzle. One thing weakening this revolutionary movement was that, whatever brilliant use the rebels made of the printing press for petitions, pamphlets, and manifestos, the anti-monarchist forces had given up one of the most powerful literary resources potentially available to a rebel cause: they had closed down the theaters.

As we have seen, English Renaissance theater had proved very sympathetic to common soldiers in battle and veterans suffering war wounds (physical and psychological), lack of employment opportunity, and arrears in pay. When the parliamentary revolution, with its strong Puritan component, closed down the theaters on religious and moral grounds in 1642, the theater's capacity for political commentary passed into the hands of royalist sympathizers—always keen supporters of the theater—whose closet dramas were sometimes printed and occasionally staged for royalists in continental exile. A good number of resistance plays came out of that closet scribbling—resistance to the new parliamentary republic and later to the Protectorate of Oliver Cromwell. These are often, by the way, cast as revenge plays, supporting the possibility of reading revenge in Renaissance plays as serious political resistance. But resistance on behalf of the status quo ante can hardly be considered revolutionary in political theory.

A case in point is an anonymous closet tragedy entitled *The Famous Tragedy of King Charles I*, clandestinely printed in 1649, just after the execution of the king. Cromwell figures as a Machiavellian villain and tyrant. Dedicated to King Charles II (the prince in exile), the play is a forthright piece of political resistance. In response to the edict that he never to return to England on pain of death, the play urges young Charles to seek foreign political alliances, to "summon all nations, to thy speedy aid," from Switzers to Moors.[67] As so often in Renaissance plays, a common soldier comes in for attention, but here his energies are harnessed for royalist aims. As a shining example of resistance to anyone inclined to assassinate Cromwell, the playwright stages the murder of Thomas Rainsborough. Although the historical Rainsborough was probably killed by monarchists, the play shows him being assassinated by one of his own common soldiers, in retaliation for the parliamentary army's perfidious execution of brave royalist military leaders who had surrendered under truce. Those who imagined a new political world, a republic, made a strategic error in leaving the drama to their enemies.

In the early sixteenth century, vagrants, down-and-outs, and thread-bare veterans had a few well-educated, literate authors willing to stand up for them: Thomas More, Beaumont and Fletcher, Massinger, Shakespeare; and such writers helped to keep issues of poverty, homelessness, injustice, and the shameful neglect of veterans in the public eye. By the mid-seventeenth century, hard-up squatters and cashiered soldiers like Gerrard Winstanley and William Everard were writing and publishing for themselves. But how might history have differed, had the great public theaters—the Globe and the Rose and the Swan—still been open when the army mutinied and the Diggers dug? What if, in that tumultuous time, Winstanley and Everard had written plays, attended by the masses? Now *there* would have been some ruffling.

Notes

1. John Harman, *A Caveat or Warning for Common Cursetors, Vulgarly Called Vagabonds,* 2nd ed. (London: Henry Middleton, 1573), sig. Aii. These terms belong to a supposed "thieves' cant"; whether such jargon existed in Harman's time or was the invention of literate authors of "rogue literature" is subject to debate.

2. Ibid., sig. Bii.

3. Ibid.

4. A. L. Beier, *Masterless Men: The Vagrancy Problem in England* (London: Methuen, 1985), 93–94.

5. J. Thomas Kelly, *Thorns on the Tudor Rose: Monks, Rogues, Vagabonds, and Sturdy Beggars* (Jackson: University Press of Mississippi, 1977), 64.

6. Ibid., 104–5.

7. John Awdeley, *The Fraternity of Vagabonds,* ca. 1561; repr. in *Awdeley's "Fraternity of Vacabondes, Harman's Caveat, Haben's Sermon," &c.,* ed. Edward Viles and F. J. Furnivall (London: Early English Text Society, 1869), 3.

8. Dates given for plays are for approximate date of first performance, as listed in Alfred Harbage, *Annals of English Drama, 975–1700,* 3rd ed., rev. Samuel Schoenbaum and Sylvia Stoler Wagonheim (London: Routledge, 1989).

9. Christopher Marlowe, *Edward II*, in *English Renaissance Drama*, ed. David Bevington et al. (New York: Norton, 2002), 1.1.33–38.

10. S. S., *The Honest Lawyer* (London: George Purslowe, 1616).

11. Nathan Field and Philip Massinger, *The Fatal Dowry*, ed. T. A. Dunn (Berkeley: University of California Press, 1969).

12. William Shakespeare and John Fletcher, *Two Noble Kinsmen*, in *The Works of Beaumont and Fletcher*, ed. Alexander Dyce (New York: Appleton, 1890), 2.1.2.

13. John Webster, *The White Devil*, ed. Clive Hart (Edinburgh: Oliver and Boyd, 1970), 3.2.

14. A. Glover and A. R. Waller, eds., *The Works of Francis Beaumont and John Fletcher* (Cambridge: Cambridge University Press, 1905–12), 1.1.

15. Stephen Greenblatt, Walter Cohen, Jean E. Howard, and Katharine Eisaman Maus, eds., *The Norton Shakespeare* (New York: Norton, 1997), 4.1.120–40.

16. Philip Edwards and Colin Gibson, eds., *The Plays and Poems of Philip Massinger* (Oxford: Clarendon, 1976), vol. 1, 3.1.22–37.

17. Ibid., 3.1.16–17.

18. Shakespeare, *Henry V*, 5.1.83–85.

19. Francis Beaumont and John Fletcher, *The Captain*, in *The Works of Francis Beaumont and John Fletcher*, ed. A. Glover and A. R. Waller (Cambridge: Cambridge University Press, 1905–12).

20. Thomas Kyd, *The Spanish Tragedy*, ed. David Bevington (Manchester: Manchester University Press, 1996), 1.2.10–11, 196, 129–30.

21. George Peele, *Edward I*, ed. Frank S. Hook. In *The Life and Works of George Peele*, ed. Charles Tyler Prouty (New Haven, CT: Yale University Press, 1952–70), vol. 2, 1.71–81.

22. Chadwyck-Healey, English Drama Full-Text Database, http://collections.chadwyck.com.

23. Henry Chettle, *The Tragedy of Hoffman, or A Revenge for a Father*, ibid.

24. John Webster, *Duchess of Malfi*, ed. John Russell Brown (London: Methuen, 1964), 1.1.59–62.

25. Despite revisionary efforts such as Ann Jennalie Cook's *The Privileged Playgoers of Shakespeare's England, 1576–1642* (Princeton, NJ: Princeton University Press, 1981), the wide mix of classes in Shakespeare's audience is still widely accepted; Alfred Harbage's classic statement that "the theatre was a democratic institution in an intensely undemocratic age" (*Shakespeare's Audience* [1941; New York: Columbia University Press, 1961], 11), while oversimplified, was substantially borne out by

Andrew Gurr's more empirical *Playgoing in Shakespeare's London* (Cambridge: Cambridge University Press, 1987). Gurr's appendix listing every named person known to have attended a London theater during this period includes, on the one hand, dukes and ambassadors, and on the other, apprentices, students, sailors, butchers, brewers, barbers, a blacksmith, a weaver, a tailor, and servants (226–46).

26. In *English Renaissance Drama,* ed. David Bevington, Lars Engle, Katharine Eisaman Maus, and Eric Rasmussen (New York: Norton, 2002), 1.186, 1.219.

27. Scene 18, stage direction.

28. Harbage, *Shakespeare's Audience,* 80.

29. Markku Peltonen, *Classical Humanism and Republicanism in English Political Thought, 1570–1640* (Cambridge: Cambridge University Press, 1995), 42.

30. James Holstun, *Ehud's Dagger: Class Struggle in the English Revolution* (London: Verso, 2000), 153–54.

31. Ibid., 166–71.

32. Ibid., 172.

33. Who actually did the writing of the army manifestos is mostly unclear; multiple authorship and multiple signatories is the norm, reflecting the army activists' principled commitment to collective action, what Holstun calls "a bottom-up model of martial praxis" (196) or an "associative martial praxis" (377). Few of the rank-and-file foot soldiers would have been literate, at least not to the level displayed in the manifestos; but they made good use of literate spokespersons. *An Agreement of the People* and *The English Soldier's Standard* may have been mainly authored by the civilian army-sympathizer William Walwyn, a largely self-educated weaver and medic. John Lilburne, soldier in the parliamentary army and author of radical petitions, hailed from a modestly well-off family and was at one time apprenticed to a clothier and later owned a brewery. Printing of these radical materials was enabled by the abolition of official censorship during the civil war era; even so, printers often took the precaution of not including the name of the print shop on the publications.

34. *The Case of the Army Truly Stated, together with the mischiefs and dangers that are imminent, and some suitable remedies, humbly proposed by the agents of five regiments of horse, to their respective regiments, and the whole Army* (London: unlisted printer, 1647); *An Agreement of the People for a firm and present peace, upon grounds of common-right and freedom; as it was proposed by the agents of the five regiments of horse; and since by the general approbation of the Army, offered to the joint concurrence of all*

the free commons of England (unlisted printer, 1647); *To the Right Honorable, the Commons of England in Parliament Assembled: the Humble Petition of diverse well-affected persons inhabiting the City of London, Westminster, the borough of Southwark, hamlets, and places adjacent* (London: H. S., 1648).

35. *A Solemn Engagement of the Army under the command of his Excellency Sir Thomas Fairfax, with a declaration of their resolutions, as to disbanding, . . . together with the representations of the dissatisfactions of the Army, . . . unanimously agreed upon, and subscribed by the officers and soldiers of the several regiments* (London: Richard Lownes, 1647).

36. Peter Chamberlen, *The Poor Man's Advocate, . . . pouring oil and wine into the wounds of the nation, by making present provision for the soldier and the poor, . . . by paying all arrears to the Parliament army* (London: Giles Calvert, [1649]).

37. *The Apology of the Common Soldiers of His Excellency Sir Thomas Fairfax's Army* (London: unlisted printer, 1647), 2, 4.

38. Ibid., 6.

39. Ibid., 8.

40. Ibid., 5.

41. In *The Clarke Papers: Selections from the Papers of William Clarke, Secretary to the Council of the Army, 1647–1649 . . .* , ed. C. H. Firth (London: Camden Society, 1891–1901; repr., London: Offices of the Royal Historical Society, 1992), 1:300, 310–11.

42. *The English Soldier's Standard to repair to, for wisdom and understanding, in these doleful back-sliding times. To be read by every honest officer to his soldiers; and by the soldiers, one to another* [sometimes ascribed to William Walwyn] ([London]: unlisted printer, 1649), 4.

43. "Edward Sexby," *Oxford Dictionary of National Biography*, ed. H. C. G. Matthew and Brian Harrison (Oxford: Oxford University Press, 2004).

44. In *Clarke Papers*, 1:329–30.

45. Edward Sexby, *Killing No Murder* ([Holland]: unlisted printer, 1657).

46. See Anthony Fletcher and John Stevenson, eds., *Order and Disorder in Early Modern England* (Cambridge: Cambridge University Press, 1985); Alan Macfarlane and Sarah Harris, *The Justice and the Mare's Ale: Law and Disorder in Seventeenth-Century England* (Oxford: Blackwell, 1981); David Underdown, *Revel, Riot, and Rebellion: Popular Politics and Culture in England 1603–1660* (Oxford: Clarendon, 1985); R. B. Outhwaite, *Dearth, Public Policy and Social Disturbance in England, 1550–1800* (Cambridge: Cambridge University Press, 1991); Laura Hunt Yungblut, *Strangers Settled Here amongst Us: Policies, Perceptions and the Presence of*

Aliens in Elizabethan England (London: Routledge, 1996). Ian Archer argues that in London, "riot was a negotiating strategy" by which apprentices and other interest groups reminded magistrates of their duties toward various sectors of society. Archer, *The Pursuit of Stability: Social Relations in Elizabethan London* (Cambridge: Cambridge University Press, 1991), 6.

47. David Petegorsky, *Left-Wing Democracy in the English Civil War: A Study of the Social Philosophy of Gerrard Winstanley* (London: Victor Gollancz, 1940), 58.

48. Robert Jütte, *Poverty and Deviance in Early Modern Europe* (Cambridge: Cambridge University Press, 1994), 43.

49. Paul Slack, *Poverty and Policy in Tudor and Stuart England* (London: Longman, 1988), 66.

50. Ibid., 73–80; cf. A. L. Beier, "Poverty and Progress in Early Modern England," in *The First Modern Society: Essays in English History in Honour of Lawrence Stone*, ed. A. L. Beier, David Cannadine, James M. Rosenheim (Cambridge: Cambridge University Press, 1989), 203–24.

51. Cited in Paul A. Slack, "Vagrants and Vagrancy in England, 1598–1664," *Economic History Review*, 2nd ser., 27, no. 3 (1974): 378.

52. Sir Thomas Smith [?], *A Discourse of the Commonweal of This Realm of England*, ed. Mary Dewar (Charlottesville: University Press of Virginia, 1969), 17, 39, 40. The attribution of this dialogue to Smith is not universally accepted.

53. Sir Thomas More, *Utopia*, ed. and trans. Robert M. Adams, 2d ed. (New York: Norton, 1992; first published in Latin, 1516), 12–14.

54. Gerrard Winstanley, *An Appeal to All Englishmen, to judge between bondage and freedom, sent from those that began to dig upon George Hill in Surrey* ([London]: unlisted printer, 1650), 5–8.

55. Gerrard Winstanley, *The Law of Freedom in a Platform: or, True Magistracy Restored* (London: J. M., 1652), 52–53.

56. William Everard and Gerrard Winstanley, *The True Levellers' Standard Advanced* (London: unlisted printer, [1649]), 6.

57. Gerrard Winstanley, *An Appeal to the House of Commons, desiring their answer: whether the common people shall have the quiet enjoyment of the commons and waste land; or whether they shall be under the will of lords of manors still* ([London: unlisted printer], 1649), 12.

58. Everard and Winstanley, *True Levellers*, sig. A2^v.

59. Ibid., 6.

60. Ibid., 6–7.

61. Ibid., 15.

62. Ariel Hessayon, "William Everard," *Oxford Dictionary of National Biography*, ed. H. C. G. Matthew and Brian Harrison (Oxford: Oxford University Press, 2004; electronic ed., 2006).

63. Petegorsky, *Left-Wing Democracy*, 73.

64. Gerrard Winstanley, *The Works of Gerrard Winstanley*, ed. George Holland Sabine (Ithaca, NY: Cornell University Press, 1941), 575.

65. Garrett Ward Sheldon, "The Political Theory of the Declaration of Independence," in *The Declaration of Independence: Origins and Impact*, ed. Scott Douglas Gerber (Washington, DC: CQ Press, 2002), 16.

66. Holstun, *Ehud's Dagger*, 251.

67. *The Famous Tragedy of King Charles I* ([London?]: unlisted printer, 1649), dedication, lines 41–47.

3

"Takin' It to the Streets"

Henry Mayhew and the Language of the Underclass in Mid-Nineteenth-Century London

A. L. Beier

Invoking the title of a popular song of the 1970s has a twofold significance. First, it is meant to highlight the hostility that the journalist
Henry Mayhew (1812–87) expressed toward popular speech, particularly of those elements of the London underclass of whom he disapproved—street vendors, vagrants, and other criminals—and, thus, to
whom he was arguably "takin' it" in his extensive publications about
them between 1849 and 1861.[1] Michel Foucault and Pierre Bourdieu
would probably agree that Mayhew was "takin' it" to these groups in
an attempt to control them—by exposing them to respectable society
and by spurring the authorities to suppress them. Second, and contrariwise, the phrase "takin' it to the streets" is intended to suggest that
popular vocabularies may have acted as forms of resistance to authority, covers for illegal activities, and expressions of countercultures
and popular solidarity.[2] Historians may wish to consider which, if
any, of these two hypotheses is valid, because the answers may tell us
something about social relations in the mid-nineteenth century.

But one might also question the premise of these two interpretations of the song's title and consider whether a single popular dialect
actually existed or whether there was a variety of vocabularies among

London's underclass. These questions are significant because contemporaries firmly believed that an underclass included criminal and dangerous elements that threatened the social order. Mayhew's documentation shows that there existed both unitary and diversified argots in the mid-nineteenth century, which raises doubts about theories of a united front of the criminal and dangerous. Yet criminality had huge symbolic significance for Mayhew, because it was the key to his vision of an underclass that, besides vagrants and other criminals, featured honest, displaced, and sweated workers, who were ultimately his greatest concern.

Theories of the Underclass

There is currently something like consensus among historians that the late eighteenth and early nineteenth centuries saw the development of a concept of a criminal class that consisted of offenders drawn to crime, not by hardship, but by their moral failings. This criminal class included "the marginal people among the urban poor—the vagrants, street-folk, prostitutes, and thieves," who were perceived to represent "the main danger to the social and moral order" in the period. The concept of a criminal class was articulated by the socially respectable in a variety of forums, including parliamentary blue books, the reports of statistical societies, and in publications by magistrates, politicians, and even poets. The idea of a criminal class enjoyed such potency that it continued to flourish into the 1850s and 1860s.[3] A more general preoccupation with the urban poor and their potentially deleterious effects upon the empire—"by carrying the ideas of London to the Colonies"—persisted in the work of C. F. G. Masterman in 1901.[4]

Arguably the key figure in recent historiography was Foucault, who in *Discipline and Punish* (1975) writes, concerning early-nineteenth-century France, that "the myth of a barbaric, immoral and outlaw class . . . haunted the discourse of legislators, philanthropists and investigators into working-class life."[5] Foucault's main point in discussing what he terms "the social base" was the rise of the penitentiary and, more broadly, what he considers a "closer penal mapping of the social body" than under the ancien régime. His view was that in the late eighteenth century there developed "penal interventions at once more premature and more numerous," particularly concerning economic infractions. These policies were accompanied by the belief in a permanent criminal class, which led in turn to the invention of the modern penal system and, more broadly, to a "carceral archipelago" that encompassed a host of public institutions associated with charity, education, housing, and health care.[6]

Recent British scholarship has affirmed the representation of a criminal class and the creation of new bodies to control it. In 1990 V. A. C. Gatrell contended that crime in Britain, as in France, was increasingly considered as a class phenomenon mainly involving the destitute and the working classes; that crime was an "artificial construct" created by a new "policeman-state" and by the development of centralized policing.[7] Still other scholars have observed that nineteenth-century rethinking of crime incorporated a new model of juvenile delinquency focusing on street crime, especially thieving, but that also included immoral acts, drunkenness, popular amusements, and bodily harm. The respectable feared that, as Britain underwent rapid industrialization and urbanization, a new breed of criminal threatened the social order. They perceived the source of the problem to lie in moral decrepitude, resulting from uncontrolled emotions and the demise of reason into "savagery," "instinctualism," and "moral insanity."[8]

Not many historians currently give much credence to the threat of a teeming, organized, and dangerous criminal element.[9] They doubt the accuracy of contemporary representations of a criminal class with special mores, a "world of its own," a subculture, or "culture of poverty," that threatened to turn the respectable world upside down.[10] It now appears that policing and prosecutions, not a crime wave, were actually key factors in upping convictions in the critical period from 1805 to 1842. Moreover, when "habitual offenders" were regularly listed from the 1870s, their overall numbers do not seem all that great.[11] There is also controversy about how great a menace the criminal classes were to public order. The evidence is varied, with anxiety about criminals turning political and becoming "dangerous" at various times—in the 1790s, in the 1830s and 1840s, and in the 1860s and 1880s—but it remains to be shown how great these threats really were.[12]

Beyond these practical issues, there remains a normative issue regarding how reality was defined in nineteenth-century perceptions of crime. Although the criminal classes might have been imagined by the respectable, whose constructions stereotyped and inflated the enormity of the peril, the effects of their perceptions were no less true to those who invented them—and to those who felt the impact of the criminal justice process. As Martin Wiener perceptively states, "criticism of the early Victorians for failing to have twentieth-century notions of realism does not take us very far." It would be misleading, he adds, to assume that the respectable "had access to a reality free from moral or sensational characteristics," since for most of them social world "*was* moral, *was* sensational in its nature."[13]

Yet the contention that crime is socially imagined, that there exist no "facts of crime," but only a "judgmental process," tends to produce a top-down view with a number of potential traps. First, it may result in teleological interpretations, which in pursuing their theories may pay too little attention to historical events and contexts. For example, this way of thinking may treat crime and punishment as signs of the "onward march of surveillance and control" in which, as Foucault maintained, their histories are principally viewed as indicators of authority from above.[14] Another potential pitfall of this approach is that crime and policy responses may be presented as signs of a "civilizing process" in which misdeeds, especially homicide, are gradually checked by elite authority in advanced societies.[15]

Moreover, top-down models are preoccupied with makers of opinion and policy to the exclusion of the criminals themselves, their personal lives, and their encounters with the authorities.[16] Admittedly, respectable members of society actively took on crime in the churches, the press, and Parliament, and they indicted, judged, and sentenced criminals in order to remove them from the streets.[17] But we should not forget that, while the criminal classes were in some measure an imagined reality, it was one that had real consequences for those at the receiving end of prosecutions and punishments. In reality, because of antagonistic testimony by the respectable, we receive a distorted view of criminals, whom we chiefly perceive through the eyes of their enemies, which leads to dehumanization. We also view criminals as objects without consciousness or culture. The upshot, seen in the work of Oscar Lewis, is to see criminals existing in a "culture of poverty," the most striking aspect of which is really a "poverty of culture" and abject hopelessness.[18] Ultimately, the great limitation of top-down models is that, whether they represent a criminal class as awful nuisances or just miserable victims, they are invariably important chiefly as objects, whether of social crises, penal systems, or civilizing improvements. A final point concerns the realities of the penal system. Foucault's thesis that new processes of incarceration assumed the reality of a new class of professional criminals, or "delinquents," was an inspired one, but his emphasis on reformers and their projects for reforming the criminal class overlooks how these projects worked in reality, how offenders actually experienced these institutions, and what convicts were like when they emerged from them. It is all right to hypothesize the invention of "a prison-machine," a system of "complete and austere institutions," but we need to know whether the machine actually produced the "docile bodies" it was supposed to.[19]

Yet crime can also be seen from below, and historians of executions have demonstrated the failings of a top-down perspective by showing the active roles taken by the condemned and the populace at hangings.[20] Henry Mayhew's publications in the *Morning Chronicle* (1849–50) and in *London Labour and the London Poor* (1851–61) provide another opportunity to see the underclass from below. Of course they are inevitably viewed through the filter of the author's lens, which censored their words and in volume four of *London Labour* produced caricatures drawn from the literature of roguery. Yet, in these texts we are able to see how Mayhew represented the underclass and the extent to which he endorsed the concepts of the criminal and dangerous classes. By examining, in particular, his recording of their speech, we can determine whether these groups really shared a common culture.

Mayhew, the Criminal, and the Dangerous

There has been a tendency to exaggerate the extent to which the phrases *criminal classes* and *dangerous classes* appear in the *Morning Chronicle* and *London Labour.*[21] Certainly Peter Razzell's assertion that the "dangerous classes" "is a phrase which appears frequently" in the newspaper articles is an exaggeration.[22] In fact, a close reading of the texts shows that, considering the size of the Mayhew oeuvre, he made some use of these descriptors, which were borrowed from the French policeman Frégier's essay of 1840, without making them the main subjects of the work.[23] Crime and criminals *were* a significant part of the writer's opus, for they represented his worst fears for the fate of the underclass. But in Mayhew the terms *criminal class* and *dangerous class* were applied to specific groups, out-and-out criminals to be sure, including thieves and vagrants, as well as street vendors, all of whom he represented as presenting a threat to society. But his use of the vocabulary of social danger must also be seen as part of his broader social and economic theories, which focused on the problems of the skilled worker and low wages.

There is no doubt that Mayhew subscribed to the belief that members of the underclass were numerous, evil, and dangerous. On occasion there were no holds barred in his language. In several articles on vagrants in the *Morning Chronicle* in 1850 he sketched their failings and the threats they posed. Using some very creative mathematics, he reported that there were "no less than 47,669 individuals of the lowest, the filthiest, and most demoralized classes, continually wandering through the country" who represented "a stream of vice and disease—a tide of iniquity and fever, continually flowing." Vagrancy was the "nursery of crime"; "habitual tramps are first the beggars, then the thieves, and, finally, the convicts of the country."[24] According to the master of the Wandsworth and Clapham Poor Law Union, whom Mayhew quoted, vagrants "form one of the most restless, discontented, vicious, and dangerous elements of society." There were four thousand in London alone, and their numbers swelled "on the eve of any threatened disturbances or any large open-air meeting," such as the Chartist gathering of 1848 on Kennington Common.[25]

The most strident and sensationalist descriptions of the dangerous and criminal classes came in *London Labour and the London Poor*. The advertisement at the beginning of the fourth volume states that "the class of individuals treated of in this volume are the Non-Workers, or in other words, the Dangerous Classes of the Metropolis." It went on to assert that the volume was a "thoughtful study of the habits and character of the 'outcast' class" that arose out of "an earnest desire to better the condition of the wretched social outcasts of whom I have now to treat." Then Mayhew produced an elaborate outline of "those who will not work"—a catalog of five main categories of crook, which was further subdivided into twenty different groups, who were broken down still more minutely into 113 types of offender. He described them as "the dishonest members of society . . . known more particularly as the criminal class."

Another of Mayhew's stated objectives played to the fear of organized crime that seemed to be growing in the early 1860s, for he promised to determine whether England was experiencing a crime wave, writing that his aim was "to ascertain whether crime pursued as a profession or business, is being augmented among us—to discover whether the criminal class, as a distinct portion of our people is, or is not, on the advance." Mayhew then regaled the reader with taxonomies of crimes and criminals supposed to have been derived from 1837 police reports, but which were garnished with slang titles added by the author and which had more than a whiff of literary invention. Although derived from contemporary cant, the result is fairly crude labeling and description that makes no bones about its literary debts.[26] Mayhew claimed that his taxonomy of offenders, whom he dubbed "voluntary non-workers," reflected the specialized crimes in which they engaged.[27]

The chapters in volume four of *London Labour* by John Binny on thieves and swindlers and Andrew Halliday on beggars reproduced stereotypes from low-life literature. Both authors were fairly open about drawing on this tradition, past and present. Out of concern for the young—"to neglect them or inadequately to attend to their welfare gives encouragement to the growth of this dangerous class"—Binny cited schools for young pickpockets, which had appeared in sixteenth-century crime reports as well as in a contemporary one in *Oliver Twist;* he later compared someone to "Fagin the Jew." He described gangs of gypsies fifty to sixty strong and a King of the Gypsies, which are well-established (and misleading) literary stereotypes of Romanies. In a section on highwaymen he referred to Dick Turpin's "bold dash," while he cited a burglar led astray by seeing a theater version of *Oliver Twist* and (twice) attending a play about the escape artist Jack Sheppard. In his chapter on beggars Halliday produced one who threw epileptic fits using soap to simulate frothing at the mouth, a story as old as Thomas Harman, who wrote about such a case in the 1560s.[28] But looking beyond the obvious purloining and the caricaturing, these chapters reinforced the theory of the criminal classes. They cited the existence of "professional" crime, claiming that pickpockets knew one another and helped comrades in jail. His "pals" held collections for an injured burglar. There was a Captain Jack, who allegedly had a team of two hundred beggars working in Pye Street.[29]

Mayhew and company linked street sellers with the criminal and dangerous classes, the costermongers (fruit and vegetable hawkers) being the best known. Early in his discussion Mayhew quoted an informant, probably a police officer, who told him that "their ignorance, and their being impulsive, makes them a dangerous class," because they supported the Chartists and hated the police. Further on in the section on costers, Mayhew wrote that they were "a social pestilence in the very heart of our land" and "that the costermongers belong essentially to the dangerous classes none can doubt." They lived in sin and had their own slang, sure signs in the low-life literature of membership of the underworld.[30]

Another group of street traders whom Mayhew negatively represented were the patterers, or "street-sellers of stationery, literature and the fine arts" and formerly known as mountebanks. Mayhew did not specifically use the language of danger regarding patterers, but one of their own kind described them as outcasts. The journalist himself outlined a litany of their abuses—begging with false papers, selling broadsheets about executions before they occurred, concubinage (one philanderer claiming five hundred conquests), and speaking a slang.[31]

Mayhew's tendency to criminalize is also evident at the beginning of the second volume of *London Labour*, where he summarized his views on the dangers posed by street traders. In a broad rhetorical sweep he described "thousands . . . ready to rush forth, on the least evidence of a rising of the people, to commit the most savage and revolting excesses." These people "have neither religious nor moral principles to restrain the exercise of their grossest passions . . . [and are] men who . . . are necessarily and essentially the dangerous classes."[32] But contrary to Gertrude Himmelfarb, Mayhew left no doubt that working people should not be confused with vagrants, who were different from the "hard-working, men of England." The "non-working" were "the very opposite to the industrious classes, with whom they are too often confounded."[33]

Language among the Underclass

One test of Mayhew's criminalization of London's underclass in the mid-nineteenth century is an analysis of the slang they spoke in their interviews with him, for one of the many rich bodies of data to be mined from the Mayhew treasure trove is popular language, which he diligently recorded. He had a sharp eye for the racy quotation and was fascinated with the slang of the underclass, which he no doubt thought added rhetorical force and credibility to his reporting. Like other men of letters, he may have found having access to underworld argot glamorous. By Mayhew's time cant's captivation of the literary world was many centuries old, tracing its earliest roots to tenth-century Islam and with later variants covering virtually the entire world.[34] Mayhew's recording of language was not confined to the slang of criminals, which is what makes it so valuable and of potential interest for the study of the underclass as a whole.

There are a number of questions one might pose concerning popular language. Was speech possibly a unifying signifier among the underclass? That would support Himmelfarb's contention that Mayhew blurred the differences between the criminal and the honest poor. Or were people's words segmented into specialist vocabularies that were peculiar to particular trades and criminal groups? What proportion of the recorded vocabulary was shared between criminals and non-criminals? For centuries writers about crime had asserted that English criminals spoke a secret slang called cant. The use of this argot was assumed to signify membership in an underworld. The language question is also of wider importance in the cultural history of the period, in which there was brewing something of a language war concerned with issues such as the incorporation of "flash" vocabulary of the underworld by the respectable and the accenting of speech, with the "rude" or lower-class accent being associated with London Cockney.[35]

From the outset of *London Labour and the London Poor*, Mayhew indicated that language was a key element. Introducing the term *street-folk* in volume one, he reported, citing ethnological studies, that society was divided into two camps—wanderers and settlers—and that each group had distinctive physiological, social, and linguistic characteristics. Nomads were differentiated from "civilized man" by their refusal to engage in regular work, their inability to plan for the future, their "passion for stupefying herbs and roots" and alcohol, insensitivity to pain, love of gambling, "love of libidinous dances" and warfare, cruelty to animals, loose concepts of property, lack of chastity among their women and "disregard of female honor," and a "vague sense of religion." Their chief and abiding sin was that they preyed on the settled population to make a living. In England wanderers ranged from the "habitual vagrant—half-beggar, half-thief—to the mechanic on tramp." In between were a great variety of criminals and street traders, of which, as stated, there were said to be five categories in London and numerous subcategories.[36] Linguistically, Mayhew reported, the "wandering hordes have frequently a different language from the more civilized portion of the community" and "a secret language of their own." They were known to "vary their speech designedly, and adopt new words, with the intent of rendering their ideas unintelligible to all but the members of their own community."[37]

Although Mayhew asserted that there was a single language used among the underclass of the mid-nineteenth century, his own evidence shows that the situation was more complex than that. This is because in the course of his many interviews Mayhew recorded the speech of representatives of many groups—ethnicities (e.g., the French, Germans, the Irish, and Italians), a variety of trades, as well as the vagrant and criminal. The record is incomplete, because a single interview would be unlikely to reproduce a person's entire vocabulary. We have also to contend with the journalist's censorship, which excluded mentions of sexual acts and which sanitized foul language.

In all, Mayhew and his collaborators recorded 3,001 instances of popular slang in the *Morning Chronicle* articles of 1849–50 and in *London Labour and the London Poor*. Slang is defined here, following the *Concise Oxford Dictionary of Current English*, as "words and phrases in common colloquial use, but generally considered in some or all of their senses to be outside of standard English; words and phrases either entirely peculiar to or used in special senses by some class or profession, cant." As examples, the *Concise Oxford* refers to the slang of artists, the racing community, schoolboys, and thieves. The dictionary's second definition of "abusive language" is less useful in discussing Mayhew, because he tended to bowdlerize rude words, substituting "h__l" for *hell*, "b____y" for *bloody*, and "d__n" for *damn*. Even though he and his coauthors spent a great deal of time on the subject of prostitution, particularly in volume four of *London Labour*, details of sexual acts were never discussed.[38]

A further limitation of the evidence is that the authors themselves used slang terms, sometimes with quotation marks, but at other times without. On occasion this means that the sole source for a term is the author, which must raise doubts about the authenticity of the record. For example, a burglar recounted how *starring the glass* was a phrase for breaking a window, but he did not use the noun *star-glazer* produced by Mayhew in his taxonomy of crooks and by Binny in his account of thieves.[39] In the case of another kind of thief, the *area-diver* or *area-sneak*, who were described as stealing from areas below stairs, no members of the underclass used the term, which was seemingly the work, once again, of Mayhew and Binny.[40] Of course, we cannot be certain that these terms were never used in popular speech, since the Mayhew record is unlikely to be a complete glossary. Moreover, it is conceivable that an author's invented slang term may later enter popular speech, as apparently did *pork pies* and *porkies,* a form of Cockney rhyming slang that meant lies and which first appeared in the comedy-drama series *Minder* on the British television network ITV in the 1980s.[41]

The author's influence, however, may be overestimated. Of the 3,001 uses of slang in the Mayhew oeuvre on the underclass, there were 227 instances (7.6 percent) in which the author and his collaborators did the speaking. On one occasion a police sergeant who informed Mayhew's collaborator Hemyng about prostitutes used the slang expression *slick off* to describe a woman who drank herself to death.[42] This evidence suggests minimal direct authorial intervention and goes some way toward exploding the thesis that cant was a fabrication of popular literati. But we should really not be surprised by the inclusion of argots in the writings of the respectable. Contributors to discussions of U (upper-class) and non-U speech have observed that the slang of criminals, while most definitely non-U, was still infectious. For example, in the 1970s terms like *lolly* (money), *nick* (to steal), and *I've been conned* entered the popular vocabulary through the medium of television. As one authority noted of this tendency to adopt and popularize argot, "we pick up the brightest new slang, Broadway, Yiddish, Cockney, and from other fertile sources of new language, to decorate our discourse with for a while."[43]

Mayhew's interviews show that popular speech had many more distinguishing features than he observed. It could be varied to suit the circumstances and to keep one's meaning from the authorities. Mayhew hinted at its secrecy in referring to the variation of speech "designedly" and for "the intent of concealing their designs and exploits," and some of his narratives confirm the point.[44] In addition, the speakers could alter their words according to circumstances. The costermongers, Mayhew reported, had a specialized slang of their own, and "if any strangers are present, the conversation is still further clothed in slang, so as to be unintelligible even to the partially initiated."[45] A young pickpocket told Mayhew that in gatherings in low lodging houses "there's people there talk backward—for one they say *eno,* for two *owt,* for three *eerht,* for four *ruof,* for five *evif,* for six *exis.*" He could count no higher, he said, because "I don't know any higher. I can neither read nor write." There is good reason to think that this form of linguistic subterfuge was not unprecedented, since the costermongers used the same ploy.[46] One of Mayhew's informants about the casual wards of workhouses reported that when "cadgers saw a stranger, they used their slang."[47]

Canting was a mutable and moveable feast. Boy crossing-sweepers-cum-tumblers did not "make no slang of our own," one of them reported, "but uses the regular one." They had nicknames for each of the police officers in their neighborhood, and when one was nearby they would shout, for instance, "Phillup," as a signal not to be seen asking for money. When one of the constables discovered the meaning of this warning, "we had to change the word."[48] A beggar also reported that they altered their cant to avoid detection: "You see the flats [short for *flatty*, or policeman] got awake to it, so in course we had to alter the patter." They changed it to a rhyming slang: "The new style of cadgers' cant," the beggars stated, "is nothing like the thieves' cant, and is done all on the rhyming principle. This way's the caper." If a cadger wanted to ask a friend to visit him, smoke a pipe of tobacco, drink a glass of rum, and play a game of cards, and if "flats" were present, he would say: "'Splodger, will you have a Jack-sur*pass* of finger-and-*thumb*, and blow your yards of *tripe* of nosey me *knacker*, and have a touch of the *broads* with me and the other heaps of *coke* at my *drum*.'"[49] Speakers could also pick up the slang and drop it when the occasion demanded. A prostitute reported to Hemyng that she sometimes used the "old slang" when she was forced to beg.[50]

In examining Mayhew's opus on the underclass, it is relevant to ask who did *not* use cant or other types of slang, for this may tell us something about the circumstances of those who *did*. Foreigners, persons with even the most tenuous claims to respectability, and solitary workers did not use much cant. Mayhew delighted in attempting to capture the accented English of foreign members of the underclass, but their usage of English slang was very limited and very likely a testimony to their limited cultural assimilation.[51] It is therefore likely that the slang of London's native underclass was unique to itself, although of course foreigners might well have used argots in their own languages.

A second group who used limited amounts of jargon came from respectable backgrounds but had "gone bad," or suffered declining economic situations. Girls from good families who became prostitutes employed very little slang. Hemyng even noted that one spoke "in a superior manner."[52] But literacy alone was not the key. A girl's social background counted for more, judging by the example of a young typographer who claimed to have read Robert Owen, and who unleashed a tirade of cant about her father, whom she described as a "macing-cove [professional cheat] what robs'" and "a well-known swell of capers gay, who cut his last fling with great applause" (i.e., he was hanged). She described herself as a *mot*, probably a corruption of the old cant term *mort* (woman) and described how she "hooked many a man by showing my ankle on a wet day."[53] But the respectable poor—according to Mayhew the "reduced" gentlepersons and tradesmen, the unemployed through no fault of their own, the low paid, and the disabled—did not speak cant much.[54]

A third group who eschewed cant were solitary workers or those who worked indoors in small numbers and whose labors only exceptionally took them into public spaces; groups like the Spitalfields weavers and the many sweated workers or "slop-workers." Needlewomen, tailors, and shoemakers used the language of private, personal experience in their interviews with Mayhew. Apart from some technical terms connected with their trades, they spoke mainly of families, of their labors, and of poverty.[55]

It is important to answer the question about possible linguistic confluence between criminal and noncriminal cultures to determine whether there was any indication of a unified popular culture. In conducting an analysis of the data, some basic parameters must be laid down. The 227 examples of words used by Mayhew and his fellow authors must be excluded, so that we are certain of actually dealing with popular speech. Of the 2,774 remaining examples, there were 1,356 (48.9 percent) that were spoken and recorded just once. Of course, the slimness of this record does not mean that the words were never uttered by other parties, just that the evidence is incomplete.

The remaining 1,418 uses of slang are interesting on the issue of confluence of groups, because they show a decidedly exogenous pattern in which more than one group of persons used a given vocabulary word. All told, 1,178 (83.1 percent), of terms spoken more than once fall into the exogenous category, that is they were used by persons beyond the immediate "tribe" (criminal group, trade, etc.) to which they belonged according to Mayhew. In contrast, just 16.9 percent were used in an endogenous manner. Frequently the latter were terms of art belonging to a particular trade, and the costermongers were striking in their specialist slang. They allegedly reversed the spelling of words so they could "shield their bargainings at market" in the fruit and vegetable trades from their Irish and Jewish competitors and other "uninitiated fellow traders." Some were said to converse in it "by the hour"; it was said to be essential to be brought up in the trade to learn the vernacular, although one lad from the country claimed to have mastered it in just three months. Communication among the costers was not confined to the actual words; it was as much by "inflection of the voice, the emphasis, the tone, the look, the shrug, the nod, the wink as by the words spoken." Mayhew thought the costers' slang was lacking in humor and was mainly about business and survival in the streets. They may even have been responsible for the much abused neologism *cool*, at least in the form of *cool it*, because they substituted it for *look* to alert one another to the presence of the police.[56]

The patterers who sold fiction on street corners also had their own special argot, which one of Mayhew's gentleman-in-decline informants reported "is not the cant of the costermonger, but a system of their own." Like that of the costers, it was incomprehensible because "it is so interlarded with their general remarks, while their ordinary language is so smothered and subdued, that unless when they are professionally engaged and talking of their wares, they might almost pass for foreigners." He gave extensive examples that he claimed to have culled from a group in a low lodging house. In a manner typical of low-life literature, the gentleman insinuated himself into their company by using a patterer's cant word. He asked them how they knew of the place, and one responded, using terms that still survive in rap music today, "We drop the main toper (go off the main road) and slink into the crib (house) in the back drum (street)." The scandalous stories they circulated were called cocks, which has an impeccable pedigree in English in signifying an incredible tale.[57] Again in the fashion of low-life literature, Mayhew's informant reported that patterers, although vagrants, were not disorganized, because "there is a telegraphic dispatch between them, through the length and breadth of the land." They communicated verbally, but also through chalking on doors of houses certain signs to show whether the denizens were friendly or hostile to wayfarers. They also carved messages on the walls of lodging houses and jails, as in "Razor George and his moll slept here the day afore Christmas; just out of 'stir' (jail), for 'muzzling a peeler' [hitting a policeman]."[58]

But colorful hucksters—and no doubt these tales lost nothing in the telling by Mayhew—were not alone in having a jargon. Mainstream trades also used argots. According to rubbish carters, there were different kinds of dirt that they removed, including "soft dirt" and "hard dirt" or "hard core," consisting of bricks, chimney pots, and slates. They characterized their masters as either "good" or "scurfs."[59] Those who caught and sold wild birds used a different jargon to describe their methods. They used a net about twelve yards on a side, which they secured to the ground by four "stars" (iron pins), which held the "wings" or "flats" (sides). A trained "call-bird" was installed in the net, which by singing loudly attracted wild ones, and the trapper drew a "pull-line" to close the trap.[60] Strolling players were also observed to "have got a slang of their own"—"mummers' slang" or a "compound of broken Italian and French" and Romany. Among the examples Mayhew gives are: "'I have got no money' is, 'My nabs has nanti dinali.'"[61] Toymakers cited a "Bristol toy maker," which meant a worker in green wood; "to planish," which was to polish by hammering; and a "head" that was steel-faced on which one planished.[62] Sailors variously described working in rigging as "dandy work," "grafting," "splicing," and "knotting." A ship's carpenter who had gone whaling described his share of whale oil as "on the lay," securing a whale before killing it as "drags," the death motion of a whale as "flurries," and boiling blubber for oil as "trying out."[63] Boot and shoemakers used the term "by-strokes" to describe the taking on of extra work, often in nonunion shops, and called those who cut out the leather "clickers."[64] For their parts, sawyers referred to a certain type of stave as "doublets," while for some reason hatters dubbed low-end hat sellers "four-and-nines."[65]

Far more numerous, though, are the 1,178 terms that people shared and that suggest a culture that went beyond particular trades. Sometimes groups would borrow from one another. The boys who became chimney sweeps, Mayhew wrote, borrowed the slang of the costers, because the sweeps were uneducated and "often betray their want of education, and are in no way particular as to their expressions, their language being made up, in a great measure, of the terms peculiar to the costermongers, especially the denominations of the various sorts of money."[66] Similar borrowers were the Italian penny-ice sellers and also a street photographer and a former banjo busker, who used the "mummers' slang."[67] There was even a possible case of social crossover through speech, for in one of his shows Punch introduced himself to the audience as "'Your most obedient, most humble, and dutiful servant, Mr. Punch.'" He concluded that "ye see I can talk as affluent as can be with the call in my mouth."[68]

As examples of cultural confluence, one may also cite examples from the vocabularies recorded by Mayhew. Take, for instance, the term *cove* or person (usually male), which originated in sixteenth-century cant.[69] By the mid-nineteenth century, as the following table indicates, the word had entered popular speech among a variety of groups and venues. Leaving aside the possibly exceptional "poet/author" as not being "of the people," here was a wide range of speakers. They tended, however, to have some specific characteristics. They were chiefly people who worked in the streets, including many costers and patterers. They also inhabited the poorer venues, such as "low lodging-houses," country lodging houses, and Rosemary Lane in the East End. Largely missing were members of respectable trades that Mayhew had interviewed for the *Morning Chronicle* articles in 1849–50, and noticeably absent were the criminals among whom the term *cove* had allegedly originated several centuries earlier. Here, then, there was blurring of the distinction between the "respectable" and "unrespectable" poor.

But clustering appears in other pieces of slang among the underclass. Where terms are used to describe the police and magistrates, it

Table 3.1. Exogenous Uses of Cant: The Term Cove

Word Reference	Source	Definition	Group/ Venue	Page	Volume
cove	street lad	person	child street sellers	474a	1
cove	coster boy	person	child street sellers	482a	1
cove	stupid runaway boy	person	child street sellers	484b	1
cove	coster?	person	costers	36	1
cove	coster?	person	costers	36	1
cove	coster?	person	costers	39	1
cove	chaunter	person	paper workers	227	1
cove	ballad singer	person: in ballad	paper workers	276	1
cove	costers	person	costers	143	1
cove	muffin seller	person	muffin sellers	202	1
cove	sewer hunter	person	sewer hunters	154a	2
cove	rubbish carter	person	rubbish carters	293a	2
cove	used clothes seller	person	Rosemary Lane	41a	2
cove	Silly Billy clown	person	street exhibitors	137a	3
cove, dry bread	patterer	poor; dry toast	paper workers	271	1
cove, first-rate	lodging-house habitué	excellent patterer	lodging houses	423	1
cove, lushy	poet/author	in ballad	paper workers	279	1
cove, lushy	coster/coalshedder	drinking man	street sellers coal	85a	2
cove, missionary	whelk dealer	missionary	whelk sellers	164	1
cove, 'riginal	coster	person	costers	22	1
cove, windmill	male beggar one	sold windmills in st.	low lodging houses	417	1
coves	patterer	men	low lodging houses	259	1
coves	gallows singer	person	paper workers	283	1
coves, corner	false reference giver	chaff at people	reference sellers	445	4
coves, shallow	patterer/ beggar	phoney shipwrecks	paper workers	244	1
coves, shallow	name given to	beg half-clad	shallow coves	435	4
coves, square	street campaigner	honest people	street campaigner	419	4

Source: Henry Mayhew, *London Labour and the London Poor,* ed. John D. Rosenberg, 4 vols (London: 1851–61; repr. New York: Dover, 1968).

was overwhelmingly street vendors who used them. As the following table shows, the terms *beak, bobby, crusher,* and *peeler* were all used to indicate the authorities, and the majority of speakers (sixteen of twenty-six) were street vendors who frequently came into conflict with the police. So even when those uttering slang appear to be exogenous, there were also actually endogenous subgroups involving particular trades that had cognate qualities.

Table 3.2. Endogenous Uses of Cant: Designating the Police

Word Reference	Source	Definition	Group/ Venue	Page	Volume
beak	cheap-john	magistrate	cheap-john	337	1
beak	street lad	magistrate	child street sellers	474b	1
beak	sharp youth	policeman?	low lodging houses	255	1
beak	patterer	police	low lodging houses	260	1
beak	patterer	policeman?	paper workers	236	1
beak	former "professional"	magistrate	thieving patterers	315	1
beak	sewer hunter	magistrate	sewer hunters	154a	2
beak	bunter	police/magistrate	prostitutes	223	4
beaks	male beggar one	police	low lodging houses	415	1
bobbies	coster	police	costers	14	1
bobbies	coster	police	costers	36	1
bobbies	man in workhouse	police	workhouse inmate	250a	2
bobbies	soldiers' prostitute	police	prostitutes	246	4
bobby	cracker seller	police constable	cracker sellers	431a	1
bobby	running patterer	policeman	paper workers	228	1
bobbys	coster	police	costers	25	1
crusher	coster	policeman	costers	123	1
crushers	street lad	police	child street sellers	474b	1
crushers	coster	police?	costers	25	1
crushers	coster	police?	costers	29	1
crushers	coster	police?	costers	30	1
crushers	costermonger	police?	rubbish carters	287b	2
peeler	author?	police	costers	20	1
peeler	author?	police	costers	35	1
peeler	stationery seller	policeman	paper workers	268	1
peelers	soldier's woman	police	prostitutes	236	4

Source: Henry Mayhew, *London Labour and the London Poor,* ed. John D. Rosenberg, 4 vols (London: 1851–61; repr. New York: Dover, 1968).

Similarly with the term *quod,* which was used for *jail* and was frequently employed by persons who had been imprisoned or whose lives put them at risk for incarceration. Seven of thirteen instances of the word's usage included persons from these groups (see table 3.3).

Table 3.3. Further Endogenous Uses of Cant: Describing Jail Time

Word Reference	Source	Definition	Group/ Venue	Page	Volume
quod	ring seller	jail	ring sellers	351a–b	1
quod	coster	jail	costers	36	1
quod	author?	in jail	paper workers	250	1
quod	thief	prison	meeting of thieves	420	1
quod	female vagrant	jail	London vagrants	405	3
quod	whistling/dancing boy	jail	street musicians	201b	3
quod	ticket-of-leave man	jail	ticket of leave men	435a	3
quod, in	old street showman	in jail	street exhibitors	73a	3
quod, in	male vagrant	jail	London vagrants	381	3
quodded	coster	jailed in workhouse	costers	125	1
quodded	former "professional"	imprisoned	thieving patterers	315	1
quodded	low lodging prostitute	jailed	prostitutes	223	4
quodded	soldier's woman	jailed	prostitutes	236	4

Source: Henry Mayhew, *London Labour and the London Poor,* ed. John D. Rosenberg, 4 vols. (London: 1851–61; repr. New York: Dover, 1968).

A final example of the inside-outside dichotomy and its limitations occurs in the use of the term *slaughter* for cheap and inferior forms of production. Again, despite the variety of voices, these forms showed definite similarities among the speakers: cabinetmakers, Spitalfields weavers, boot- and shoemakers, and retailers of the *slaughterhouse,* or cheap production, knew about the sweated trades that produced them. There should be no surprise that these groups shared a jargon (see table 3.4).

The evidence I have presented suggests that there *were* confluences of vocabularies among the underclass of mid-nineteenth-century London, but that they were limited in extent. That almost half of the examples culled from Mayhew involved just a single occupational or criminal group should give one pause about accepting theories about the existence of linguistically unified criminal and dangerous classes with a wider reach into popular culture. If Mayhew's exposure of the

Table 3.4. Yet Further Endogenous Uses of Cant:
Slaughterhouses and *Slaughterers*

Word Reference	Source	Definition	Group/ Venue	Page	Volume
slaughter-house	author quotes	cheap production	street seller coal	81a	2
slaughter-house	better chairmaker	cheap middleman	cabinetmakers	150	V
slaughter-house	Spitalfields weaver	making cheap goods	Spitalfields weaver	60	I
slaughter-houses	women's man	produce junk	boot/shoemakers	159	III
slaughter houses	poor workmen call	retailers in swag shops	swag shops	333	1
slaughter houses	author quotes	cheap producers	boot/shoemakers	154	III
slaughterers	poor workmen call	retailers in swag shops	swag shops	333	1
slaughterers	garret master	wholesalers	casual workers	302a	2
slaughterers	author quotes	furniture warehouses	furniture sellers	22b	2
slaughterers	cabinetmaker	cheap employers	poor cabinetmakers	192	V

Source: Henry Mayhew, *The Morning Chronicle Survey of Labour and the Poor: The Metropolitan Districts*, ed. Peter Razzell, 6 vols. (London, 1849–50; repr., Firle, Sussex: Caliban Books, 1980); Mayhew, *London Labour and the London Poor*, ed. John D. Rosenberg, 4 vols. (London, 1851–61; repr., New York: Dover, 1968).

Note: Roman numerals for volumes refer to the *Survey.* Arabic numerals for volumes refer to *London Labour and the London Poor.*

speech of the underclass was an attempt to "take it to" them, he was in considerable measure erecting and attacking a straw man. For centuries English and continental writers had "documented" the speech of a supposed underworld of vagrants, thieves, and prostitutes, and part of the work of Mayhew and company evidently belonged to that tradition.[70] To the extent that these journalists incorporated cant into a stereotyped view of the underclass as degenerate, threatening, and a coherent class, they were "taking it to" their subjects.

Yet the Mayhew record shows that speech clusters actually existed among cognate occupations, especially those with relationships to the streets and prisons of the public sphere. These clusters suggest that a common slang did exist in varied and possibly numerous groups among the underclass. At the level of respectable fears, the existence of such argots should not be underestimated, because they clearly frightened the respectable, drove public debate, inspired legislation, and influenced policies of policing and the judicial system. To some, after all, departures from standard language can be frightening and contentious. The issue of people's speech can also be contentious: witness recent debates in the United States about "Ebonics" and hostility to Spanish-speaking immigrants, which have sparked efforts to take it to them by making English the official national language.

It remains to be seen whether the slang of the underclass in mid-nineteenth-century London fostered popular solidarity and empowerment. Specialized vocabularies may have maximized success in running street businesses and committing crimes, but their speech may also have alerted the authorities to their presence there. Where then were the points of solidarity? Physically, the underclass were scattered around London in the neighborhoods that journalists and novelists called rookeries, and reformers like Masterman as late as 1901 described as "these unknown regions."[71] Mayhew and company, besides recording popular speech, captured in print and pictures a vibrant portrait street life, including the people, the work they did (or did not), gathering places, housing, and popular entertainments. The scenes of Saturday night in the market in the New-cut suggest an animated community of stallholders, street sellers, their customers, and people from the neighborhood.[72] Similarly lively, according to Mayhew, was the Jewish neighborhood in Pettycoat Lane:

> The savor of the place is . . . peculiar. There is fresh fish, and dried fish, and fish being fried in a style peculiar to the Jews; there is the fustiness of old clothes; there is the odor from the pans on which (still in the Jewish fashion) frizzle and hiss pieces of meat and onions; puddings are boiling and enveloped in steam; cakes with strange names are hot from the oven; tubs of big pickled cucumbers give a sort of acidity to the atmosphere; lemons and oranges abound; and al-together the scene is not only such as can only be seen in London, but only such as can be seen in this one part of the metropolis.[73]

That Mayhew had a remarkable sense of places and the people that occupied them is apparent from the scene he described in Church Lane, Bloomsbury, in a section of his book innocuously entitled "street-sellers of salt." He observed a neighborhood in which

> Stretching across the narrow street, from all the upper windows, might be seen lines crossing and recrossing each other, on which hung yellow-looking shirts, stockings, women's caps, and handkerchiefs looking like soiled and torn paper, and throwing the whole lane into shade. Beneath this ragged canopy, the street literally swarmed with human beings—young and old, men and women, boys and girls, wandering about amidst all kinds of discordant sounds. The footpaths on both sides of the narrow street were occupied here and there by groups of men and boys, some sitting on the flags and others leaning against the wall, while their feet, in most instances bare, dabbled in the black channel alongside the kerb, which being disturbed sent up a sickening stench. Some of these groups were playing cards for money, which lay on the ground near them. Men and women at intervals lay stretched out in sleep on the pathway; over these the passengers were obliged to jump; in some instances they stood on their backs as they stepped over them, and then the sleeper languidly raised his head, growled out a drowsy oath, and slept again.[74]

Mayhew also described in grim detail the world of the bone-grubber and pure-finder between the London and St. Katherine's docks and Rosemary Lane. There he found, a "wretched locality . . . , redolent of filth and pregnant with pestilential diseases" to which "all the outcasts of the metropolitan population" were drawn. There they found both the positive and negative sides of takin' it to the streets. On the one hand they experienced solidarity by "finding fitting associates and companions in their wretchedness (for there is doubtlessly something attractive and agreeable to them in such companionship)." But they also went there because the authorities were takin' it to them: "for the purpose of hiding themselves and their shifts and struggles for existence from the world."[75]

It also remains to be seen whether the popular culture reported by Mayhew deserves the position accorded it in accounts of the Victorian underworld; that is, as a narrative of crime tout court. Rather, I believe that within Mayhew's overall oeuvre that culture, to be understood, must be contextualized. His concern about criminality and his hostility to the jargons of the underclass should be considered in the light of their symbolic significance for him. For, with the exception of the fourth volume of *London Labour,* Mayhew was principally concerned to highlight three issues concerning London's underclass, only one of which concerned the dangerous and criminal. First, he sought to underscore the hardships of the low paid, which he systematically and—for the most part sympathetically—chronicled. Second, he wanted to link their difficulties to a labor system he perceived to be in decline—that of the society man or the skilled, independent artisan. Third, his narrative, while often disjointed and rhetorical, targeted street vending and crime as the fate of the low-paid craft workers. There never seemed a doubt in his mind that the street vendors and criminals were the dishonorable, while the poorly remunerated and desperate artisans were the honorable. If the two groups sometimes blurred into one another, it was because the harsh reality, in Mayhew's view, was that skilled craft workers were rapidly joining the ranks of the underclass.

Notes

1. Henry Mayhew, *The* Morning Chronicle *Survey of Labour and the Poor: The Metropolitan Districts,* ed. Peter Razzell, 6 vols. (London, 1849–50; repr., Firle, Sussex: Caliban Books, 1980); Mayhew, *London Labour and the London Poor,* ed. John D. Rosenberg, 4 vols. (London, 1851–61; repr., New York: Dover, 1968).

2. Peter Burke, introduction to *The Social History of Language,* ed. Peter Burke and Roy Porter, Cambridge Studies in Oral and Literate Culture, no. 12 (Cambridge: Cambridge University Press, 1987), 11–13.

3. Victor Bailey, "The Fabrication of Deviance: 'Dangerous Classes' and 'Criminal Classes' in Victorian England," in *Protest and Survival: Essays for E. P. Thompson,* ed. John Rule and Robert Malcolmson (London: Merlin Press, 1993), 232–35, 239–42. This section of this chapter is reprinted, with some changes, from "Identity, Language, and Resistance in the Making of the Victorian 'Criminal Class': Mayhew's Convict Revisited," *Journal of British Studies* 44, no. 3 (2005): 499–502.

4. Charles F. G. Masterman, ed., *The Heart of the Empire: Discussions of Problems of Modern City Life in England* (London: T. Fisher Unwin, 1901; repr., New York: Barnes and Noble, 1973, ed. Bentley B. Gilbert), preface, viii–ix. I owe this reference to Paul Ocobock.

5. Michel Foucault, *Discipline and Punish: The Birth of the Prison* (New York: Vintage Books, 1979; orig. pub. as *Surveiller et punir: Naissance de la prison* [Paris: Gallimard, 1975]), 275. Foucault's work was anticipated in considerable measure by Louis Chevalier, *Classes laborieuses et classes dangereuses à Paris pendant la première moitié du XIXe siècle* (Paris: Plon, 1958).

6. Foucault, *Discipline and Punish*, 78–82, 296–98.

7. V. A. C. Gatrell, "Crime, Authority and the Policeman-State," in *The Cambridge Social History of Britain*, ed. F. M. L. Thompson, 3 vols. (Cambridge: Cambridge University Press, 1990), 3:250, 278, 287.

8. For youth, see Heather Shore, *Artful Dodgers: Youth and Crime in Early Nineteenth-Century London* (Rochester, NY: Boydell, 1999; repr., 2002), 7, 17, 29–31, 34; also see Gatrell, "Policeman-state," 278–79. Quotations are from Martin J. Wiener, *Reconstructing the Criminal: Culture, Law, and Policy in England, 1830–1914* (Cambridge: Cambridge University Press, 1990), 14–27.

9. Bailey cites various authorities that separated the working and criminal poor. Bailey, "Fabrication of Deviance," 223, 232, 234. Cf. Shore, *Artful Dodgers*, 53, 151; David Philips, *Crime and Authority in Victorian England: The Black Country, 1835–1860* (London: Croom Helm, 1977), 126–27, 287; Clive Emsley, *Crime and Society in England, 1750–1900*, 2nd ed. (London: Longman, 1996), 173. For more recent evidence of the blurring of lines between working and crime, criminals and the police, see Dick Hobbs, *Doing the Business: Entrepreneurship, the Working Class, and Detectives in the East End of London* (Oxford: Oxford University Press, 1988), 117, 149–50.

10. Quotations from Wiener, *Reconstructing the Criminal*, 20; G. Himmelfarb, "The 'Culture of Poverty,'" in *The Victorian City: Images and Realities*, ed. H. J. Dyos and M. Wolff 2 vols. (London: Routledge and Kegan Paul, 1973), 2:711, 730. But for doubts about a subculture, see Gatrell, "Policeman-state," 303 (while stating on p. 299 that "professional" crime certainly existed); Emsley, *Crime and Society*, 173.

11. Shore, *Artful Dodgers*, 17, 29–32; Wiener, *Reconstructing the Criminal*, 14, 17; S. J. Stevenson, "The 'Habitual Criminal' in Nineteenth-Century England: Some Observations on the Figures," *Urban History Yearbook*, 1986, 48–49. Stevenson notes that lower levels of policing tended to produce fewer registrations of offenders (44).

12. Bailey, "Fabrication of Deviance," 224–25, 236–37, 250.

13. Wiener, *Reconstructing the Criminal*, 29 (emphasis in original).

14. Ibid., 6–8. There is the further difficulty with the Foucault model that it tends to treat the authorities as monolithic. See the evidence of police resistance to the enforcement of middle-class morals on the London working classes gathered by Stephen Inwood, "Policing London's Morals: The Metropolitan Police and Popular Culture, 1829–1850," *London Journal* 15, no. 2 (1990): 135, 137, 142.

15. Eric A. Johnson and Eric H. Monkonnen discuss the Norbert Elias paradigm. Johnson and Monkonnen, eds., *The Civilization of Crime: Violence in Town and Country since the Middle Ages* (Urbana: University of Illinois Press, 1996), 1–13.

16. An outstanding exception to this statement is Shore, *Artful Dodgers.*

17. For an early example of elite involvement in the reform of policing and punishment, see A. L. Beier, "Foucault *Redux?* The Roles of Humanism, Protestantism, and an Urban Elite in Creating the London Bridewell, 1500–1560," in *Crime, Gender, and Sexuality in Criminal Prosecutions*, ed. Louis A. Knafla, Criminal Justice History, no. 17 (Westport, CT: Greenwood, 2002).

18. For a powerful attack on Oscar Lewis's formulation and evidence, see Charles A. Valentine, *Culture and Poverty: Critique and Counter-proposals* (Chicago: University of Chicago Press, 1968), ch. 3.

19. Foucault, *Discipline and Punish*, 135, 249, 251. Foucault did cite resistance to some forms of forced labor and efforts by workers' newspapers to resist the isolation of delinquents from the urban working classes (241, 286–87). Cf. Gatrell, "Policeman-state," 302–3, for a statement that professional criminals were "usually conceived within and sheltered by the urban poor."

20. Peter Linebaugh, *The London Hanged: Crime and Civil Society in the Eighteenth Century* (Cambridge: Cambridge University Press, 1992); V. A. C. Gatrell, *The Hanging Tree: Execution and the English People, 1770–1868* (Oxford: Oxford University Press, 1994); but esp. Thomas W. Laqueur, "Crowds, Carnival and the State in English Executions, 1604–1868," in *The First Modern Society: Essays in English History in Honour of Lawrence Stone*, ed. A. L. Beier, David Cannadine, and James M. Rosenheim (Cambridge: Cambridge University Press, 1989), 332.

21. This chapter will not consider Mayhew and Binny, *The Criminal Prisons of London and Scenes of Prison Life* (London: Griffin, Bohn, 1862; repr., London: F. Cass, 1968), which focuses on prisons and whether they reformed criminals.

22. P. Razzell, introduction, *Morning Chronicle*, 1:2. Admittedly the author adds, "Mayhew only used it to rebut the assumptions and fears which it concealed."

23. Himmelfarb, *Idea of Poverty*, 393; but somewhat contradictorily, she did not believe the dangerous classes of England posed the same threat as their counterparts in France or Germany (395–97).

24. Mayhew, *Survey*, 3:47.

25. Ibid., 3:47, 50, 69, 74.

26. Mayhew, *London Labour*, IV, v, 1, 23–27, 29–30, 33. For differing views of the 1860s, see Jennifer Davis, "The London Garrotting Panic of 1862: A Moral Panic and the Creation of a Criminal Class in Mid-Victorian London," in *Crime and the Law: The Social History of Crime in Western Europe since 1500*, ed. V. A. C. Gatrell, B. Lenman, and G. Parker (London: Europa, 1980), 190ff.; S. J. Stevenson, "The 'Habitual Criminal' in Nineteenth-Century England: Some Observations on the Figures," *Urban History Yearbook*, 1986, 37–60.

27. Mayhew, *London Labour*, 4:30–31.

28. Ibid., 4:33, 275, 302, 304, 314, 326, 347, 376, 434–35. For early modern examples, fictional and real, see ch. 7 in Beier, *Masterless Men: The Vagrancy Problem in England, 1560–1640* (London: Methuen, 1985).

29. Mayhew, *London Labour*, 4:255–56, 324, 352, 432.

30. Ibid., 1:11, 20, 101 (which includes some remarks by Mayhew defending the costers).

31. Ibid., 1:213–23.

32. Ibid., 2:5. The hyperbole was qualified when he stated that these were "men who have no knowledge of the government of the country but as an armed despotism, preventing their earning their living, and who hate all law, because it is made to appear to them merely as an organized tyranny," presumably a reference to restrictions on street-traders' rights. He added an explanation if not a defense of their dangerousness, which he said arose "from our very neglect of them," so that we "rail at or deplore" their existences.

33. Ibid. 3:45, 50. Cf. ibid., 410–29, esp. 428–29. But Mayhew's stories of immoral, criminal behavior among vagrants were tempered in *London Labour* by a series of lengthy autobiographies, which with great humanity spelled out how sweated labor, unemployment, and family crises led to mendicancy, and which ended with one of his occasional attacks on the rich in which he told them to "get down from your moral stilts."

34. Peter Burke, introduction to *Languages and Jargons: Contributions to a Social History of Language*, ed. Burke and Roy Porter (Cambridge: Polity, 1995), 5; C. E. Bosworth, *The Mediaeval Islamic Underworld*, 2 vols.

(Leiden: E. J. Brill, 1976), 1:153; A. Dauzat, *Les argots: Caractères, evolution, influence* (Paris: Delagrave, 1956), cited by Bosworth, 1:152.

35. A. L. Beier, "Identity, Language, and Resistance in the Making of the Victorian 'Criminal Class': Mayhew's Convict Revisited," *Journal of British Studies,* 44, no. 3 (2005): 512–14, and the sources cited there.

36. Mayhew, *London Labour,* 1:2–3.

37. Ibid., 1:2.

38. H. W. Fowler and F. G. Fowler, eds., *The Concise Oxford Dictionary of Current English,* 5th ed. (Oxford: Oxford University Press, 1964); Mayhew, *London Labour,* 1:16, 21, 25, 31, 33, 46, 69, 100.

39. Mayhew, *London Labour,* 4:25, 281, 293, 339.

40. Ibid. 4:25, 291.

41. The etymology of these terms, which are presumably substitutes for "dirty lies" or some such equivalent, is a matter of dispute between myself and my friend Professor Clive Emsley of the Open University. Although Emsley, as a Londoner and a historian of crime, has excellent credentials in this area, it seems that that he is mistaken in thinking that "porkies" was in common parlance before *Minder.*

42. Mayhew, *London Labour,* 4:237; cf. Hemyng's use of the terms "legged" and "bullies" without quotation marks, ibid., 4:252, 264.

43. Richard Buckle, *U and Non-U Revisited* (London: Viking, 1978), 38, 42–43.

44. Mayhew, *London Labour,* 1:321.

45. Ibid., 1:11.

46. Ibid., 1:411 (emphasis in original); for the costers, see ibid., 1:23–24.

47. Ibid., 3:396.

48. Ibid., 2:496, 498.

49. Ibid., 1:418 (emphasis in original).

50. Ibid., 4:245.

51. Ibid., 1:94, 2:8, 337, 3:414 (Irish); 2:8 (Jewish), 2:454 (Moroccan); Mayhew, *Survey,* 3:190 (German), 77, 192 (French), 245; Mayhew, *London Labour,* 3:77, 139 (Italian).

52. Mayhew, *London Labour,* 4:243–44, 260–62, 269–71.

53. Ibid., 4:256.

54. Ibid. 1:91, 269–70, 3:414–16

55. Mayhew, *Survey,* 1:57–8, 60–61, 62–63, 112, 115, 121, 135, 138–39, 141, 144, 148–49, 149–50, 155–56, 157–59.

56. Mayhew, *London Labour,* 1:23–4.

57. Ibid., 1:218, 222, 234, 292; *Concise Oxford Dictionary of Current English,* s.v. *cock.* Note that Mayhew put a negative spin on the term when he associated it with phony love letters. Mayhew, *London Labour,* 1:238.

58. Ibid., 1:218–19.

59. Ibid., 2:281, 289.

60. Ibid., 2:58.

61. Ibid., 3:139.

62. Ibid., 3:217, 230.

63. Ibid., 4:92, 12.

64. Mayhew, *Survey,* 3:121, 125, 155, 156.

65. Ibid., 5:63–64, 74; 6:154, 159.

66. Ibid., 2:364. Mayhew adds, however, that he has met with sweepers "whose language was that in ordinary use, and their manners not vulgar."

67. Ibid., 2:139, 364; 3:206.

68. Ibid., 3:54. The call may refer to a "signaling-whistle." *Concise Oxford Dictionary.*

69. *Concise Oxford Dictionary.*

70. Lee Beier, "Anti-language or Jargon? Canting in the English Underworld in the Sixteenth and Seventeenth Centuries," in *Languages and Jargons: Contributions to a Social History of Language,* ed. Peter Burke and Roy Porter (Cambridge, MA: Polity, 1995), 64–69.

71. Masterman, "Realities at Home," in *Heart of the Empire,* 15.

72. Mayhew, *London Labour,* 1:9–10.

73. Ibid., 2:10–11.

74. Ibid., 2:89–90.

75. Ibid., 2:143–44.

4

Vagrant India

Famine, Poverty, and Welfare under Colonial Rule

David Arnold

CRITICAL UNDERSTANDING OF the nature and significance of vagrancy in colonial India is best situated within a wider discussion of poverty and welfarism. This essay divides the colonial era into three main phases, covering the periods 1770–1840, 1840–1900, and 1900–47, and works from three basic premises. The first is that consideration of the idea of welfare in British India call for a long-term perspective— as much in order to identify the factors that inhibited the growth of a welfare ideology as those that favored its eventual (and only partial) emergence. The essay accordingly surveys the colonial *longue durée* from the Bengal famine of 1770, which occurred shortly after the English East India Company assumed control of eastern India, up to the landmark Health Survey and Development Committee, which reported in 1946, on the eve of Indian independence. A second premise is that recurrent famine had a significant bearing both on how vagrancy manifested itself in India and how welfare ideas and practices were formulated. However, the absence of overt famine after 1908, before concepts of state welfare became widely disseminated and officially endorsed, poses questions about the exact nature of the famine/welfare relationship.

The third premise is that measures to counter destitution and vagrancy in India cannot be understood simply in terms of state policy (or even the racial bias inherent in colonial policy) but also need to be considered in relation to civil society. One of the singular characteristics of post-independence India has been a failure to establish a welfare state. As Sunil Amrith has observed "the idea that the state ought to be held responsible for the provision of public healthcare is not one that has rooted itself in Indian political culture."[1] India has looked instead to indigenous traditions of poor relief and social welfare, and the period under discussion witnessed the growth of community and political organizations that offered their own welfare programs.

Encountering Poverty

Two interconnected events set the agenda for the early colonial period. The first was the Bengal famine of 1770, which devastated eastern India (causing as many as ten million deaths) and set back agricultural production for decades.[2] The second was the establishment of the Permanent Settlement in 1793, which sought to resolve problems of rural management and revenue extraction in Bengal by entrusting land control to Indian landlords (*zamindars*) in return for a fixed rent. The famine was partly attributed to a deficient monsoon and resulting food shortages, but the rapacity of East India Company officials helped strip the countryside of food at a time of heightened vulnerability. That the famine erupted in Bengal, hitherto the most bountiful of all Indian provinces, was a profound shock to British expectations. One response was to seek ways in which the seemingly frail agrarian economy could be rendered more secure and the livelihood of the population guaranteed. The Permanent Settlement conceived the zamindars as an "improving" elite, whose enlightened management of their estates would enhance the well-being and productivity of their tenant farmers.[3] The settlement delegated primary responsibility for peasant welfare to the zamindars, who held judicial as well as revenue powers over their peasants (*ryots*).[4]

Science and technology were also invoked to help create a more secure and productive agrarian society. This included the establishment at Calcutta in 1786 of a botanic garden, whose first superintendent,

Robert Kyd, advocated the introduction and dissemination of new plants to supplement the seemingly narrow range of Indian food staples and commercial crops.[5] The program of agrarian improvement was extended through the founding of the Agricultural and Horticultural Society in Calcutta in 1820 by the Baptist missionary William Carey. Transferring to India the lessons of Britain's agricultural revolution appeared to offer a practical means of combating famine, ridding the countryside of unproductive "wastes" and jungle, improving animal husbandry, and transforming the supposedly indolent and custom-bound peasantry into an industrious workforce. When Carey spoke of "the future welfare of India" he partly had in mind associating "Native Gentlemen" with the task of agricultural improvement,[6] though, in practice, the society relied heavily on European agency. Yet, even though successive governors-general praised the society and lauded its ambitions, they were loath to commit state revenues for the purpose. Equally, many naturalists became more interested in the ornamental aspects of Indian botany than in the need to revitalize Indian agriculture, and by the late 1830s there was general disappointment that so little of practical benefit had been achieved.[7] What the investigations of the early colonial period did, however, was to naturalize the idea of poverty in India, to see it as inherent in its awkward climate and capricious monsoons, its deficient harvests and outmoded agrarian practices, deflecting attention away from the impoverishing effect of "de-industrialization" and the high revenue assessments instituted by the British.

At this early stage of colonial rule the peasant was identified as the bedrock of Indian society but also as famine prone and eking out a precarious existence from the land. Two other aspects of the initial colonial response to Indian poverty and distress deserve notice. One was the assumption that Indian society already possessed, as the Famine Commission of 1880 later put it, structures that were "admirably adapted for common effort against a common misfortune." These included the "corporate body" of the Hindu joint family, but also long-standing relations of "moral obligation" and "mutual assistance," as between landlord and tenant, master and servant, alms giver and alms receiver, "which are of the utmost importance in binding the social fabric together, and enabling it to resist any ordinary strain." These ancient institutions, along with "salutary habits of frugality and foresight," allowed India to pass "comparatively unscathed though periods of dearth." Hence, in the colonial view, "Any form of relief calculated to . . . break down these habits, by showing them to be superfluous, would be an incalculable misfortune."[8]

In part these views reflected a tendency on the part of the British to Orientalize and romanticize certain aspects of Indian society and to minimize their own responsibilities. But the famines of the nineteenth century did appear to show the continuing value of indigenous forms of charity and poor relief. Some of these stemmed directly from Indian traditions of philanthropy,[9] while others were of a more recent, hybrid nature. For example, the Monegar *choultry* (rest house) first established during the 1780–81 famine in Madras, was run by a joint committee of Indians and Europeans. Sited just outside the city, the choultry fed crowds of hungry migrants who flocked in from the surrounding countryside during repeated famine episodes.[10] Throughout the nineteenth century, in this and in many other towns and cities, landlords and merchants distributed grain or cooked food to thousands of the famine-struck.[11] It was one of the enduring features of Indian famines, right up to 1943, that, although they originated in the countryside, their impact was most fully felt when the starving poor descended on the cities in search of food and shelter and so brought their plight to the attention of the urban population. However, by the 1830s many Europeans had grown critical of Indian charity, seeing it as disorganized, inadequate, and, especially when it was directed at high-status groups like Brahmins, more likely to encourage the idle than sustain the genuinely needy.[12]

The other noteworthy aspect of relief in this early period was the extent to which it reflected the racial exclusionism of the colonial regime. Asylums were established from the early 1780s onward for the care of European and mixed-race (Eurasian) orphans: modeled on similar institutions in eighteenth-century Britain, by the 1830s they accommodated as many as three thousand children across India.[13] European churches also provided relief for poor members of their congregations or through "friend-in-need" societies helped European and Eurasian paupers.[14] Indian destitutes were dealt with differently: some were rounded up by the police and dumped at city hospitals and dispensaries; many ended up in jail convicted of looting or petty theft.[15] Indians were deemed too numerous to receive systematic relief and, anyway, as the influential administrator and evangelical Charles Grant argued, giving further weight to the naturalization of Indian poverty, they lived in a country where climate and custom had combined "to keep down the standards of wants among the Indian poor. The tropical climate minimizes the need for food and artificial warmth, and so simplifies the mere act of living."[16] William Tennant, a Calcutta chaplain, similarly observed that while poverty and nakedness were universal in India this did not signify the same degree of suffering as in Europe: "An Hindoo," he averred, "feels himself comfortable on the same fare on which an Englishman would languish and starve."[17] India appeared to permit levels of poverty (for Indians) that in Britain would have been almost unimaginable or for which the austerity of the workhouse was the necessary solution. India was beyond the workhouse.

That is not to say that metropolitan debates over poor laws and workhouses passed India by. On the contrary, they sharpened awareness of the peculiarities of the Indian situation. Thus, the 1837–38 North Indian famine saw widespread use of such terms as *paupers, vagrants,* the *able-bodied* and *deserving poor* that echoed poor-law legislation in Britain.[18] But, despite the rhetoric, there was extreme reticence about adopting similar measures in India. As Lance Brennan noted, "While the British were committed to the maintenance of the eligible poor in England, they refused to consider this as a possibility in normal times in India, preferring to rely upon the private charitable institutions and practices of the people over whom they ruled. They were prepared to interfere only when whole populations were endangered by widespread famine. The last thing they wished to consider was an Indian equivalent of the New Poor Law."[19]

As a further illustration of this principle of colonial difference, in Calcutta in the late 1830s the problem of vagrancy on the city's streets was so intense that the District Charitable Society, set up in the wake of the 1837 famine and drawing on both European and Indian funds, decided to abandon distribution of gratuitous relief. It asked the government for permission to build a workhouse that would attract only the most desperately needy and require them to labor for their subsistence. The society urged the government to pass a vagrancy act, offering its own draft ("in strict analogy with that introduced into England at the suggestion of the Poor Law Commissioners") as an inducement.[20] The government approved the workhouse but rejected vagrancy legislation, partly because of the scale of the problem. It was anyway wary of offending Hindu and Muslim sentiment by seeming to outlaw religious mendicants or prohibit almsgiving.[21] When vagrancy legislation was introduced in India in the 1870s it was, as we shall see shortly, for the very different purpose of confining European—not Indian—vagrants.

Famine and Vagrancy in the Age of Laissez-Faire

The 1830s and 1840s can be seen as marking a shift in colonial thinking about poverty and destitution. Significant in this was the persistence of famine and the severe mortality and economic dislocation it occasioned. The 1837–38 famine was followed by a series of similar episodes, particularly between 1866 and 1908, affecting vast swaths of the subcontinent and resulting in millions of deaths from starvation and disease.[22] One state response was to look to modern technology and public works for a solution—initially through the construction of irrigation canals, and subsequently, from the 1850s, of railroads. The severity of the 1837–38 famine stimulated the idea of public works as a legitimate state response to drought and dearth, one that did not contravene laissez-faire orthodoxy. One enthusiast anticipated that the effect of the new canals on the countryside between the Ganges and Jumna rivers would be that "this great tract will become the garden of the North-Western Provinces; and we shall hear no more of those devastating famines, which have hitherto swept across it, bringing physical wretchedness and moral degradation in their train."[23] Decades later, the Indian Irrigation Committee advised, more cautiously: "The whole of India can never be protected from famine by irrigation alone, but irrigation can do much to restrict the area and to mitigate the intensity of famine."[24] Railroads assumed still greater prominence as a means of facilitating the rapid movement of grain to needy districts in times of dearth (as well as providing works of "permanent utility" on which the famine-poor labored in return for relief). The 1880 Famine Commission endorsed this strategy by calling for the building of an additional twenty thousand miles of railroads as one of the most urgent and effective ways of curbing famine.[25]

But while the state looked to technological solutions to the famine problem, its economic policy was generally constrained by laissez-faire doctrine. Although the impact of free-trade ideology on state responses to dearth and famine became evident as early as 1806, it was not until the 1830s, and particularly the 1860s and 1870s, that the full significance of state abstention from the market became apparent.[26] The determination not to interfere in the grain trade, nor to force down prices, import food stocks, or prohibit hoarding and export, provoked food riots and other forms of protest. It also left many officials perplexed: there always was a dissenting view that Indian famine was a catastrophe so far beyond conventional "dearth" and "distress" as to be outside the normal laws of political economy. However, in the wake of the English poor law and the Irish famine, the state's abstentionist policy was coupled with an insistence that any relief should not be gratuitous, for fear this would encourage idleness, but only (except in extreme cases of debility and destitution) given in return for labor. Famine wages and relief conditions were to discourage all but the most needy and, even then, allowed them only the minimum necessary for survival.[27]

Malthusian pessimism pervaded official thinking, with the underlying assumption that the impecunious poor had brought their fate largely on themselves: "Poverty, ignorance, apathy, improvidence, fatalism, tropical reproduction amongst men"—along with "poverty of soil and deficient rainfall in nature"—were, according to one official who had witnessed the South Indian famine of 1876–78, "the causes that bar progress and produce famines."[28] Strict adherence to the principles of political economy was frequently invoked and enjoined upon subordinate officials. Thus Sir Richard Strachey expressed his "earnest hope that no temporary impulse of sympathy with present suffering, no selfish . . . effort to escape at any cost the pain of witnessing it, may be permitted to stand in the way of that real benevolence which is founded on sound principles drawn by intelligence from the lessons of experience."[29] Historians, however, have tended to take the view that "behind the façade of theoretical argument [in support of laissez-faire] there was the fear that the Government would have to assume a gigantic financial responsibility in undertaking to feed a vast population during the period of a famine."[30] More than 60 percent of state income was derived from land revenue and protecting that tax base was an essential part of state policy.

The widespread famine of 1876–78 did, however, force the government of India to acknowledge that even under laissez-faire it had an obligation to protect its subjects. In January 1877 it declared that "human life shall be saved at any cost and at any effort; no man, woman or child shall die from starvation," though it added: "Distress they must often suffer; we cannot save them from that. We wish we could do more, but we must be content with saving life and preventing extreme suffering."[31] Viceroy Lord Lytton's minute on famine policy in August that year restated the imperative of state abstention from the grain trade, "so long as that trade was active," but also the need to provide relief works for those demonstrably in need. The government was further obliged "to avert death from starvation by the employment of all means practically open to the resources of the State and the exertions of its officers; but to discharge this duty at the lowest cost compatible with the preservation of human life from wholesale destruction."[32] The Famine Commission of 1880 went further, declaring that in a crisis beyond the ability of individuals to obtain relief for themselves the state must act. "It . . . becomes a paramount duty of the State to give all practical assistance to the people in time of famine, and to devote all its available resources to this end, and this duty is emphasized by the fact that the Government stands in the place of landlord to the agriculturists, who form the great mass of the population."[33] The commission prepared the way for the provincial famine codes that gave detailed guidance on the timing and nature of relief measures. The codes have been seen as a major achievement of British rule, though they were unable to prevent the famines that between 1896 and 1901 again devastated large parts of India.[34]

From the perspective of destitution and vagrancy, two further aspects of these Victorian famines warrant attention. First, the onset of famine gave rise to a mass mobilization of the rural poor, as poor peasants, rural artisans, and laborers left their homes in search of food, drifting into towns and districts still relatively unaffected by drought and dearth. Although famine migration was a significant factor behind the exodus of Indian labor across the subcontinent and overseas, the "irrational" wandering of large numbers of the famine-poor alarmed British officials—it facilitated the spread of disease, made relief administration more difficult, imperiled law and order, and left many cultivators far from their fields when, eventually, agricultural activity resumed. Many destitutes found their way to relief camps, but others, as in the Madras Presidency (1876–78), found refuge in dispensaries, jails, even in the lock hospitals intended for prostitutes.[35] Wandering on such a vast, unregulated scale was one factor in impelling the authorities to institute local relief measures designed to keep the famine-struck close to home. But it can also be understood as part of a more general concern to curtail the unsupervised movement of the poor, including those "wandering tribes" who, from 1871 onward, were brought under the provisions of the Criminal Tribes Act.[36]

Second, private charity was mobilized to fill the void left by the paucity of state relief, but in the novel form of provincial and all-India funds. There was a recognition that during "ordinary times" Hindu and Muslim charitable practices assisted the aged and infirm "as a religious duty." When "times of trouble" arose this "deeply-rooted institution of private charity" continued for a while to supplement state relief, but as distress grew more acute private charity "naturally contract[ed]" and needed to be absorbed into an "organized system of charitable relief on a wider basis, in which all the better classes of the community participate[d]."[37] In appealing for private charity in 1868 the lieutenant governor of the North-Western Provinces pledged that the state would aid the "helpless poor" and, where necessary, provide them with work. "But the support of the sick and aged, the young and tender, and the infirm, must mainly be the care of private charity."[38] In the South Indian famine of 1876–78 this involved a well-publicized nonofficial campaign in which collections made in India were supplemented by donations made in Britain through the Mansion House Committee and elsewhere in the empire.[39] Perhaps fearing how negatively this might reflect on the state's own response, in many subsequent famines officials were deputed to help elicit private charity (even posting poor boxes in their offices for the purpose). The viceroy and provincial governors also leant their support. Thus, in February 1900 the viceroy, Lord Curzon, appealed to Europeans and Indians alike to give to the famine-struck, thereby "obeying a summons that lies at the root of all religion and is the consecration of our common humanity."[40]

Huge funds were raised in this way (more than three million rupees in 1900–1901 alone), but these exercises in state-sponsored charity were not unproblematic. Charitable committees were expected to supplement state measures, not rival them. They were directed to use their funds to help individuals not covered by state relief (such as assisting purdah women "who would rather have died" than attend public relief works, providing clothing and other "additional comforts," and advancing loans to cultivators who had no security and so were ineligible for state benefits).[41] Although the committees included both European and Indian members, in general the Europeans—officials, businessmen, missionaries, and clergymen—predominated and there was some disagreement as to how funds should be raised and expended. The issue of poor-law legislation for India again arose, to be dismissed once more as inappropriate: "any legislative enactment in this direction, so far as it related to the Native residents of India, would be altogether opposed to Native public feeling," declared the European secretary of the Central Committee Relief Fund in 1869. He added, "As long as the professed religion of the great mass of the people made religious mendicants objects of veneration and solicitude, as long as the generous dole of lavish and indiscriminate charity is a practice not only enjoined by the belief of the people, but largely in vogue amongst the richer and better-educated classes, it would be inexpedient to take any steps for the establishment of workhouses."[42]

Not for the first time, the need to conciliate "native" opinion was used as an argument for state inaction.

Famines, and the contrast between Indian poverty and apparent state indifference they appeared to illuminate, were one of the principal ingredients in the emerging anticolonial critique of the late nineteenth century.[43] But in 1888, when Lord Dufferin instituted an inquiry to assess the extent of distress among the poorer classes of India, he reached a reassuring conclusion. Responses from district officials showed wide regional variation (in Bihar, for instance, 40 percent of the population were said to be in a state of "agricultural degradation"), but the overall verdict was remarkably complacent, for it appeared that "in normal years the people seem to enjoy a rude plenty." The secretary of state concurred, observing that "in ordinary seasons even the poorest of Her Majesty's Indian subjects get enough food to keep them in fair health and strength," and that the standard of living across India had generally improved over the past thirty years. "It may be true," he added, "that the condition of the poorest classes in India is not so depressed as the condition of the very poor in the crowded cities of Europe." But even so, "these conditions do not absolve the British Government in India from the duty which it has undertaken of mitigating, as far as may be possible, the evils of drought and famine."[44]

The guarded state response to the widespread famines in which many millions of Indians perished stands in sharp contrast to the policy pursued with respect to European vagrancy. This only became a serious issue for the British after the Mutiny of 1857, as increasing numbers of European soldiers and sailors were discharged in India or were dismissed (often for drunkenness or abusive behavior) by the railroad companies that had employed them as train drivers, guards, and stationmasters. The issue was one of both race and class. The European elite looked down on these "loafers," believing that their actions (tramping from place to place, demanding food from villagers, begging in the streets and bazaars) were demeaning to the white race and might incite racial hostility. The numbers involved were small— a few hundred in any one year—but in 1871 the government of India moved quickly to legislate against them (a revised Vagrancy Act was passed in 1874). In a parody of the English poor law, white vagrants were arrested and confined to workhouses, where their conditions were far from arduous and which mostly served to detain them (and to keep them out of the public eye) until they could be put on a ship and deported back to Britain. Except in error, Indians and Eurasians were never brought under the provisions of this vagrancy legislation.[45]

The Move to Welfare

In 1908 the last in the long series of famines ended. Although widespread hunger and malnutrition remained, there were no further major famine episodes in British India, apart from that in Bengal in 1943, which occurred in the exceptional circumstances of World War II. While famine reigned, ideas of welfare remained, in official discourse, little more than generalized pieties. But a more precise notion of welfare did emerge, especially after World War I. One reason for this was growing official recognition of the problem of rural poverty (while largely absolving the British of blame for it) and the attempt to redress it through rural cooperative societies and debt relief measures.[46] More substantially, though, the invocation of welfare ideology came from several different directions, mostly from outside the formal state structure. One element in this was the medicalization of welfare, especially through the growth of the women's medical movement. Initially, as represented by the Dufferin Fund, established in 1885, this took the form of employing women doctors to care for female patients who for reasons of caste and religion might not be seen by male (especially white male) doctors. But over the course of the following decades, particularly after 1918, the investigation of women's health gave rise to expressions of more urgent concern. By the 1930s one of the principal contexts in which the idea of "welfare" was mooted was in relation to the special needs of women (and, by extension, children). For instance, from 1933 the All-India Institute of Hygiene and Public Health in Calcutta had a small Maternity and Child Welfare Centre, and in 1937 a special committee was appointed by the Central Advisory Board of Health to report on "maternity and child welfare work" in India.[47] The pursuit of women's and children's welfare, though often articulated, even by colonial officials, in terms of national need (and often with a eugenic tinge),[48] in practice drew only to a limited extent on state funds and personnel, relying heavily instead on voluntary organizations like the Indian Red Cross and the Calcutta-based Ramakrishna Mission. Yet, as India's public health commissioner observed in 1937,

> The children of the nation are one of the State's most valuable assets and few countries are now content to leave the protection and welfare of their future citizens entirely to the head of the family or to the humanitarian efforts of philanthropists or of voluntary organizations. . . . The stage seems to have been reached in India when transition from voluntary direction to official control must take place if further developments are to be made, and the problem during the next few years will be to preserve a suitable balance between governmental and voluntary effort. The duties and responsibilities of guardianship of the nation's children must be shared by individuals and by the State.[49]

Two further developments arguably encouraged this move toward welfare, if only through their evident insufficiency. One was the growth of local government institutions, entrusted from 1888 with primary responsibility for public health. The powers of these bodies were strictly circumscribed, as was their income, which relied heavily on unpopular local taxes.[50] Municipal councils and rural boards strove to promote their own limited version of welfare by setting up dispensaries and clinics, forming malaria eradication brigades, and appointing midwives, vaccinators, and sanitary inspectors. A second development was the growth of an industrial workforce. From a relatively early date, factories were subjected to a regime of inspection, though this was often a thinly veiled disguise to prevent Indian mills from competing effectively with their British rivals. In this context, the importance of the "welfare of the operative" was occasionally invoked, though in practice treated as a secondary consideration.[51] By the 1920s, however, a stronger welfare dimension had emerged, as some factory owners recognized the value of having a healthier workforce, less prone to absenteeism, and as a result of pressure from the International Labour Organization (the government of India having ratified the International Labour Convention of 1919), though here too noncompliance was widespread.[52]

More substantially, the idea that, under a colonial order widely seen as remote and uncaring, Indians should provide for their own welfare had been growing since the late nineteenth century. This idea partly arose from the continuing strength of indigenous traditions of philanthropy, now bolstered by a new class of businessmen and industrialists, like the Parsi magnates of Bombay and the Hindu *mahajans* (leading merchants: literally, "big men") of North India.[53] A sense of competition was also engendered by the activities of Christian missionaries, who in addition to their proselytizing (and the educational and medical facilities used to promote it) were suspected of using famine relief and the setting up of orphanages for famine children to spread their religion. For instance, the Church Missionary Society opened an orphanage at Agra following the 1837–38 famine and sought to use it as the base for building a Christian community in the district. Organizations like the Arya Samaj responded by collecting their own funds for famine orphans in the hope of keeping the children within the Hindu fold.[54]

Welfare activities also arose in the 1890s and 1900s in connection with a host of newly formed religious and social reform organizations, such as the Ramakrishna Mission or the Poona-based Servants of India Society. Others with a more explicitly communal base, like the Sri Narayana Dharma Paripalana Yogam in the princely state of Travancore, served the needs of a particular caste (in this case, the "depressed" Ezhavas), and sought through marriage reform, by the encouragement of temperance and vegetarianism, education, health, and "industrious habits," to raise its social standing and "respectability."[55] Among the declared aims of the Nadar Mahajana Sangam, which similarly aimed to improve the status of a low-caste community in the southern districts of the Madras Presidency, were to "promote the social, material, and general welfare of the Nadars," to "take practical measures for [their] social, moral, and intellectual advancement," and to "foster and promote the spirit of union and solidarity among the members of the community."[56] Of course, many of these objectives remained mere statements of intent and not evidence as such of actual welfare provision. Nonetheless, welfarism became one of the building blocks of modern communal identity and solidarity. By the 1920s and 1930s it was not uncommon, too, for political organizations, such as the Indian National Congress, to undertake welfare activities—such as flood and famine relief, the distribution of food and cloth to the poor, or, as in the case of the Harijan campaign, led by Mohandas Karamchand Gandhi in the mid-1930s, to help the untouchables. Gandhi's rejection of the modern state and his preference for self-help and "service" organizations that would promote village uplift or Harijan well-being were part of a more general move to take welfare roles and responsibilities away from the state and entrust them to local activists and communities themselves.[57]

Significantly, though, service and uplift tended to be the dominant idioms through which these multifarious nongovernmental campaigns presented themselves, stressing a philanthropic or communal approach, rather than an idea of welfare based on individual rights and collective needs—a distinction evident in Gandhi's emphasis on duty rather than rights. Even so, by the 1940s the idea of welfare—of catering for the needs of the poor, destitute, homeless, and half-starved—had become widespread in India. Laissez-faire had ceased to be a cardinal feature of state policy, but there remained an underlying official belief that the responsibilities of the colonial state toward its subjects were necessarily limited by lack of funds, by the political and cultural gulf between rulers and ruled, and by a continuing preference for delegating responsibility to voluntary and religious organizations. The Congress Party was almost alone when, in its deliberations in the late 1930s on India's postcolonial future, it began to sketch out a more interventionist role for the state—and even then, despite the stated concern for "national reconstruction and social planning," it was directed more toward industrial development and technoscience than welfare provision.[58] It was only toward the end of World War II (prompted by the Beveridge Report of 1942 in Britain) that an explicit language of state welfarism entered official discourse in India.

One illustration of this shift—in language at least—was the commission of inquiry into the Bengal famine of 1943, which was appointed in July 1944 and published its final report the following year. Chaired by Sir John Woodhead, the committee included W. R. Aykroyd, a pioneer of nutritional science research in India since the mid-1930s. The report made it clear that the state "should recognize its ultimate responsibility to provide enough food for all" and not merely protect its subjects from death by starvation. It was now "abundantly clear that a policy of *laissez-faire* in the matter of food supply and distribution can lead nowhere and would probably end in catastrophe." The report recognized that the government of India had long since "accepted the duty of preventing widespread deaths from famine," but this was now no longer enough. "The further obligation of taking every possible step, not only to prevent starvation, but to improve nutrition and create a healthy and vigorous population, has not yet been fully recognized and accepted."[59]

While skirting the actual concept of welfare, the report concluded by calling for a "new spirit." "At present," it declared, "all governments are preparing plans of reconstruction and development in the postwar period. A new spirit and determination are abroad. But it is one thing to draw up plans, another to carry them out. A great responsibility rests on governments, administrators and government servants of all grades, in organizing and stimulating the work of 'nation building.'" With an appreciative glance at Russia (another "backward and illiterate nation" currently transforming itself), the report ended with the "earnest hope that, in her future development as an independent nation, India will find in her own tradition the vision and faith, which will enable her to create a new life for her people"[60]—suggesting that nothing so ambitious could reasonably be expected from a fast-fading colonial power.[61]

A further expression (couched in even more explicitly public-health terms) of the new welfare ethos was the Health Survey and Development Committee, chaired by Sir Joseph Bhore. Appointed in October 1943 but not reporting until 1946, the committee included Indians as well as Europeans, women as well as men, physicians, and civil servants. Presenting a detailed analysis of the medical deficiencies of India at the time and calling for "radical" change, the committee argued for greater state provision for the health of women and children, for urban, industrial, and rural populations, and for greater attention to be given to nutrition and other vital areas of healthcare. It placed particular stress on the fact that half the current mortality in India was "preventable and should therefore be prevented."[62] Echoing Beveridge, the report stated, "No individual should fail to secure adequate medical care because of inability to pay for it." The new health program should "lay special emphasis on preventive work," and "the doctor of the future" should be a "social physician protecting the people and guiding them to a healthy and happier life."[63] But, despite the emphasis on state responsibility and initiative, the Bhore Committee reported at a time when the government was half paralyzed by the imminent approach of independence and partition. At this late hour, with control over India crumbling, the government of India was unlikely to institute wide-ranging measures along the lines of the British welfare state. If there were to be such an entity, it would have to come after the British had withdrawn from the increasingly costly enterprise of empire. In practice, the promise of the Bhore Committee report was never realized.[64]

One can see in British India in the nineteenth and early twentieth centuries several sets of ideas, policies, and practices that diverged from the British case and yet contained many parallels and connections with it. From a relatively early stage, the idea of poverty—visible, unremitting, often catastrophic, and almost always on a scale almost unimaginable in modern Europe—was so widespread as to be almost ubiquitous. Vagrancy, at least as far as it affected Indians, was seen as a part of the wider problem of poverty and the periodic eruption of major famines or as part of the need to improve Indian agriculture, to tie the population more closely to the land and discourage "aimless" or "criminal" wandering. In terms of British responses to endemic rural poverty, a laissez-faire, market-dominated approach sought to minimize state responsibility and intervention, but there also existed, as a kind of subtext, a more statist view of an obligation to protect the rural poor from extreme destitution and starvation and to create, through public works, an infrastructure to ameliorate the worst effects of drought, poverty, and disease. It was not until the mid-1940s (and so too late to make a difference to colonial India) that the balance shifted decisively toward the latter.

Contradictions in the colonial camp were matched by those among the Indian population. There was a resilient tradition of Indian philanthropy (for which the elimination of poverty was one goal) that, despite criticism of its inefficiency and want of discrimination, survived and rearticulated itself during the colonial period. This perhaps paralleled the "vast, ramshackle mass of voluntary, self-governing, local, parochial and philanthropic provision" said to exist in late-nineteenth-century Britain.[65] But it often functioned alongside state or semistate relief measures, or was characterized by a community-specific focus and by an ideal of "service" rather than an entitlement to "welfare." To some extent this philanthropic, reformist tradition was encouraged by a competitive ethos (particularly relative to Christian missionaries), by criticisms of colonial neglect, and latterly by the antistate ideas of Gandhi and his followers. But conversely, the idea of the state (stripped of its colonial self-interest and neglect) as the only body with sufficient resources and authority to alleviate mass poverty and forge a better society, the idea of a "development Raj,"[66] appealed to many Indian intellectuals from the mid-nineteenth century onward and informed the attitudes of Jawaharlal Nehru and the Congress planners of the 1930s and 1940s. Yet even here there was a tendency to see the state less as a vehicle for the creation of a welfare society than as a regulator of economic change, with the finer points of welfare relegated, as in the past, to nonstate philanthropy and communal self-help.

Notes

1. Sunil Amrith, "Political Culture of Health in India: A Historical Perspective," *Economic and Political Weekly* 42 (January 13, 2007): 114.

2. Binay Bhushan Chaudhuri, "Agricultural Growth in Bengal and Bihar, 1770–1860," *Bengal Past and Present* 95, no. 1 (1976): 290–340.

3. Ranajit Guha, *A Rule of Property for Bengal: An Essay on the Idea of Permanent Settlement* (Paris: Mouton, 1963).

4. In the 1820s Thomas Munro, governor of Madras, promulgated an alternative revenue (*ryotwari*) system, which removed intermediaries between cultivator and state while establishing a periodic review of the revenue assessment, thus assuming that the peasants' welfare would result from their following the "yeoman path to enrichment." David Ludden, "India's Development Regime," in *Colonialism and Culture*, ed. Nicholas B. Dirks (Ann Arbor: University of Michigan Press, 1992), 269.

5. Richard H. Grove, *Green Imperialism: Colonial Expansion, Tropical Island Edens, and the Origins of Environmentalism, 1600–1860* (Cambridge: Cambridge University Press, 1995), 332–48.

6. William Carey, "Prospectus of an Agricultural and Horticultural Society in India," *Transactions of the Agricultural and Horticultural Society of India* 1 (1829): xiii. On improvement, see Richard Drayton, *Nature's Government: Science, Imperial Britain, and the "Improvement" of the World* (New Haven, CT: Yale University Press, 2000).

7. Secretary, Government of India, to Secretary, Madras, May 29, 1837, F/4/1809: 74529, Oriental and India Office Collections (hereafter, OIOC), British Library, London; [Richard Temple], "The Agri-Horticultural Society of India," *Calcutta Review* 22, no. 44 (1854): 341–59.

8. India, *Report of the Indian Famine Commission*, pt. 1 (London: HMSO, 1880), 35.

9. David L. White, "From Crisis to Community Definition: The Dynamics of Eighteenth Century Parsi Philanthropy," *Modern Asian Studies* 25, no. 2 (1991): 303–20; Douglas E. Haynes, "From Tribute to Philanthropy: The Politics of Gift Giving in a Western Indian City," *Journal of Asian Studies* 46, no. 2 (1987): 339–60.

10. In 1824 the Monegar choultry management fed up to fifteen thousand people a day. Madras Public Proceedings 10, July 27, 1824, OIOC.

11. On local charity, see C. R. Baird Smith, *Report on the Famine of 1860–61* (n.p., 1861), 14–15; William Digby, *The Famine Campaign in Southern India*, 2 vols. (London: Longmans, Green, 1878), 2:12–13, 27–28.

12. Sanjay Sharma, *Famine, Philanthropy, and the Colonial State: North India in the Early Nineteenth Century* (New Delhi: Oxford University Press, 2001), 185–91; Digby, *Famine Campaign*, 2:2–3, 8.

13. David Arnold, "European Orphans and Vagrants in India in the Nineteenth Century," *Journal of Imperial and Commonwealth History* 7, no. 2 (1979): 106–9; Christopher Hawes, *Poor Relations: The Making of a Eurasian Community in British India, 1773–1833* (Richmond, Surrey: Curzon Press, 1996), ch. 2.

14. Digby, *Famine Campaign*, 2:27.

15. A recurrent issue of Indian jail administration was how to prevent prisons from becoming "hotels for the starving poor," especially during famines. It was sometimes said that the state had a responsibility to keep such individuals out of jail but at the same time accepted that in India the "systematic relief of pauperism" remained far off. G. S. Sutherland, quoted in *Report of the Indian Jail Conference* (Calcutta: Home Secretariat Press, 1877), 21.

16. Memorandum on Poverty in India, Willoughby Mss Eur E 308/51, OIOC (I owe this reference to Shruti Kapila). Cf. Frederick Henvey, "the necessities of life in a tropical climate are few and simple," *A Narrative of the Drought and Famine Which Prevailed in the North-West Provinces 1868–70* (OIOC), 2.

17. William Tennant, *Indian Recreations*, 2nd ed., 2 vols. (London: Longman, Hurst, Rees, and Orme, 1804), 1:85.

18. Sharma, *Famine*, 140–44.

19. L. Brennan, "The Development of the Indian Famine Codes: Personalities, Politics, and Policies," in *Famine as a Geographical Phenomenon*, ed. Bruce Currey and Graeme Hugo (Dordrecht, Netherlands: Kluwer, 1984), 93.

20. Special Committee of the District Charitable Society to the governor-general, Lord Auckland, May 30, 1840, F/4/1949: 84682, OIOC.

21. Legislative Department to Court of Directors, February 4, 1841, F/4/1949: 84682, OIOC.

22. Leela Visaria and Pravin Visaria, "Population," in *The Cambridge Economic History of India*, vol. 2, *c. 1757–c. 1970*, ed. Dharma Kumar (Cambridge: Cambridge University Press, 1983), 528–31.

23. [C. R. Baird Smith], "Canals of Irrigation in the N.W. Provinces," *Calcutta Review* 12, no. 23 (1849): 165.

24. *Report of the Indian Irrigation Committee, 1901–1903* (London: HMSO, 1903), pt. 1, 125–26.

25. Ian J. Kerr, *Building the Railways of the Raj, 1850–1900* (Delhi: Oxford University Press, 1995), 43.

26. S. Ambirajan, *Classical Political Economy and British Policy in India* (Cambridge: Cambridge University Press, 1978), ch. 3.

27. Ira Klein, "When the Rains Failed: Famine, Relief, and Mortality in British India," *Indian Economic and Social History Review* 21, no. 2 (1984): 185–214; Mike Davis, *Late Victorian Holocausts: El Niño Famines and the Making of the Third World* (London: Verso, 2001), ch. 1.

28. F. A. Nicholson, *Manual of the Coimbatore District in the Presidency of Madras* (Madras, India: Government Press, 1887), 276.

29. Quoted in India, *Report of the Famine Commission,* pt. 1, app. 1, 7.

30. B. M. Bhatia, *Famines in India,* 3rd rev. ed. (Delhi: Konark Publishers, 1991), 107.

31. Quoted in David Hall-Matthews, "Famine Process and Famine Policy: A Case of Ahmednagar District, Bombay Presidency, India, 1870–94" (D.Phil. thesis, Oxford, 2002), 191. For an in-depth discussion of famine policy and its effects, see David Hall-Matthews, *Peasants, Famine and the State in Colonial Western India* (Houndmills, Basingstoke, UK: Palgrave Macmillan, 2005, ch. 5.

32. C. H. Philips, ed., *The Evolution of India and Pakistan, 1858 to 1947* (London: Oxford University Press, 1962), 669.

33. Ibid., 672.

34. Jean Drèze, "Famine Prevention in India," in *The Political Economy of Hunger,* vol. 2, *Famine Prevention,* ed. Jean Drèze and Amartya Sen (Oxford: Oxford University Press, 1990), 19–35.

35. David Arnold, "Famine in Peasant Consciousness and Peasant Action: Madras, 1876–78," in *Subaltern Studies* 3, ed. Ranajit Guha (Delhi: Oxford University Press, 1984), 90–103; Sarah Hodges, "'Looting' the Lock Hospital in Colonial Madras during the Famine Years of the 1870s," *Social History of Medicine* 18, no. 3 (2005): 390–95.

36. Neeladri Bhattacharya, "Pastoralists in a Colonial World," in *Nature, Culture, Imperialism: Essays on the Environmental History of South Asia,* ed. David Arnold and Ramachandra Guha (Delhi: Oxford University Press, 1995), 77–84.

37. *Indian Famine Charitable Relief Fund 1897 and Madras Provincial Committee, Report on the Operations of the Executive Committee* (Madras, India: Government Press, 1897), 9–10.

38. [North-West Provinces], *Report on Operations of the Central Committee Relief Fund, North-Western Provinces, 1868–69* (Allahabad, India: Government Press, 1870), 1.

39. Between July and November 1877, £692,603 was received from overseas and Rs 3,05,756 raised locally: most was spent on providing peasants with seed grain and bullocks. Digby, "Memorandum on Private Relief in the Madras Famine," January 22, 1879, *Report of the Indian Famine Commission,* part 3, 121–27.

40. *Report of the Operations of the Bengal Branch of the Indian Famine Charitable Relief Fund, 1900* (Calcutta: Bengal Secretariat Press, 1901), app. B, iv.

41. *Report on Operations . . . 1868–69,* 25; *Report of the Operations . . . 1900,* 2–3, app. B, v.

42. Minute, August 23, 1869, in *Report on Operations . . . 1868–69*, 41A.

43. Dadabhai Naoroji, *Poverty and Un-British Rule in India* (London: Swan Sonnenschein, 1901).

44. *Result of Enquiries made in 1888 by Lord Dufferin into the Condition of the People of India* (London: HMSO, 1902), 4, 11, 29–30.

45. Arnold, "Orphans," 114–23; Harald Fischer-Tiné, "Britain's Other Civilising Mission: Class Prejudice, European 'Loaferism' and the Workhouse-System in Colonial India," *Indian Economic and Social History Review* 42, no. 3 (2005): 295–338. Between 1876 and 1897, 5,682 European vagrants were confined to workhouses, and 586 were deported (316–17).

46. See, for example, Malcolm Lyall Darling, *The Punjab Peasant in Prosperity and Debt* (London: Oxford University Press, 1925).

47. M. I. Neal-Edwards, "Annual Report of the Maternity and Child Welfare Centre for 1937," in *Annual Report of the All-India Institute of Hygiene and Public Health Calcutta, 1937*, 45–57; "Extracts from the Report of the Public Health Commissioner for 1937," *Journal of the Association of Medical Women in India* 27, no. 4 (1939): 275–83. On the child welfare movement, see Margaret I. Balfour and Ruth Young, *The Work of Medical Women in India* (London: Oxford University Press, 1929), ch. 9.

48. See Sarah Hodges, "Indian Eugenics in an Age of Reform," in *Reproductive Health in India: History, Politics, Controversies*, ed. Sarah Hodges (Hyderabad, India: Orient Longman, 2006), 115–38.

49. "Report of the Public Health Commissioner," 281.

50. On the scant funding for rural boards, see A. P. Pillay, *Welfare Problems in Rural India* (Bombay: D. B. Taraporevala Sons), 14, 130.

51. Lord Elgin to secretary of state, February 26, 1896, Home (Judicial), 467, February 1896, National Archives of India, New Delhi.

52. Samita Sen, *Women and Labour in Late Colonial India: The Bengal Jute Industry* (Cambridge: Cambridge University Press, 1999).

53. Christine Dobbin, *Urban Leadership in Western India: Politics and Communities in Bombay City, 1840–1885* (Oxford: Oxford University Press, 1972), 21, 218; C. A. Bayly, *The Local Roots of Indian Politics: Allahabad, 1880–1920* (Oxford: Clarendon, 1975), 73.

54. Kenneth W. Jones, *Socio-Religious Reform Movements in British India* (Cambridge: Cambridge University Press, 1989), 53, 100.

55. Robin Jeffrey, *Politics, Women and Well-Being: How Kerala Became a 'Model'* (Houndmills, Basingstoke, UK: Macmillan, 1992), 51–2; Koji Kawashima, *Missionaries and a Hindu State: Travancore, 1858–1936* (Delhi: Oxford University Press, 1998), 171–75.

56. Cited in Robert L. Hardgrave, *The Nadars of Tamilnad: The Political Culture of a Community in Change* (Berkeley: University of California Press, 1969), 132.

57. For Gandhi's ashram-based programs, see Mark Thomson, *Gandhi and His Ashrams* (London: Sangam Books, 1993). For ideas of service in colonial India, see Carey Anthony Watt, *Serving the Nation: Cultures of Service, Association and Citizenship* (New Delhi: Oxford University Press, 2005).

58. Nehru, speech to the National Academy of Sciences, March 5, 1938, in *Selected Works of Jawaharlal Nehru*, gen. ed. S. Gopal, 16 vols. (New Delhi: Orient Longman, 1976), 8:811. For the Congress Planning Committee and the Bhore Commission, see Roger Jeffery, *The Politics of Health in India* (Berkeley: University of California Press, 1988), 112–14; Pramit Chaudhuri, "Changing Perceptions to Poverty in India: State and Poverty," *Sankhya* 55, no. 3 (1993): 310–21.

59. *The Famine Inquiry Commission: Final Report*, Madras, 1945, 113–14. Aykroyd's interventionist stance was also evident in his *Notes on Food and Nutrition Policy in India* (New Delhi: n.p., 1944).

60. *Famine Inquiry Commission*, 331–32.

61. But the report did encourage the government of India to declare in 1946 that its policy was "to promote the welfare of the people and to secure a progressive improvement of their standard of living. This includes the responsibility of providing enough food for all, sufficient in quantity and of requisite quality." The aim in future was "not only to remove the threat of famine, but also to increase the prosperity of the cultivator, raise levels of consumption and create a healthy and vigorous population." India, *A Statement of Agriculture and Food Policy in India* (Delhi: Government of India, 1946), 1–2.

62. India, *Report of the Health Survey and Development Committee*, 4 vols. (Delhi: Government of India, 1946), 1:11.

63. Ibid., 4:v–vi.

64. On the reasons for this, see Amrith, "Political Culture of Health," 114–21.

65. José Harris, "Political Thought and the Welfare State, 1870–1940: An Intellectual Framework for British Social Policy," *Past and Present* 135 (May 1992): 116.

66. Ludden, "India's Development Regime," 260–64.

5

Vagrancy in Mauritius and the Nineteenth-Century Colonial Plantation World

Richard B. Allen

DESERTION, ILLEGAL ABSENCE, and vagrancy figure prominently in studies of labor relations and social control in the colonial plantation world. Historians have paid considerable attention in recent years to marronage in the slave plantation societies that flourished in the Americas between the late seventeenth and early nineteenth centuries and to colonial responses to the threat that fugitive slaves and maroon communities posed to local socioeconomic systems.[1] The indentured or free contractual laborers who replaced slaves as field hands in many plantation colonies after the abolition of slavery and who labored in the new plantation systems that were established during the mid- and late nineteenth century have also been a subject of scholarly interest.[2] However, as Doug Munro noted some time ago, studies of labor relations and social control in the postemancipation era have frequently done little more than replicate the kinds of information reported by commissions of inquiry that investigated the conditions under which indentured laborers lived and worked.[3] A tendency to focus on the legal and quasi-legal dimensions of the indentured experience, to describe the content of local "master-servant" ordinances, and to recount the details of these workers' lives are common features of these studies.[4]

As recent work on postemancipation labor resistance and accommodation demonstrates,[5] much remains to be done to deepen our understanding of labor relations and social control in the nineteenth- and early-twentieth-century colonial plantation world. Delving further into the complex dynamics of coercion and worker agency is crucial to understanding how social order was (or was not) maintained in such societies. Central to such endeavors is the need to assess the ways in which and the extent to which desertion, illegal absence, and vagrancy shaped the contours of colonial life.

Three areas of particular concern can be discerned.[6] First, students of plantation systems have frequently not asked basic questions about the act of desertion or vagrancy itself: for example, how many persons deserted from their employers or were arrested and convicted for desertion or vagrancy? What percentage of the local population or workforce engaged in such acts? What were the characteristic features of these acts—their duration, the age, sex, and occupation of those involved? Meaningful discussions about the nature and dynamics of social control require at least some sense of the number and kinds of persons who were involved in these various forms of labor resistance over time.

A second source of concern is the ahistorical nature of much of the previous work on these subjects. Once again, many historians have not asked basic questions about the extent to which and the ways in which this activity changed, and why it did—or did not—do so. Coming to grips with these questions requires not only ascertaining how many people engaged in such acts at various points in time, but also being sensitive to changes in the ideology of desertion and vagrancy on the part of both workers and their employers. Doing so can require transcending the propensity in plantation historiography to treat the pre- and postemancipation eras in isolation from one another. That desertion and vagrancy ordinances were often modeled on fugitive slave laws points up the structural continuities that could exist between pre- and postemancipation systems of labor control.[7]

Lastly, social control and labor resistance are often examined within highly circumscribed social, economic, and political contexts.

The tendency to emphasize the role that racism played in shaping colonial attitudes and policies toward desertion, illegal absence, and vagrancy, often to the exclusion of other factors, illustrates this tendency toward compartmentalized approaches to the study of these societies and economies.[8] So does the failure to situate discussions of social control and labor resistance in colonies in appropriate imperial frameworks. The need to analyze these phenomena more holistically is highlighted by work on peasant protest in southern Asia,[9] while an overview of maroon activity in the Indian Ocean world underscores the need to compare the ways in which these phenomena varied from colony to colony.[10]

What we know about postemancipation Mauritius provides an opportunity to examine the dynamics of social control and labor resistance in the nineteenth-century colonial plantation world in such broader contexts. Mauritius was the crucial test case for the use of free contractual labor in the wake of slave emancipation,[11] and the success of the Mauritian experience with indentured labor led to the emigration of more than two million men, women, and children to British, Dutch, French, and Spanish colonies—and beyond—between 1834 and the first decades of the twentieth century, when the indentured labor trades came to an end.[12] Like their Mauritian counterparts, many of these workers lived in a world in which desertion, illegal absence, and vagrancy were an integral part of a life that would be shaped and reshaped by the complex interplay between local social, economic, and political institutions and changes in global commodities markets.

Vagrancy in Mauritius

Official concern in Mauritius about vagrancy dates to 1835, when, following the formal abolition of slavery on February 1 of that year, the colony's government promulgated an ordinance that stipulated that all persons sixty years of age or under who were able to work but had no occupation, employment, or known means of subsistence could be punished as vagabonds. This ordinance, directed at the island's new freedmen, sought to criminalize behavior that could threaten the integrity of the workforce needed to maintain the colony's rapidly expanding sugar industry.[13] Although disallowed by the secretary of state for the colonies because of its blatantly repressive nature, the 1835 ordinance was a harbinger of subsequent attempts to use the charge of vagrancy to control the island's agricultural workers, and its indentured Indian immigrants in particular, that lasted into the latter part of the nineteenth century.[14]

Mauritian authorities were not, of course, the first to rely on vagrancy laws to control or mobilize labor. In England the use of such legislation for these purposes can be traced back to the mid-fourteenth century.[15] Laws dealing with vagrants remained a regular feature of English life during succeeding centuries; the continuing difficulties of reining in the relative independence of English workers resulted in the passage of as many as twenty-eight vagrancy statutes between 1700 and 1824.[16] Work on Argentina and Brazil has likewise emphasized the extent to which such statutes were used during the second half of the nineteenth century to control or mobilize labor.[17] Vagrancy legislation in British East Africa during the first half of the twentieth century would be designed for the same purposes.[18]

Scholars have appreciated that vagrancy ordinances were often adaptive responses to significant changes in local socioeconomic relationships. Vagrancy legislation provided British officials in northern Nigeria, for instance, with the legal cover needed to deal with fugitive slaves as they sought to manage the transition from a slave to a nonslave economy during the early twentieth century and avoid alienating indigenous elites in the process.[19] Work on the postbellum United States demonstrates that the transition from slave to free labor and the attendant reliance on vagrancy statutes entailed a subtle reconceptualization of the justification for involuntary labor in which compulsion came to be viewed as an appropriate, if not necessary, means of guaranteeing the sanctity of the free-labor contract.[20] There can be little doubt that similar ideas underpinned the Mauritian experience with vagrancy.

As the royal commissioners who investigated the living and working conditions of indentured Indian immigrants in Mauritius in 1872 observed, desertion, illegal absence, and vagrancy were, at least in theory, separate and distinct offenses. Desertion and illegal absence usually involved a breach of contract between a worker and his or her employer, while vagrancy constituted a more serious offense against society as a whole. The royal commissioners also noted, however, that these offenses often remained indistinguishable from one another.[21] Reports on the Mauritian prison population during the 1850s and early 1860s, for instance, did not distinguish between those imprisoned for desertion and those incarcerated for vagrancy. Even when local ordinances distinguished between these two offenses, it was not unusual for other ordinances to blur the distinction between them again. Ordinance 4 of 1864, to cite a prominent example, considered desertion to be an act of vagrancy. The issuance of Ordinance 31 of 1867 (commonly known as the Labour Law of 1867) underscored the depth of governmental concern about desertion, illegal absence, and vagrancy by consolidating and reaffirming police and judicial powers to deal with these offenses.

The ultimate goal of such legislation, as the planter Adolphe de Plevitz observed in 1871, was to provide the colony's planters with the legal tools they needed to force the colony's Old Immigrants to remain working on their estates.[22] The distinction between "old" and "new" immigrants had first been defined in law in 1847. New Immigrants were those indentured laborers who had not completed a mandatory five years of "industrial residence," a residence that usually entailed working on a sugar estate. Old Immigrants, who had either completed their industrial residence or otherwise freed themselves of this obligation, were technically free to earn their living in a manner of their own choosing. In practice, however, both planters and government officials expected Old Immigrants to continue working on the island's sugar estates.

As the archival record makes clear, many Old Immigrants declined to do so and pursued other livelihoods. Their desire to free themselves from the bonds of estate wage labor became a source of increasing concern during the late 1840s as large numbers of Indian immigrants who had reached the colony during the late 1830s and early 1840s completed their industrial residence and took steps to secure greater control over their lives. The concern that this trend evoked is illustrated by a letter three colonists sent to Governor Sir William Gomm in April 1847 in which they complained about the "large Population of do-nothings" who had quit the estates to avoid work and the resultant overstocking of the island with Indian shopkeepers, peddlers, and bazaar vendors.[23] Four years later, a colonial census revealed that Indian immigrants accounted for a significant percentage of the colony's residents who pursued nonagricultural occupations, including 31.2 percent of all persons engaged in commerce and 44.7 percent of all domestic servants. The 1861 census revealed an even larger Indian immigrant presence among persons who earned their living from commerce, domestic service, diverse crafts and trades, and the professions. This trend toward ever greater Indian immigrant participation in various sectors of colonial economic life continued through the 1860s, as the 1871 census would confirm.[24]

Attempts to suppress vagrancy in mid-nineteenth-century Mauritius must be viewed in light of these socioeconomic developments. The seriousness with which colonial authorities viewed this problem is apparent in the annual report on the colony for 1854, in which Acting Governor Major-General Hall castigated vagrancy as "an evil which, in addition to the loss it entails on the employer of labour, is fraught with moral and social mischief, and is, I believe, the source and basis of much of the crime of the island." Only the most strenuous efforts by government, Hall continued, would allow the colony to rid itself of this "monster evil."[25]

Attempts to suppress vagrancy in Mauritius must also be viewed in the context of high rates of worker absenteeism and desertion during the 1840s, 1850s, and 1860s. Indentured laborers on the island frequently had to endure difficult living and working conditions and, like their enslaved predecessors, many resorted to flight from their employers as one way to cope with the abuses to which they were subjected. The public outcry in Britain and India over the mistreatment of the earliest indentured workers on the island prompted the government of India to suspend emigration to Mauritius in late 1838;[26] when immigration resumed late in 1842, it did so under governmental supervision in an attempt to minimize further abuse.

Living and working conditions for many of the island's estate workers, however, remained difficult throughout the remainder of the nineteenth century.[27]

Information on illegal absence and desertion during the 1840s is sketchy, but the figures at our disposal indicate the general scale of this activity. In 1845, 6 percent of the island's 35,000 Indian estate workers were estimated to have deserted their employers, while another 11 percent had been temporarily absent without leave.[28] The following year, 7.7 percent of 33,651 estate workers enumerated in the colony were reported to be deserters, while another 6.2 percent had been absent from work for less than two weeks.[29] Other sources suggest that desertion and absenteeism rates averaged 11.9 percent a year on sugar estates between 1845 and 1850, and 7.9 percent a year on other kinds of estates during the same period.[30]

These rates were comparable to marronage rates among Mauritian slaves between 1820 and 1826, when the equivalent of 11 to 13 percent of the colony's bondmen and bondwomen fled from their masters.[31] They are also generally consistent with the limited information at our disposal on desertion rates in other parts of the plantation world during the latter part of the nineteenth century. In Assam, for example, some 10 percent of tea plantation laborers in the Surma Valley and 15 percent of those in Sylhet District deserted between 1882 and 1885; between 1882 and 1901, almost 5 percent of the region's plantation workers managed to desert successfully from their employers, while a far larger percentage of the workforce tried unsuccessfully to do so.[32] From 17.3 to 33.7 percent of the Hawaiian workforce deserted or refused to work during the 1880s and 1890s.[33] The number of runaways in Samoa fluctuated between 10.6 and 12.6 percent between 1891 and 1894.[34] Approximately 4 percent of Natal's indentured Indian population were charged with refusing to work between 1900 and 1910, a figure that does not take full account of worker desertion.[35] Desertion rates could occasionally reach truly staggering levels, as in Tucumán, Argentina, where more than 40 percent of registered workers were reported to be runaways in 1889.[36]

Data on vagrancy per se do not exist in Mauritius before 1852, while the figures available after 1852 are problematic, given their frequent failure to distinguish between vagrants and deserters. During the early and mid-1850s, colonial authorities pointed to the increasing number of imprisonments for vagrancy and desertion to illustrate the seriousness of the problem they faced. The number of persons imprisoned for vagrancy in Port Louis, for example, rose from 3,202 in 1852 to 4,546 in 1857 (table 5.1). Instructions that the police were not to harass Indian laborers unnecessarily led to a dramatic decline in the number of persons imprisoned for these offenses in 1858 and 1859, but the early 1860s witnessed a dramatic resurgence in the number of such imprisonments. Official reports are silent about the reasons for this increase, but this trend was a source of official annoyance and frustration. In his annual report for 1862, the protector of immigrants noted that although there had been a marked decline that year in the number of arrests for vagrancy compared to 1861, that decrease did not "arise from a diminution in vagrancy, but rather from Deserters eluding detection, by making use of forged tickets, or tickets belonging to other Immigrants." The magnitude of this problem, he continued, was illustrated by the fact that Indian immigrants had made 30,075 applications for duplicate tickets and passes during 1862.[37]

Although it is difficult to ascertain the scale of vagrant activity before 1861 with any precision, a sense of its magnitude can be inferred from the fact that the equivalent of 4 percent of all male Indian immigrants were imprisoned for vagrancy or desertion each year between 1852 and 1863. The extent of this activity becomes more readily apparent between 1861 and 1871, when an average of 12.7 percent of all Indian males may have been arrested for vagrancy each year. These figures, coupled with low conviction rates following such arrests (an average of less than 45 percent each year during this period), give credence to the 1872 royal commissioners' statement that enforcement of the colony's vagrancy and labor laws amounted to nothing less than unbridled harassment of the island's Indian population.[38]

Unfortunately, many other features of postemancipation Mauritian labor relations remain hidden from view. The annual reports of the protector of immigrants—the single most important source of information about desertion, illegal absence, and vagrancy on the island—first become available only in 1859, a quarter century after indentured

Table 5.1. Desertion, Illegal Absence, and Vagrancy in Mauritius, 1852–71

| | Vagrancy | | | | Desertion and Illegal Absence | |
| | Arrests | | Committals to Prison[b] | | Complaints[c] | |
Year	Number	% MIP[a]	Number	% MIP	Number	% CWF[d]
1852	—	—	3,202	4.0	—	—
1853	—	—	3,483	4.0	—	—
1854	—	—	—	—	—	—
1855	—	—	4,404	4.4	—	—
1856	—	—	4,480	4.4	—	—
1857	—	—	4,546	4.3	—	—
1858	—	—	2,687	2.2	—	—
1859	—	—	2,444	1.7	—	—
1860	—	—	5,132	3.9	12,346	20.3
1861	23,371	15.7	5,925	4.0	11,306	16.1
1862	16,668	11.0	4,904	3.2	12,829	15.8
1863	—	—	7,335	4.9	15,098	21.2
1864	18,834	12.5	—	—	16,037	19.6
1865	18,382	11.4	—	—	12,802	16.4
1866	19,416	12.0	—	—	9,420	13.1
1867	16,884	11.5	—	—	5,971	10.1
1868	22,357	15.8	—	—	6,773	10.1
1869	23,916	17.2	—	—	6,272	9.0
1870	16,880	12.0	—	—	4,235	5.5
1871	12,096	8.5	—	—	3,366	4.4

Sources: AIR 1860–62, 1864–71; PP 1857–58 XL [2403], 154; PP 1859 XXI Sess. 2 [2567], 173; PP 1860 XLIV [2711], 122; PP 1861 XL [2841], 113; PP 1862 XXXVI [2955], 123; PP 1863 XXXIX [3165], 94; PP 1865 XXXVII [3423], 119; PP 1875 XXXV, Appendix G (Nos. 44, 45).

[a] Arrests for vagrancy as a percentage of the male Indian population.

[b] For vagrancy and desertion, 1852–61; for vagrancy, 1862–63.

[c] Filed by employers and overseers against Indian immigrant workers.

[d] Complaints as a percentage of the contractual work force.

immigration to the colony began. Although the protectors filed their annual reports well into the twentieth century, these and other contemporary sources frequently contain little information about important details such as the demographic structure of the deserter/vagrant population, the length of desertions and illegal absences, and the extent to which people engaged in such activity alone or in groups. The fact that the great majority of the island's deserters and vagrants were males, for example, must be inferred from census data and information about the composition of the contractual workforce.[39]

Information on the incidence of vagrancy in each of the island's nine districts between 1864 and 1871 sheds additional light on the scale and intensity of this activity. These data demonstrate that vagrancy rates varied, sometimes substantially, from year to year not only in the colony as a whole, but also in its various districts. We may note, for instance, that an average of almost 47 percent of all arrests for vagrancy during this eight-year period were made in Port Louis, the colony's capital, while the districts of Grand Port and Pamplemousses together accounted for another 23.6 percent of all such arrests each year. Average annual conviction rates for vagrancy during this period likewise often varied from district to district, ranging from a high of 60.4 percent in Pamplemousses to a low of 30.9 percent in Black River. The percentage of contractual laborers who were arrested for vagrancy each year also varied widely from district to district over this eight-year period. In the island's rural districts, the average annual percentage of such arrests ranged from a low of only 6.6 percent in Flacq to a high of 25.1 percent in Black River. In Port Louis, on the other hand, the equivalent of 83.7 percent of the city's contractual workers were arrested for vagrancy on average each year during the same period.

Significant year-to-year fluctuations in this activity can also be discerned within individual districts. In Moka and Pamplemousses, for example, high conviction rates for vagrancy in 1864 and 1865 gave way to noticeably lower conviction rates for the same offense by 1870 and 1871. In Black River the trend was just the opposite. The impact of vagrant activity on local socioeconomic life could also vary widely. In Pamplemousses, the equivalent of 44 percent of the district's contractual laborers were arrested for vagrancy in 1868 compared to only 13.1 percent of the district's workforce in 1865. In Black River, Flacq, and Plaines Wilhems, on the other hand, the ratio between the number of arrests for vagrancy and the number of contractual laborers in the district remained relatively constant during the period in question. Data from Port Louis are of particular interest, revealing as they do that the equivalent of 127, 123, 145, and 112 percent of the city's contractual workforce were arrested for vagrancy in 1867, 1868, 1869, and 1870, respectively.[40] Figures such as these underscore the city's importance as a place where many Indian immigrant vagrants and deserters, like fugitive slaves before them,[41] sought refuge because the town and its environs offered greater opportunities for individuals to find gainful employment and evade detection by the police.

Our ignorance about many details of local socioeconomic life makes it difficult to explain why the patterns to vagrant activity outlined above varied so much from year to year. As the 1872 royal commissioners appreciated, the attitude of district magistrates toward vagrants and deserters could be one important factor. The commissioners noted that the willingness of two magistrates in Rivière du Rempart and Savanne to examine carefully the cases of alleged vagrancy brought before them and to apply the vagrancy statutes properly contributed to the relatively low conviction rates in these districts. The attitude of these two magistrates stood in sharp contrast to that of their colleagues in other districts, who, the commissioners reported, were much more willing to condemn deserters for vagrancy in an arbitrary and indiscriminate manner.[42]

The size and efficiency of the colony's police force was another important variable. During the first decades of the nineteenth century, colonists complained frequently about what they perceived to be police failure to pursue fugitive slaves, complaints given substance by the fact that in 1826, only eleven of forty-two rural *détachements* charged with pursuing maroons appear to have done so vigorously.[43] Police inefficiency at that time may be traced partly to low levels of government funding to suppress marronage,[44] and partly to periodic lapses in the political will to do so. Similar problems, coupled with uncertainties about who ultimately controlled the local police, apparently continued well into the mid-nineteenth century.[45]

Developments during the 1860s and 1870s would reveal, however, that governmental attitudes, policies, and personnel were not the only factors that shaped the course of postemancipation labor relations in Mauritius. During the late 1860s and early 1870s, colonial authorities noted that desertion and vagrancy were becoming less of a problem than had hitherto been the case. The number of complaints against contractual workers for desertion and illegal absence began to decline markedly after 1865, while arrests for vagrancy dropped significantly in 1870 and 1871 (table 5.1). Other data likewise point to significant changes in the tenor and tone of local labor relations at this time. The number of complaints that contractual workers lodged against their employers and overseers also began to decline sharply during the late 1860s, falling from an average of 6,690 a year between 1865 and 1869 to 3,541 a year between 1870 and 1874. The average number of such complaints fell still further, to an annual average of 2,737, between 1875 and 1879.[46]

Many contemporary observers of colonial life attributed these developments to the impact of the Labour Law of 1867. In his annual report for 1869, the protector of immigrants attributed the marked improvement he discerned in the social and moral condition of the colonial workforce to the decrease in vagrancy made possible by the Labour Law.[47] The United States consul in Port Louis likewise agreed that vagrancy had ceased to be as serious a problem by the early 1870s as it had been since he reported; the vagrancy laws were now "working satisfactorily."[48] Others, however, were less sanguine about the Labour Law's effectiveness. The 1872 royal commissioners noted that the number of laborers actually employed on the colony's sugar estates had declined, rather than increased, since this law's passage and, moreover, that its impact on vagrancy was a subject of debate even among the colony's police officers.[49]

Unlike many modern students of indentured labor systems, the royal commissioners understood, if only implicitly, that concentrating on the legal and quasi-legal aspects of desertion, illegal absence, and vagrancy could yield only limited insights into the nature and dynamics of postemancipation labor relations. Mauritian authorities tinkered continuously with local labor laws during the mid-nineteenth century as they sought to exercise more effective control over the island's agricultural workforce. Their own reports reveal, however, that their attempts to do so had met with, at best, only partial success as large numbers of Indian immigrants demonstrated their unwillingness to comply with these colonial rules. Such realities underscore the need to examine desertion, illegal absence, and vagrancy in light of other considerations, not the least of which is the socioeconomic context within which local labor legislation was enacted, enforced, and defied.[50]

The 1860s and 1870s witnessed several developments that had a marked impact on Mauritian labor relations. The domestic labor market became much less unsettled during these decades than it had been during the first years of Indian immigration as Old Immigrants increasingly replaced New Immigrants as the single largest component of the colony's agricultural workforce and agricultural laborers in general began to sign longer-term contracts with the same employer. The demographic composition of this workforce also started to change as increasing numbers of Mauritian-born Indians entered the workforce. By 1885, for example, Indo-Mauritians comprised 28 percent of all contractual workers, compared to less than 8.5 percent of such workers just twelve years earlier.[51]

The 1860s also witnessed the beginnings of a major restructuring of the Mauritian sugar industry, a restructuring that provides an important backdrop against which the dramatic decline in the incidence of desertion and vagrancy must be viewed. Although the local sugar industry had attracted significant metropolitan investment during the 1830s and 1840s, a severe financial crisis in 1848 precipitated by the collapse of four of the five London banking houses that financed the local crop, ushered in an era that lasted well into the twentieth century, during which the colony remained heavily dependent on domestically generated capital.[52] This domestic capital base depended in turn on the world market price for sugar and the industry's profitability.[53] The dramatic expansion of beet sugar production that began during the 1860s and the attendant downward pressure on the world price of sugar set the stage for a growing capital liquidity crisis that placed substantial pressure on local planters to maximize production. Doing so included controlling labor costs, which could account for as much as half of an estate's operating expenses, and mobilizing labor resources more efficiently.[54] A financial crisis in 1865 and a series of natural disasters that struck the island between 1866 and 1868 provided additional incentives to do so.

As the data on desertion and vagrancy at our disposal attest, thousands of indentured laborers suffered the consequences of these economic realities. The fact that an average of 47.7 percent of all convicted vagrants between 1864 and 1871 served between two and four weeks in jail, where they were promptly employed on public and other works, underscores the importance of the vagrancy laws as a means of mobilizing labor. However, such undertakings were also expensive, and by the mid-1870s there is evidence that the colony's planters were resurrecting a strategy they had used earlier in the century to control costs and mobilize labor during another period of economic crisis.

Central to this strategy was the subdivision, or *morcellement*, and sale of undeveloped or more marginal estate lands to anyone with the desire to acquire such small holdings and the cash in hand to do so. The attendant creation of a class of small planters allowed estate owners to shift some of their production costs on to the shoulders of these individuals, who could also serve as a reservoir of seasonal laborers. Many former free persons of color and ex-apprentices met these criteria and participated in the *petit morcellement* that began around 1838 and lasted until the late 1840s.[55] Many Old Immigrants found themselves in a comparable position thirty years later, on the eve of the *grand morcellement* that began in earnest around 1875 and continued well into the twentieth century.[56] Their control of significant financial resources clearly contributed to their ability to participate in this process. The 1872 royal commissioners noted, for example, that 5,256 Indian immigrants had leased land to or from other persons between 1864 and 1871, and that the value of these leases was estimated at £122,000.[57] Indian immigrants also began to purchase ever greater amounts of real property, spending an average of 222,615 rupees (Rs) each year to do so between 1864 and 1887.[58] They would spend ever greater sums as the grand morcellement steadily gained momentum. Indian immigrants invested an average of Rs 1,217,097 in real property each year between 1888 and 1894, a sum than exceeded the average annual net value of specie imports and exports during the same seven-year period by 42.5 percent.[59] The importance of Indian participation in this process is illustrated further by limited data from the mid-1890s that point to a strong correlation between the incidence of sharecropping on sugar estates and levels of Indian investment in real property in the island's rural districts.[60]

Given the economic problems that became increasingly serious as the 1870s progressed, it took no great effort on the part of both planters

and colonial authorities to appreciate that it would be counterpro-
ductive to unduly harass that segment of the population on whom
this strategy's success, and ultimately the colony's economic survival,
depended. The result was the erosion of an expensive and already
fraying system of labor control and the attendant preoccupation with
desertion, illegal absence, and vagrancy. The ultimate expression of
this process came early in 1886 when the Vagrant Depot at Grande
Rivière Nord-Ouest, established by Ordinance 4 of 1864 to house the
thousands of persons being convicted of vagrancy each year, was closed
and its remaining inmates were transferred to the central prison in
Port Louis.[61]

Labor control and resistance will remain important topics of research
and debate in colonial plantation studies. They will do so in part because these topics are central to assessing whether the postemancipation era witnessed, as Hugh Tinker asserted more than thirty years
ago, the creation of a "new system of slavery" that would endure well
into the twentieth century.[62] The Tinkerian paradigm, which echoes
the concerns of many nineteenth-century abolitionists, continues to
exert considerable influence because it links the well documented
conditions under which many indentured laborers lived and worked
with a highly emotive concept that summarizes not only the exploitation and oppression to which these men and women were subjected
but also their apparent lack of freedom and attendant inability to shape
the course of their own lives in meaningful ways.[63]

    In recent years, however, several scholars have argued that this
characterization of postemancipation colonial plantation labor relations is at least something of a misnomer.[64] These critiques have
emphasized the importance of the legal distinctions between free
contractual and slave laborers, the many similarities in their procure-
ment, treatment, and living conditions notwithstanding. Although
they raise important questions about the Tinkerian paradigm, the
continuing preoccupation with the legal dimensions of the indentured experience underscores the need to expand our conceptual and
methodological approaches to the study of these societies and economies in general, and the nature and dynamics of desertion, illegal
absence, and vagrancy in particular.

As the Mauritian case study demonstrates, doing so can entail answering unasked questions about the nature and dynamics of local labor relations and social control, such as how many workers engaged in acts of desertion or vagrancy and the extent to which in which this activity changed through time. Doing so also requires situating desertion, illegal absence, and vagrancy firmly within larger social, economic, and political contexts that can include significant demographic changes in indentured populations and the restructuring of local economies in the wake of transformations in global commodities markets. Coming to grips with the ideology of resistance and accommodation on the part of both indentured servants and their masters is another important task to be undertaken. The letters and petitions that indentured immigrants sent to colonial authorities are one potentially important source of such information.[65] Finally, we must consider the role of worker agency in all of its myriad forms in shaping not only the tenor and tone of local labor relations, but also a wider range of colonial socioeconomic relationships. While many indentured workers never achieved as much control over their lives as they would have liked, there can be little doubt that they remained active participants in the complex dance of life that was the postemancipation colonial plantation experience.

Notes

AIR—Colony of Mauritius, variously entitled annual reports of the Protector of Immigrants/Immigration Department
CO—Colonial Office records, British National Archives, Kew
PP—British Parliament Sessional Papers

1. For a review of this literature, see Richard B. Allen, "Maroonage and Its Legacy in Mauritius and in the Colonial Plantation World," *Outre-mers: Revue d'histoire* 89, no. 336/337 (2002): 131–52.
2. Recent studies include Walton Look Lai, *Indentured Labor, Caribbean Sugar: Chinese and Indian Migrants to the British West Indies, 1838–1918* (Baltimore, MD: Johns Hopkins University Press, 1993); Marina Carter, *Lakshmi's Legacy: The Testimonies of Indian Women in Nineteenth Century Mauritius* (Rose Hill, Mauritius: Éditions de l'Océan Indien, 1994); Carter, *Servants, Sirdars and Settlers: Indians in Mauritius, 1834–1874* (Delhi:

Oxford University Press, 1995); Carter, *Voices from Indenture: Experiences of Indian Migrants in the British Empire* (London: Leicester University Press, 1996); K. O. Laurence, *A Question of Labour: Indentured Immigration into Trinidad and British Guiana, 1875–1917* (New York: St. Martin's, 1994); Rosemarijn Hoefte, *In Place of Slavery: A Social History of British Indian and Javanese Laborers in Suriname* (Gainesville: University Press of Florida, 1998); Madhavi Kale, *Fragments of Empire: Capital, Slavery, and Indian Indentured Labor in the British Caribbean* (Philadelphia: University of Pennsylvania Press, 1998); Dorothy Shineberg, *The People Trade: Pacific Island Laborers and New Caledonia, 1865–1930* (Honolulu: University of Hawai'i Press, 1999).

3. Doug Munro, "Patterns of Resistance and Accommodation," in *Plantation Workers: Resistance and Accommodation,* ed. Brij V. Lal, Doug Munro, and Edward D. Beechert (Honolulu: University of Hawaii Press, 1993), 1–43.

4. For example, Kay Saunders, "Troublesome Servants: The Strategies of Resistance Employed by Melanesian Indentured Labourers on Plantations in Colonial Queensland," *Journal of Pacific History* 14, no. 3 (1979): 168–83; Kusha Haraksingh, "Control and Resistance among Overseas Indian Workers: A Study of Labour on the Sugar Plantations of Trinidad, 1875–1917," *Journal of Caribbean History* 14 (1981): 1–17; O. Nigel Bolland, "Systems of Domination after Slavery: The Control of Land and Labor in the British West Indies after 1838," *Comparative Studies in Society and History* 23, no. 4 (1981): 591–619; Bolland, "Labour Control and Resistance in Belize in the Century after 1838," *Slavery and Abolition* 7, no. 2 (1986): 175–87; David Vincent Trotman, *Crime in Trinidad: Conflict and Control in a Plantation Society, 1838–1900* (Knoxville: University of Tennessee Press, 1986); Jan Breman, *Taming the Coolie Beast: Plantation Society and the Colonial Order in Southeast Asia* (Delhi: Oxford University Press, 1989); Michael J. Gonzales, "Resistance among Asian Plantation Workers in Peru, 1870–1920," in *From Chattel Slaves to Wage Slaves: The Dynamics of Labour Bargaining in the Americas,* ed. Mary Turner (London: James Currey, 1995), 201–23. For recent studies of master-servant legislation, see Douglas Hay and Paul Craven, eds., *Masters, Servants, and Magistrates in Britain and the Empire, 1562–1955* (Chapel Hill: University of North Carolina Press, 2004).

5. Lal, Munro, and Beechert, *Plantation Workers;* Richard B. Allen, "Indian Immigrants and the Legacy of Maroonage: Illegal Absence, Desertion and Vagrancy on Mauritius, 1835–1900," *Itinerario* 21, no. 1 (1997): 98–110; Allen, *Slaves, Freedmen, and Indentured Laborers in Colonial Mauritius* (Cambridge: Cambridge University Press, 1999), esp. 55–75.

6. Allen, "Maroonage," 138–39.

7. On the redefinition of labor laws between the slave and free-labor eras, see Mary Turner, "The British Caribbean, 1823–1838: The Transition from Slave to Free Legal Status," in Hay and Craven, *Masters, Servants,* 303–22.

8. Doug Munro, "The Labor Trade in Melanesians to Queensland: An Historiographical Essay," *Journal of Social History* 28, no. 3 (1995): 609–27; Kevin D. Smith, "A Fragmented Freedom: The Historiography of Emancipation and Its Aftermath in the British West Indies," *Slavery and Abolition* 16, no. 1 (1995): 101–30; Richard B. Allen, "The Intellectual Complacency of Contemporary Plantation Studies," *Historian* 57, no. 3 (1995): 582–86; Allen, "Indentured Labor and the Need for Historical Context," *Historian* 63, no. 2 (2001): 390–94.

9. Michael Adas, "From Footdragging to Flight: The Evasive History of Peasant Avoidance Protest in South and South-East Asia," *Journal of Peasant Studies* 13, no. 2 (1986): 64–86.

10. Edward A. Alpers, "Flight to Freedom: Escape from Slavery among Bonded Africans in the Indian Ocean World, c. 1750–1962," in *The Structure of Slavery in Indian Ocean, Africa and Asia,* ed. Gwyn Campbell (London: Frank Cass, 2004), 51–68. For recent work on slave resistance outside the Americas, see Edward Alpers, Gwyn Campbell, and Michael Salman, eds., *Slavery and Resistance in Africa and Asia* (London: Routledge, 2005).

11. I. M. Cumpston, *Indians Overseas in British Territories, 1834–1854* (London: Oxford University Press, 1953), 85.

12. For an excellent survey of the indentured labor trades, see David Northrup, *Indentured Labor in the Age of Imperialism, 1834–1922* (Cambridge: Cambridge University Press, 1995).

13. Allen, *Slaves, Freedmen,* 22–23.

14. See Saloni Deerpalsingh, "An Overview of Vagrancy Laws, Its Effects and Case Studies, 1860–1911," in *The Vagrant Depot of Grand River, Its Surroundings and Vagrancy in British Mauritius,* ed. Vijayalakshmi Teelock (Port Louis: Aapravasi Ghat Trust Fund, 2004), 47–83.

15. See A. L. Beier, "'A New Serfdom': Labor Laws, Vagrancy Statutes, and Labor Discipline in England, 1350–1800," chapter 1 of this volume.

16. Nicolas Rogers, "Vagrancy, Impressment and the Regulation of Labour in Eighteenth-Century Britain," *Slavery and Abolition* 15, no. 2 (1994): 104.

17. Donna J. Guy, "The Rural Working Class in Nineteenth-Century Argentina: Forced Plantation Labor in Tucumán," *Latin American Research Review* 13, no. 1 (1978): 135–45; Martha Knisely Huggins, *From*

Slavery to Vagrancy in Brazil: Crime and Social Control in the Third World (New Brunswick, NJ: Rutgers University Press, 1985), 50.

18. See Andrew Burton and Paul Ocobock, "The 'Travelling Native': Vagrancy and Colonial Control in British East Africa," this volume.

19. Paul E. Lovejoy and Jan S. Hogendorn, *Slow Death for Slavery: The Course of Abolition in Northern Nigeria, 1897–1936* (Cambridge: Cambridge University Press, 1993), 65, 85–86.

20. Amy Dru Stanley, "Beggars Can't Be Choosers: Compulsion and Contract in Postbellum America," *Journal of American History* 78, no. 4 (1992): 1265–93; Stanley, *From Bondage to Contract: Wage Labor, Marriage and the Market in the Age of Slave Emancipation* (Cambridge: Cambridge University Press, 1998), esp. ix–x, 99.

21. Report of the Royal Commissioners Appointed to Enquire into the Treatment of Immigrants in Mauritius [hereafter 1872 Royal Commission], paras. 2026, 2040, PP 1875 XXXIV.

22. 1872 Royal Commission, p. 10 (para. 17). See also Carter, *Sirdars, Servants,* 198–99.

23. CO 167/84—Address to Sir William Gomm by W. W. West, M. Baudot, and Ed. Rouillard, April 20, 1847, enclosed in Despatch No. 141, Sir William Gomm to Earl Grey, July 3, 1847.

24. Allen, *Slaves, Freedmen,* 144–48.

25. Major-General Hall to the Rt. Hon. Sidney Herbert, May 3, 1855, PP 1856 XLII [2050], 178.

26. On immigrant living and working conditions between 1834 and 1838, see the reports of the commissions of inquiry based in Mauritius (PP 1840 XXXVII [58], 18–35, 45–68, and PP 1840 XXXVII [331], 12–94, 107–83) and Calcutta (PP 1841 XVI [45], 4–12).

27. On various aspects of indentured life, see Northrup, *Indentured Labor,* esp. 120–29; Carter, *Voices from Indenture.*

28. 1872 Royal Commission, para. 236. Other sources put the number of deserters and illegal absentees that year at 6.8 percent and 5.1 percent, respectively (Carter, *Servants, Sirdars,* 225).

29. Messrs. Gobarz, J. Currie, P. N. Truquez, and E. Dupont to David Barclay and John Irving, agents for Mauritius, July 22, 1846, PP 1847–48 XLIV [61], 2–3.

30. Carter, *Servants, Sirdars,* 225.

31. Richard B. Allen, "Marronage and the Maintenance of Public Order in Mauritius, 1721–1835," *Slavery and Abolition* 4, no. 3 (1983): 224.

32. Behal and Mohapatra, "Tea and Money," 163. On prosecutions in Assam for breach of contract, see Prabhu P. Mohapatra, "Assam and the

West Indies, 1860–1920: Immobilizing Plantation Labor," in Hay and Craven, *Masters, Servants*, 455–80.

33. Edward D. Beechert, "Patterns of Resistance and the Social Relations of Production in Hawaii," in Lal, Munro, and Beechert, *Plantation Workers*, 53.

34. Doug Munro and Stewart Firth, "Samoan Plantations: The Gilbertese Laborers' Experience, 1867–1896," in Lal, Munro, and Beechert, *Plantation Workers*, 117. This rate fell to about 4 percent a year between 1895 and 1898.

35. Tayal, "Indian Indentured Labour," 543–44.

36. Guy, "Rural Working Class," 140. Guy also reports desertion rates among registered workers of 3.67 percent in 1876, 4.76 percent in 1882, and 8.35 percent in 1895.

37. AIR 1862, para. 39.

38. 1872 Royal Commission, para. 704.

39. Indian immigrant women comprised less than 2 percent of all agricultural laborers under contract throughout the nineteenth century.

40. Richard B. Allen, "Vagrancy and Labour Control in Mid-Nineteenth-Century Mauritius," in Teelock, *Vagrant Depot*, esp. 40–42.

41. Allen, "Marronage and the Maintenance of Public Order," 222–23; Satteeanund Peerthum and Satyendra Peerthum, "'Shattering the Shackles of Slavery': The Rural Maroons in Port Louis with Some Comparisons with Cape Town, 1811–1835," in *Maroonage and the Maroon Heritage in Mauritius*, ed. Vijaya Teelock (Réduit: University of Mauritius Press, 2005), 73–80.

42. 1872 Royal Commission, paras. 2047–53.

43. Allen, "Marronage and the Maintenance of Public Order," 226. On slave patrols in the American South, see Sally E. Hadden, *Slave Patrols: Law and Violence in Virginia and the Carolinas* (Cambridge, MA: Harvard University Press, 2001).

44. Allen, "Maroonage and Its Legacy," 146.

45. Louis-José Paul, *Deux siècles d'histoire de la police à l'île Maurice* (Paris: Éditions L'Harmattan, 1997).

46. Allen, *Slaves, Freedmen*, 68.

47. AIR 1869, para. 55.

48. Nicolas Pike, *Sub-tropical Rambles in the Land of Aphanapteryx* (New York: Harper and Brothers, 1873), 474.

49. 1872 Royal Commission, paras. 879–83.

50. Allen, *Slaves, Freedmen*, 71–72.

51. Ibid., 72.

52. Richard B. Allen, "Capital, Illegal Slaves, Indentured Labourers and the Creation of a Sugar Plantation Economy in Mauritius, 1810–1860," *Journal of Imperial and Commonwealth History* (forthcoming).

53. Allen, *Slaves, Freedmen*, 6, 22.

54. According to contemporary sources, the services of an adult male indentured laborer cost planters £12 to £18 a year during the mid-1840s, compared to the £3 to £4 that had been required to maintain an adult male slave for a year (Second Report of the Select Committee on Sugar and Coffee Planting, paras. 3286, 3483 and Statement no. 3 following para. 4021, pp 1847–48 XXIII [137]). The projected wage bill for indentured workers in 1851, 1856, and 1857 equaled 29.2 percent, 34.2 percent, and 23.7 percent, respectively, of sugar export earnings during these three years (Allen, "Capital, Illegal Slaves"). The average annual minimum estate-wage bill equaled 31.2 percent of the value of sugar exports from 1860 to 1864, and 28 percent of the value of such exports from 1865 to 1869 (Allen, *Slaves, Freedmen*, 69–70). These figures cover wages only and do not include other related costs (housing, rations, clothing, and medical care) that planters had to bear.

55. For a fuller discussion, see Allen, *Slaves, Freedmen*, 114–27.

56. Ibid., 138–44.

57. 1872 Royal Commission, para. 2947.

58. The rupee became the colony's official currency in 1876, with an initial value of two shillings (£1 = Rs. 10). The value of the rupee fluctuated from slightly less than 1s. 1d. to 1 s. 4d. from 1894 through 1898, before stabilizing at 1s. 4d. from 1899 to 1918.

59. Allen, *Slaves, Freedmen*, 142.

60. Richard B. Allen, "Indian Immigrants and the Restructuring of the Mauritian Sugar Industry, 1848–1910," *Journal of Mauritian Studies*, n.s., 1, no. 1 (2001): esp. 64–66.

61. See Satyendra Peerthum, "History of the Vagrant Depot of Grand River North West (1864–1886)," in Teelock, *Vagrant Depot*, 84–119.

62. Hugh Tinker, *A New System of Slavery: The Export of Indian Labour Overseas, 1830–1920* (London: Oxford University Press, 1974; 2nd ed., London: Hansib, 1993).

63. See Maureen Tayal, "Indian Indentured Labor in Natal, 1890–1911," *Indian Economic and Social History Review* 14 (1977): 519–47; M. D. North-Coombes, "From Slavery to Indenture: Forced Labour in the Political Economy of Mauritius, 1834–1867," in *Indentured Labour in the British Empire, 1834–1920*, ed. Kay Saunders (London: Croom Helm, 1984), 78–125; Ravindra K. Jain, "South Indian Labour in Malaya, 1840–1920," in

Saunders, *Indentured Labour*, 158–82; Rana P. Behal and Prabhu P. Mohapatra, "Tea and Money versus Human Life: The Rise and Fall of the Indenture System in the Assam Tea Plantations, 1840–1908," *Journal of Peasant Studies* 19, nos. 3–4 (1992): 142–72; P. Ramasamy, "Labour Control and Labour Resistance in the Plantations of Colonial Malaya," *Journal of Peasant Studies* 19, nos. 3–4 (1992): 87–105.

64. Edward D. Beechert, "Reflections," in Lal, Munro, and Beechert, *Plantation Workers*, 319; Bridget Brereton, "The Other Crossing: Asian Migrants in the Caribbean. A Review Essay," *Journal of Caribbean History* 28, no. 1 (1994): 99–122; Carter, *Servants, Sirdars*, 1–6; Northrup, *Indentured Labor*, 154.

65. For the kinds of information that can be extracted from these sources, see Carter, *Lakshmi's Legacy;* Carter, *Voices from Indenture.*

6

Doing Favors for Street People

Official Responses to Beggars and Vagrants in Nineteenth-Century Rio de Janeiro

Thomas H. Holloway

OVER THE COURSE of the nineteenth century, through the processes of political independence and state formation, Brazil participated in a more general modernization of public institutions—and the principles on which their actions were based—associated with the nation-state. Once conceived as extensions of the will of the theoretically absolute monarch, public institutions came to be thought of as the ways in which the state translated the collective will of the citizenry into concrete policies to solve the problems facing the nation.[1] Much of the political debate of the era involved drawing and redrawing the boundaries between public and private, official and personal, and the accepted realm of state intervention and areas left to tradition, custom, and deeply ingrained cultural expectations. The process of defining a phenomenon as a problem for which a solution should be found often involved the expansion of state authority and activity, at the expense of unquestioned assumptions long established. Public begging and charity was one area of behavior and social relations in which such debates took place and in which new policies were formulated and acted on through new institutional structures.

Also, in the transition from colony to nation, continuing through the subsequent decades, Brazilian institutions underwent a progressive specialization of functions in an increasingly complex public bureaucracy with a rationalized relationship among the various functions of the state—a process Max Weber analyzed with deliberation and acumen in Europe. During the eighteenth-century era of enlightened absolutism, the concept of police and policing emerged to incorporate a range of administrative areas, from public works to ensuring the provisioning of the city, and including the personal and collective security with which the police became associated as their functions became more specialized over time.[2] Policing in the general, older sense included dealing with public behavior that had existed since ancient days and continues today—public begging. As Rio de Janeiro's police system grew and expanded after independence, public begging remained within the purview of police control and regulation, especially as such behavior was criminalized by the progressive Criminal Code of 1831. As a thoroughly updated definition of unlawful behavior, the 1831 code was a definitive step in overcoming the absolutist legacy of the colonial era, and it was an important step in the maturation of the independent Brazilian nation-state.[3] Through the ensuing decades, what should be done about beggars and begging remained in the realm of police activity, whether the solutions were defined as charitable and benevolent or repressive and punitive.

The problem with begging was not necessarily asking for alms in itself. In fact, by Catholic tradition acts of charity toward those whom they deemed deserving demonstrated the compassion of the givers.[4] In a sense, the worthy beggar was doing the giver a favor by providing the opportunity to engage in charitable acts. But in nineteenth-century Rio de Janeiro, begging became an issue for the police because of two related problems that grew to dominate elite discourse on begging and what to do about it. One issue was the relationship between begging and more offensive activities, including overstepping the line between asking for alms and accepting when offered, and taking without asking. If the former was charity, the latter was theft. Petty theft was one of a range of minor offenses that many street people engaged in, along with public drunkenness, rowdy socializing, and disorderly conduct variously defined, which fell within the range of behavior the police were expected to repress or keep within acceptable bounds.

A related question involved the increasingly problematic distinction between "true" beggars—whose debased condition, extreme poverty, and inability to engage in gainful employment made them the deserving object of charity—and "false" beggars, who were unworthy of charity because, according to elite observers, they begged out of sloth, dereliction, and trickery. True beggars were the objects of pity and well-meaning paternalistic assistance to alleviate their plight. False beggars, in contrast, were considered to be engaged in immoral acts of deceit, exploiting the charitable impulse and good will of the public. They were therefore subject to unmasking, detention, and correction or punishment. The 1831 Criminal Code provided a detailed list of circumstances under which begging was a criminal offense. Begging was false if it happened where there were public establishments for beggars to seek charity, or when a private person offered to support the beggar. When those who begged were capable of working, even in places where there was no public asylum, it was deemed false. When beggars falsely claimed to have wounds or other illnesses, it was false begging. Begging was not allowed in groups of four or more, unless the beggars were members of the same nuclear family. Wives accompanying their beggar husbands and boys guiding the blind were also exempted from the limitation on begging in groups of more than three.[5] These distinctions notwithstanding, the very presence of beggars in the public space of the city came to be defined as problematic, and their numbers grew despite a variety of efforts by police authorities that were by turns paternalistic and repressive. Beggars were viewed as unsightly, unseemly, unsanitary, and made a bad impression on visitors to the city. Moreover, begging was seen as a prelude to and context for petty criminality. Life on the streets was detrimental to desirable qualities of morals, morale, and work discipline.

A Shelter for Beggars

In order to illustrate the ways in which these discursive perspectives on begging evolved through time and were transformed into administrative and regulatory action, it is useful to review the record of the police institutions of Rio de Janeiro as they attempted to deal with the beggar problem. With the transfer of the Portuguese royal court to Brazil in 1808, an intendant of police was established in the capital city of Rio de Janeiro, following the administrative structures already existing in Lisbon, which were modeled on French precedent. Municipal administration was thus invigorated, but there is little to indicate that public begging per se was seen as particularly problematic at the time. The intendancy remained in place when the heir apparent to the Portuguese throne, who became Pedro I of Brazil, declared independence in 1822. The police institutions and legal structures inherited from colonial times were replaced in Brazil by the new Criminal Code of 1831, and the office of chief of police was created at the lower levels of the new judicial hierarchy in the Code of Criminal Procedures of late 1832. During his term as Rio's first chief of police (1833–44), spanning the regency period (1831–40) and the first years of the Second Empire, Eusébio de Queiroz initiated polices in several areas that provided the rationale and the institutional structure for police action that long outlasted his time in office. One such activity was the effort to control beggars and vagrants. As Queiroz declared in an 1838 memo proposing a new set of measures, "begging is a matter that occupies the attention of police in all civilized countries. Its extinction is impossible, however, and the most that can be sought is to diminish its bad effects." At the time he had taken over as police chief, six years earlier, the standard practice had been to deposit beggars in the common jail, which was recognized to be "a school capable of converting those who were merely vagrants and beggars into criminals and thieves." Between 1833 and 1838 Queiroz had established a series of shelters where beggars could spend the night, attempted to create a workshop where they might be usefully occupied, and ordered some arrested now and then, thus "reducing the number of those who habitually sleep in the streets and in the doorways of churches."[6]

In September 1838 an opportunity arose for a new push against the chronic problem when the government of Rio de Janeiro Province completed construction of a jail of its own across Guanabara Bay in Niterói. Some sixty of the prisoners who had come from the province and were occupying space in jails in the city of Rio were moved to the new facilities, freeing up one of the two large rooms in the prison on Santa Bárbara Island for holding mendicants incapable of working. With undue optimism, Queiroz told the minister of justice that he "did not want to lose the opportunity to end the problem of street beggars." He issued a general warning that after a grace period of a few days, any invalid beggars found on the streets would be rounded up and sent to the newly vacated section of the Santa Bárbara prison. In a characteristic stance on the issue now called civil liberties, Queiroz said that those affected by the police sweep

> would not be deprived of their freedom, because they will be permitted to leave upon signing a promise not to continue begging, and they would only be locked up at night. Thus those who are invalid and truly in need will find a way to satisfy all the necessities of life, without luxury it is true, but in a way analogous to their circumstances, without having to wander the streets of the city—an activity enjoyed only by those addicted to begging.

He confidently anticipated one criticism of the plan, providing at the same time his own view of the mindset of poor people and the socioeconomic conditions in Brazil:

> We should not be concerned that the very existence of an establishment where beggars are provided for will make their numbers increase, and that people without urgent need will want to enter. Living in one of the bays of [the former jail on] Santa Bárbara [Island], with meager sustenance and nightly lockup, may be considered a benefit for the truly invalid, but it is not the sort of life to be envied by the vagrants and unemployed of a country such as this one, where anyone who wants to work, however proletarian he may be, does not die of hunger. Such concerns might be valid in some countries of Europe, where the strongest desire to work at times is insufficient to provide a living.

In justifying the new approach to an old problem, Queiroz mixed high-minded paternalism with practicality. "After meditating on the matter," he told the minister of justice, "I believe that this is a plan by which, with the humanity due to the truly unfortunate, we will purge the beggars from the streets of this city." He added the important consideration that no additional budget allocations would be necessary, because the upkeep of those cared for in the Santa Bárbara prison would cost no more than the criminals from Rio Province previously kept there.[7]

To put the scheme in operation Queiroz ordered justices of the peace, the magistrates responsible for precinct-level police activity at the time, to arrest everyone who fell under Article 296 of the 1831 Criminal Code, which declared begging a crime punishable by up to one month in prison with hard labor.[8] Invalids were to go to the beggars' asylum established in the former jail on Santa Bárbara Island. Able-bodied detainees were taken to the house of correction, after which they were sent to the officer in charge of military conscription; those declared fit were placed in the service of the army or navy. The navy had certain standards of physical fitness for conscripts who were to join the crews of warships, but Queiroz suggested that useful employment might also be found on unarmed vessels or on the grounds of the naval arsenal for those unable to serve on men-of-war, and "in this way not only will we remedy the manpower shortage our navy suffers, but the city will also be free of the vagrants and false beggars who flood it."[9] The director of the arsenal, less enthusiastic about the prospects, responded that he would be able to accept only men fit to sail.[10]

The roundup of undesirables was a success in the short run, primarily due to a reward of ten mil-réis for each able-bodied beggar brought in. That cash bonus amounted to more than a week's normal pay per mendicant arrested, and Queiroz enthusiastically noted that police agents "spared no effort in discovering them." The cost of paying these rewards would soon decline, Queiroz assured the minister of justice, when "the number of such vagrants and beggars will drop to almost nothing, because of the arrests themselves and because people will either hurry to find honest work, or leave the city." The police chief reported that in less than a week no less than 104 beggars fit for work had been removed from the streets of the city and were serving their one-month term of prison with labor in the house of correction, breaking rock for use in filling the nearby marsh. If the city government would provide the carts, he went on, the extra workers could make considerable progress in actually transporting the material to the site of the fill.[11]

In principle, this plan was neatly tied together. Give policemen a direct reward for making arrests. Use the labor gang system of the house of correction to occupy the able-bodied in the useful task of filling the city's swampy lowlands, and then send them off to military service. Use the fortuitously available facilities on Santa Bárbara island to provide an existence for the infirm, but not so luxurious as to promote the accumulation of those not in dire straits. While the officials had designed numerous and detailed procedures to handle beggars, the root of the original phenomenon—the profusion of beggars and vagrants in the city—was never specified beyond invoking a series of negative terms. Beggars "infest" and "flood" the city, with "bad effects," but the underlying nature of the problem was considered so obvious and unquestioned as to dispense explicit comment.

The sweep of 1838 illustrates how the political and social elite perceived the issue, and the associations they made among poverty, charity, the obligation of the able-bodied to work, and the obligation of the state to remove the social detritus from public view. It also illustrates how these concerns were translated into specific policies through the existing institutional structure and the available physical facilities. It did not end the presence of beggars in Rio de Janeiro, nor was it the first or last of similar efforts by police authorities.

When Queiroz reviewed efforts to establish a beggars' shelter in mid-1841, he did not mention the Santa Bárbara Island initiative of less than three years earlier. Apparently that plan had not achieved the hoped-for success. Harking back to his early career as a district magistrate, he recalled a meeting of the police commission in 1832 that "resolved to establish a shelter where beggars could spend the night, to avoid sleeping in the streets, with great danger for themselves, for passersby, and even offending decency and public morality." A shed adapted for the purpose had later been taken over as a storage facility for the streetlight service, and several other buildings served as temporary shelters until early 1839, when the army designated the last one, a storehouse adjacent to the military academy in

São Francisco Square, for demolition. Since that time, the police chief lamented, beggars have "continued to sleep in the entryways of churches and in the streets, which is public and notorious." With this preface, and noting that the policy of sentencing able-bodied beggars to a month at hard labor was working well, he asked the minister of justice to arrange for a building that could serve as a shelter for the invalid and indigent. Either the police must "furnish a shelter where these people can at least spend the night," he said, "or we must tolerate their continued infestation of the streets." With the provision that the facility be located close to the center of the city he made several suggestions, including the possibility of constructing a new building for this purpose if an existing one could not be found.[12] After looking over the possible sites, the administrator of government properties in the city was hard pressed to make a recommendation "Unfortunately," he concluded, "no one likes these people as neighbors, and with good reason, due to the necessary sanitary measures."[13]

Throughout this period the police continued to lock up beggars under Article 296 of the Criminal Code for a month of hard labor. In May 1849, for example, an escapee from the house of correction was described as "not a criminal serving a sentence, but a beggar there for correction."[14] The policy of sending only the physically fit to the house of correction remained in force, however, and authorities were reluctant to send the sick, infirm, and small children to the adjacent house of detention; they were after all, "true" beggars. Without an adequate shelter for the true beggars, there was little choice between jail on the one hand, and the medical facilities of the Santa Casa de Misericordia charity hospital on the other. In April 1845 some details of the characteristics of "true" beggars appeared in a request that some people arrested for vagrancy and remanded to jail be sent instead to the Santa Casa instead, "since they cannot do any work whatever." They included "José Faustino de Santa Ana, more than sixty years old, with an inguinal hernia and in deformed condition; João Benguela, more than forty years old, with one arm missing and the other entirely crippled; Pedro Congo, nearly eighty years old and in a state of marasmus [chronically undernourished]; and Maria Luisa de Nazarete, who has chronic dysentery and cannot work at anything."[15]

In 1850 the police chief made yet another effort to deal with the problem, this time based on complaints, relayed through precinct-level police officials, that the growing number of vagrants and beggars was "prejudicial to public morals." They "disturbed the peace and tranquility of residents" of the waterfront area between the imperial palace and the Santa Casa hospital, particularly under the walkway built over the Rua Direita (now Rua Primeiro de Março), and around the imperial stables adjacent to the palace. These were reasons enough to address the problem, said the chief, but another issue made action particularly urgent in this case because this was the stretch of waterfront closest to the anchorage, where most passengers landed: "I refer to the picture of immorality, the indictment against our civilization, that this situation presents to the view of foreigners just arriving on our shores." As a result, the police chief asked for permission "to put an end to this scandalous abuse" by locking the offenders away, assuring the minister of justice that he would only remand to the house of correction those not accepted at the army and navy arsenals for conscription because there might be too many for the military to absorb in a short time.

In his penciled notes for a reply, the minister of justice asked rhetorically whether it might be possible to regulate the vagrants in question by forcing them to register with the police. Providing his perceptions on the psychology of beggars, while at the same time revealing something of his own cultural pretensions, Paulino José Soares de Souza suggested, "The necessity of going to the police and declaring they are poor, in order to ask for alms in the streets, will diminish their numbers substantially. This is the case at least with Brazilians, who will want to be anything except poor. 'Poverty,' said Rousseau, 'is not a vice, but it is a serious defect.'" More formally, his response was that only those sentenced to prison with labor for having committed a crime could be sent to the house of correction, which was not to be used as a holding tank for people not falling under the provisions of the Criminal Code.[16]

In 1850 the first yellow fever epidemic in Rio de Janeiro's history created a major public health crisis. As sick people fell in the streets and survivors wandered, disoriented and pleading for assistance, officials declared that the beggar problem was contributing to the public health problem. The minister of the empire reported that an urgent measure was to "provide asylum for the beggars whose appearance and presence in the streets does as much to invoke repugnance by their lack of cleanliness as they do to invoke the pity, if not the duty, of those who govern."[17] Public health as a policy issue in the modern sense emerged in Brazil only at the beginning of the twentieth century, after the germ theory of disease propagation was generally accepted and prophylactic measures became available.[18] In the middle of the nineteenth century officials saw public health as an issue only when it added to the more generalized problems of personal security and acceptable public behavior.

Finally, in August 1854, a building near the Santa Luzia church was remodeled for use as a beggars' shelter at considerable expense and was opened under regulations reflecting the goals of the police and the experience gained from previous efforts. Mendicants found in the streets, public places, and doorways of churches were to be brought to the shelter at night, from which those able to work were to be sent to the house of correction. All those who spent the night in the shelter were to be registered, records were taken of their names, ages, reason for inability for work, and other details of their condition. The staff was to include a doorkeeper charged with maintaining order and cleanliness in the establishment and registering the entries, to be assisted at night by three policemen, who would take turns on guard.[19]

In 1856 the chief of police praised the efforts of the government to "save the capital of the empire from the sad spectacle beggars offer to the public view, spending the night anywhere, in the doorways of churches, and even in the streets." The conditions in the shelter, however, were not intended to provide the "idle and vagrant with a place where they might find those pleasures that can only be obtained through labor," so he had the police doctor examine people in the shelter and then sent those found reasonably fit to the house of correction where the director was to put them to work as he saw fit, "providing the same rations they would get in the shelter." José Thomaz Nabuco de Araújo, the minister of justice, formally approved this more informal procedure that did not involve criminal charges, noting that it was within the provisions of the 1854 regulations.[20]

Later that year, during a cholera epidemic, people found wandering in the street were sent to the beggars' asylum for food and shelter, and the practice of supplying food to street people unable to work was continued after the public health crisis subsided. For an indication of the scale of this operation in the following period, during all of 1860 a total of ninety-one beggars entered the shelter (sixty-three males and twenty-eight females); and at the end of the year there were forty-one people in the establishment (twenty-six male and fifteen female).[21] In 1862, movement through the shelter had dropped to just thirty people, and there were sixteen in residence at the end of the year, evenly balanced by sex. It is impossible to say what proportion of all beggars on the streets of Rio these numbers represent, but it is likely only a small fraction. The total population of Rio de Janeiro at this time was approximately 210,000.[22] Again, the police chief urged that the separate beggars' shelter be closed down, and its services be added to those provided by the house of correction, primarily to save on rent and administrative expenses of a separate building, but also so that "useful labor" might be found to occupy those able to work.[23]

The shelter continued to exist as a separate entity, however, and an activity was found to make use of the client population in generating income to offset expenses. During 1865 the inspector in charge bought 240 hundredweight of worn-out rope from the nearby naval arsenal, which had been replaced in the course of rerigging navy vessels. The occupants of the beggars' shelter were put to work unraveling the cordage by hand to produce oakum (caulking material), which was then sold in the port, most of it back to the navy, for ship repair. The profit from the oakum-making activities came to 614 mil-réis, or less than 10 percent of the total operating expenses for 1865 of 6,964 mil-réis. The income from making oakum from old rope was used for expenses not covered in the regular operating budget, such as buying fabric for making clothing for the shelter inhabitants and cleaning supplies. In the eyes of officials, at least the rope-recycling operation kept idle hands occupied.[24]

In 1866 the chief of police criticized the practice of sending vagrants to a month of labor prescribed in the Criminal Code, suggesting that it did more harm than good: "Serving his sentence, the vagrant or vagabond acquires neither skills nor habits of work, but it is enough time to extinguish the last flicker of self respect." After such a term in prison, the vagrant "returns to his cohorts more daring, having lost the fear of punishment." The chief preferred the practice of obliging vagrants to sign promises to seek honest employment, the violation of which meant a jail term considerably longer than one month. During 1865 police agents had obtained such promises from sixty-four individuals, of which twenty-three were Brazilian and forty-one foreign. Of the latter, thirty-four were Portuguese, three English, two Spanish, one Belgian, and one from the United States.[25] The Portuguese caught in these nets were probably immigrants who had fallen on hard times. It is likely that some of the other non-Brazilians were merchant seaman down and out in a tropical port. Although slaves comprised approximately a quarter of the city's population in 1865, they were normally dealt with under regulations aimed specifically on slaves. If slaves were picked up for vagrancy, they were sent directly to the jail dedicated to holding slaves, pending notification to the person's owner to retrieve their human property. For slaves, formal promises to seek honest employment did not apply.

Commenting on the level of vagrancy and the petty crimes associated with it, the police chief in 1869 declared that "poverty should not be considered a causal factor, because in our country there is superabundance of work available, and resources [for living] are easily obtained." He went on to decry "the excessive number of vagrants who infest the city, and who are found in all public places with the intent to exercise their criminal industry, the majority being of Portuguese nationality." He noted that some of the women who spent time in the beggars' shelter, after being "regenerated by the regimen there" were "turned over to private individuals to work as domestic servants." He again urged that a building be specially constructed for this function, which was "one of the urgent needs of this city, where pauperism is on the increase, especially with the importation of foreigners given to vagrancy and drunkenness, who then turn to begging." A new asylum would also make it possible to rigorously apply the punishments set forth in the Criminal Code.[26]

The inspector in charge of the beggars' asylum conveyed his own experienced observations to the police chief in an 1871 report that deserves to be quoted at length, as an expression of official attitudes distinguishing false from true beggars:

> I must note that beggars, properly speaking, who wander the streets asking for alms, are very few, even though their numbers seem to be increasing. The majority of them are men and women vagrants given to drunkenness and petty crime [*malandrice*]. Taking advantage of tolerance, and counting on the benevolence and public charity of the country, these people abandon labor to plead for alms by day, disguised as beggars, and by night they are transformed into sneak thieves [*ratoneiros*]. I believe that if such tolerance were suspended, and energetic measures were employed so that everyone found begging were remanded directly to the beggars' asylum, this crowd would disappear. Most of them are foreigners who intrude into houses and churches disguised as beggars, although in fact some among them are property owners, and many others are money lenders who, after a time, return to their countries of origin with fortunes, as experience has shown. I am convinced that if such measures were put into practice, the beggars' shelter would [only] house those who are really beggars. If the vagrants were taken into custody by the police to be dealt with as the case warrants, they would be convinced of the prohibition, and would not continue in the vice of begging, to which they have become accustomed, and would look for work.

He noted further that from 1866 to 1869, from among the beggars entering the asylum, he had sent 208 men to the naval arsenal in Rio to be put into service in the naval squadrons then operating in the Paraguayan War. In the same period, some 160 men and women who entered the asylum were contracted as domestic servants to private parties who had sought them out, and most of them were still in the homes to which they had been sent. This showed, the inspector proclaimed, that "most of the people who have come into the asylum as beggars are vagrants disguised as beggars. Keeping them in the asylum for a time has made them of some use to society and to themselves, and many have been rehabilitated, dedicating themselves to labor, as I have indicated." He further expressed his conviction that if they could be assured that begging would cease in the downtown commercial districts, business would make monetary contributions to the operation of the beggars' asylum in amounts sufficient to pay the institution's operating costs.[27]

In an 1874 report the minister of justice, discussing the beggars' asylum as a "preventive institution," provided a well-developed rationale for the desirability of such an establishment, in the larger context of the problem of maintaining public order and security. Since the creation of the asylum some twenty years before, the minister declared, it had been of considerable public utility:

No longer are found, as was the case in former times, so many unfortunates who, due to lack of physical capacity, or moral abasement, or through habits of idleness, were not able to obtain the means to sustain themselves, and found themselves obliged to take recourse in private charity, which was not always prompt or adequate. We no longer see them wandering the streets despairing of their condition, resentful against a society that abandoned them, thus becoming enemies of that society and the constant object of vigilance by the police.

Today, gathered in that modest establishment [the beggars' shelter], they are occupied in labor that is light and easy, but of some utility, as is seen in the yearly reports. And while they do not thus repay the state for the small expense it incurs in their sustenance, they do become accustomed to a useful occupation, and thus escape the criminal activity to which they would otherwise be driven by poverty.

Among the idlers who roam the city are many minors who are not yet subject to the action of the courts, but who for lack of support and protection become perverted, acquiring vices that impose new needs, which then draw them to theft and more serious crimes. Upon entering life, man has inclinations, or natural dispositions, that may then be directed toward virtue, shaped by good example, and fortified by sentiments of family and religion. But the orphan, the foundling, the child of illicit unions (I am not including misery and pauperism, which fortunately are not known here); the young vagrants, the idle, the indigent, without anyone to direct their first steps, cultivate their intelligence, or awaken and cultivate their moral sentiments, go straight down the road to corruption due to the abandonment in which society leaves them. Society does not provide support and tutelage for them, even though it might pay dearly for this negligence by the need to punish them in the future.[28]

In early 1876 one of the city's major newspapers issued a call for more diligent action by the police in controlling the perceived increase in the beggar problem. In an open letter to the chief of police, the *Jornal do comércio* asked,

Is it not possible to put a stop to the shameful scenes repeated every day in this city, especially in the Campo da Aclamação [a large public park, now Praça da República], by the immense number of troublemakers and vagrants of both sexes, who respect nothing and mock everything, with no action by the appropriate authorities? Is there no way to enforce existing laws requiring labor of those who do nothing but bother and insult the honest and peaceful population? We live in a policed city, yet we see ourselves troubled and deprived of security of person and property, condemned to stand by helplessly and watch the farcical dance of the those who commit all manner of mischief in the streets of the city, with impunity. What sort of capital do we live in? Will no forceful and decisive action be taken by the authorities whose mission is to guarantee the liberty and welfare of citizens, in order to efficiently repress the independence of such audacious people and prevent the complete breakdown of good customs, respect for the law, and for social order?

Two days later, in direct response to this editorial outcry, the internal orders of the day of Rio's uniformed police force included the urgent call for the arrest of anyone suspected of being vagrant and disorderly (*desordeiros*).[29] Taking beggars off the streets had long been included in the standing orders of Rio's street patrolmen, but this incident shows that police institutions were responsive to such public outcries.

An Asylum of Mendicity

In October 1875 a new Asilo de Mendicidade (asylum of mendicity) was authorized. The new facility was not opened until four years later, in July 1879, as part of the house of correction complex, still under the administrative supervision of the chief of police. It replaced the old Albergaria de Mendigos (beggars' shelter) that had been the focus of such efforts since 1854. The new establishment was intended to provide lodging for those who by their physical condition or advanced age "were not able to provide themselves with the necessities of life through their own labor." Also eligible were children under fourteen years of age, and "idiots, imbeciles, and the insane." Those who accepted the services of the new establishment were not free to come and go as they pleased but were, in effect, incarcerated. Residents tacitly agreed to abide by regulations intended to ensure its orderly functioning, subject to disciplinary action that in a homeless shelter of today would seem draconian. Punishment for violations of the internal rules ranged from extra work details to being put on a regimen of bread and water for up to three days to confinement in a darkened cell for up to eight days. Those approved for residence in the asylum would be free to leave at such time as "by means of their own earnings [peculio—the same term used for funds slaves accumulated for self-purchased freedom], from donations or the protection of a trustworthy person, they could live without begging."[30] In other words, once a person admitted indigence and made use of the support afforded by the new asylum, the only way out was to prove that one would not be a burden to society upon release.

Despite the more formal title, new installations, and increasingly elaborate bureaucratization, the press often looked askance at official claims that the new institution was serving the purpose for which it was intended. In May 1880, for example, the English-language *Rio News* published the following note, laced with thinly disguised irony:

A few days ago the minister of justice visited the *Asilo de Mendici-dade* and took lunch. He found everything in fine order—in short a model institution. On the 1st the chief of police made a similar visit—unexpectedly it seems—and found it in satisfactory condition. In view of this circumstance, would it not be in order to now remove a few beggars from the streets to the asylum? On Saturdays the city is overrun with them and they tax the time and pockets of businessmen to a degree which should never be permitted in any community. A beggars' asylum is of precious little use when the beggars are allowed to run about at will.[31]

Who Was Doing Favors for Whom?

During the period discussed here, there was little indication that the various and recurring institutional efforts to deal with the "beggar problem" had the long-term effect of significantly reducing the number of beggars, vagrants, and other assorted street people in Rio de Janeiro. On the contrary, the problem seemed to grow proportionally with the growth of the city itself, and in any case the actual numbers of people "served" by the system remained small relative to the perceived scale of the problem to be solved. In this regard, it is impossible to say how many beggars roamed the streets of Rio at any given time during the period under study, and thus it is difficult to assess the relative efficacy of the various punitive and palliative measures emanating from state institutions. What we do know is that both police authorities and the press perceived begging as a problem, and that both the perception and the activity were ongoing. Neither the provision of sustenance and shelter adequate for survival of the "true" beggars nor the routine arrest and punishment of the "false" beggars seemed to have more than a temporary and limited effect. With some variations of scale, intensity, and vehemence, the negative descriptions of the phenomenon, explanations for it, as well as prescriptions for it, remained as a recurring feature of elite discourse.

One possible explanation for why more street people did not take advantage of the services offered is one that emerges in later historical periods. In accepting the largesse of the state, people had to accept the authority of the state over their behavior and conform to the norms the state chose to impose. In other words, by entering the institutional structures aimed at helping them, beggars lost the freedom to decide for themselves when to drink alcohol, the freedom to engage in affective or conflictive relationships that the state considered illicit or immoral, and even the freedom to decide on the mundane details of daily life. It may also be that public begging continued to be a viable source of sustenance, however meager, for those who engaged in it, and that the punitive aspects of the state response to begging were seen as a tolerable part of the risk environment beggars dealt with. Moreover, if the people who gave their pocket change to the deserving poor believed it was a small step toward achieving a state of grace, such attitudes and the resulting actions might have continued to create incentives for beggars to continue to ply their trade, even in the face of periodic campaigns of state-sponsored repression.

A question that logically arises from this experience is why the developing state, through its emerging institutional structures, did not do more to deal with the beggar phenomenon so consistently identified as a problem. One possible answer is that among false beggars, police action such as the threat of arrest, summary beatings, and the month of hard labor, did serve as a deterrent and made street people wary and circumspect, limiting the scale of the problem. In order for the streets of the city to be considered adequately secure and free of bothersome beggars, some level of mendicant activity was apparently tolerable by the public and to the authorities who acted in their name. The functional definitions of "acceptable bounds," "adequately secure" and "tolerable levels" are difficult to specify with the information at hand.

The situation of the true beggars is more intriguing. The question here might be posed as to why the police did *anything* for them, if the people involved were not deemed criminals. As expressed in recurring reports, it was partly a question of appearances. Even true beggars were dirty, bothersome, made a bad impression on visitors, and set a bad example for those on the edge of such behavior themselves. More generally, however, these were the indigent, the helpless, the incapacitated—hapless souls who truly needed and *deserved* the largesse of those who could provide for them the means of survival. The emerging state presumed to act in the name of the nation's citizenry, a category that in functional terms did not include beggars or vagrants. As the boundary between private and public responsibility shifted through the period toward the latter, officials and institutions in the state structure can be seen as acting on the collective will, impelled by ideological precepts and cultural values presumably shared by the people who made up the collectivity—the citizenry of the upstanding, the self-sufficient, and the morally virtuous.

The individual capable of dispensing charity to those less fortunate could achieve a minimal level of grace by doing so. By extension, the consolidating state, acting in the name of its citizens, should engage in the benevolent paternalism of charity through more sustained and institutionalized policies. And the efforts of the state had approximately as much overall and long-term effect in resolving the so-called beggar problem as did the individual act of dropping a coin into the grubby hand extended in supplication.

Notes

1. As used here, the term *modernization* and the contrast between traditional and modern refer to the multifaceted changes affecting western Europe and historically related areas roughly in the century from the mid-1700s to the mid-1800s, marked by the maturation of capitalism and the emergence of the nation-state. For interpretive essays focused on controlling the behavior of the population as the nation-state emerged, see Michel Foucault, *Discipline and Punish: The Birth of the Prison* (New York: Vintage, 1979); Max Weber, *Economy and Society*, 3 vols. (New York: Bedminster, 1968). As Mark Poster observes in discussing *Discipline and Punish,* Foucault "might have chosen a Weberian frame for his work." Poster, *Critical Theory and Poststructuralism: In Search of a Context* (Ithaca, NY: Cornell University Press, 1989), 121. Foucault himself made several mentions late in his life of a Weberian point of reference in his thinking; see, for example, David Couzens Hoy, ed., *Foucault: A Critical Reader* (Oxford: Basil Blackwell, 1986), 22.

2. Elysio de Araujo, *Estudo histórico sobre a polícia da capital federal* (Rio de Janeiro: Imprensa Nacional, 1898), 10–27. An 1868 dictionary of the Portuguese language, while noting derivation from Greek *polis* (city), recognized the emergence of a narrower conception of *polícia*, with the following definition: "Government and good administration of the state, of the security of citizens, public health, subsistence, etc. Today refers particularly to cleanliness, lighting, security, and all matters with respect to vigilance over vagrants, beggars, thieves, criminals and seditious persons, etc." The same source defines a second usage of *polícia*, derived from Latin *polire* (to polish), as "culture, polish, the perfecting of a nation, the process of civilization" and warns that the two meanings, each with its own origin and connotation, should not be confused with one another. José Maria d'Almeida and Araujo Corrêa Lacerda, *Diccionario encyclopedico ou novo· diccionario da lingua portuguesa*, 3rd ed., 2 vols. (Lisbon: F. A. da Silva, 1868), 2:743. In thinking about what their role in society should be, Rio's police authorities did consider these two areas of activity or connotations of the term—repressing criminality and civilizing the urban lower classes—to be extensions of one another. For a broader context, see Thomas H. Holloway, *Policing Rio de Janeiro: Repression and Resistance in a Nineteenth-Century City* (Stanford, CA: Stanford University Press, 1993). For a discussion of the broader use of the term *police* in old regime France, see Robert Schwartz, *Policing the Poor in Eighteenth-Century France* (Chapel Hill: University of North Carolina Press, 1988), 3.

3. Brazil was declared independent from Portugal on September 7, 1822 and had a constitution by 1824, but the administrative structures of the new state took some time to develop. Vicente de Paula Azevedo, "O centenário do código criminal," *Revista dos tribunais* 77 (1931): 441–61.

4. A key scriptural passage declaring the necessity of charity to gain redemption is Matthew 25:31–46. Also, see the discussion of the persistence of Catholic charity in eighteenth-century Spain in Paul Ocobock's introduction to this volume.

5. Article 296 of the 1831 Criminal Code included begging in the chapter on vagrants and beggars, in the section on "police crimes," such as offenses against "religion, morals, and good customs; secret societies; illegal assembly." The code decreed the maximum punishment for the offense of begging thus delineated would be one month in prison, either simple cellular confinement or engaged in labor, according to the capacity of the beggar; Antonio Luiz Ferreira Tinôco, *Codigo criminal do Imperio do Brazil* (Rio de Janeiro: Senado Federal, Conselho Editorial, 1886), 513.

6. Relatório do Ministro da Justiça, 1833 (Rio de Janeiro: Imprensa Nacional, 1834), 25.

7. Arquivo Nacional do Rio de Janeiro (hereafter ANRJ) IJ6 187 (Ofícios do Chefe da Polícia da Corte), September 24, 1838.

8. Under the conditions of the 1831 Criminal Code, once a mendicant's asylum was officially established in Rio de Janeiro, public begging automatically became a criminal offense.

9. ANRJ IJ6 187 (Ofícios do Chefe da Polícia da Corte), September 27, 1838.

10. ANRJ IJ6 190 (Ofícios do Chefe da Polícia da Corte), October 2, 1838.

11. ANRJ IJ6 187 (Ofícios do Chefe da Polícia da Corte), September 28, 1838.

12. ANRJ IJ6 196 (Ofícios do Chefe da Polícia da Corte), July 30, 1841.

13. ANRJ IJ6 196 (Ofícios do Chefe da Polícia da Corte), August 20, 1841.

14. ANRJ IJ6 179 (Ofícios da Polícia Militar da Corte), May 11, 1849.

15. ANRJ, III7 42 (Ofícios do Calabouço), April 15, 1845.

16. ANRJ IJ6 214 (Ofícios do Chefe da Polícia da Corte), June 3, 1850.

17. Relatório do Ministro do Império, 1851, annex (Rio de Janeiro: Imprensa Nacional, 1852), 10.

18. Nancy Stepan, *Beginnings of Brazilian Science: Oswaldo Cruz, Medical Research and Policy, 1890–1920* (New York: Science History Publications, 1976).

19. ANRJ IJ6 218 (Ofícios do Chefe da Polícia da Corte), August 14, 1854.

20. ANRJ IJ6 222 (Ofícios do Chefe da Polícia da Corte), February 4, 1856.

21. Relatório do Chefe de Polícia, 1861, annex to Relatório do Ministro da Justiça, 1861, (Rio de Janeiro: Imprensa Nacional, 1862), 4.

22. Censuses of Rio de Janeiro counted 97,162 in 1838, 205,906 in 1849, and 228,743 in 1872. See Holloway, *Policing Rio*, 295.

23. Relatório do Chefe de Polícia, 1863, annex to Relatório do Ministro da Justiça, 1863, (Rio de Janeiro: Imprensa Nacional, 1864), 7.

24. Relatório do Chefe de Polícia, 1866, annex to Relatório do Ministro da Justiça, 1866, (Rio de Janeiro: Imprensa Nacional, 1867), 6. One mil-réi was roughly equivalent to 45 U.S. cents in 1866.

25. Relatório do Chefe de Polícia, 1866, annex to Relatório do Ministro da Justiça, 1866 (Rio de Janeiro: Imprensa Nacional, 1867), 2. For more on the social composition of Rio's population and the major division of the lower-class population into slave and free, see Holloway, *Policing Rio*.

26. Relatório do Chefe de Polícia, 1869, annex to Relatório do Ministro da Justiça, 1869 (Rio de Janeiro: Imprensa Nacional, 1870), 56–57, 62.

27. Ofício do Inspector do Asylo de Mendigos, em 14 de março de 1871, annex to Relatório do Ministro da Justiça, 1871 (Rio de Janeiro: Imprensa Nacional 1872), 34.

28. Relatório do Ministro da Justiça, 1874 (Rio de Janeiro: Imprensa Nacional 1875), 29–30.

29. *Jornal do comércio* (Rio de Janeiro), January 11, 1876, 3; Arquivo Geral da Polícia Militar do Rio de Janeiro, Ordem do Detalhe, January 13, 1876.

30. Relatório do Ministro da Justiça, 1879 (Rio de Janeiro: Imprensa Nacional, 1880), 74.

31. *Rio News*, May 5, 1880, 3.

7

Vagabondage and Siberia

Disciplinary Modernism in Tsarist Russia

Andrew A. Gentes

"FAIRLY OFTEN YOU see a person flee from the road and scamper into the taiga," Petr A. Kropotkin wrote in his diary while passing through Eastern Siberia in 1862. "The number going about as vagabonds [*brodiagi*] is huge. . . . They're on Irkutsk's boulevards and in the mountains (albeit only a few); very many travel along the rivers, and they're all fast-moving, faster than the Angara [River] below Irkutsk."[1] Twenty-five years later, an editorial entitled "The Struggle with Brodiagi and Warnings from Siberians Regarding the Ulcer of Exile" appeared in the *Eastern Observer*. The newspaper's editor, author Nikolai M. Iadrintsev, frequently addressed the connection between exile and vagabondage (*brodiazhestvo*), and wrote here, "At any one time there is a minimum of thirty thousand brodiagi in Siberia."[2]

Neither of these writers was an impartial critic of tsarism: Kropotkin became a leading exponent of anarchism during the 1860s, and Iadrintsev had been exiled as a Petersburg university student to Archangel Province for "Siberian separatism." Nevertheless, the belief that brodiagi were plaguing Siberia finds expression in official sources as well. "The number of military deserters and brodiagi escaping along the Main Siberian Road . . . is steadily growing," Irkutsk's provincial administration reported as early as 1820, adding that brodiagi were "extremely burdensome" on the region's population.[3] Writing in 1875, Irkutsk Province's chief of gendarmes called them "the principal source of all possible crimes";[4] and S. M. Dukhovskoi, the Amur Territory's governor-general from 1893 to 1898, characterized up to half the exile-settlers assigned to Transbaikalia as brodiagi.[5]

Establishing that Russians throughout the nineteenth century believed brodiazhestvo a nearly unmanageable problem is easy enough; determining brodiagi's numbers or whether they were the principal source of all possible crimes is considerably more difficult. Scholarship on vagrancy and its association with crime demonstrates that modernization's disorienting effects conditioned perceptions of vagabonds' numbers and impact. Factors such as land dispossession, agricultural disasters, rapid urbanization, and vagaries of the wage-labor systems that replaced bonded-labor systems variously explain the burgeoning numbers of migrant laborers, beggars, and others labeled vagrants in England, France, and elsewhere.[6] Such factors however fail to explain the situation in preemancipation Russia, where serfdom coexisted with brodiazhestvo until 1861. For example, droughts and other natural disasters tended to afflict Russian agriculture worse than those of its counterparts, but because serfs had already lost all migratory privileges in 1649, few risked leaving the village, even if their owners did not (as they often did) provide for them in times of need. Therefore, land dispossession and itinerant labor are irrelevant in the Russian case. Serfdom similarly limited urbanization. The above factors are more relevant to the postemancipation period, when land reallocations combined with population growth decreased land availability and rapid urbanization and the new wage-labor system created the kind of impoverished lumpenproletariat first seen in Birmingham and Manchester. Nevertheless, I argue that vagabondage is best understood as a Foucauldian knowledge-technology functioning within a modern disciplinary apparatus.[7] Although Michel Foucault is vague concerning the origins of power relations within this apparatus, the conflicts produced may be said to consist for the most part of decision makers trying to impose order on perceived deviants as part of a normalizing process, all of which renders the vagrant as much an invention of modern technology as the internal combustion engine.

What, then, do brodiagi and brodiazhestvo reveal about the modernizing disciplinary process in tsarist Russia? Numerous studies look at prerevolutionary modernization, but nothing has been written on Russian vagabondage. I therefore offer three proposals. First, the tsarist government used brodiazhestvo to classify and regulate a society that, especially by the early nineteenth century, was steadily falling apart. Official attitudes toward brodiazhestvo reflected a larger process of "systematization" whose intention was a "well-ordered police state."[8] Second, the peasant commune's use of brodiazhestvo reflected tensions within rural society and was itself a major form of oppression. The peasantry's possession of extralegal punitive powers was a characteristic of Russia's uneven development and, as Stephen Frank has noted, necessitated by the government's limited police control over the countryside.[9] Third, the literature of the time shows that Iadrintsev and other writers constructed brodiagi as icons to serve their own agendas; mythified these persons and their behavior; and in so doing identified brodiazhestvo as a major fault line within this disintegrating society. This fault line separated Russia's "two cultures," in Abbott Gleason's words: privileged society and the people, or *narod*.[10] Finally, my use of *brodiagi* and *brodiazhestvo* indicates that although I recognize similarities with phenomena elsewhere, the differences between these phenomena, especially when Siberia and the exile system are factored in, seem to me more useful in understanding Russian modernization. Like Australia, the American colonies, and New Caledonia, Siberia partially functioned as a penal colony; but in contrast to these other locations it served that function much longer and for many more people, and its contiguity with the motherland rendered the problems there of immediate concern.

Origins of Brodiazhestvo

Brodiazhestvo first became a political issue coincident with the development in Russia of the service-state ethos—an ethos that subordinates society to the state and assigns to each subject a utilitarian and instrumentalist function. Accordingly, efforts by landowners and government officials to tie peasants to the land began in earnest during the reign of Ivan III (the Great; 1462–1505), and culminated with the 1649 Law Code (Ulozhenie) that definitively eliminated serfs' migratory rights. It is significant that this code also designated Siberia as a destination for exiles. Hereon serfs and exiles were assigned to specific locations while those commoners found elsewhere became increasingly susceptible to charges of brodiazhestvo, not only from government officials and church leaders but also from fellow commoners, who often accused them of witchcraft.[11] "Those people first called 'free,' who later received the sobriquet 'idlers' [guliashchie], were eventually called 'brodiagi,'" wrote S. V. Maksimov in 1900. "Free people existed before the Muscovite Ivans [Ivan III and Ivan IV (r. 1533–84)], guliashchie during their reigns and until that of Peter [the Great (r. 1689–1725)] ..., and brodiagi after him and up to our day."[12]

Indeed, Peter greatly expanded the campaign against brodiazhestvo. More than any European ruler, he marshaled human capital to serve the state. Coming to power at the close of Europe's most belligerent period in history, when 95 percent of the years between 1500 and 1700 witnessed a war somewhere on the continent, Peter inherited a legacy of insecurity in a polity that had utterly collapsed a century earlier during the Time of Troubles (1598–1613). Peter's greatest nemeses were Sweden and the Ottoman Empire, both of which controlled vast territories Russia eventually annexed after years of fighting. These and other powers benefited from a head start in the military-technological revolution that began in the sixteenth century, and this partly explains why, early on, Peter was captured by the Ottomans and humiliated by Sweden at Narva. The tsarist state was also pressured by the mercantile competition arising out of development of the worldwide economy.[13] These and other external threats in turn led to greater pressure on society to conform, and rendered Peter's enforcement of the service-state ethos as much a part of his grand strategy as the navy or the metallurgical industry, for here was a do-or-die philosophy by which he subjugated all those under his control, forcing even the lowliest to serve in one or another capacity. As serfdom embraced expanding numbers of peasants and the military and bureaucracy called for ever more recruits and officials, a new epistemology that saw individuals as separate fiscal units commodified human beings as never before. To improve tax collection the Petrine government assigned every subject to a social estate (*soslovie*), and for this reason specifically targeted the guliashchie. "The struggle with 'the free and the itinerant' became part of a whole system of combating fugitives," writes Evgenii Anisimov,[14] and under the new disciplinary apparatus the criminalization of such persons allowed them to be drafted by the military, assigned to a new penal labor regime called *katorga*, or exiled to Siberia. As Adele Lindemeyr has shown in her study of poverty in Russia, efforts to order society continued through the eighteenth and nineteenth centuries, with laws against vagrancy and begging that "de-sanctified the poor" (to borrow A. L. Beier's words), so that "holy fools" once appreciated as recipients for pietistic almsgiving now became deviants and louts who had to be excised from society and put to use as soldiers, penal laborers, or exile-settlers.[15] If unable to perform these services satisfactorily—perhaps because they were mentally ill, physically disabled, or enfeebled—Siberia's vast expanses provided a solution and thus became their home for as long as they could survive, though the journey into this freezing hell killed many before they arrived.

Little information exists on brodiazhestvo during the rest of the eighteenth century, though the granting of exilic authority to landowners and peasant communes by Elizabeth Petrovna (r. 1741–61) and Catherine the Great (r. 1762–96) suggests the state continued to regard it a major problem. In any case, this extension of authority meant brodiagi and their ilk could now be punished by administrative as well as judicial procedures. Documented growth of Siberia's exile population further suggests that efforts to punish brodiagi continued apace. A. D. Kolesnikov has estimated that Russia deported up to thirty-five thousand males to Siberia between 1761 and 1781, though because many would have been accompanied by family members, the total number of adults was probably closer to sixty thousand.[16] Certainly not all were exiled for brodiazhestvo; but what is known about the subsequent application of this charge suggests brodiagi accounted for significant numbers of deportees at this time. Moreover, Catherine's government encouraged landowners to hand over serfs for compulsory settlement by granting credits against military recruitment quotas as well as payments of several rubles per head. Despite rules forbidding it, many took advantage of this provision to rid themselves of problem serfs and those too sick or old to work. In 1802 a Senate investigator found that of a group of 1,454 such colonists assigned to the Irkutsk region, 260 were epileptic and 91 mentally afflicted; and that many others were over the age limit of forty-five, crippled, or otherwise incapacitated.[17] Again, not all were exiled as brodiagi. But note should be taken of comparable instances in other cultures where undesirables with fixed locations have been labeled vagrants; and societies routinely exclude the physically and mentally disabled. In Russia the deportation of persons manifestly unfit for colonization demonstrates how little control Petersburg exerted over the countryside, as well as the nobility's tendency to hijack state policy for their own benefit.

Observing the increase in publications devoted to "migratory criminals," Frank has concluded that anxiety over brodiagi grew during the late nineteenth century.[18] However, such publications are somewhat misleading insofar as they coincided with the rapid growth of the publishing industry and readership in Russia. Among at least landowners and government leaders, anxiety was certainly widespread in the years *before* emancipation, when both serfdom's supporters and opponents invoked fears of a jacquerie similar to the Pugachev Uprising of 1773–75. Like his predecessor Stenka Razin, Emelian Pugachev counted among his followers large numbers of brodiagi and fugitive exiles. Elites' fears therefore found solid basis in a long tradition of ragtag *brodiaga* armies like that led against Moscow in 1603 by Khlopko Kosolapyi ("the Pigeon-Toed"). Sixty years later, fugitive exiles and mutinous Cossacks led by the exile Nikifor Chernigovskii managed to establish an independent state in southeastern Siberia; and in 1724 "a gang numbering in the thousands under the leadership of the fugitive soldier Klopova built a fort in Penza Province."[19] Despite some cross-cultural similarities, "bandit armies" in Russia were especially gigantic and dangerous, indicative yet again of the government's tentative hold over the countryside. Elites may also have found the Taiping Rebellion of 1850–64 unsettling, not just because it coincided with the height of the serfdom debate but because the millenarian notions informing it recalled peasant tales about the reappearance of a presumably dead tsar who crushes the nobility and redistributes the land. Russian history is replete with pretenders who capitalized on this myth, ranging from Pugachev, who at times claimed to be the murdered Peter III, to Marija Szimanskaja, an exiled Pole who during the 1830s walked from Krasnoiarsk to Irkutsk proclaiming herself Mariia Pavlovna, daughter of the similarly murdered Paul I, telling villagers that Nicholas I's dead brother was really alive and would soon rise up to free the oppressed.[20]

In short, brodiazhestvo was an important aspect of early Russian modernization. The fears, myths, and policy concerns associated with it carried over into tsarism's final century of existence.

Brodiazhestvo and Disciplinary Modernism

As M. J. D. Roberts and others have shown, England's Vagrancy Act of 1822 allowed prosecution of any number of acts considered deviant. The elasticity of this and similar laws elsewhere made them useful policing tools, since arrest and conviction were far easier under "vagrancy" than almost any other charge. As Foucault observes, "Power produces, it produces reality; it produces domains of objects and rituals of truth. The individual and the knowledge that may be gained of him belong to this production." Roland Barthes similarly writes, "What is invested in the concept is less *reality* than a *certain knowledge of reality.*" Barthes calls the resultant products "myths," adding that their "expansive ambiguity" renders them serviceable to authority, which places them in "a chain of causes and effects, motives and intentions."[21] Research on the corporealization of authority during the modern era[22] also helps to account for the upsurge of vagrancy legislation.

Russia may therefore be understood to have come into possession of a modern disciplinary apparatus simultaneous with England, for on February 23, 1823, Alexander I (r. 1801–25) promulgated the Brodiagi Regulation (*Ustav o brodiagakh*), the most significant brodiazhestvo legislation issued before 1917. Prior to 1823 the government seems to have assigned most able-bodied brodiagi to the military; but in the wake of the Napoleonic Wars a growing sense of professionalism, as well as the emperor's desire to insure the army's integrity, led to their being exiled to Eastern Siberia instead. The Brodiagi Regulation created a vicious circle that increased the number of both exiles and brodiagi. Whereas brodiagi such as Dmitris Zakharevich and Leon Parfenov (each arrested in Vilna Province in 1824) would now be deported,[23] recruitment quotas would almost certainly have risen (especially during wartime) to make up for the loss of recruits, which in turn explains the apparent increase in the number fleeing the draft and the army. "Nearly unwavering consistency distinguished the number of brodiaga-deserters who fled the difficulties of military service," writes Maksimov of the period after 1823;[24] and if arrested and not identified, such fugitives would have been exiled as brodiagi. In 1834 only 5 percent of brodiazhestvo cases were acquitted,[25] which further explains why brodiagi came to account for such large numbers of exiles. Between 1827 (when detailed statistics began) and 1846 they made up 62 percent (48,566) of administrative exiles (77,909) and 30 percent of all exiles (159,755).[26] In 1833, 2,314 brodiagi were exiled, whereas the second-largest cohort (those convicted of stealing either property or money) totaled only 1,680.[27] During 1838–60, brodiagi and deserters accounted for 31 percent of all those exiled. Moreover, the dismal lives facing growing numbers of "soldiers' widows" may explain the rise in female exiles' numbers after 1823 as well.[28]

State authorities used brodiazhestvo to remove a variety of deviants deemed noxious for one reason or another. Peasants who rebelled in Staraia Russa in 1831, as well as others involved fifteen years later in the so-called potato riots in Viatka and Kazan provinces, were exiled as brodiagi. There is some evidence the state used brodiazhestvo to control non-Russian communities. In 1840 Petersburg announced "decisive measures for eradicating the brodiazhestvo of Gypsies" by reporting that Nicholas I (r. 1825–55) had approved a plan to settle them in "state settlements" early the following year. They were to be deported, settled, and administered "as per the [1822] 'Regulation on Exiles.'"[29] Later statistics showed that for 1842 Kiev had by far the largest number of brodiazhestvo arrests (2,758) of all imperial provinces and that Poltava, another Ukrainian province, ranked fifth.[30] The number of Gypsies then in Ukraine is uncertain, but the region is known to have also included large numbers of Poles and Jews, who may account for some of those arrested. Also, Nicholas approved the establishment of penal battalions for brodiagi, deserters, and petty criminals. As of July 1830, eight such battalions were operating in the southern districts of Odessa and Novorossiia; and by 1847 these penal battalions accounted for 5,500 prisoners assigned to public works in Moscow, Brest-Litovsk, Kronshtadt, Kiev, Ekaterinoslav, and other cities.[31] Despite the 1823 regulation, under Nicholas the military—with its discipline, rigidity, and conformity—remained the model for dealing with brodiagi.

Following emancipation, the absence of both alternative penal strategies and meliorating social policies explain the continuing deportation of brodiagi (the battalions were discontinued; practically no prisons or workhouses existed; charity was a private, not a government, affair). From 1867 to 1876 the courts sentenced 23,383 individuals to "exile to resettlement" (ssylka na vodvorenie).[32] First created in 1848 "under extraordinary pressure from the overcrowding of prisons,"[33] this category was soon directed only at brodiagi but remained purely nominal, since exiled brodiagi were assigned to peasant villages or penal labor instead of (nonexistent) penal settlements (vodvoreniia). "The actual conditions of this exile category render it, like the crime of brodiazhestvo itself, a complete anomaly, unjustified by any reasoning," reported the Main Prison Administration's director in 1886.[34] Courts nevertheless continued to vigorously prosecute brodiagi. As of 1898, brodiagi exiled "to resettlement" accounted for 13 percent (36,683) of all Siberia's nonpenal labor exiles.[35]

Civilian authorities' reasons for deporting people were mundane by comparison. Since the 1760s, landowners and communal village assemblies had been using exile to rid themselves of troublemakers or economically burdensome individuals. So ubiquitous was the use of brodiazhestvo to deport elderly and mentally or physically afflicted serfs that in August 1827 the Senate "forbid the removal to Siberia for brodiazhestvo of the aged, deaf, mute, and blind." The following year, senators amended this decision by assigning new destinations for certain brodiagi: the elderly were to be sent to workhouses while those originating in the southern provinces would go to the Caucasus, and Muslim brodiagi to fortresses in Finland. Female brodiagi were still to be exiled to Siberia, because of the region's shortage of Russian women.[36]

Determining the proportion of these and later expulsions that originated with village assemblies is difficult. For one thing, data for 1827 through 1846 conflate brodiagi exiled by civilian authorities with those exiled by government officials. Nevertheless, several factors suggest peasants were primarily responsible for the nearly fifty thousand brodiagi exiled to Siberia during these years, as well as the majority of those afterward. First, most such exiles came from the countryside. Of a cohort of 718 brodiagi exiled between 1835 and 1846, 588 originated among the peasantry. Peasants also accounted for 90 percent of a cohort of 9,564 persons exiled under the equally vague and elastic charge of "bad behavior," which, like brodiazhestvo, communes used to administratively deport undesirables.[37] Second, because of the lack of government control over the countryside as well as landowners' habitual absence or disinterest, communes largely policed themselves, even when a bailiff was present. "The social oppression of serf over serf ... distinguished the structure of authority," writes Steven Hoch of the preemancipation village;[38] and legislation passed in 1857 confirmed the commune's right to exile those who "took up" brodiazhestvo throughout the remainder of the tsarist era. Third, after 1861 a combination of land dues, population growth, and declining productivity imposed new pressures on the peasantry, so that despite no longer being serfs, they continued to engage in predatory relations that often led to banishment. That they did is supported by the fact that communes' exilic authority was a highly contentious issue during the late imperial period, primarily because it was largely responsible for Siberia's growing exile population. For instance, a 1900 Ministry of Justice report paints a damning picture of conditions for administrative exiles and their effect on the region. The Imperial Cabinet nonetheless quashed ministerial attempts to curb communes' authority. From 1892 to 1896 village assemblies administratively exiled 23,500 people to Siberia, whereas the government administratively exiled only 730; and of nearly 300,000 nonpenal labor exiles in Siberia as of 1898, 146,656 had been banished by communes. The proportion among this number accused of brodiazhestvo cannot be determined, but the latter figure ties into the final indicator of communes' central role in persecuting brodiagi: their right not to accept the return of those previously exiled or otherwise removed for punishment. Repeatedly supported by legislation throughout the nineteenth century, this privilege resulted in tens of thousands of "unacceptables" (*nepriniatye*) being reexiled by either administrative procedure or judicial sentence "to resettlement," and thus effectively rendered brodiagi. "Unacceptables" accounted for 81 percent (32,476) of all administrative exiles between 1882 and 1886, as well as a significant proportion of the 13,233 assigned to the resettlement category from 1887 to 1898.[39]

The expansion of a service-state ethos that commodified human beings largely explains the emergence of brodiazhestvo as a criminal, or at least deviant, behavior. Government officials and landowners labeled as brodiagi those whose value was low, nonexistent, or might be better realized by assignment to a new service function such as soldiery or colonization. At the same time, large numbers of peasants fled enserfment, military recruitment, and taxation and, whether under the noms de jour *guliashchie* or *brodiagi*, tried to become "free." Whereas landowners, the government, and the courts deported significant numbers of people, the peasants themselves, albeit acting under economic pressure, were the main actors in their own oppression.

Brodiazhestvo and Siberia

In Siberia, brodiazhestvo was a problem for reasons different than those in European Russia. In addition to the nominal brodiagi deported there, many of those wandering the countryside were fugitive exiles and many of them were violent criminals. In 1883, for example, Panteleimon Rudenko, previously exiled to the Sakhalin penal colony, escaped and murdered an exile-settler and a peasant before being captured.[40] The archives are filled with orders like those from an

Irkutsk constable to Oëk Canton officials "to thoroughly hunt down" Anisim Prokofev, Ivan Zasilev, the schismatic Serafim, and other exiles missing in the region.[41] In general, Siberian brodiagi were by-products of a penal system whose management undermined the modern disciplinary intent behind it. Most exiles were simply dropped into peasant communities that barely tolerated them, let alone gave them land parcels. That many had been deported because they were already unproductive peasants only compounded the problem, and so after exhausting their government stipends they took to begging, sold their clothes, and obtained "loans" from peasants who charged 100 percent interest. Large numbers found their way to district townships to scrounge a living on the streets, so that small cities like Kainsk, Mariinsk, and Ialutorovsk were inundated by half-naked supplicants blocking doorways with outstretched hands. Siberia's prisons were similarly easy to walk away from. Evfimiia Kashaeva (a.k.a. Agafia) was able to slip out of an Irkutsk jail in 1883 by pretending to be the visiting wife of a male prisoner.[42] That same year, Krasnoiarsk officials bashfully reported, "on the 28th of this past May, the exiled prisoners Nikifor Kondratev and Zakhar Kurylkin, held in the local prison, having been allowed to go outside the gates to the scales for weighing prisoners' bread, escaped."[43] Of the 7,458 penal laborers assigned to Nerchinsk District's mines and factories as of February 1859, four thousand were listed as "on the run" (v begakh).[44] Depending on the exilic category, Siberian administrators could not account for the whereabouts of between 10 and 50 percent of those exiled between 1887 and 1898.[45] These figures reflect to some extent poor record keeping, and only a portion of those who fled would have assumed a brodiaga lifestyle; nevertheless, Iadrintsev seems to have been correct in claiming many thousands of exiles were wandering throughout Siberia at any given time. Whereas regulations and institutions show the state animated by a goal to discipline those who entered the penal system, the lack of systematization significantly undermined this goal's realization.

Violent offenders' lengthy penal labor sentences were a prime motivation to escape; and even when captured, they concealed their identities so as to be punished more lightly as brodiagi. Many would escape for this reason alone. In 1865, Irkutsk police reported the arrest of an "unknown person, without papers, who calls himself Ivan Ivanov." An Andrei Andreev was arrested several weeks later.[46] Political exile P. F. Iakubovich recorded much more colorful pseudonyms than these, however:

> Ivan-the-Suffering, Petr-the-Enduring, Semen-Many-Griefs-Seen, Hightail-to-the-Hill, Beaten-to-Pieces, And-I'm-Following-Him, Thirty-Two-Years-Forgotten, and so forth and so on in that vein. The following surnames were also favored: Almazov [of Diamonds], Brilliantov [of Gems], Lvov [of Lions], Orlov [of Eagles], Sokolov [of Falcons], Burin [Stormy], Vetrov [of the Winds], Skobelev [of Adzes], Gurko [the Georgian], and similar fine-sounding and boastful names.[47]

Yet the most common pseudonym by far was Nepomniashchii—"Not Remembering." For example, in 1856 Uspensk Canton officials reported to the Nerchinsk land court, "Iakov Nepomniashchii has been shown [to be] Ivan Kononov." However, confusion continued over the next several years regarding this particular Nepomniashchii's true identity.[48] Anton Chekhov's 1890 census of Sakhalin's penal population revealed the Nepomniashchii clan to be remarkably procreative,[49] and Iadrintsev reported counting forty members in a single prison. "It cannot be said that *nepomniashchie* result from mistakes in our judicial procedures," he reasoned. "More correctly, they have earned themselves the right to exist."[50]

Residents and authorities blamed brodiagi for spreading crime and immorality. "He who has not lived long in Siberia cannot understand how terrible the reverberations of exile have been on its inhabitants," intoned the Irkutsk newspaper *Siberia,* "how much innocent blood has been shed thanks to the wandering masses of drunken, embittered, unsheltered people here; how much moral evil these wretches have spread and how many unbearable hardships have been imposed on local inhabitants by exiles' actions!"[51] Ishim's city duma concluded that brodiagi were limiting commerce and poisoning the behavior of others. "Because of exiles," noted its 1875 minutes, "the Ishim middle class's immorality has become so proverbial that our city thoroughfares are known to be dangerous several hundred versts in advance of arriving in Ishim."[52] Western Siberia's governor-general additionally explained. "In the spring and summer, when those who are escaping to their homes from undermanned and ineffective supervision are on the run and hiding in the woods, it is rare that the countryside, along well-trodden paths, is without theft, rare that the cities are without villainous attempts on life, rare that the road is without dead bodies."[53]

In Irkutsk Province, 2,145 crimes were recorded in 1886, including 162 murders and 764 thefts or robberies. Of the 857 convictions secured in these cases, exiles and brodiagi accounted for 375, including two of the three convictions for bestiality.[54] Clearly, in Siberia brodiazhestvo was different than in Russia. "In Russia, the brodiaga goes about modestly and quietly, only at night," explains Iadrintsev, but in Siberia, "it is another matter." They routinely abduct women and girls from fields and woods and "the elderly, female pilgrims, children, and all defenseless people are subject to assault and robbery from brodiagi."[55] Russian and foreign visitors alike shared Iadrintsev's view. Diarizing on Siberia's phenomenal midge population, Kropotkin notes, "They are the fate of the brodiagi," then adds: "The brodiagi; now there's a children's game—'capturing brodiagi.' A children's game, though recently it was no game." He goes on to describe three exiled brodiagi's escape, murder of a convoy guard, and eventual arrest.[56] "We've encountered brodiagi with pots on their backs," Chekhov writes in a letter to his sister while en route to Sakhalin, "these gentlemen stroll freely along the whole of the Siberian Road. They'll knife an old woman to steal her skirt for their puttees, tear the metal sign off a road marker for some use, knock in the skull of a passing beggar or gouge out the eyes of a brother exile, but won't touch passengers in vehicles. Generally, traveling here is completely safe as far as robbery goes."[57] And the Englishman Charles Hawes, who visited Sakhalin in 1901, describes traveling with a loaded rifle along a road where two brodiagi had accosted a merchant's son a week earlier: "Fortunately, before they had seriously injured him, he was recognized, and, with the delightful *naïveté* and *sang-froid* of the Sakhalin *brodyagi,* they exclaimed, 'It wasn't you we wanted, but your father!'"[58]

As these accounts suggest, Siberian brodiagi not only fascinated writers but were also constructed by them. The literature on brodiagi relates to that on the Russian peasantry, though brodiagi's association with crime and—in the emerging parlance of the time—"the criminal nature" rendered them much more titillating. Similar to what Cathy Frierson has written about constructions of peasant icons,[59] brodiaga icons met the needs of an emerging middle-class readership. Four writers are particularly notable in this regard: N. M. Iadrintsev, S. V. Maksimov, P. F. Iakubovich, and V. M. Doroshevich. Each belonged to the postemancipation *intelligentsiia*, which meant being both a social and—as censorship allowed—a political critic. Theirs was the voice of a small middle class espousing newfound values and seeking to redefine the body politic through literature, which in prerevolutionary Russia was particularly coherent because of the small number of intellectuals, as well as influential, as the reforms that followed Dostoevskii's, Tolstoi's, and Chekhov's books on the criminal justice system suggest.[60] Yet, the above four writers lived within a narrow privileged stratum far removed from the narod, and this led to their portraying the brodiaga as an other. Collectively, their writings reveal to some extent the influence of the popular genre of bandit and crime stories that embodied both commoners' fantasies of personal rebellion and freedom and elites' fears of disorder and criminality. By framing brodiagi as a discrete and threatening subspecies, these writers evoked middle-class insularity, anxiety, and insecurity in a rapidly changing Russia. But other motives were at work as well, for they used brodiaga icons to level necessarily veiled criticism against state and society. Doroshevich, in particular, combined a tendency to subspeciate with descriptions of individual brodiagi, through whom he then questioned human nature and the morality of the penal justice system.

Iadrintsev was most conflicted when describing brodiagi. He argued that Siberia had degraded into "an enormous prison without a roof," yet also mythified this landscape as a repository of ancient Russian values. As part of efforts to demonstrate the disastrous effects of government policies he iconized brodiagi as being primarily to blame for regional crime; yet he also portrayed them as renegades whose very lifestyle mocked authority. "As in the ancient, so in the new Rus, escape and brodiazhestvo were the natural protests of the individual against restraints [imposed by authorities]," he writes in *Russian Society in Prison and Exile* (1872). Iadrintsev credits brodiagi's forerunners, the guliashchie, with first settling peripheral regions later incorporated into the empire. These runaways embodied both the Russian "soul" and the expansionary promise of the Russian "tribe," yet at the same time formed a distinct ethnographic group. "This generation of brodiagi," he similarly writes of his contemporaries, "have their own history, passed on through oral tradition. . . . The brodiagi cooperative, like any cooperative, creates its own types and ideals. In their souls, all brodiagi hope to become the ideal brodiaga—the hero." This hero is the archbandit, cunning, fearless, and adventurous: "he should be an outstanding thief; he should not lack for money; he should carouse and carry on a bitter struggle with the authorities and the peasantry."[61]

Iadrintsev considered brodiazhestvo to be as much a state of mind as a lifestyle, as his taxonomy of six kinds of brodiagi shows. There are the "worker-brodiagi," for example, who in European Russia tend to labor on peasants' or landlords' farms or as fisherman on the Caspian Sea or Don River, but in Siberia more often work in the mines. Entrepreneurial Siberian peasants may nevertheless have as many as five brodiagi in their employ, and Iadrintsev claims that eighty such worker-brodiagi were discovered in a village of one hundred in Tomsk Province, though "the majority help peasants only during harvest time, living the rest of the time as brodiagi." His use here of the verb *brodiazhit* (to vagabond) indicates that whereas a brodiaga might be a laborer, a laborer can never be a brodiaga. "Brodiagi assume various professions" he can therefore write without contradiction, "they serve as sentries, beekeepers, herdsmen, millers, and so on, working as well in the crafts. . . . There are tailors, cobblers, glassblowers, brewers, saddlers, locksmiths, and joiners." Yet another category of brodiagi goes about as sorcerers (*znakhari*), capitalizing on peasant beliefs in magic and herbal remedies. With their satchels of roots, herbs, ground bone, and pebbles, znakhari cure bewitched women, cleanse households of bedbugs and cockroaches, and target

Cupid's arrows; as lineal descendents of King Solomon, they tell fortunes by appealing to the Oracle of Solomon or gazing into mirrors, for which they earn up to five kopeks or ten eggs per session. Renowned znakhari are sometimes approached for darker purposes: one told Iadrintsev that women often asked him to poison their husbands. Indeed, the small category of female brodiagi includes many peasant girls who have run off with these charismatic figures, and though some brodiaga unions include offspring, "brodiaga-women" typically abandon their children in villages and, reports Iadrintsev, at least one is known to have sold her children to a peasant family for eight rubles.[62]

Siberian brodiagi are most abundant when the call of the cuckoo signals the arrival of spring and exiles flee their locations to form the human tsunami peasants call General Cuckoo's army. Iadrintsev writes that groups of as many as forty brodiagi can be seen straggling along the Great Siberian Road leading from the Nerchinsk mines, where most penal laborers were sent. Such is the lack of police that most follow the major roads, though some proceed through the taiga or along the rivers, gathering other fugitives from factories and settlements. He details several routes by which brodiagi, if they want, may return to European Russia.[63] Like the earliest Russian explorers, these are accomplished trackers and woodsmen who know the landscape and are fearless, bold, and independent. For Iadrintsev, brodiagi are products of a government that seeks to control rather than serve society. He models them as tricksters and changelings whose freewheeling ways spoof this government and invert its values. Despite frequently alluding to them as a scourge, he idealizes them as Russia's heart and soul, typifying them with his construction of the hero.

Maksimov's description of brodiagi partly resembles that of Iadrintsev. After discussing the history of fugitive escape in Russia he writes, "Fugitives evincing a uniquely Russian type of vagabonds in Siberia who go by the names *varnaki* and *chaldony* are a numerous and certainly peculiar class of people." But unlike Iadrintsev, he portrays brodiagi as an urban problem. "Before us are the brodiagi—people without vocation, having no known residence or means of existence, employed by neither workshops nor factories," verbigerates Maksimov. "They are the prototype of all kinds of villains to be encountered as an unavoidable phenomenon anywhere commerce is permitted and defended by law, where there exists criminal industry—that vegetation which receives its nutrition in large cities."[64] Brodiagi are the excrescence of a commercial and industrial development that Slavophilic Russians like Maksimov loathed because they believed it was destroying Mother Russia. They are in some ways pitiful, but above all dangerous and contemptible. Maksimov's is therefore really a critique of modernization itself, a response to the replacement of sacred with secular values, to the supersession of the city over the countryside. His brodiagi iconize this process and provide one more reason to resent it.

The political exile Iakubovich found brodiagi contemptible as well—rather ironic, considering that before his arrest he belonged to the People's Will, a revolutionary party advocating popular socialism. Yet he explains that his romantic image of the narod evaporated during his march with them into Siberia in 1887. Like Maksimov, Iakubovich uses *brodiagi* as a synonym for that caste of hardened criminals who form prison society's elite, occupy all the best positions literally and figuratively, and institute a reign of terror over other prisoners they contemn as "the herd" or "locusts." Senior members call themselves Ivans and parade about in red blouses and sashes, manhandling lesser exiles' wives with impunity. After describing their fearsome activities, Iakubovich concludes, "These people are for the most part depraved, having what is called *ni foi, ni loi* for a soul, though they are tight with one another and in the [deportation] party comprise the real state within the state." In this account, brodiagi are a constant in the criminal and prison worlds and comprise all professional criminals regardless of their actual crimes, though Iakubovich does add that "brodiagi's ranks have greatly thinned" because of new regulations, and that several prison massacres occurred during the 1880s, when "the locusts raised their heads."[65] Nonetheless, brodiagi remain an animal force forming part of the oppressive tsarist system: they have no origins, no individual existence or identity, but instead function collectively as archdemons in the exilic inferno Iakubovich describes. This unsympathetic portrait of society's wretched outcasts is particularly remarkable for having been republished in a

Soviet edition of 1964, since these masses are in no wise credited with even deserving to be liberated from their bonds. Iakubovich's brodiaga is invested with the same middle-class fears of unbridled willfulness and sexuality that reemerged in Russia after the 1917 revolution.

Doroshevich replicates Iakubovich's use of *brodiagi* to refer to prison elites and professional criminals, and he repeats the story of the massacres. However, unlike the previous authors, this investigative journalist (as he would be called today) creates sympathetic portraits of the brodiagi and other prisoners he met on Sakhalin in 1897. Most evocative is that of "the brodiaga Sokolskii," a former actor from Moscow with whom Doroshevich (also a theater critic) discusses favorite actors. Doroshevich recalls that he "noticed a peculiar oddity about Sokolskii."

> It was as if he could not finish saying something. . . . He would arrive, sit, turn around in his chair, talk about some frivolities, and leave. . . . He appeared to have something he simply could not get off his tongue.
>
> I tried to lead him to it in the following conversation.
>
> "Sokolskii, is there something you want to tell me? Please, be candid . . ."
>
> "No, no. . . . It's nothing, nothing. . . . Really, it's nothing. Goodbye, goodbye!"[66]

It transpires that Sokolskii wants to ask Doroshevich for money but is ashamed. Doroshevich of course gives him a few rubles, which prevent his being murdered by the Tatar convicts who run the prison's loan-sharking concession. An intelligent, cultured, sensitive man who somehow found himself in a barbaric world of Tatar thugs and other shadowy figures, this "brodiaga" was above all a victim. Sokolskii's victimization is heightened by the absence of any explanation of how he became a brodiaga. Instead, Doroshevich idealizes him as a counterpoint to the dehumanizing penal system he roundly condemns throughout his book. Sokolskii is meant not to typify brodiagi but rather to suggest that judicial mistakes have been made, and that these mistakes and others can nevertheless be corrected through Christian charity. In this sense, Doroshevich combines Maksimov's lament for traditional piety with the middle class's faith in progressive improvement. He plays the role in these vignettes of a modern intellectual well-versed in Lombrosian criminology who nevertheless patronizes the holy fool. His brodiagi are well-meaning simpletons who provide him opportunities to demonstrate these qualities, as in his story of "the brodiaga Ivanov"—"a beardless, moustacheless youth" who clerks in a government chancery until one day, his supervisor crudely insults him and Ivanov botches a murder attempt before botching his own suicide. Doroshevich quotes his suicide note:

> I request no one be found guilty in my death, it was my desire to shoot myself.
>
> (1) I fail in everything.
>
> (2) They don't understand me.
>
> (3) I request that it be written (to the address shown in Revel[67]) that I die loving only her.
>
> (4) Do not bury my body, but if you will, cremate it. Please!
>
> (5) I request a prayer be made to the Lord God, whom I understand not with reason, but believe in with all my soul.
>
> —Brodiaga Ivanov

Ivanov is sent to the infirmary to recover from his bullet wound. Doroshevich visits and comforts him when he breaks into tears protesting that he's an educated man. "The poor fellow," concludes Doroshevich, "he'd inserted 'cremate' into his suicide note probably to show that he was educated. . . . Before me lay a boy, a proud, tearful boy—but he was in penal labor."[68] Readers may sympathize with Doroshevich's agenda to humanize brodiagi and other deviants, but it's no less a shaping device for this. Like children, they are made to be adorable, disingenuous, and good, and therefore not responsible for their actions. Like children, they are shown to need guardians with broader, more mature understandings who will make decisions and keep them from harm's way. Such paternalism, increasingly embraced by the nascent middle class as the old regime sank below the horizon, perpetuated Russia's disciplinary tradition.

Against the backdrop of the long service-state tradition, the tsarist government during its final decades presaged Soviet social engineering projects via policies that russified and dictated school curricula, colonized the Russian Far East, and privatized agriculture (to name but a few). Social engineering is an almost inevitable corollary of modernization; but the Russian government could ill afford what it was spending on these and similar policies. At the same time, the emerging middle class was demanding a greater say in politics and seeking to strengthen its position with links to the narod by dispensing educational and medical services as well as propaganda. It assumed the right to join the debate over what to do with this population. Analysis of brodiazhestvo indicates that while this debate objectified or iconized the nonprivileged, they themselves were excluded from participating in it. The tendency by the government and intellectuals to regard the general populace as an inert mass to be disciplined or molded carried over into the Soviet period, during which exceptional vengeance was reserved for brodiagi and others who deviated from a new set of normative structures. By looking at the conflicts centered on this "extremity"[69] of human behavior, much is revealed about the workings of society as a whole.

Notes

GAIO	Gosudarstvennyi arkhiv Irkutskoi oblasti
GARF	Gosudarstvennyi arkhiv Rossiskoi Federatsii
RGIA DV	Rossiskii gosudarstvennyi istoricheskii arkhiv Dal'nego Vostoka
d	*delo* (sheaf)
f	*fond* (collection)
k	*karton* (carton)
l	*list* (sheet)
op	*opis'* (listing)

The transliteration style used here is a modified form of the Library of Congress system without diacritical marks, which have, however, been retained in the notes. All dates reflect the Julian calendar used in pre-Soviet Russia and that during the nineteenth century was twelve days behind the Gregorian calendar.

1. Petr A. Kropotkin, *Dnevniki raznykh let* (Moscow: "Sov. Rossiia," 1992), 60.

2. *Vostochnoe obozrenie* (St. Petersburg), September 3, 1887.

3. GAIO, f. 435, op. 1, d. 133, l. 108.

4. Quoted in A. V. Shavrov, ed., "Dal'nii Vostok glazami nachal'nika zhandarmskogo upravleniia," *Otechestvennye arkhivy* 1 (1993): 88–100, quote at 95.

5. Rossiskii gosudarstvennyi istoricheskii arkhiv Dal'nego Vostoka (RGIA DV), f. 1, op. 1, d. 1383, lines 4–37 [l. 7].

6. E.g., A. L. Beier, *Masterless Men: The Vagrancy Problem in England, 1560–1640* (New York: Methuen, 1985); Lionel Rose, *"Rogues and Vagabonds": Vagrant Underworld in Britain, 1815–1985* (New York: Routledge, 1988); M. J. D. Roberts, "Public and Private in Early Nineteenth-Century London: The Vagrant Act of 1822 and Its Enforcement," *Social History* 13, no. 3 (1988): 273–94; Olwen Hufton, "Begging, Vagrancy, Vagabondage and the Law: An Aspect of the Problem of Poverty in Eighteenth-Century France," *European Studies Review* 2, no. 2 (1972): 97–123; Sue Davies, "Working Their Way to Respectability: Women, Vagrancy and Reform in Late-Nineteenth-Century Melbourne," *Lilith* 6 (1989): 50–63; Jeffrey S. Adler, "Vagging the Demons and Scoundrels: Vagrancy and the Growth of St. Louis, 1830–1861," *Journal of Urban History* 13, no. 1 (1986): 3–30.

7. Michel Foucault, *Power/Knowledge: Selected Interviews and Other Writings, 1972–1977,* ed. Colin Gordon, trans. Colin Gordon et al. (New York: Pantheon, 1980), 51–52, 142, 184; Foucault, *Discipline and Punish: The Birth of the Prison,* trans. Alan Sheridan (New York: Pantheon, 1977), 194.

8. George L. Yaney, *The Systematization of Russian Government: Social Evolution in the Domestic Administration of Imperial Russia, 1711–1805* (Urbana: University of Illinois Press, 1973); Marc Raeff, *The Well-Ordered Police State: Social and Institutional Change through Law in the Germanies and Russia, 1600–1800* (New Haven, CT: Yale University Press, 1983).

9. Stephen P. Frank, *Crime, Cultural Conflict, and Justice in Rural Russia, 1856–1914* (Berkeley: University of California Press, 1999).

10. Abbott Gleason, *Young Russia: The Genesis of Russian Radicalism in the 1860s* (New York: Viking, 1980), 1.

11. Valerie A. Kivelson, "Male Witches and Gendered Categories in Seventeenth-Century Russia," *Comparative Studies in Society and History* 45, no. 3 (2003): 606–31, [622].

12. Sergei V. Maksimov, *Sibir' i katorga*, 3rd ed. (Petersburg: Izd. V. I. Gubinskago, 1900), 218.

13. Michael Roberts, *The Military Revolution, 1560–1660: An Inaugural Lecture Delivered before the Queen's University of Belfast* (Belfast: M. Boyd, 1956); Immanuel Wallerstein, *The Modern World-System*, vol. 2, *Mercantilism and the Consolidation of the European World-Economy, 1600–1750* (New York: Academic Press, 1980).

14. Evgenii V. Anisimov, *The Reforms of Peter the Great: Progress through Coercion in Russia* (Armonk, NY: M. E. Sharpe, 1993), 229.

15. Adele Lindenmeyr, *Poverty Is Not a Vice: Charity, Society, and the State in Imperial Russia* (Princeton, NJ: Princeton University Press, 1996), 36ff.

16. A. D. Kolesnikov, "Ssylka i zaselenie Sibiri," in *Ssylka i katorga v Sibiri (XVIII–nachalo XX v.)*, ed. Leonid M. Goriushkin et al. (Novosibirsk: Nauka, Sibirskoe otd-nie, 1975), 51; Alan Wood, "Siberian Exile in the Eighteenth Century," *Siberica* 1, no. 1 (1990): 38–63, [56, 59].

17. G. Peizen, "Istoricheskii ocherk kolonizatsii Sibiri," *Sovremennik* 9 (1859): 9–46, [29–30].

18. Frank, *Crime*, 140–41.

19. Maksimov, *Sibir'* (1900), 326–27; V. A. Aleksandrov and N. N. Pokrovskii, "Mirskie organizatsii i administrativnaia vlast' v Sibiri v XVII veke," *Istoriia SSSR* 1 (1986): 47–68; N. M. Iadrintsev, *Russkaia obshchina v tiur'me i ssylke* (St. Petersburg: Tip. A. Morigerovskago, 1872), 352–54.

20. A. S. Nagaev, *Omskoe delo, 1832–1833* (Krasnoiarsk: KGU, 1991), 122–23; A. P. Okladnikov et al., eds., *Istoriia Sibiri s drevneishikh vremen do nashikh dnei*, 5 vols. (Leningrad: Nauka, Sibirskoe otd-nie, 1968) 2:475–76.

21. Foucault, *Discipline*, 194; Roland Barthes, *Mythologies* (New York: Hill and Wang, 1972), 119, 124; emphasis mine.

22. For example, Emily Michael and Fred S. Michael, "Corporeal Ideas in Seventeenth-Century Psychology," *Journal of the History of Ideas* 50, no. 1 (1989): 31–48.

23. GARF, f. 1183, op. 1, d. 137, lines 60–61, 66–67.

24. Maksimov, *Sibir'*, 207.

25. S. S. Ostroumov, *Prestupnost' i ee prichiny v dorevoliutsionnoi Rossii* (Moscow: Izd-vo Moskovskogo Universiteta, 1980), 22, table 8.

26. Evgenii N. Anuchin, *Izsledovaniia o protsente soslannykh v Sibir' v period 1827–1846 godov: Materialiy dlia ugolovnoi statistiki Rossii* (St. Petersburg: Tip. Maikova, 1873), 21, 23, tables.

27. *Statisticheskiia svedeniia o ssyl'nykh v Sibiri, za 1833 i 1834 gody (Izvlechenie iz otcheta o delakh Sibirskago Komiteta)* (St. Petersburg: Tip II Otdeleniia Sobstvennoi E. I. V. Kantselarii, 1837), 35–38, app. to table 1.

28. Sergei Maksimov, *Sibir' i katorga,* 3 vols. (St. Petersburg: Tip. A. Transhelia, 1871) 2:320, 338–39, tables.

29. "Rasporiazheniia: O poriadke soderzhaniia i preprovozhdeniia Tsygan, dlia vodvoreniia ikh v kazennykh seleniiakh," *Zhurnal ministerstva vnutrennykh del* 36, no. 4 (1840): xxvi–xxxii.

30. "Materialy dlia otechestvennoi iuridicheskoi statistiki," *Zhurnal ministerstva vnutrennykh del* 4 (1843): 490–92, table.

31. I. Ia. Foinitskii, *Uchenie o nakazanii v sviazi s tiur'movedeniem* (St. Petersburg: Ministerstva putei soobshcheniia, 1889), 290–91, 295n1.

32. N. M. Iadrintsev, *Novyia svedeniia o sibirskoi ssylke: Soobshchenniia S.-Peterburgskomu Iuridicheskomu Obshchestv,* 2, table; appendix to Iadrintsev, *Sibir' kak koloniia: K iubileiu trekhsotletiia: Sovremennoe polozhenie Sibiri. Eia nuzhdy i potrebnosti. Eia proshloe i budushchee* (St. Petersburg: Tipografiia M. M. Stasiulevicha, 1882).

33. G. S. Fel'dstein, *Ssylka: Eia genezisa, znacheniia, istorii i sovremennogo sostoianiia* (Moscow: T-vo Skoropechatni A. A. Levenson, 1893), 146.

34. Nachal'nik Glavnago tiurcmnago upravleniia, *O ssylke,* December 28, 1886, 10; in Russian State Library, Moscow, W 15/63.

35. *Ssylka v Sibir': Ocherk eia istorii i sovremennago polozheniia* (St. Petersburg: Tipografiia S.-Peterburgskoi Tiur'my, 1900), 14–18, apps., table.

36. Maksimov, *Sibir'* (1900), 207.

37. Anuchin, *Izsledovaniia,* table, 66–67.

38. Steven L. Hoch, *Serfdom and Social Control in Russia: Petrovskoe, a Village in Tambov* (Chicago: University of Chicago Press, 1986), 189–90.

39. *Ssylka v Sibir',* 59–60, 94, 98–99, 144ff. and appendices, tables, 3–5, 6–13, 14–18, 19–26.

40. RGIA DV, f. 701, op. 1, d. 202, lines 17, 18, 19–21.

41. GAIO, f. 28, op. 1, d. 4, lines 27, 29–30, 32, 53. All documents date from 1852.

42. GARF, f. 122, op. 6, d. 432, l. 2.

43. Ibid., d. 431, l. 13.

44. Leonid M. Goriushkin, ed., *Politicheskaia ssylka v Sibiri: Nerchinskaia katorga* (Novosibirsk: Sibirskii khronograf, 1993), doc. 74, p. 139.

45. *Ssylka v Sibir'*, 39–40, apps., tables.

46. GAIO, f. 137, op. 2, d. 13, lines 120–21, 156–57.

47. Petr F. Iakubovich, *V mire otverzhennykh: Zapiski byvshego katorzhnika*, 2 vols., (Moscow: "Khudozhestvennaia literatura," 1964), 1:81.

48. RGIA DV, f. 1408, op. 1, d. 1, lines 58, 66–67, 68, 99, 101.

49. Rukopisnyi otdel' Biblioteki imeni Lenina, f. 331.

50. Iadrintsev, *Russkaia*, 434.

51. *Sibir'* (Irkutsk), April 5, 1887.

52. Reproduced in Iadrintsev, *Novyia*, 12. One verst is about two-thirds of a mile.

53. Reproduced ibid., 18.

54. *Obzor Irkutskoi gubernii za 1886 god* (Irkutsk: Gubernskaia Tipografiia, 1887), 29, app., table 8.

55. Iadrintsev, *Russkaia*, 491–92.

56. Kropotkin, *Dnevniki*, 247.

57. Anton P. Chekhov, *Sobranie sochinenii*, 12 vols. (Moscow: Gos. Izd-vo Khudozh. lit-ry, 1960–64) 11:423–24.

58. Charles H. Hawes, *In the Uttermost East* (New York: C. Scribner's Sons, 1904), 376.

59. Cathy A. Frierson, *Peasant Icons: Representations of Rural People in Late Nineteenth-Century Russia* (New York: Oxford University Press, 1993)

60. See Dostoevskii, *Notes from the House of the Dead;* Tolstoi, *Resurrection;* Chekhov, *Sakhalin Island.*

61. Iadrintsev, *Russkaia*, 351, 400–403.

62. Ibid., 403–5, 409, 463–67.

63. Nikolai M. Iadrintsev, *Sibir' kak koloniia v geograficheskom, etnograficheskom i istoricheskom otnoshenii* (St. Petersburg: Izdanie I. M. Sibiriakova, 1892), 268; Iadrintsev, *Russkaia*, 385–86, 388–89.

64. Maksimov, *Sibir'* (1900), 210, 216–17.

65. Iakubovich, *V mire*, 1:33, 35–36.

66. Vlas M. Doroshevich, *Sakhalin (Katorga)*, 2 vols. (Moscow: Tipografiia Tovarichestva I. D. Sytina, 1903), 1:137.

67. Present-day Tallinn, in Estonia.

68. Doroshevich, *Sakhalin*, 2:135.

69. Foucault, *Power/Knowledge*, 96–97.

8

"Tramps in the Making"

The Troubling Itinerancy of America's News Peddlers

Vincent DiGirolamo

"THE NEWSBOY IS forever restless," wrote the young settlement house worker Ernest Poole in 1903. "He works only when the crowds are thickest, and shapes all his habits to suit the changing, irregular life of the metropolis, and its life makes the life of his boyhood. Sometimes this spirit of the street gets into his blood, and he moulds his whole later existence into an unceasing passion for travel." Poole estimated that there were at least five thousand newsboys in New York, most under sixteen, many under twelve. "Hundreds are homeless," he told his readers, "and of these some are constantly wandering—to Chicago, San Francisco, and New Orleans, to London and the cities of the Continent, wandering always—but returning always, sooner or later, to the home that taught them to be homeless." Poole labeled this occupational subclass "wandering newsboys" and warned they were "tramps in the making."[1]

To bolster his argument, Poole told about a boy named Joe who was well cared for by his parents but started selling papers on the sly to earn spending money. He grew independent and rebellious. "When eleven years old he suddenly disappeared," said Poole. "He was gone some weeks, and saw Pittsburgh and Chicago both from the street's own standpoint." Joe's passion for the road increased, and at age fifteen he spent several months in Europe. His parents tried to cure him of this compulsion by sending him to trade schools. He showed promise as a mechanic and, at seventeen, took a job at a steel mill. He worked the night shift for several months and then relapsed. "Early one morning, after a long night's strain of work, the old passion must have returned with a power he could not resist," surmised Poole. Joe's body was found several miles out of town by the side of the railroad tracks: "He had started off for one more ride in the old exciting way. 'Wanderlust' had done its work."[2]

Joe's flight was probably as much a response to the grinding realities of factory work as to the siren song of the road, but Poole gave more credence to the latter and thus turned his gritty exposé of newsboy life into a kind of urban fable or morality play. He never gave Joe's last name, hometown, or death date, but presented him as an archetypal figure whose sad end might shock readers into action. A recent graduate of Princeton University, Poole was just twenty-two when he moved into the University Settlement on New York's Lower East Side. His first task was organizing basketball games for neighborhood boys, but his easy rapport with the kids led to an assignment from the New York Child Labor Committee to investigate newsboys to help win passage of a state law regulating juvenile street work. An aspiring writer who revered journalist Jacob Riis, Poole threw himself into the job. He chummed around with the boys for weeks, plying them with cigarettes, suppers, and stage shows—tricks he had learned from his father who used to round up a dozen Chicago street boys every Christmas Eve and treat them to new outfits and a night on the town. "By such bribes I got the facts and stories I wanted about their jobs and lives," Poole recalled in his autobiography. "In true reformer fashion then I centered on the worst ones, the toughest and the wildest, the hundreds down by City Hall near what was then still Newspaper Row. For these were the real street Arabs who slept at night in doorways or under Brooklyn Bridge close by."[3]

Poole was not the only social investigator to focus on tramps and street children. His idol Riis documented the poverty and squalor of both types in his 1889 classic *How the Other Half Lives*. Trinity College sociology professor John J. McCook surveyed scores of tramps and dozens of Hartford, Connecticut, newsgirls in the 1890s. Vagabond writer Josiah Flynt industriously churned out books and articles telling of innocent boys being "seduced" into the hobo life. And novelist Jack London, who peddled papers as a ten-year-old in Oakland, California, and hopped his first freight train over the Sierra Nevadas at age sixteen, recorded his own adventures in his 1907 memoir *The Road*. But Poole, more than any of his contemporaries, saw a direct link between the hustling newsboy and the shiftless tramp. He thus fused two of the most troubling social problems of the day: child street labor and adult vagrancy.

While his article presents a valuable ethnographic snapshot of New York street children, Poole's overt legislative agenda cast serious doubts about his findings. Did tramps really prey on newsboys? Was news peddling the first step to "Hobohemia" and ultimately ruin—or was this the product of a muckraker's vivid imagination? What role did mass-circulation newspapers play in destroying—or perhaps sustaining—the lives of the poor children who sold them? And how did their relationship change over time?

Writing almost fifty years ago, Raymond Williams called attention to "a quite widespread failure to co-ordinate the history of the press with the economic and social history within which it must necessarily be interpreted."[4] Scholars have since done much to illuminate the role of newspapers in the rise of democracy, spread of literacy, assimilation of immigrants, and commercialization of culture. They have also begun to investigate the job experiences of printers, reporters, illustrators, and other "news workers."[5] Their studies have enriched our understanding of changing notions of citizenship and the republic, but an even broader focus and less celebratory narrative is needed. Historian John Nerone has posited that journalism is fundamentally a system of relationships—"structured connections between various institutions of the state and civil society (the police, the New York Stock Exchange, major league baseball) and various constituencies in the public."[6] The interactions of children, tramps, and the press have largely escaped historical notice, but I believe they offer crucial insights about each of these parties and the meaner workings of American enterprise and society.

Here I draw on a variety of written and visual sources to trace the intersecting and sometimes indistinguishable experience of tramps and newsboys from the mid-nineteenth century to the early twentieth. My aim is to show how the American press has long exploited the leg- and lung-power of a rootless underclass of hawkers and carriers, both young and old, and to document how these people have in turn relied on the news trade to provide a subsistence living and more. Theirs was a reciprocal, though by no means equal, relationship as it involved some of America's least powerful individuals and most powerful institutions. At no time was their mutual dependence more evident than during the devastating economic depressions of the 1850s, 1870s, 1890s, and early 1900s, decades in which the social experience and cultural meaning of childhood, vagrancy, and beggary were in flux.

Tiers and Terms of the Trade

Although often seen as an indigenous national type, the American newsboy is a direct descendent of the itinerant newsmen, broadside peddlers, *corrantos* sellers, petty chapmen, flying stationers, running patterers, ballad singers, colporteurs, paper caddies, postboys, and mercurie girls who cried their wares on the streets of London, Paris, and other European cities in the seventeenth and eighteenth centuries. They belonged to a small subset of street vendors who specialized in the written word. They were naturally the most literate of hawkers, but their learning conveyed little status. In fact, they were widely regarded as rogues and vagabonds. One English proclamation of 1551 specifically called for the "reformacion of Vagabondes, tellers of newes, sowers of sedicious rumours, players, and printers without license & diuers other disordred persons."[7] As Linda Woodbridge has pointed out, peddlers' low reputation stemmed partly from their competition with settled merchants who paid rent, taxes, and wages, and thus resented competition from itinerants.[8] Those who dealt in news and opinion posed a political threat as well, given the potentially subversive nature of their wares. Up to the mid-nineteenth century,

European monarchs and aristocrats kept the press in check via strict licensing acts, libel laws, and stamp taxes. But American newspapers flourished due to constitutional protections, common schools, and cheap postal rates. By the early 1800s the number and circulation of newspapers in the United States surpassed all other countries.[9]

The commercial distribution of newspapers in America was a highly stratified business involving wealthy merchants and the outcast poor. At the top were proprietors of big wholesale firms. Below them came the thousands of retail vendors who operated shops or stands, often with the help of wives and children. Many of them functioned as wholesalers themselves, supplying hawkers, carriers, or other dealers. Next in line came the men, women, and children who acquired regular pitches and routes. At the bottom of the pyramid dwelled the hawkers, young and old, who owned nothing but their labor power.

Newspaper peddling in nineteenth-century America is best understood as part of an informal economy that coexisted with more formal and measurable economic activities. Informal, shadow, or hidden economies consist of small-scale, labor-intensive enterprises that take place on a local, face-to-face basis, such as growing and selling produce, cleaning houses, or giving lessons. Such businesses tend to be household centered yet are indispensable to major industries and deeply imbedded in national, even international markets. Although the adjective *shadow* suggests a nebulous kind of trade, there is no more enduring form of economic activity.[10] From this perspective, newspaper peddlers were major, not minor, economic actors in nineteenth-century urban America; they numbered into the tens of thousands and their work was integral to the fortunes of a major industry. One of the small ironies of industrialization is that it was accompanied, and in many ways underpinned, by an increased reliance on this essentially preindustrial form of labor and exchange. While more and more people were compelled to work for wages in an unstable, boom-and-bust economy, many, particularly the young, old, and disabled, took refuge in their ability to peddle. They sold a wide array of goods and services from matchsticks to shoe shines, but most of all newspapers. The invention of steam presses in the 1830s made American newspapers one of the first modern mass-produced commodities and their distribution required a host of Old World hawkers and carriers, mostly children.

Newspaper publishers originally sought adult vendors. One of the first advertisements in the *New York Sun* in 1833 began: "TO THE UNEMPLOYED—A number of steady men can find employment by vending this paper. A liberal discount is allowed to those who buy and sell again."[11] But men, even the unemployed, did not think there was enough money to be made hawking a penny paper and so it fell to the poorest boys of the city to do the job. What they lacked in efficiency they made up for in appeal. Some boys prospered by developing routes or recruiting smaller boys—rarely girls—to sell or deliver papers for them. Other cheap papers soon sprang up in New York and then spread to Baltimore, Philadelphia, Boston, and beyond.

A handful of boys plied their trade between cities. New York boasted four ferry piers with regular runs to Brooklyn, Staten Island, and Jersey City, and six steamboat docks serving Hartford, New Haven, Providence, Philadelphia, and Albany. On an excursion up the Hudson River in 1837, a journalist noted that "these varlets of newsboys" would shatter the customary repose of steamship travel with their cries—"Here's the Star!" "Here's the Express!" "Would you like a New Era, sir?" "Take a Sun, miss?"—which he called "the babel of a metropolis."[12] Upon docking, the boys easily found buyers for their now exotic New York papers and picked up local sheets to peddle on the return trip or back home. One boy who specialized in this maritime trade, Charles Barton, would reputedly "effect his object if the devil stood in the way."[13]

Genteel urbanites such as former New York mayor Philip Hone decried these new "cash papers" and the "gang of troublesome ragged boys" who hawked them.[14] Police sometimes arrested newsboys who desecrated the Sabbath with their din or disorderliness. But newspapers defended their young vendors as "winged Mercuries," "Time's Arrows," "loyal subjects of Queen Journalia," "little Gabriels of the literary world," and "brazen-throated members of the Fourth Estate."[15] Publishers routinely ran flattering articles and illustrations of these children, praising their enterprising "sauciness" as the spirit of the age (fig. 8.1).

FIG. 8.1. Charles A. Barry, "Itinerant News-Boy," 1854. In Charles Augustus Poulson Scrapbook Collection, *Illustrations of Philadelphia*, vol. 7, page 144, Library Company of Philadelphia

Their numbers continued to grow and by midcentury newsboys were more likely to be counted as vagrants than workers or merchants. In 1849, New York City's first police chief, George Matsell, polled his ward captains and determined there were at least three thousand "vagrant, idle and vicious children" in the city, fully two-thirds of whom were girls between eight and sixteen years of age. He guessed the actual number was closer to ten thousand, which he likened to a "corrupt and festering fountain endlessly flowing into the brothels and prisons." Matsell, who later displayed the same flair for language as editor of the *National Police Gazette*, divided the youths into five quasi-occupational classes that included scavengers, crossing sweepers, "baggage smashers," peddlers who sold fruits, nuts, socks, toothpicks and other items, and boys from respectable homes who nevertheless loitered on street corners.[16]

Newsboys now became synonymous with rooting beasts and nomads. They were called waifs and strays, urchins and guttersnipes, little wanderers and little vagrants, Bedouins of the street and bohemians of trade, apaches and street arabs. The latter epithet, invoked so casually by Poole, originated in 1848 when the British philanthropist Lord Shaftesbury told Parliament that "City Arabs" were like "tribes of lawless freebooters, bound by no obligations, and utterly ignorant or utterly regardless of social duties."[17] The word *newsboy* itself did not just refer to a male youth who sold newspapers but was a euphemism for any child—boy or girl—who had to survive on the streets. Writers and reformers commonly referred to the "newsboy class" or the "newsboy race."[18] Rev. Charles Loring Brace, founder of the Children's Aid Society, opened the first Newsboys' Lodging Houses in New York City in 1854, but it was open to working boys of all occupations. One regular lodger, a match peddler named Johnny Morrow, titled his 1860 memoir *A Voice from the Newsboys* and concluded by asking sympathy for "that class of human beings known as 'Newsboys;' under which class, however, are properly included all those unfortunate children of poverty in cities, who have to live in the streets mostly by their own *wits* or *resources,* whether it be by *peddling newspaper, sweeping crossings, selling stationery,* or any other little traffic which they may carry on."[19]

Whatever their specialty, newsboys developed their own occupational jargon, some of which suggests they were on intimate terms with vagrancy. *Bumming* referred to roving the streets at night without sleep. *Grubbing* meant begging. And *snoozing* signified sleeping out. Those who did so regularly were called *sleepouts* while runaways earned the title *kip outs*.[20] The mobility of newsboys is also evident in the names they gave themselves, many of which were based on their place of origin or favorite destination. Among those who worked in New York in the 1870s were Rockaway, Kalamazoo, and Country. Two newcomers to the Philadelphia scene in 1880 were simply dubbed Fresh and Recently.[21] Like hobo road names, newsboy monikers ensured anonymity while permitting a kind of fellowship within the trade. A closer look at the ways in which these boys kept themselves fed, washed, and sheltered reveals the central role of the press in their struggle for existence.

Down and Out in Newsdom

Hunger—gut-rumbling, breath-souring, head-spinning hunger—was a fact of life among the urban poor in the 1850s. Yet it was more than just a physical sensation; it was a social force. Hunger shaped class relations by turning individuals of all ages into willing workers. Morrow called hunger "the tyrant of animal life" and the most compelling force behind his trade. His father denied him breakfast and supper, he said, so "that I might obtain food for myself from those of my customers who were charitably disposed." Some newsboys helped vendors set up their stands in exchange for coffee and a roll; others ran errands for cooks and waiters or traded newspapers for a scrap of meat or a piece of bread.[22]

Cities could be gastronomic emporiums, even for children who counted their earnings a penny at a time. Newsboys usually ate from fellow vendors or in "penny restaurants," where a portion of everything on the menu, from roast beef and rice to apple pie and coffee, could be had for a cent.[23] Boys occasionally splurged for a hearty breakfast or a sumptuous dinner. After the rush for morning papers was over at nine o'clock, Johnny Morrow would sometimes spend nine cents for a cup of coffee and a dozen griddle cakes at a saloon. And after big paydays, he said, it was not uncommon for newsboys "to march into a restaurant and order a dinner of venison or woodcock, with sauces, which would not be despised by an alderman."[24] Such a feast could be had for twelve cents in New York, but prices were often higher elsewhere. Danny Sullivan, one of the more nomadic newsboys of the period, complained that a six-cent beefsteak in New York cost twenty cents in Boston. Fortunately, his favorite dish was the more affordable mackerel—"splendid fish, that."[25] Known as the Newsboy Professor, Sullivan lived off and on at the Newsboys' Lodging House in New York, but took periodic jaunts throughout the country, always packing a carpetbag full of papers, cards, and toys to sell while on the road. In the fall of 1857 he set off on a four-month trip that took him through Albany and Troy, New York, as well as Springfield and Boston, Massachusetts. Asked how he got by, he cracked wise: "I threw cards— peddled papers—killed Irishmen to sell them for soap-fat, and niggers to make blacking—any thing for an honest living."[26]

Many newspapers operated cheap cafés or sublet space to victuallers to attract news peddlers and keep them close at hand. Among the first to do so was the *New York Sun,* which opened an oyster cellar and saloon in its offices in 1844. James Gordon Bennett, whose *Herald* stood across the street, suggested that the *Sun*'s entry into the seafood business reflected its utter failure in the field of journalism, but Bennett soon opened the Union Restaurant in his own cellar.[27] The *New York Tribune* was home to two restaurants. The first, Butter-Cake Dick's, was an all-night eatery where three cents bought a cup of coffee and a heavily buttered biscuit that was the house specialty. Newsboys of the 1850s were always welcome, as the proprietor, Richard Marshall, was himself a former newsboy. In 1875 the *Tribune* let space to German immigrants John Koster and Albert Bial, whose restaurant became the foundation of their popular music hall. However, it served beer and rum on the premises, which some felt dishonored the memory of *Tribune* founder Horace Greeley, a lifelong temperance man.[28] Newspaper cafés were not just a New York phenomenon. The *San Francisco Herald* sublet its basement in 1861 to a man who operated a "low-down dive" that served whiskey along with more substantial fare, and the *Montreal Witness* opened a newsboy's lunchroom in the rear of its offices in 1868.[29] These places generated valuable income and swelled the ranks of hawkers in the neighborhood.

Staying clean was of less concern to newsboys than staying fed, and it was not necessarily good for business. A prosperous appearance might cause a boy to lose sales to his more needy-looking competitors. Yet boys with filthy clothes and dirty faces also risked alienating customers, attracting the attention of authorities, or being labeled a bummer by their peers. Bathing was an uncommon event even for boys who had homes, since few tenement apartments came equipped with tubs, showers, or hot water. Some boys were known to take footbaths behind horse-drawn street sprinklers.[30] A more thorough washing could be had at free or cheap public baths.[31] The first such institution in New York was built by the Association for the Improvement of the Condition of the Poor in 1852. The city used public funds and private donations to open several more baths by the 1870s. Children did not flock to these places voluntarily but were usually marched there en masse by schools or missions. The experience was not always pleasurable. Speaking about a later period, Baltimore newsboy Abe Sherman recalled that three cents bought just three minutes at a public bath: "They'd bang on the door if you didn't get out. Bang on the door and drag you out."[32]

Public fountains and water pumps were the first public baths, but the sight of children scrubbing themselves in these venues annoyed some urbanites and amused others. We can only speculate how it made the children feel. A glib human-interest story in *Appleton's Weekly* of 1871 inadvertently reveals how embarrassing it could be for a boy to wash in public. "At an unusually early hour one morning," begins the account, "I happened to discover where my newsboy, Billy by name, made his semiweekly toilet. It was at one of the park pumps. He had turned down his collar, and placed his hat within his reach on the top of the pipe, and was disporting himself like a grampus." The reporter joked that he could always tell the days of the week by the boy's complexion, for Monday and Thursday washdays left him streaked with grime rather than clean. Unwilling to respect the boy's privacy, the reporter saluted him: "He looked up dripping. . . . He felt criminal. He blushed scarlet. Had I caught him carrying the pump away, he could not have been more abashed."[33]

River bathing was a more discrete alternative when the weather was fine. Johnny Morrow noted that he and his friends regularly enjoyed summer dips in the East or Hudson rivers.[34] In 1876, however, authorities in New York banned river bathing, which prompted newsboys to appeal to the *New York Times* for help. "I always read the Times, because it gives me ideas and is never foolish in the expression of its views," wrote one boy on behalf of his coworkers. "I am a newsboy, and a poor boy, and I know just how acceptible [*sic*] a bath is in the heat of Summer. Can you not in some way use the influence of your paper so as to get us the privilege of making ourselves clean by bathing in the river? It would go far to make better citizens, at any rate more clean and healthy ones, of us, and we will not forget THE TIMES."[35] Newsboys clearly felt they had rights in the matter and were not averse to collectively demanding them.

Children who grabbed meals from vendors, bathed in public, and slept rough on the streets were not necessarily orphans, outcasts, or runaways. Many of them had homes, however humble or inhospitable. Poor families often lived in small tenement apartments overcrowded with relatives, lodgers, or work materials. Morrow's family of eight, for example, lived in a one-room apartment on Forty-fourth Street that measured thirty feet by twenty feet. The children slept five to a bed in one corner, while his parents and a newborn slept in another corner. A third was occupied by his father's carpentry bench, from which he produced stools that his children peddled on the street for twelve to fifteen cents apiece.[36] Under such cramped conditions boys who slept out on occasion were hardly missed, though their labor and earnings often were. Chief Matsell reported that in warm weather even sons of "respectable" parents absented themselves from their families for weeks, returning home only for clean clothes or meals. Morrow's description notwithstanding, parents who allowed their sons—but rarely their daughters—to fend for themselves were not necessarily guilty of neglect or abandonment, but were practicing a deliberate and effective method of childrearing that enabled boys to acquire the skills, self-assurance, and social network necessary to make a living in an urban economy that offered few opportunities.[37]

It was a rare boy who braved the streets alone in nineteenth-century America without friends or relatives. Street children fought, robbed, and abused each other. Sleeping rough could be dangerous. One boy showed up at the Newsboys' Lodging House in October 1855 with a broken nose and a woeful tale. "I slept in boxes about the Herald office, and some of the boys were bad to me," he said. "They knocked me about nights and laughed at me; said I was never a doin' nothing."[38] But street children also looked out for each other. When asked how he was able to survive on the streets of New York, a twelve-year-old who lived in a box on Twenty-second Street told Brace that "the boys fed him."[39] Children generally slept out in groups, which provided a measure of protection. They made their beds in an ingenious array of places—in old crates and hogsheads along the waterfront; under steps and bridges; on benches and barges; in wagons, market stalls, and the backs of saloons. Two newsboys, little warmed by the irony, slept one winter in a burned-out safe on Wall Street.[40]

Unsold papers were sometimes their only bedding. During his first night on the streets in the early 1870s, New York newsboy Tom Carroll observed attentively as a young colleague bedded down in a dark hallway off Frankfort Street. "The latecomer took a bundle of newspapers from under his arm and carefully proceeded to prepare his bed," recalled Carroll. "First, he spread a number of sheets on the floor; then built a pillow from the major part, and, at last, proceeded to cover himself with the remaining papers." When the boy invited Carroll to share the warmth of his makeshift bed, he was only too happy to comply.[41]

Such ingenuity was not uncommon. Tramps, newsboys, and the lower classes in general put newspapers to use in ingenious ways. They wore them under their clothes for warmth, stuffed them in their holey shoes, and folded them into hats. Poor and homeless children used newspapers to start their barrel fires, wipe their bottoms, and make the swords, kites, and balls that sufficed as toys. In debunking stories of richly dressed foundlings, Jacob Riis said, "They come in rags, a newspaper often their only wrap."[42] Newspapers were, in short, part of the material culture of working-class childhood, more ephemeral but no less historically significant than the cradles, blankets, and rocking horses cherished by upper-class families and now found in children's museums.

One of the most favored sleeping locations was over steam gratings, which newsboys called "iron bedsteads."[43] These provided snuggling warmth on raw nights, but could also inflict severe burns on exposed skin. The most convenient gratings were located above the giant steam presses of metropolitan dailies. In the summer of 1850 the *Tribune* noted that the police regularly scared up thirty or forty boys sleeping downtown along Nassau and Ann streets.[44] Brace said he frequently saw "ten or a dozen of them, piled together to keep one another warm, under the stairs of the printing-offices."[45] Few publishers felt such scenes reflected poorly on their enterprise. On the contrary, many thought they were doing a public service by providing work for the boys and a safe place to catch some winks. Besides, it was handy to have them nearby for early morning editions or the occasional "midnight extra," such as the one issued by the *Tribune* after passage of the Kansas-Nebraska Act in 1854.[46]

Criers and Casualties of War

The Civil War spurred the proliferation of tramps and newsboys. The war led to a boom in the number and circulation of newspapers in the North and an accompanying rise in the ranks of their vendors. According to a Detroit newspaper, newsboys became "a noticeable feature of the town" with the first battle of Bull Run in July 1861.[47] In New York newsboys totaled "many thousands," according to one journalist, and spanned "all the seven ages of man."[48] Widely perceived as war orphans, the boys received more public sympathy and charity than their predecessors. Newsboys did not just serve anxious civilians on the home front but also catered to news-starved soldiers in the field. The Union army provided a burgeoning market for newspapers, prompting hundreds of vendors of all ages to follow hometown brigades into the field of battle (fig. 8.2). Some boys and men

FIG. 8.2. Newspaperman, ca. 1860s. Library of Congress LC-B814-1378

worked independently, but others attached themselves to regiments and secured passes to ride free on railroads and steamers.

The ranks of newsboys continued to grow after the war, as did those of now homeless veterans. Like the "rufflers" in sixteenth-century England discussed by Woodbridge in chapter 2, men who served in the American Civil War also tramped in hopes of finding work, food, and the respect of a forgetful nation. Many historians attribute the postwar increase in vagrancy to the war itself. They point out that military service took young men away from their homes and gave them the camping and foraging skills necessary to survive on the road; it taught them to ride in or on top of boxcars and left some with psychic wounds that made readjustment to a settled civilian life difficult.[49] Yet the economic slumps that followed the war probably did more to create the multitude of roving ex-soldiers unwelcome in polite society.

One young veteran who met with shabby treatment upon his discharge from the army was eighteen-year-old Joseph Pulitzer. The tall, wraith-thin Hungarian had served honorably with the First New York Lincoln Cavalry, but in the fall of 1865 he was reduced to huddling around the potbellied stove in the lobby of French's Hotel on Park Row with other jobless veterans. When guests complained, the porter turned the men out. Pulitzer slunk off to St. Louis, where he survived scrubbing boats, repairing levees, and waiting tables. He eventually found work writing for a German-language newspaper and gained enough standing and capital to win election to the state legislature and buy a bankrupt newspaper at auction. He turned the *St. Louis Post-Dispatch* into a profitable defender of the poor and working classes. In 1883 he returned to New York to buy up the ailing *World* and seven years later erected the magnificent copper-domed Pulitzer Building where French's Hotel once stood.[50]

Pulitzer's triumph over poverty and vagrancy was clearly exceptional, but the newspaper industry proved a refuge for many veterans. In 1879, Massachusetts passed a law providing them with free peddlers' licenses, wounded or not.[51] Other states granted them preference in operating newsstands outside post offices and other public buildings. Likewise, trade unions and mutual-aid societies used news peddling as a kind of welfare provision for widows and orphans, helping them to buy papers or a stand.[52]

The postwar years also saw the passage of legislation detrimental to vagrants and vendors. Both northern and southern states passed a spate of vagrancy laws that made it a crime to beg and wander without "visible means of support."[53] Recently emancipated blacks were particularly vulnerable to these statutes. The founding of the New York Society for the Prevention of Cruelty to Children (SPCC) in 1874 further helped to define news peddling as a mendicant, or wandering, occupation. The society viewed the ragged children who peddled papers at night to be victims of neglect and acquired police powers to detain them. The Cruelty, as it was known, became a feared institution in working-class wards. News peddlers and their families resisted its interference but the SPCC flourished nonetheless. By decade's end it had offices in thirty-four cities in the United States and fifteen abroad.[54]

The licensing of newsboys also served to prevent homeless, drifting, and truant children from using the news trade as a front for beggary or a refuge from destitution. Boston had a licensing scheme in place as early as 1857, when Danny Sullivan passed through. It was probably overwhelmed during the wartime newspaper boom, but a new plan emerged in November 1867, when the city began issuing leather badges to newsboys and bootblacks for a $1.25 fee, refundable upon return of the badge. Boston required all recipients to attend school during some portion of the day and restricted the number of licenses to three hundred.[55] The Chicago Common Council passed a similar ordinance in January 1862 requiring newsboys to buy a license for fifty cents and display a "tasty" (tasteful) leather badge. It limited the number to a hundred.[56] Detroit tried to license its newsboys during the war but the effort failed. It finally instituted a badge system in 1877, partly as a response to the children's labor militancy. In July the newsboys struck the *Detroit Evening News* over its pricing policy, and their "generally unruly character" led to the passage of an ordinance in November requiring each newsboy to obtain a yearly license and badge for ten cents from the police sanitary commission. Months later an amendment stipulated that the badges were to be issued "only on satisfactory assurance of good conduct." Enforcement was minimal; twice a year police were ordered to send all boys who had no badges to the juvenile home to secure them. But within four years 4,200 boys had passed through the system.[57]

Newsboys were not the only itinerant workers in the industry; printers and reporters also found casual work on newspapers. The International Typographical Union issued traveling cards granting members work at union shops wherever they went. Thousands of journeymen took advantage of this benefit, and their numbers increased every year between 1857 and 1892.[58] Writing in 1878, detective Allan Pinkerton conjectured that "there is not a newspaper or job office in the world that has not its tramp-printer, and that does not count upon periodical visitation from that irrepressible individual."[59] He said the first thing a tramp does when he "strikes a town" is to "hunt up the printing offices and ask the foremen for work. Even if none is available, he can usually arrange to pass the night somewhere on the premises in return for setting a few thousand ems in the morning." Tramp printers would also "nick the office," begging spare change from fellow printers, most of whom would not begrudge a fellow tradesman a few coins.

Reporters, too, had a special affinity with the footloose. Before they began to professionalize in the 1890s, journalists were widely known as bohemians because of their kinship with gypsies and artists in lifestyle and temperament. In 1868, a San Francisco newspaper defined a bohemian as "a writer that wanders from one subject to another, a "*ménager* of trifles."[60] Journalists wandered literally as well, offering stories to a variety of papers as "free lances." In 1871 the *New York Sunday Mercury* "engaged over sixty men to report incidents of one Fourth of July," reported a trade journal, "and it is such occasions that give occupation to the 'bummers' of the press."[61]

Whatever their age or occupation, transients also shared common lodgings. "Young and old, the intelligent and the ignorant, the criminal and the newsboy, all are found in the 'ten-center,'" observed Josiah Flynt, which he ranked as the second-lowest type of lodging houses because they provided bunks, not just hammocks. Nevertheless, he said they were cesspools "into which are drained all sorts of vagabonds."[62] Newspapers, meanwhile, used them as sources of cheap labor. Low lodging houses were the first places circulation managers looked for help when extras were issued, strikes threatened, or circulation wars flared. In October 1883, for example, when adult news

FIG. 8.3. Grant E. Hamilton, "A Suggestion to J. G. B.—How to Utilize Tramps," *Judge* 4, no. 104 (1883): 16

vendors refused to sell the *New York Herald* for less than three cents a copy, the paper recruited a hundred hawkers from lodging houses, including the Newsboys' Lodging House, which provided half the required vendors.[63] The humor magazine *The Judge* mocked the practice in a cartoon showing a mob of flush-nosed, stubble-chinned tramps rushing from the *Herald* office crying their papers (fig. 8.3). The dilettantish publisher James Gordon Bennett Jr. peers imperturbably through an office window beside a sign reading: "Notice— Tramps Wanted—Orphans Wanted—Widows Wanted—Cripples Wanted—To Sell the Herald at 2 cts."[64]

Those unfortunates who could not afford the hospitality of ten-centers often found shelter in the offices or back alleys of newspapers. Little had changed in this regard since the 1840s and 1850s, although few journalists dared defend the practice anymore and Jacob Riis could now employ the latest photographic technology—*Blitzlichtpulver*, or flash powder—to document it. His 1889 photograph "Three A.M. in the *Sun* Office" shows four newsboys sleeping in a clump on the floor of the *New York Sun* while two workmen gaze drowsily through

FIG. 8.4. Jacob Riis, "Three A.M in the Sun Office," ca. 1889. New York Public Library

a cage at the photographer. He, not the newsboys, was the unusual sight (fig. 8.4).

Vagrant children and adults also frequented charity soup kitchens and one-cent coffee stands, which Riis and others felt contributed to their profligacy (fig. 8.5). "We have watched these coffee stands and inquired about them carefully, said Charles D. Kellogg, superintendent of New York's Charity Organization Society, in 1890, "and we are convinced that they are patronized principally by tramps, who thus find an added facility for living without labor, and by newsboys, who thus have more money to gamble by policy-making, and to attend the theaters."[65] Apparently the only thing more worrying than their shared poverty was their shared charity.

Just as individual street children appealed for alms, so too did the organizations that cared for them. The Children's Aid Society, for example, received about half its income from state and local government and half from private donors.[66] Soliciting support, or "going begging," as it was called, was a necessary part of its work. The CAS

FIG. 8.5. Victor Perard, "Coffee at One Cent." In Jacob Riis, *How the Other Half Lives: Studies among the Tenements of New York* (1889; repr. Boston: Bedford Books, 1996).

used the iconography of the Homeless Waif to great effect, printing thousands of handbills featuring a woodcut based on an Oscar Gustav Rejlander photograph on one side and an appeal for aid on the other (fig. 8.6). "It is a sad picture," observed the social affairs magazine *The Forum* in 1886. "The little waif sits on a stone step, with his head bent over and resting on his hands, stretched across bare knees, his flowing hair covering his face, and his tattered clothes and bare feet betokening utter wretchedness. Turning the leaf, we are informed that twenty dollars will enable the society to give the boy a home."[67]

Riding the Wanderlust Express

Nothing increased the number and mobility of tramps and newsboys in the postwar years more than expansion of railroads. New rail lines encouraged the formation of large distribution companies that

FIG. 8.6. Oscar Gustav Rejlander, "Homeless," 1863.
Albumen print 20.2 x 14.9
cm, George Eastman
House, Miller-Plummer
Fund, NEG: 34952
84:0081:0001

transported metropolitan newspapers far afield and gave the unemployed greater range in their search for work or recreation. Railway
newsstands popped up in stations all along these lines and one by
one fell under the control of conglomerates. Two distinct types of
newsboys emerged: neatly uniformed "news butchers," or "train
boys," who plied passengers with snacks, beverages, and reading material, and footloose "hobo newsies" who "beat" rides on freight or
passenger trains. One such boy, twelve-year-old John Mason, traveled
from his home in Beardstown, Illinois, to New York City in 1884. His
stated aim was not work but pleasure, "to see something of the
world." Riding mainly on freight cars, he made his way through
Cincinnati, Pittsburgh, and Philadelphia before arriving at his destination. We know his story because he came to the attention of the
New York Society for the Prevention of Cruelty to Children on his
second day in the city when he tussled with a local newsboy over a
dime. Each accused the other of trying to steal the money. A judge
dismissed the case but held Mason on charges of vagrancy, as preferred by the SPCC, and provided for the boy's return to Illinois.[68]

Another hobo newsie originally from New York told his story to a
Milwaukee reporter in 1883 and revealed much about the vagabond
lingo and lifestyle. The boy did not give his name and claimed to have

never known his age or his parents. He said he grew up in a place where he "used to get a licking most every day." It had been almost two years since he ran away and fell in with an older boy named Joe Grubbs, who let him ride with him to Milwaukee. "O, he's the boss chap he is. He can beat any of us selling papers or telling a whopper." They traveled by train without charge by the conductor. Once in Milwaukee they started selling papers. They usually earned a dollar or more a day, and avoided paying lodgings, entertainment, or travel. "Sleep anywhere I get a chance," he explained, "like some of the other fellers. Go into the depot and lie down on the bench and snooze till 'buttons' comes around and orders me out. I wait till he goes off and try it again. If he hangs around too long I skip off to a stable or a barn and keep myself warm that way. That's in winter, you know. In summer it don't make any difference where I sleep. I ain't particular, I ain't."

The boy explained that state fairs provided the main impetus to travel:

Summer's the times, when the fairs are going on. A fair's the place to make money. I'm honest, but some of the boys don't mind cheating. Some of 'em are regular gamblers, too. The show lasted two months and I scooped in dead oodles of swag. Oh, no, I didn't go there alone. There was a big crowd of us [Milwaukee boys], and a lot of Chicago roosters. . . . The way we do is to catch on to the trains on the back of the sleeper. Sometimes the porter is a bully sort of a chap and don't care, but most of 'em are mean. . . . when they make us git off we have to get in under the cars and catch on to the trucks. Risky kind of business, too. First time I tried it I got scared nearly to death. The train went so fast that I got dizzy seeing the ground fly away back so fast right under me, but I held on, bet your bottom dollar. . . . I am used to it now and kinder like it to see the rocks and the stones and the ties fly back like a streak 'o lightning and cross over a river and see the water a rushing one way and me a going another way. . . . One time there was forty of us kids under a train and the porter got on to it. Well you ought to have seen us get out in a jiffy. It looked like a lot of rats let loose out of a trap. The porter caught one of the bootblacks and made him black all the boots in the sleeper for nothing. Darn mean cuss, he was. He was on the same car when we went back, and we didn't ask any odds of him neither. We had cash then and we bought our tickets and rode down in the smoker. That was after the fair was over.[69]

Jack London also traveled with a gang during his first "push" east from Sacramento. There were a dozen in their party, plus about forty local boys who crowded on to the train and whooped it up with the sole purpose of sabotaging their friends' furtive departure, or at least making it more interesting. London used language similar to Poole in diagnosing himself; he said he became a tramp because of the "wander-lust in my blood that would not let me rest."[70] Yet he also took part in a mass push of historic proportions, which occurred for political not physiological reasons. During the depression of 1894 thousands of unemployed men and boys set out for Washington, D.C., to demand government jobs and relief. They were known as the Commonweal of Christ, or Coxey's Army, after Ohio quarry owner Jacob Coxey, who headed the movement. One contingent was led by printer Charles T. Kelley, a former newsboy who had survived the depression of 1877 living at the Newsboys' Home in Chicago. General Kelley, as he was called, organized six hundred protesters in San Francisco. Traveling on foot and by freight train, their numbers grew to two thousand, including London. Kelley's group got bogged down in Iowa and Coxey's Army as a whole failed to achieve its legislative goals but for a time gained supporters from all classes and regions.[71]

Traveling alone or in gangs, tramps usually preferred to earn a stake by begging, or "mooching," when they hit a town, but peddling papers was the next best thing in communities that did not tolerate begging. Men such as the one photographed selling the *Denver Republican* in the early 1900s could easily alter their status as vagrants by carrying a stack of newspapers (fig. 8.7). He appears to be the epitome of the "gentleman hobo" with his with his bowler hat, bow tie, and shabby clothes, yet his papers mark him as a legitimate merchant. Even if only a ruse, the papers did not preclude one from employing his best hard luck stories on passersby. So accustomed was

FIG. 8.7. Harry Mellon Rhoads, "Street Vendor from Denver Republican Newspaper," ca 1900–1910. Western History/ Genealogy Department, Denver Public Library

the public to patronizing homeless vendors that philanthropists in New York, St. Louis, Chicago, and Pittsburgh founded periodicals with the sole purpose of giving street people a legitimate way to earn money and raise consciousness about their plight.[72] These publications were forerunners of such contemporary homeless newspapers as the *Big Issue* in London, *StreetWise* in Chicago, and *Real Change* in Seattle.

While most tramp newsboys at the turn of the century rode the rails in search of work, adventure, and occasionally social justice, Jack Ross had a more personal mission: to find his parents. Ross traveled the country for twelve years, from 1898 to 1910, looking for the couple that had abandoned him in the care of an aunt when he was a child. "As soon as he was old enough," reported the *Rochester Herald*, "Ross took a bundle of newspapers and started to pay his own way. He drifted around the country, traveling on the bumpers of freight trains and the head ends of baggage trains. He became well known in many newspaper offices throughout the country where he found employment." Newspapermen ran stories about his Telemachus-like quest and eventually helped him locate his father, a fire captain in Elizabeth, New Jersey, and his mother and sister. A photograph of Ross circa 1910 shows a strapping, big-eared youth framed against the looming office buildings of downtown Rochester (fig. 8.8). The pin on his left lapel marks him as a bona fide vendor registered with the city.[73]

By this time scores of cities and about a dozen states required newsboys to obtain permits and wear official pins or badges. Most newspapers welcomed these regulations as a means of disciplining their hawkers and quieting reformers who sought a total ban on juvenile street trading. Adult vendors and their associations also supported licensing because it limited competition from children. Even some newsboy clubs backed the laws for the same reason. In 1924 the Newsboy Club of Springfield, Massachusetts, proposed to "run off" all boys selling without a license.[74] The likes of Danny Sullivan would no longer be welcomed there. While usually viewed as part of the Progressive effort to regulate child street labor, newsboy licensing schemes also worked to ward off transients and protect the property rights of newsstand operators and boys who "owned" routes and corners. In this sense, the licenses resemble the passes imposed by colonial authori-

FIG. 8.8. Albert R. Stone, "The Wandering Newsboy," ca. 1910 (portrait of Jack Ross). Albert R. Stone Negative Collection, Rochester Museum and Science Center, Rochester, NY

tion on villagers in Papua New Guinea in the 1920s. As Robert Gordon shows, the pass system was intended to stanch the flow of rural migrants into urban areas and eliminate illegal squatter settlements and other threats to private property.

Incredible as it might seem, some newsboys did not restrict themselves to domestic travel but went abroad, taking the working-class equivalent of the Grand Tour. Poole mentioned that the ill-fated Joe spent several months in Europe when he was fifteen. He also told of a sixteen-year-old newsboy named Mike who, after traveling across the United States, got the urge "to do Europe." Mike secured a position as a cabin boy with the American Steamship Company, and his first voyage took him to England, where he enjoyed three days ashore. From habit he stole a ride on the underside of a train from Southampton to London. He said the accommodations were "stingier" than those on American trains due to the narrower-gage tracks. Once in London, he and an English boy went partners on a lantern and earned money lighting people's way home through the legendary London fog. Then they saw the town in high style.

Perhaps the most well traveled newsboy at the turn of the century was Jimmie Sullivan, a.k.a. Jimmie the Globetrotter. A hawker of the *New York Morning Journal* since the age of five, Jimmie claimed to have made his first trip overseas as a six-year-old after his mother died and his father abandoned him. He told the *Journal* that he had crossed the Atlantic seventeen times in his fourteen years, mostly as a stowaway on ships plying British and French ports. One voyage, which began on a British troopship, took him to Australia and the Far East. He started out from Portsmouth, England, but was discovered and put off in Malta. There he boarded a man-o'-war, which took him to Alexandria, Egypt, where he was put off again. He then befriended an Englishwoman who passed him off as her son and thus passed through Chinese and East Indian waters. He earned his keep on board by blacking boots and eventually returned home to the Bowery to tell his story. It is possible that Jimmie was an inveterate liar as well as traveler, but if so he fooled the *Journal*. Exaggerated or not, his were the kind of "highly colored yarns" that Poole said helped beguile "the raw recruits of the newsboys."[75]

Newspapers contributed to this mythology in other ways as well. In 1901 three American and two French dailies sponsored a round-the-world race by newsboys as an elaborate stunt to boost circulation. The *New York Journal, Chicago American, San Francisco Examiner,* and *Le Journal* and *Le Matin* of Paris each dispatched a newsboy to girdle the globe. The winner was seventeen-year-old Charles Cecil Fitzmorris of Chicago, who completed the trip in sixty days, thirteen hours, twenty-nine minutes, and forty-two and four-fifths seconds.[76] While child labor reformers like Poole wrote volumes exposing the corrupting nature of street work, the three Hearst dailies capitalized on the romance and worldliness of their newsboys.

Prushuns and Jockers

The most effective way for reformers to overcome the public's apathy about the dangers of news peddling was to stress children's sexual vulnerability. This tactic worked successfully in the early 1900s to severely limit the rights of girls to sell papers on the street and to curb the freedoms of boys as well. Most investigators spoke euphemistically about the "moral dangers" of the street or the road. In his magazine journalism, for example, Josiah Flynt told of tramps who lured newsboys away from home with their "ghost stories" about life on the road (fig. 8.9). But in an essay written specially for Havelock Ellis's multivolume *Studies in the Psychology of Sex*, Flynt shed all Victorian reticence and described with clinical precision the

FIG. 8.9. M. Trautschold, "Telling 'Ghost Stories.'" In Josiah Flynt, "Tramping with Tramps," *Century Illustrated Magazine* 47, no. 1 (1893): 102

seduction ritual and sexual practices of adolescent and adult tramps, or "prushuns" and "jockers" in the hobo's vernacular.[77] "The tramps gain possession of these boys in various ways," he said. "A common method is to stop for awhile in some town, and gain acquaintance with the slum children. They tell these children all sort of stories about life 'on the road,' how they can ride on the railways for nothing, shoot Indians, and be 'perfeshunnels' (professionals), and they choose some boy who specially pleases them. By smiles and flattering caresses they let him know that the stories are meant for him alone, and before long, if the boy is a suitable subject, he smiles back just as slyly."

Flynt estimated that there were seven thousand boy tramps in the United States in 1899 and that about five hundred spent each winter in New York City. Their average age was fourteen, but some were as young as nine or as old as seventeen. They were distinguishable, he said, by their "shambling gait, rounded shoulders, harsh voices and exaggerated 'tough manner.'" Each was compelled by "hobo law" to beg for his jocker and gratify his sexual desires. Some did so under threat of punishment, he said, but most learned to enjoy this treatment. He said the usual method of intercourse was "'leg-work' (intercrural), but sometimes *immissio penis in anum*, the boy, in either case, lying on his stomach."[78]

Flynt went on to describe brutal gang rapes and tender partings between men and boy lovers. Yet he also acknowledged, along with many tramp memoirists, that most youths enjoyed platonic, even fatherly, relationships with older tramps. St. Louis newsboy Robert Saunders, who made three long rail trips in the early 1910s, claimed he learned valuable, even lifesaving lessons about hopping freight trains, begging for meals, and finding jobs from more experienced hoboes.[79] It's also worth noting that the abuse went both ways; some teenagers made a sport of preying on tramps. The autobiographical writings and oral histories of Chicago newsboys Nels Anderson, Philip Marcus, and Clifford Shaw are full of stories about how they "jackrolled" (beat and robbed) drunken hoboes and homosexual strollers in the city's "main stem," or transient district. "It was bloody work," said Shaw, "but necessity demanded it—we had to live."[80]

Tramp newsboys could be equally ruthless on behalf of the news-papers that hired them. Many of them were "toughs" in their late teens or twenties who could be called in to break strikes or win circulation wars. As outsiders, they paid no heed to turf rights and brazenly sought clashes with local boys. Tramp newsboys usually worked only long enough to earn a few dollars for food or to replenish their trav-eling stake. Publishers let them sleep on the premises or put them up in flophouses and paid them cash bonuses and sales commissions.[81] Shortly after it came under the control of William Randolph Hearst in 1900, for example, the *Chicago American* paid "sluggers" $3.50 a day plus $10 for every newsboy they beat up—$80 a day and $225 a head in today's money.[82]

A U.S. Children's Bureau report characterized tramp newsboys as the most corrupted and corrupting of all news peddlers. It said a bitter rivalry between evening newspapers resulted in an increase in their number in Atlanta and Omaha in 1926. Local newsboys and their parents said these men encouraged younger boys to steal by acting as fences for stolen goods, enticed them into their poker and dice games, cheated them, stole their money, knocked them around, introduced them to prostitutes, and used the "younger newsboys for immoral purposes."[83]

Newspaper executives generally had a higher opinion of hobo newsies. Sidney Long, who ran the *Wichita Eagle* and headed the In-ternational Circulation Managers Association, preferred to call them "professional hustlers" or "wandering newsboys." The country was "full of them," he recounted in a 1928 memoir. "Years ago they used to ride the freight trains and the bumpers on the passenger trains. Now they either ride on the cushions or they have their own little car or they start out and walk and catch rides wherever they can. Sometimes they go clear across the continent." Whenever one of these hustlers would show up in a new town, said Long, he would seek out the man in charge of street circulation and tell him about his experience, which was usually obvious the moment he opened his mouth. "His very language is his card," said Long. He noted that these young men were especially valuable in starting up a paper: "All you have to do is to send out a few wires to the street circulators within three or four hundred miles of your town and in these fellows will flock. When you are through with them, they are gone. You don't know from where they come and you don't know where they go but they put the deal over for you mighty good and pretty straight."[84]

Long's memoir and the Children's Bureau studies reveal two unexpected truths about tramp, or hobo, newsboys. First, they were not lone drifters who blew in and out of town like tumbleweeds, but members of a reliable labor force that could be mobilized quickly through established networks. Second, many felt little or no compunction about betraying their brothers-in-trade. Tramps in the 1870s and 1880s were often considered radical agitators who traveled from strike to strike in order to stir up trouble. Those who belonged to the anarcho-syndicalist Industrial Workers of the World in the early 1900s reinforced their reputation as rabble-rousers. As Frank Tobias Higbie has shown, many hobos were indeed class-conscious critics of industrial capitalism.[85] Yet the accounts of tramp newsies remind us that a certain number regularly sided with management over labor; these drifters may have flouted bourgeois customs of settled domesticity, but when bosses called they willingly did their bidding.

This was not just a northern phenomenon. A 1921 study of newsboys in Dallas, Texas, found that their ranks included a "more or less shiftless" class of newsboy who passed through the city on an irregular basis. They constituted a relatively unknowable minority, yet the Southern Methodist University sociologists who headed the study generalized that these casual newsboys were "recruited from the submerged migratory group—in and out of Dallas—here a week and gone; camping on the outskirts; children of junkers and horse-traders—from families that pick cotton in the summer and fall, drift to Dallas for three months in the winter and are in Arkansas, Oklahoma or South Texas in the spring."[86] For all its ambiguity, the study attests to the links between urban and rural youth labor markets and the fact that sometimes the same people were involved in the sowing and reaping of industrial as well as agricultural products.

In sum, vagrant men and boys used the news trade in a variety of ways. They peddled papers to earn a stake while on the road, to earn money when other work was not available, and as an alternative to work they found repugnant. Some gravitated to newspaper offices and alleys even if they were not interested in selling papers so they could find old friends or make new ones. Others sought shelter or a place to sleep in relative safety. Publishers varied in their willingness to accommodate these drifters, but their insatiable desire for vendors made newspapers more hospitable toward them than any other place in the city. Tramps were not necessarily bogeymen who lured innocent boys astray. Nor were newsboys impressionable victims of a dangerous trade, as Poole suggested. Rather, they found friendship and betrayal, protection and coercion, sex and violence in each other's company. Although newsboys symbolized enterprise and tramps laziness in American popular culture, they actually shared much in common. Both formed a wandering proletariat whose search for work and recreation took them far from home and family. In whatever city they found themselves, however, they could always count on the calculated kindness of the capitalist press.

Notes

1. Ernest Poole, "Newsboy Wanderers Are Tramps in the Making," *New York Evening Post*, January 26, 1903, repr. in *Charities* 10, no. 7 (February 14, 1903): 160–62.

2. Ernest Poole, *Child Labor—The Street* (New York: New York Child Labor Committee, 1903), 7–8. Poole reworked this material for several articles. In addition to those cited above, see Poole, "The Little Arabs of the Night," *Collier's Weekly* 30 (March 7, 1903): 11; "Waifs of the Street," *McClure's* 21 (May 1903): 40–48; "Dutch and the Skinner," *Everybody's Magazine* 10 (1904): 223–29. These pieces culminated in his novel *The Voice of the Street* (New York: A.S. Barnes, 1906).

3. Ernest Poole, *The Bridge: My Own Story* (New York: Macmillan, 1940), 68. Poole matriculated at Princeton during the years Walter A. Wyckoff, the university's first sociology professor, taught there. Nicknamed Weary Willie the tramp by his students, Wyckoff based his first book, *The Workers: An Experiment in Reality, the East* (New York: Scribner's, 1897), on an eighteen-month tramp he had taken across America in 1891 and 1892 to learn firsthand about labor, poverty, and vagrancy. There is no record of Poole's having taken a class with Wyckoff. Thanks to Kristen

Turner, archivist at the Seeley G. Mudd Manuscript Library, Princeton University. On Wyckoff, see Daniel Rodgers, "The Tramp and the Policy Doctor: The Social Sciences at Princeton," *Princeton University Library Chronicles* 58, no. 1 (1996): 57–90.

4. Raymond Williams, "The Growth of the Popular Press," in *The Long Revolution* (New York: Columbia University Press, 1961), 173.

5. See Ava Baron, "An 'Other' Side of Gender Antagonism at Work: Men, Boys, and the Remasculinization of Printers' Work, 1830—1920," in *Work Engendered: Toward a New History of American Labor*, ed. Ava Baron (Ithaca, NY: Cornell University Press, 1991), 47–69; Hanno Hardt and Bonnie Brennen, eds., *Newsworkers: Toward a History of the Rank and File* (Minneapolis: University of Minnesota Press, 1995); Joshua Brown, *Beyond the Lines: Pictorial Reporting, Everyday Life, and the Crisis of Gilded Age America* (Berkeley: University of California Press, 2002); April F. Masten, *Laborers in the Field of the Beautiful: Women, Art, and Democracy in Mid-Nineteenth-Century New York* (Philadelphia: University of Pennsylvania Press, 2007).

6. John Nerone, "Journalism," in *Encyclopedia of American Cultural and Intellectual History*, ed. Mary Kupiec Cayton and Peter W. Williams, 3 vols. (New York: Scribner's, 2001), 3:417. See also Kevin G. Barnhurst and John Nerone, *The Form of News: A History* (New York: Guilford, 2001).

7. C. J. Ribton-Turner, *A History of Vagrants and Vagrancy and Beggars and Begging* (1887; Montclair, NJ: Patterson Smith, 1972), 95. Selected for their buxomness as well as their lungpower, "mercurie girls" were grown women who hawked seditious news pamphlets in London in the 1630s. See Leslie Shepard, *The History of Street Literature* (Newton Abbott, Devon: David and Charles (Holdings) Ltd., 1973), 84; and Anthony Smith, *The Newspaper: An International History* (London: Thames and Hudson, 1979), 36, 56–58. On the literary and pictorial representation of early street criers, see Karen F. Beall, *Kaufrufe und Strassenhändler: Eine Bibliographie* (Cries and itinerant trades: A bibliography), trans. into German by Sabine Solf (Hamburg: Dr. Ernst Hauswedell, 1975).

8. Linda Woodbridge, "The Peddler and the Pawn: Why Did Tudor England Consider Peddlers to Be Rogues?" in *Rogues and Early Modern English Culture*, ed. Craig Dionne and Steve Mentz (Ann Arbor: University of Michigan Press, 2004), 150–51.

9. Paul Starr, *The Creation of the Media: Political Origins of Modern Communications* (New York: Basic Books, 2004), 48.

10. On the informal economy, see Ivan Illich, *Gender* (New York: Pantheon, 1982), 45–66; Louis A. Ferman, Stuart Henry, and Michele Hoyman,

eds., *The Informal Economy,* special issue of *The Annals of the American Academy of Political and Social Science* 493 (September 1987) (Beverly Hills: Sage Publications, 1987); Gracia Clark, ed., *Traders versus the State: Anthropological Approaches to Unofficial Economies* (Boulder, CO: Westview, 1988); Cyril Robinson, "Introduction: Exploring the Informal Economy," *Crime and Social Justice* 15, nos. 3–4 (1988): 3–16; Alejandro Portes, Manuel Castells, and Lauren A. Benton, eds., *The Informal Economy: Studies in Advanced and Less Developed Countries* (Baltimore, MD: Johns Hopkins University Press, 1989); David Dewar and Vanessa Watson, *Urban Markets: Developing Informal Retailing* (London: Routledge, 1990); Jane L. Collins and Martha Gimenez, eds., *Work without Wages: Comparative Studies of Domestic Labor and Self-Employment* (Albany: SUNY Press, 1990); M. Estellie Smith, ed., *Perspectives on the Informal Economy* (Latham, MD: University Press of America, 1990); J. J. Thomas, *Informal Economic Activity* (New York: Harvester Wheatsheaf, 1992). For a critique of the concept see Philip Harding and Richard Jenkins, *The Myth of the Hidden Economy* (Milton Keynes, UK: Open University Press, 1989).

11. *New York Sun,* September 4, 1833, 1.

12. N. P. Willis, "The Four Rivers," *New-Yorker* 3, no. 25 (September 9, 1837): 389.

13. "The News Boys," *Flash* 1, no. 9 (August 14, 1842): 2.

14. Philip Hone, *The Diary of Philip Hone, 1828–1851,* ed. Allan Nevins (New York: Dodd, Mead, 1927), 195.

15. Gerald T. McDonald, Stuart C. Sherman, and Mary T. Russo, comps., *A Checklist of American Newspaper Carriers' Addresses, 1720–1820* (Worcester, MA: American Antiquarian Society, 2000), vii; *Chicago Magazine The West as It Is* 1, no. 2 (April 15, 1857), 101; "Journalism in New York," *Chicago Tribune,* August 30, 1867, 2.

16. George Matsell, "Semi-annual Report of the Police Department, May–October 1849," in *Juvenile Depravity and Crime in Our City: A Sermon,* ed. Thomas L. Harris (New York: Charles B. Norton, 1850), 14; New York Children's Aid Society, *Second Annual Report* (New York: The Society, 1855), 3, 11.

17. *Oxford English Dictionary.* Americans who picked up the phrase included Charles Dawson Shanly in "The Small Arabs of New York," *Atlantic Monthly* 23 (March 1869): 279–86; George C. Needham, *Street Arabs and Gutter Snipes: The Pathetic and Humorous Side of Young Vagabond Life in the Great Cities, with Records of Work for Their Reclamation* (Boston: D. L. Guernsey, 1884). According to Needham, the term *street*

Arab was used to designate the young nomads of the streets, while *gut-tersnipe* was employed for a class of children "too utterly weak, both mentally and physically, to cope with the more sturdy Arab," while *waif* was a generic term "embracing many grades of young unfortunates."

18. See, for example, Mary Mapes Dodge, "The Artist and the Newsboy," *New York Independent,* November 19, 1863.

19. Johnny Morrow, *A Voice from the Newsboys* (New York: A. S. Barnes and Burr, 1860), 127; emphasis in original.

20. *Newsboy* 14, no. 10 (May 1976); Myron E. Adams, "Children in American Street Trades," *Annals of the American Academy of Political and Social Science* 25 (May 1905): 37–38.

21. "The Boot-Black's Story," *Saturday Evening Post* 55, no. 22 (December 25, 1875), 5; Mary Wager-Fisher, "The Philadelphia Newsboys; and Their Annual Fourth of July Dinner," *Wide Awake* 11, no. 1 (July 1880): 16–23. Reprinted in *Newsboy* 14, no. 1 (August 1975): 18. Some newsboys carried these names their whole lives, including my father and his five brothers. They peddled papers and shined shoes in Somerville, Massachusetts, before migrating to Monterey, California, in the early1930s, and were still known around town as "Boston" sixty years later, long after they had lost their accents and gone into other lines of work.

22. Edward W. Townsend, "A Street Waif's Luck," *Harper's Young People,* January 1, 1895, 162; "Danny Cahill, Newsboy," *Harper's Young People,* March 19, 1895, 345.

23. W. A. Rogers, "The Penny Restaurant," *Harper's Weekly,* December 8, 1877, 967–68.

24. Morrow, *Voice,* 43, 129, 131.

25. "The 'Professor's' Account of His Travels" (September 11, 1855), in Children's Aid Society, *Third Annual Report* (New York: M. B. Wynkoop, 1856), 42.

26. "Visit from the 'Newsboy Professor,' Returned from Boston," in *Sketches and Incidents in the Office of the Children's Aid Society, by W. C. D.* [W. Colopy Desmond], *Part the First* (December 2, 1857) (New York: Children's Aid Society, 1857), 130.

27. *New York Herald,* October 25, 1844, 2; "Little Broken Nose" (October 1, 1855), in Children's Aid Society, *Third Annual Report,* 43.

28. James L. Ford, *Forty-Odd Years in the Literary Shop* (New York: Dutton, 1921), 210–11.

29. J. B. Graham, *Handset Reminiscences: Recollections of an Old-Time Printer and Journalist* (Salt Lake City: Century Printing, 1915), 112; "Brevities," *Hartford Daily Courant,* July 1, 1868, 2.

30. Paul Frenzeny, "Street Arabs Taking a Foot-Bath," *Harper's Weekly*, August 3, 1872, 606.

31. Joseph Becker, "New York City—Opening of the Free Public Baths: Street Arabs Taking an Early Morning Plunge," *Frank Leslie's Illustrated Newspaper* 56, no. 1447 (June 16, 1883).

32. Carl Schoettler, "Abe Sherman, 'Oldest Newsboy,' Dead at 89," *Baltimore Evening Sun*, April 16, 1987, repr. in *Best Newspaper Writing, 1988*, ed. Don Fry (St. Petersburg, FL: Poynter Institute for Media Studies, 1988), 171. See also Marilyn Thornton Williams, *Washing "The Great Unwashed": Public Baths in Urban America, 1840–1920* (Columbus: Ohio State University Press, 1991).

33. "People in the Parks," *Appleton's Journal* 6, no. 123 (August 5, 1871): 155.

34. Morrow, *Voice*, 49.

35. "River Bathing," *New York Times*, July 2, 1876, 5.

36. Morrow, *Voice*, 38–40.

37. For an interesting contemporary application of this theory of child rearing, see Lewis Aptekar, "Family Structure in Columbia: Its Impact on Understanding Street Children," *Journal of Ethnic Studies* 17, no. 1 (1989): 104.

38. Children's Aid Society, *Third Annual Report*, 43.

39. Charles Loring Brace, *The Dangerous Classes of New York and Twenty Years' Work among Them* (New York: Wynkoop and Hallenbeck, 1872), 228.

40. Ibid., 100.

41. Carroll grew up and transformed himself into a successful writer. See Owen Kildare, *My Mamie Rose: The Story of My Regeneration* (New York: Baker and Taylor, 1903), 47–48.

42. Jacob Riis, *How the Other Half Lives: Studies among the Tenements of New York* (1889; Boston: Bedford Books, 1996), 182. On the material culture of middle-class children in America, see Karin Calvert, *Children in the House: The Material Culture of Early Childhood, 1600–1900* (Boston: Northeastern University Press, 1994).

43. Oliver Dyer, "The *New York Sun*—Its Rise, Progress, Character, and Condition," *American Agriculturalist*, December 1869, 463–67, Eckel Collection.

44. Christine Stansell, *City of Women: Sex and Class in New York, 1789–1860* (Urbana: University of Illinois Press, 1986), 206; *New York Tribune*, June 3, 1850.

45. Brace, *Dangerous Classes*, 100.

46. "The News Boys' Lodging-House," *New York Dispatch*, May 28, 1854, repr. in Brace, *Sermons for Newsboys* (New York: Scribners, 1866), 224.

47. "Then and Now, Newspaper Distributing in Detroit in the '50s," *Friend Palmer Scrapbook* 13 (May 26, 1896): 70, Detroit Public Library; Silas Farmer, *The History of Detroit and Michigan* (Detroit: S. Farmer, 1889), 693, Eckel Collection.

48. "The New York Newsboys," *Leisure Hours*, November 1, 1869, 717, Eckel Collection; Helen Campbell, *Darkness and Daylight: Lights and Shadows of New York Life* (Hartford, CT: A. D. Worthington, 1892), 112.

49. See Tim Cresswell, *The Tramp in America* (London: Reaktion Books, 2001), 34–35; Kenneth L. Kusmer, *Down and Out, On the Road: The Homeless in American History* (New York: Oxford University Press, 2002), 35–37.

50. Sam B. Armstrong, *The Story of the* St. Louis Post-Dispatch, 7th ed. (St. Louis: Pulitzer Publishing, 1962), 4.

51. Massachusetts Society for the Prevention of Cruelty to Children, *Amended Manual of Laws of Massachusetts Concerning Children* (Boston: Massachusetts Society for the Prevention of Cruelty to Children, 1890), 123–24.

52. The news trade functioned similarly in England, where one "gentleman's son" recalled in 1877 that after the death of his father his old friends "got me papers to sell, and others sent sister some music-scholars; and that's how we live." See "Only a Newsboy," *Newsvendor*, no. 155 (April 11, 1877): 5; John Benson, *The Penny Capitalists: A Study of Nineteenth-Century Working-Class Entrepreneurs* (Dublin: Gill and Macmillan, 1983), 101.

53. Amy Dru Stanley, "Beggars Can't Be Choosers: Compulsion and Contract in Postbellum America," in *Labor Law in America: Historical and Critical Essays*, ed. Christopher L. Tomlins and Andrew J. King (Baltimore, MD: Johns Hopkins University Press, 1992), 128–59.

54. Linda Gordon, *Heroes of Their Own Lives: The Politics and History of Family Violence* (Harmondsworth, UK: Penguin, 1988), 27.

55. "Boot Blacks and Newsboys," *Boston Daily Evening Traveler*, March 5, 1868, 2.

56. "Licensed News Boys," *Chicago Tribune*, January 29, 1862, 4; "Licensing Newsboys," *Chicago Tribune*, January 31, 1862, 4; "Newsboys' Licenses," *Chicago Tribune*, February 10, 1862, 4; "The Newsboys," *Chicago Tribune*, September 26, 1864, 4.

57. "A Newsboys' Riot," *Detroit Evening News*, July 21, 1877, 4; Farmer, *History of Detroit*, 693. According to an 1883 city guide, there were nearly

twelve hundred street trading children in Detroit that year, one hundred of whom were bootblacks and the rest newsboys. They ranged in age from ten to fifteen, the average being twelve. See Thomas S. Sprague, *Sprague's Visitors Guide and Dictionary of Detroit and Vicinity* (Detroit: the author, 1883), 48. The Detroit ordinance, long in disuse, was repealed during the Great Depression. *Detroit News,* May 17, 1935.

58. Jules Tygicl, "Tramping Artisans: Carpenters in Industrial America, 1880–90," in *Walking to Work: Tramps in America, 1790–1935,* ed. Eric H. Monkkonen (Lincoln: University of Nebraska Press, 1984), 92. See also Paul Fischer, "A Forgotten Gentry of the Fourth Estate," *Journalism Quarterly,* Spring 1965, 169.

59. Allan Pinkerton, *Strikers, Communists, Tramps and Detectives* (1878; New York: Arno Press, 1969), 52.

60. "Characters about Town: The 'Bohemian,'" *San Francisco Golden City,* January 26, 1868, cited in Gunther Barth, *City People: The Rise of Modern City Culture in Nineteenth-Century America* (New York: Oxford University Press, 1980), 67.

61. "New York Reporter," *American Newspaper Reporter and Advertisers Gazette,* March 20, 1871, 217.

62. Josiah Flynt, "The City Tramp," *Century Illustrated Magazine* 47, no. 5 (March 1894): 710.

63. "What the Newsdealers Are Doing," *New York Tribune,* October 2, 1883, 5.

64. Grant E. Hamilton, "A Suggestion to J. G. B.—How to Utilize Tramps," *Judge* 4, no. 104 (October 20, 1883): 16. Publishers have had few qualms about using the homeless as a source of cheap labor. Indeed, as recently as the vendors' strike in 1990, the *New York Daily News* solicited hundreds of homeless people from shelters across New York City. At one point, trucks simply dropped off bundles of freshly printed papers outside the shelters. See James Barron, "Daily News Uses Homeless to Sell Paper," *New York Times,* November 10, 1990, B1, 27.

65. Charles D. Kellogg, "Blundering Charity," *Independent,* December 11, 1890, 2.

66. Michael B. Katz, *In the Shadow of the Poorhouse: A Social History of Welfare in America* (New York: Basic Books, 1986), 107.

67. "The Homeless Waif," n.d., Eckel Collection, box 9b; David Dudley Field, "The Child and the State," *Forum* 1 (April, 1886): 8. The Shaftesbury Society in England also adopted Rejlander's photograph for its publicity campaigns. See Stephanie Spencer, "O. G. Rejlander's Photographs of Street Urchins," *Oxford Art Journal* 7, no. 2 (1884): 23–24.

68. New York Society for the Prevention of Cruelty to Children, *Tenth Annual Report for 1884* (New York: The Society, 1885, 54.

69. *Milwaukee Journal,* 1883.

70. Jack London, *The Road* (New York: Macmillan, 1907), 152.

71. Henry Vincent, *The Story of the Commonweal* (Chicago: W. B. Conkey, 1894; New York: Arno Press, 1969), 125–62; London, *Road,* 57, 175–95. See also Carlos Schwantes, *Coxey's Army: An American Odyssey* (Lincoln: University of Nebraska Press, 1986); Kusmer, *Down and Out,* 58, 181; Nell Irvin Painter, *Standing at Armageddon: The United States, 1877–1919* (New York: Norton, 1987), 117–21.

72. "'The Newsboys' Magazine,'" *New York Tribune,* March 3, 1903, 6; "The 'Newsboys' Magazine,'" *Book and News-Dealer* 14, no. 161 (April 1903): 41. "Mr. Roosevelt Displeased with 'Newsboys' Magazine' Methods," *New York Tribune,* January 11, 1905, 2.

73. *Rochester Herald,* May 15, 1910, n.p.

74. "Study of Newsboys in Springfield, Mass.," *Monthly Labor Review,* January 1924, 97–98.

75. "'Jimmie the Devil'—A Persistent Globe Trotter Visits the Journal Office," *New York Journal* (n.d.), Heig Scrapbook, Eckel Collection, repr. in *Newsboy* 19, no. 3 (October 1980): 10; Poole, "Waifs of the Street," 42.

76. "A Newspaper Race," *Newspaper Owner and Modern Printer,* September 11, 1901, 14. Fitzmorris beat the previous record holders: journalists George Francis Train, who accomplished the feat in sixty-seven days in 1890, and Nellie Bly, who did it in seventy-two days in 1889, and of course the fictional Phileas Fogg, who took eighty days in Jules Verne's 1872 novel. Train's trek was sponsored by the *Tacoma Ledger* and Bly's by the *New York World.* See Robert F. Karolevitz, *Newspapering in the Old West: A Pictorial History of Journalism and Printing on the Frontier* (New York: Bonanza Books, 1965), 160. Three New York reporters repeated the stunt in 1936, when J. R. Ekins of the *World-Telegram* won with a time of eighteen and a half days. See Edwin Emery, *The Press and America: An Interpretive History of the Mass Media,* 3rd ed. (Englewood Cliffs, NJ: Prentice Hall, 1972), 320.

77. The etymology of *prushun* is uncertain. Some speculate it is a corruption of the words *impressionable* or *protégé,* yet it may well owe its origin to the famed horsemen of the Franco-Prussian War of 1870–71, an ironic reference since boy tramps were usually ridden by their jockers. Tramp memoirist John Lewis Everson (1875–1945) believes *prushun* is a variant of the ambiguous terms *prunse, prunsing,* and *prunchon.* See Everson, *The Autobiography of a Tramp* (n.p.: W. L. Everson, 1992), ch. 14.

78. Intercrural sex is sometimes known as the Princeton First Year. Josiah Flynt, "Homosexuality among Tramps," in Havelock Ellis, *Studies in the Psychology of Sex*, vol. 2, *Sexual Inversion* (Philadelphia: F. A. Davis, 1915), app. A.

79. Frank Tobias Higbie, *Indispensable Outcasts: Hobo Workers and Community in the American Midwest, 1880–1930* (Urbana: University of Illinois Press, 2003), 181–82; Robert S. Saunders, "A Montage of the River," (c.1966), 60; and "The Road," 7–8, 71–72. Robert S. Saunders Papers, Western Historical Manuscripts Collection, University of Missouri–St. Louis. Thanks to Kristine Stilwell.

80. Nels Anderson, "The Mission Mill," *American Mercury* 8 (August 1926): 489–91; Anderson, *The Hobo: The Sociology of a Homeless Man* (Chicago: University of Chicago Press, 1923); Anderson, *The American Hobo: An Autobiography* (Leiden, Netherlands: E. J. Brill, 1975); Philip Marcus, "Newsboys. When papers was a penny apiece . . ." WPA L.C. Project Writers' Unit, Chicago, May 18, 1939, xii. Library of Congress; Clifford R. Shaw, *The Jack-Roller: A Delinquent Boy's Own Story* (1930; Chicago: University of Chicago Press, 1994), esp. ch. 7.

81. U.S. Department of Labor, Children's Bureau, *Children Engaged in Newspaper and Magazine Selling and Delivering*, Pub. 227 (Washington, DC: Government Printing Office, 1935), 50–51.

82. "An Academy of Crime," *Los Angeles Times*, May 28, 1905, VI 10.

83. U.S. Department of Labor, Children's Bureau, Nettie P. McGill, *Children in Street Work*, Pub. 183 (Washington, DC: Government Printing Office, 1928), 18, 75, 177–80.

84. Sidney D. Long, *The Cry of the News Boy* (Kansas City, MO: Burton, 1928), 46–47, Eckel Collection.

85. In addition to the essay in this volume, see Higbie, *Indispensable Outcasts*.

86. Civic Federation of Dallas, "The Newsboys of Dallas," Dallas, May 1921, 4.

9

Between Romance and Degradation

Navigating the Meanings of Vagrancy
in North America, 1870-1940

Frank Tobias Higbie

WHEN AMERICAN REFORMERS "discovered" unemployment and vagrancy during the 1870s, they launched a debate about work and poverty that remained vigorous for decades and in some ways still resonates in contemporary politics. Who were these people without jobs who wandered from town to town, begging for meals and straining the meager social services of local communities? Were they honest workers cast into poverty by forces outside their control, or had their own character flaws, addictions, and manias driven them from the company of ordinary workers? Was tramping, like the frontier, a safety valve for overburdened urban labor markets, or was it a degrading perversion of normal life?[1]

Consider the life histories of two "vagrants" with very different outcomes. Anton Johannsen was born in Germany in the 1870s and as a child moved with his family to Clinton, Iowa. He began working at age twelve, and at eighteen he left town in order to avoid his father's wrath after he was fired from his job for loafing. Over several years in the late 1880s to early 1890s, he gained a wealth of experience and work skills as a hobo, one of the millions of men who traveled by freight train in search of seasonal work in construction and extractive industries. Claiming the qualifications of a skilled carpenter he took jobs only to be fired in a few days when the foreman discovered his incompetence. Little by little, he learned the craft and the work culture. He also began to think critically about American social and economic conditions thanks to the socialist tramps he met on the road. Like other transients he worked, he begged for food and handouts, he went hungry, and he spent time in jail. But eventually he returned home, married, and later moved to Chicago, where he became a leader of the anarchist community and the labor movement. His life story became the subject of a famous Progressive Era "human document," Hutchins Hapgood's *The Spirit of Labor* (1907). Johannsen considered his experiences as a vagrant a valuable education in economics, politics, and psychology that helped him with his career.[2]

A second laborer, Earl Coole never made it that far, and what we know of his life comes from a coroner's inquest. In the summer of 1915 the seventeen-year-old was working for a farmer near Aberdeen, South Dakota. As the harvest finished, he drew his pay and headed into town for a little excitement. As he walked along the tracks he met two harvest hands that had worked their way up from Arkansas. These two were packing a bottle of bootleg liquor, and they sold some to Coole, who promptly slugged back a few shots. His fast friends left him there by the tracks, staggering and holding his head in his hands. An hour later Coole lay unconscious on the tracks as a freight train came around the bend and, despite the engineer's slamming on the brakes, crushed his young body.

Both Anton Johanssen and Earl Coole would have been called vagrants, and both were part of a much larger phenomenon I term the hobo migration. Between 1865 and the 1930s millions of laborers participated in this migration, cycling between seasonal work in agriculture, railroad construction, logging, and mining. Known variously has hoboes, tramps, and migrant workers, they were mainly young men, equally from urban and rural homes, and racially and ethnically similar to the working-class and rural populations around them. In the springtime, they hired out on railroad building and maintenance crews, living in remote areas along the railway lines, often in converted rail cars. In late summer they found work in the Great Plains wheat harvest, joining poor farmers, unemployed urban workers, and the occasional student in a labor market that by 1920 was drawing as many as one hundred thousand workers each summer. As the harvest ended, some workers flowed into the northern timber industry. Others wintered in transient districts of large cities, picking up odd jobs or living off their accumulated earnings; or they returned to family farms and working-class homes.

The divergent fates of Johannsen and Coole highlight the difficulty of encompassing and defining "vagrancy." Some vagrants settled into relatively normal lives. Like Johannsen, more than a few prominent men recounted their tramping experiences in memoirs and interviews: writers Carl Sandburg and Jack Conroy, historian Philip Taft, and radical leaders like William Z. Foster and Ralph Chaplin, among others.[3] Others were literally torn apart by the experience, their names and life histories lost to us, or filed with coroners' inquests. For at least one historian, the difference was clear: the smart ones got out, the others succumbed.[4] But this is too easy. Historians usually encounter tramps through the words and statistics of others: police, sociologists, employers, and journalists. Compared to the millions who spent some time on the road, we have very few memoirs and interviews that offer the voice of those who survived. Most disappeared after their brief interaction with the historical record, and we are hard pressed to say with any certainty what happened to them.

Like the people of other times and places explored in this volume, North American hoboes are a geographically and temporally specific manifestation of the discourses and experiences linked to vagrancy. As a mass social phenomenon that lasted more than fifty years, the hobo migration is a particularly useful point of reference for understanding the meanings of vagrancy. It created a powerful set of discourses that would influence sociological understandings of migration, poverty, and masculinity for years after the migration had faded. These sociological discourses in turn had their impact on how historians have defined and described the experience of vagrancy and of the working-class and immigrant communities from which many so-called vagrants emerged and returned to. It is in this context that vagrancy is most clearly part of regional migration patterns that were in turn linked to national and transnational flows of people, commodities, and ideas.

Vagrancy Discourse and Hobo Historiography

As the other essays in this volume make clear, ideas about vagrancy and experience of vagrancy did not always fit together neatly. Pioneered by the English, talk of vagrancy has always been a discourse of social control that criminalizes certain populations in order to facilitate selective punishment. Vagrants are those who are liable to be arrested for vagrancy. In some cases, as in postrevolutionary China, they are a relatively well defined group—beggars. In other cases, like colonial Kenya, vagrancy came to define entire working-class populations. In many cases, talk of vagrancy is aimed at young working people, and especially those young working people who embody their society's shift from agricultural to industrial production. For better or for worse, vagrants symbolize a very modern set of potentialities: freedom from social norms, and the danger of people set free.

In nineteenth-century North America those who wrote harshly about tramps had, paradoxically, often looked to the experience of tramping for their personal liberation from the hassles of materialism and the moral expectations of their middle-class communities. The most famous of these writers were men who had gone "undercover" to investigate the tramps. Commenting on his undercover work during the 1877 railway strike, the detective Allan Pinkerton quipped, "No person can ever get a taste of the genuine pleasure of the road and not feel in some reckless way . . . that he would like to become some sort of a tramp." Others went beyond dabbling in trampdom, embracing the underworld so completely that they lost their own identity. Born into a prominent midwestern family, Josiah Willard ran away from home as a teenager and lived for years as a tramp, taking on the road name Cigarette. When he returned to middle-class life in the 1890s he made a name for himself with a series of popular articles on tramps under the pen name Josiah Flynt, and even took a job advising railroad managers how to keep tramps off their trains. When he died young—probably from alcoholism—his friends eulogized him as a man who longed to escape himself: give him "the disguise of a vagabond, or whisky with which to fortify himself, and the man's spirit sprang out of its prison of flesh, like an uncaged bird."[5]

Sociologists of the early twentieth century would aim for a more objective relationship with their research, but they too relied heavily on participant observation to validate the information they received from working-class informants. Because sociology was only then emerging as a separate discipline, some early-twentieth-century studies looked a lot like their predecessors. Reflecting the drive for social reform and economic rationalization, freelancers like the Protestant minister Edwin Brown and the personnel executive Whiting Williams went undercover and wrote popular studies that suggested reforms and programs that they believed would lessen or eliminate tramping. Others went undercover as part of more systematic studies. As graduate students, the social scientists Frederick Mills and Peter Speek shipped out with hoboes, lumberjacks, and railroad workers as part of the massive U.S. Commission on Industrial Relations research project between 1912 and 1914.[6] Similar studies were underway in Canada, most prominently by Edwin Bradwin, an adult educator working in the railroad, timber, and mining camps of the Canadian north in the years before World War I. Interest in vagrancy continued after World War I with two major U.S. studies. One by economist Don Lescohier focused on the Great Plains wheat harvest and its workers. The other, Nels Anderson's *The Hobo: The Sociology of the Homeless Man* (1923), drew on the author's own experience as a transient worker and on his participant-observation in Chicago's migrant districts.[7]

By 1930 the hobo migration in the North American West was in deep decline because of mechanization in harvesting, mining, and timber. In the context of the Great Depression, vagrancy took on a different, or at least more complex look. The image of Dorothea Lange's Migrant Mother now competed with that of unattached male workers.[8] During the 1950s and 1960s, studies of vagrancy per se turned increasingly to the down-and-out in the declining urban skid rows.[9] The emergence of the New Social History brought a number of studies of nineteenth-century vagrancy as historians began to mine quantitative data and other artifacts of earlier sociological investigations. Historians of crime and policing like Eric Monkkonen, scholars of unemployment like Paul Ringenbach and Alexander Keyssar, and several unpublished dissertations tried to recover the experience of tramping, while Amy Dru Stanley connected the discourse of tramping to broader postemancipation debates on free labor and women's citizenship and economic rights.[10]

Since 2001 at least three monographs have dissected vagrancy, broadly defined. Tim Creswell's *The Tramp in America*, takes the perspective of critical geography to assess the ways in which tramps' mobility undermined efforts to stabilize capitalist society, and the various cultural projects to define the tramp in a way that would work with capitalism. Covering the tramp through the lens of homelessness are Kenneth Kusmer's *Down and Out, on the Road: The Homeless in American History* and Todd DePastino's *Citizen Hobo: How a Century of Homelessness Shaped America.* Both books connect vagrancy to issues of urbanization, housing, and welfare policy. DePastino's book also discusses the differential valuing of geographic and seasonal mobility for the rich and poor in America— the rich, after all, were also very mobile—and so places the ideology of home and homelessness at the center of twentieth-century American history.[11]

My own approach to vagrancy has drawn more from the social history of working-class and immigrant communities than from the historiography of the welfare state. I consciously avoided the lenses of vagrancy and homelessness in writing my book *Indispensable Outcasts,* preferring to situate my analysis in the context of labor markets and communities. This approach echoes other histories of internal migration, especially Gunther Peck's *Reinventing Free Labor* and Cindy Hahamovitch's *Fruits of Their Labor.*[12] Peck's study looks at "floating labor" in three different sites across North America, drawing on sources in several languages to explore the structures of labor markets, the experiences of workers, and the power of immigrant middlemen who supplied workers to the North American labor market. In contrast, Hahamovitch looks at the seasonal migration of agricultural workers up and down the Atlantic Coast during the early twentieth century. Although urban immigrants played a role in these labor markets early on, an increasing number of workers were African Americans from the rural South looking to supplement family incomes. Hahamovitch also explores the expanding role of the federal state in mobilizing and disciplining migrant workers during the New Deal.

These and other studies reflect a turn toward a more dynamic understanding of community among social historians. Beginning in the 1980s immigration historians had urged studies that could explain interactions between ethnic groups as well as life within the ethnic community. The turn away from a focus on immigrant assimilation eventually prompted the exploration of "transnational" aspects of migrant life, defining community as something that could transcend the bounded geographic space of the ethnic neighborhood. In a similar vein, at least two generations of labor historians have been breaking away from what sociologist Sonya Rose has called the "quintessential worker problem."[13] The search for a normative working-class experience, Rose argues, created a distorted image of working-class life that left out the experiences of women, minorities, and others with restricted access to the best-paid, most steady jobs. As a result of these interpretive developments, the subjects of labor and immigration history have multiplied and diversified. Vagrants, agricultural workers, farmers, and others marginal to labor history, because of their tenuous connection to full time wage labor and their lack of labor unions, now must be drawn deeper into the mainstream of social history.

Who Were the Hoboes?

There are few hard statistics on the hobo migration. The census did not identify migrants, and in any case they would have been as liable to undercounting as are poor workers in our day. Early-twentieth-century economist Carleton Parker figured that more than 10 million men worked in unskilled occupations.[14] During the first three decades of the twentieth century, the U.S. census counted roughly 30 percent of the labor force as lumbermen, farm laborers, and nonfarm laborers. Obviously, not all these people were hoboes, but these occupations were subject to extreme seasonal variations, as were the skilled craftsmen and factory workers. As the labor economist William Leiserson wrote in 1916, because of seasonal and business cycle related unemployment, "practically every wage-earner" passed through the ranks of "floating labor" at some point in his life.

A focus on the West North Central states (Kansas, Missouri, Iowa, Nebraska, South Dakota, North Dakota, and Minnesota) highlights the demographic similarities between those likely to be seasonal migrants and the rest of the population.[15] Based on a sample of the 1910 manuscript census, the region's males over ten years old were 97 percent white, 80 percent U.S. born, and 96 percent literate. Laboring men (lumber workers, farm laborers, and nonfarm laborers) were 95 percent white, 79 percent U.S. born, and 92 percent literate. There were significant differences between men classed as farm laborers and nonfarm laborers, although anecdotal evidence suggests a good deal of crossover between the two groups. Farm wage laborers had a median age of twenty-one, making them younger than nonfarm laborers and the male population generally. Only about 12 percent of farm wage laborers were foreign born, with Scandinavians and Germans the largest immigrant groups; however, children of immigrants were a significant subsection of this group. Nonfarm laborers counted in the 1910 census sample were older, more likely to have families, and more likely to be foreign born. These workers had a median age of thirty, in line with the general male population of working age. Thirty-six percent of nonfarm laborers were foreign born, a significantly greater proportion than in the general population of the region. Scandinavians and Germans were most numerous, with significant numbers of Italians, Mexicans, Eastern Europeans, and Greeks. In addition, the census sample included more nonwhite workers (about 10 percent) among nonfarm laborers than in the region's overall population, reflecting the employment of African Americans and Asians in railroad construction and maintenance, and Native Americans in lumber work.

The migrant workforce was split into a surprising array of occupations, often reflecting the colorful language of the western laboring subculture. In addition to harvest hands and lumberjacks there were several types of railroad laborers (gandy dancer, snipe, and jerry) and various occupations within the construction industry, such as skinner (teamster), mucker (ditchdigger), dino (explosives specialist), and splinter belly (wooden-bridge worker). To a certain extent, these occupational lines could be identified by special clothing and language, but in many cases individual migrants moved between different occupations simply by purchasing the right type of clothing before going to the employment office. Beyond these occupational categories, the most obvious manifestation of hierarchy within the laborers' subculture was the oft-cited hobo/tramp/bum trinity. Middle-class investigators picked up on these distinctions through the writing and speeches of ex-tramps like Ben Reitman. Although there were many variations on the theme, all posited a hierarchy of character in which hobo was at or near the top and bum at the bottom. Reitman had it that "the hobo works and wanders, the tramp dreams and wanders and the bum drinks and wanders." A similar version stated, "A hobo is a migratory worker. A tramp is a migratory non-worker. A bum is a stationary non-worker." Nels Anderson added the "seasonal worker" above the hobo because the seasonal worker followed a definite pattern, whereas "the hobo, proper, is a transient worker without a program."[16]

Despite these efforts to parse distinctions, the key to understanding the meaning of vagrancy in North America is the mixing of so-called vagrants with more stable workers in the widely dispersed job sites of extractive, transport, and agricultural industries. Census and survey data indicate that the vast majority of unskilled laborers in the upper Midwest actually lived with families, rather than being homeless. Between two-thirds and four-fifths of laborers counted in the census samples for 1900, 1910, and 1920 were either heads of household, children, or lived with relatives. Data on thirty-two thousand harvest workers collected by the U.S. Department of Agriculture between 1919 and 1921 confirms this impression. About a third of the harvest workers interviewed normally worked for wages in agriculture. Two-thirds were usually nonagricultural workers—half of whom were skilled workers and half laborers. No more than a fifth of all the harvest workers interviewed by the USDA were classed as migratory workers without homes. Considering the normal image of harvest workers as hobos and tramps—that is, as vagrants—it is striking that 80 percent had homes to return to at the close of the harvest season.[17]

If they did not go directly home after the harvest, many workers went on to find work in another seasonal industry, especially in timber, mining, and railroad construction. Whether or not their contemporaries would have called them vagrants, many working-class people were compelled to piece together a living from work in various industries. These migration patterns, into and out of seasonal labor markets, reflect both the economistic notion of the "labor reserve" and the survival strategies of poor working-class and rural people. Marx famously predicted that capitalism would push more workers into unemployment, creating a permanent pool of reserve labor that would hold wages down. Cut off from traditional forms of subsistence economy, the labor reserve would become the lumpen proletariat, a dangerous unorganizable class that threatens both capitalism and the organized workers who seek its overthrow. Non-Marxian economists consider these issues from the perspective of the "secondary labor market" of workers who, for whatever reason, do not have full-time wage work. They are the temporarily unemployed, the young, the excluded, the addicted, and the disabled. They are also women who normally work in the home but periodically enter the labor market to raise family income.

Local and regional seasonal work opportunities were vital to the survival strategies of poor urban and rural households generally, not just to the lives of those identified as vagrants and hoboes. Examples of these relationships can be found across North America. Harald Prins has shown that Mi'kmaq tribespeople, whose traditional lands span northern Maine and the Canadian Maritime Provinces, have migrated between community reserves and seasonal employment in logging and potato harvesting for more than 150 years. In a similar way, as Cindy Hahamovitch has written, the Atlantic Coast vegetable and fruit harvests drew southern African Americans, many of them farmers and sharecroppers, into a migrant system that stretched from Florida to New England. In the Mississippi Delta, African Americans migrated for railroad and lumber work, eventually establishing permanent residence in the expanding sawmill towns of Louisiana and Arkansas. In the Southwest, Mexican American, Mexican, and Native American farmers worked in mines and on railroads not as an end in itself, but as a means to sustain their rural communities, farms, and extended family networks.[18]

Migration was never a one-way affair from rural community to urban labor market, and neither did the migrants experience a neat "proletarianization" in which they were stripped completely of their access to community resources. Instead, seasonal labor was both a measure of economic stress on the home community and an opportunity to maintain that community through a strategic engagement with wage labor. On the flip side, wherever seasonal labor demand brought outsiders to local communities, their presence highlighted the integration of small-town and rural life with translocal markets (sometimes national, sometimes global), and raised issues about the stability of families and the safety of local residents. This is one of the primary reasons—and not simply because they were young men— that migrant workers in various regions became associated with the negative image of dangerous and disconnected vagrants.

Many of those without homes were, as Vincent DiGirolamo explains elsewhere in this volume, poor boys and young men hard pressed by hunger to find work of any kind. Like Henry McGuckin, they often hit the road after a fight with a parent. Or like Philip Taft, they were living more or less on the street when the opportunity for work in the West presented itself. With railroads close at hand, working-class youths could get out of town easily. These were certainly the migrants who were most likely to be identified as hoboes and tramps, and the most likely to be prosecuted as vagrants. Commenting on his time as a migrant, Fred Thompson remembered, "the very unpleasant sense of singularity when on a summer day one walks through a small town with a winter overcoat over one arm, knowing he will need it to keep warm that night, even though it marks him as a pesky go-about meanwhile."[19] Yet despite their harrowing personal stories of hunger, pain, and loneliness on the road, McGuckin, Taft, and Thompson each survived to live more or less productive lives.[20]

The early-twentieth-century world of hoboes and harvest hands was the location of two emergent subcultures that became lightning rods for criticism by outsiders, and it played a central role in the local version of vagrancy discourse. McGuckin, Taft, and Thompson shared more than the experience of hoboing. Each of them was an activist in the militant social movement known as the Industrial Workers of the World. The IWW, or the Wobblies, began as a dissident trade union federation in 1905, but became associated with migrant workers in the West, especially after the 1915 founding of its Agricultural Workers' Organization. For nearly a decade, the AWO maintained a presence in the wheat harvest of central North America and spread its influence into nearby seasonal labor markets in timber, mining, and the emergent oil industry of Texas and Oklahoma.[21]

Unlike most other American unions of the period, the IWW was truly international with branches in Canada, Mexico, Australia, and South America. This loose international network of radical unionists was created by globe-hopping migrant workers, and in turn facilitated the international and even global scope of the hobo migration. The Mexican migrant Primo Tapia spent time working the Great Plains wheat harvest and was a member of the IWW. When he returned home, he applied his lessons in organizing to local land struggle during the Mexican Revolution. Another migrant, F. G. Peterson came to the United States from Denmark around 1907. He worked his way across the continent, joined the IWW, and became an organizer, and in 1911 he briefly fought in the Mexican Revolution before fleeing back to the United States. Another immigrant we know only as Doyle was born in Ireland, came to North America in the 1890s, and claimed to have traveled much of the Western Hemisphere, including the major cities of South America. William Z. Foster, who later became a leader of the U.S. Communist Party, worked his way to Europe in order to observe conditions of workers there and participate in an international syndicalist labor congress.[22]

Local and federal authorities brutally repressed the IWW during World War I, imprisoning most of its key leadership. Nevertheless, the union survived and grew in the early 1920s, going into decline in large part due to its own internal factionalism, and the decline of the hobo migration that sustained so many of its members. The reasons for its endurance were clearly linked to its role in providing an infrastructure of community for migrant workers. IWW halls in towns throughout the West were warm places to visit with well-stocked libraries. As one former Wobbly recalled, "If it had not been for my contact with the IWW and what I gained from them, I would have probably become a criminal. . . . Like many migratory workers, I had left the mill of religion behind me. I couldn't even be threatened with hell. I had no respect for institutions, because I saw how they worked. I had no way to evolve a sense of values that would make me a social being."[23]

The early life of St. Louis carpenter Robert Saunders captures much of the complex dynamic between the potentially liberating and degrading aspects of migrant life. Saunders's life is the subject of a fascinating dissertation by Kristine Stilwell, which makes it clear that migrants—that is, vagrants—were deeply linked to communities and to wider trends in cultural and social life.[24] Born in 1893, Saunders spent most of his adult life as a husband, a father, a carpenter, and a union leader—hardly the image of the downtrodden tramp. But between 1911 and 1916 he hit the road eight times. He first took to the road as a teenager, more for adventure than for money, and throughout his life he treasured the opportunity to see new places and meet new people. Like many other hobo migrants, Saunders worked a vast array of jobs: urban industry, agriculture, extraction, and transportation. His first successful travels took him to Chicago and Indianapolis, where he worked in factories. Then he went west to work in the wheat harvest, in a salt production facility on San Francisco Bay, and many times as a railroad construction worker. He also joined the IWW and he soon became a professional organizer. But there were downsides to Saunders's adventures. He was frequently hungry, and often fell sick from bad food and water in work camps. He was thrown in state prison for his part in a Kansas City restaurant workers' strike. While working as an organizer he came into regular contact with the criminals who robbed harvest hands, and he came very close to becoming a criminal himself. On one of his last rides on a freight train, Saunders nearly fell under the wheels. For several hours he clung to a one-inch-thick steel rod beneath a boxcar, unable to move until the train pulled into the next station. Nevertheless, he considered his experiences an important form of education. As he recalled in his unpublished memoir, "Among the [ho]boes I met more men who thought in abstract terms than in any other group that I have been thrown in with all my life."[25]

A distinct but overlapping subculture among migrants was that of homosexual men, a reality that encapsulated for mainstream society the dangerous aspects of vagrancy. As the economist Carleton Parker noted without much elaboration, "There are social dangers which a group of demoralized, womenless men may engender under such conditions [that are a] greater menace than the stereotyped ill effects of insanitation and malnutrition." Most disturbing for many observers society was the prevalence of sexual relationships between men and young boys, thought to be endemic to the vagrant world. These were the jocker and the prushun (in tramp jargon), sometimes known more explicitly as the wolf and lamb, or simply husband and wife.[26] So common was the association between hoboing and intergenerational sex, many memoirists made a point of stating that their relations with older men were totally platonic.[27]

In his groundbreaking sociological study, *The Hobo*, Nels Anderson documented a wide-ranging culture of homo- and heterosexuality among laboring men. But Anderson's most detailed information on homosexuality remained unpublished in his field notes. Among Anderson's informants who described their early encounters with homosexuality was an eighteen-year-old laborer living on Chicago's main stem (transient district). This "Boy Tramp" told Anderson that he had his first experience while working in the wheat harvest. In Kansas he traveled with a man who took a keen interest in his well-being. While waiting in a wheat belt town for work to begin, the older man suggested that the two walk out of town to a haystack that would make a good sleeping spot. "When they reached the stack," Anderson's notes recounted, "the man tried to force a union" with the informant, who "opposed him for an hour or so, but finally submitted."

Anderson's informant soon parted company with this man but encountered others like him. While working in Nebraska and the Dakotas the next year, "he met the same types of men, had the same advances, and again yielded. This time he yielded with less coaxing than before. He began to get a certain pleasure out of the practice, and even put himself in the way of men who seemed to be interested." According to Anderson, the Boy Tramp had overcome "any scruples he may have had" and strongly argued the merits of homosexuality.[28]

Anderson's field notes represent just the tip of the iceberg according to Peter Boag. Drawing on prison and police records from Washington, Oregon, and Idaho, Boag argues that homosexual relationships—especially those between men and boys—were in fact the defining feature of the Pacific Northwest's seasonal migration of unskilled laborers. Although the world of seasonal migrants was a homosocial male world throughout North America, Boag points out that gender ratios were especially skewed in the Pacific Northwest where there were fifteen males for every female. The region's male population was also younger than the U.S. average, more likely to be unmarried, and more heavily immigrant. Boag argues that "local authorities clearly utilized laws against same-sex sexual activities as only one part of a larger middle-class campaign to persecute working-class men of racial and ethnic minority backgrounds, particularly the foreign-born."[29] More so than is denoted with a simple notion of vagrancy as lacking a domicile, these mobile workers were deemed vagrants because of their association with radicalism, foreignness, and transgressive sexuality.

The meaning of vagrancy in North America lies in the balance between images of romance and degradation, and between experiences of liberation and privation. The migrant workers of the North American West were often called vagrants, and frequently found themselves in jail for the crime of lacking money, a job, and a known address. Like other workers circulating at the periphery of transitional political economies, their work and their marginalization were central to the smooth functioning of the society that excluded them. The U.S. and Canadian West relied on highly mobile populations. It was no crime to move from place to place, nor was being broke and on the road a guarantee of incarceration. But refusing to work at "going wages," belonging to the IWW, or engaging in same-sex relationships could easily land a migrant in jail on charges of vagrancy. At the same time, the idea of being a vagrant often attracted both middle-class and working-class people—especially young men—because it offered the trade-off of high wages for relatively brief periods of unpleasant work. The fourteen-hour days of the wheat harvest, after all, were always temporary and therefore more tolerable. For some men, the opportunity to have sex with other men added a powerful layer of desire to the compulsion to find work and earn a living. To the middle-class individuals who went undercover, the tramp world also offered freedom from the expectations of respectability. One person's liberation is another's moral degradation, and ultimately most men were on the road because they had few other choices. They needed to earn money for themselves and their families, and they made the best of a bad situation. The bipolar view of tramping as both romantic and degrading facilitated the circulation and selective repression of laborers, creating opportunities to earn a living at the same time that it limited the chances to escape work.

Notes

Portions of this chapter are drawn from chapters 3 and 5 of Frank Tobias Higbie, *Indispensable Outcasts: Hobo Workers and Community in the American Midwest, 1880–1930* (Urbana: University of Illinois Press, 2003). My thanks to Lee Beier, Paul Ocobock, Aminda Smith, Abby Margolis, and Gerry Ronning for their helpful comments and suggestions.

1. Paul T. Ringenbach, *Tramps and Reformers, 1873–1916: The Discovery of Unemployment in New York* (Westport, CT: Greenwood, 1973).

2. Hutchins Hapgood, *The Spirit of Labor* (1907; Urbana: University of Illinois Press, 2004).

3. Carl Sandburg, *Always the Young Strangers* (New York: Harcourt, Brace, 1953); Douglas Wixson, *Worker-Writer in America: Jack Conroy and the Tradition of Midwestern Literary Radicalism, 1898–1990* (Urbana: University of Illinois Press, 1994); Maurice Neufeld, ed., "Portrait of the Labor Historian as a Boy and Young Man: Excerpts from the Interview of

Philip Taft by Margot Honig," *Labor History* 19 (Winter 1978): 39–71; Charles A. Hale, "Frank Tannenbaum and the Mexican Revolution" *Hispanic American Historical Review* 75 (1995): 215–46; Elsie Gluck, *John Mitchell, Miner: Labor's Bargain with the Gilded Age* (New York: John Day, 1929), 14; James R. Barrett, *William Z. Foster and the Tragedy of American Radicalism* (Urbana: University of Illinois Press, 1999); Ralph Chaplin, *Wobbly: The Rough-and-Tumble Story of an American Radical* (Chicago: University of Chicago Press, 1948).

4. David T. Courtwright, *Violent Land: Single Men and Social Disorder from the Frontier to the Inner City* (Cambridge, MA: Harvard University Press, 1996).

5. Allan Pinkerton, *Strikers, Communists, Tramps and Detectives* (New York: G. W. Dillingham, 1878), 26; Josiah Flynt, *My Life* (New York: Outing Publishing Co., 1908), 349.

6. Gregory Woirol, *In the Floating Army: F. C. Mills on Itinerant Life in California, 1914* (Urbana: University of Illinois Press, 1992); Edmund W. Bradwin, *The Bunkhouse Man: A Study of Work and Pay in the Camps of Canada, 1903–1914* (1928; Toronto: University of Toronto Press, 1972).

7. Nels Anderson, *The Hobo: The Sociology of the Homeless Man* (1923; Chicago: University of Chicago Press, 1961); Don D. Lescohier, *The Labor Market* (New York: Macmillan, 1919).

8. Carey McWilliams, *Factories in the Field: The Story of Migratory Farm Labor in California* (Boston: Little, Brown, 1939); McWilliams, *Ill Fares the Land: Migrants and Migratory Labor in the United States* (Boston: Little, Brown, 1942); James Gregory, *The Southern Diaspora: How the Great Migrations of Black and White Southerners Transformed America* (Chapel Hill: University of North Carolina Press, 2005).

9. Samuel E. Wallace, *Skid Row as a Way of Life* (Totowa, NJ: Bedminster, 1965).

10. Eric H. Monkkonen, ed., *Walking to Work: Tramps in America, 1790–1935* (Lincoln: University of Nebraska Press, 1984); Ringenbach, *Tramps and Reformers;* Alexander Keyssar, *Out of Work: The First Century of Unemployment in Massachusetts* (New York: Cambridge University Press, 1986); Amy Dru Stanley, "Beggars Can't Be Choosers: Compulsion and Contract in Postbellum America," *Journal of American History* 78 (March 1992): 1265–93; Lynne Marie Adrian, "Organizing the Rootless: American Hobo Subculture, 1893–1932" (Ph.D. diss., University of Iowa, 1984); Allen G. Applen, "Migratory Harvest Labor in the Midwestern Wheat Belt, 1870–1940," (Ph.D. diss., Kansas State University, 1974).

11. Tim Cresswell, *The Tramp in America* (London: Reaktion, 2001); Todd DePastino, *Citizen Hobo: How a Century of Homelessness Shaped America* (Chicago: University of Chicago Press, 2003); Kenneth Kusmer, *Down and Out, on the Road: The Homeless in American History* (New York: Oxford University Press, 2002).

12. Higbie, *Indispensable Outcasts;* Gunther Peck, *Reinventing Free Labor: Padrones and Immigrant Workers in the North American West, 1880–1930* (New York: Cambridge University Press, 2000); Cindy Hahamovitch, *Fruits of Their Labor: Atlantic Coast Farmworkers and the Making of Migrant Poverty, 1870–1945* (Chapel Hill: University of North Carolina Press, 1997). See also Josef Barton, "Borderland Discontents: Mexican Migration in Regional Contexts, 1880–1930," in *Repositioning North American Migration History: New Directions in Modern Continental Migration, Citizenship, and Community,* ed. Marc S. Rodriguez (Rochester, NY: University of Rochester Press, 2004), 141–205; Howard Lamar, "From Bondage to Contract: Ethnic Labor in the American West, 1600–1890," in *The Countryside in the Age of Capitalist Transformation: Essays in the Social History of Rural America,* ed. Steven Hahn and Jonathan Prude (Chapel Hill: University of North Carolina Press, 1985).

13. Donna Gabaccia, Franca Iacovetta, and Fraser Ottanelli, "Laboring across National Borders: Class, Gender, and Militancy in the Proletarian Mass Migrations," *International Labor and Working-Class History* 66 (Fall 2004): 57–77; Sonja Rose, "Class Formation and the Quintessential Worker," in *Reworking Class,* ed. John R. Hall (Ithaca, NY: Cornell University Press, 1997), 133–66; Alice Kessler-Harris, "Treating the Male as 'Other': Redefining the Parameters of Labor History," *Labor History* 34 (Spring–Summer 1993): 190–204.

14. Carleton Parker, *The Casual Laborer and Other Essays* (New York: Harcourt, Brace, and Howe, 1920), 116.

15. The following analysis is based on the Integrated Public Use Microdata Samples (IPUMS), released 1995, http://www.hist.umn.edu/~ipums/, drawn from Higbie, *Indispensable Outcasts,* 102–5.

16. Anderson, *Hobo,* 87, 90.

17. Don D. Lescohier, "Sources of Supply and Conditions of Employment of Harvest Labor in the Wheat Belt," USDA Bulletin 1211 (Washington, DC: Government Printing Office, 1924), 3–5; Lescohier, "Hands and Tools of the Wheat Harvest," Survey 50 (July 1, 1923), 412. See also Lescohier, "Harvest Labor Problems in the Wheat Belt," USDA Bulletin 1020 (Washington, DC: Government Printing Office, 1922); Lescohier, "Conditions Affecting the Demand for Harvest Labor in the Wheat

Belt," USDA Bulletin 1230 (Washington, DC: Government Printing Office, 1924).

18. Harald E. L. Prins, "Tribal Network and Migrant Labor: Mi'kmaq Indians as Seasonal Workers in Aroostook's Potato Fields, 1870–1980," in *Native Americans and Wage Labor: Ethnohistorical Perspectives*, ed. Alice Littlefield and Martha Knack (Norman: University of Oklahoma Press, 1996), 45–65; Hahamovitch, *Fruits of Their Labor*; William Jones, *The Tribe of Black Ulysses: African American Lumber Workers in the Jim Crow South* (Urbana: University of Illinois Press, 2005); Paul Garon and Gene Tomko, *What's the Use of Walking if There's a Freight Train Going Your Way? Black Hoboes and Their Songs* (Chicago: Charles H. Kerr, 2006); Kurt M. Peters, "Watering the Flower: Laguna Pueblo and the Santa Fe Railroad, 1880–1943," in Littlefield and Knack, *Native Americans and Wage Labor*, 177–97; Neil Foley, *The White Scourge: Mexicans, Blacks, and Poor Whites in Texas Cotton Culture* (Berkeley: University of California Press, 1997); Chris Friday, *Organizing Asian American Labor: The Pacific Coast Canned-Salmon Industry, 1870–1942* (Philadelphia: Temple University Press, 1994); Sarah Deutsch, *No Separate Refuge: Culture, Class, and Gender on an Anglo-Hispanic Frontier in the American Southwest, 1880-1940* (New York: Oxford University Press); Devra Weber, *Dark Sweat, White Gold: California Farm Workers, Cotton, and the New Deal* (Berkeley: University of California Press, 1994); Colleen M. O'Neill, *Working the Navajo Way: Labor and Culture in the Twentieth Century* (Lawrence: University Press of Kansas, 2005).

19. Fred Thompson to Henry McGuckin Jr., June 10, 1974, Charles H. Kerr Company Records, box 7, Newberry Library, Chicago.

20. Henry McGuckin, *Memoirs of a Wobbly* (Chicago: Charles H. Kerr, 1987); Neufeld, "Portrait of the Labor Historian"; Fred Thompson to Henry McGuckin Jr., June 10, 1974, Charles H. Kerr Company Records, box 7, Newberry Library, Chicago; David Roediger, ed., *Fellow Worker: The Life of Fred Thompson* (Chicago: Charles H. Kerr, 1994).

21. On the IWW, see, among many others, Melvyn Dubofsky, *We Shall Be All: A History of the Industrial Workers of the World* (New York: Quadrangle, 1969); Higbie, *Indispensable Outcasts*, ch. 4; Nigel Anthony Sellars, *Oil, Wheat, and Wobblies: The Industrial Workers of the World in Oklahoma, 1905–1930* (Norman: University of Oklahoma Press, 1998).

22. Paul Friedrich, *Agrarian Revolt in a Mexican Village* (Chicago: University of Chicago Press, 1977), 67–70; John R. Commons, ed., *Trade Unionism and Labor Problems, 2nd Series* (Boston: Ginn, 1921), 102; untitled notes on "Doyle," 1921, Don D. Lescohier Papers, box 1, folder 1, State

Historical Society of Wisconsin, Madison; James R. Barrett, *William Z. Foster and the Tragedy of American Radicalism* (Urbana: University of Illinois Press, 1999), 26–27, 43–49. On international aspects of the IWW, see Verity Burgmann, *Revolutionary Industrial Unionism: The Industrial Workers of the World in Australia* (Cambridge: Cambridge University Press, 1995); Francis Shor, "Left Labor Agitators in the Pacific Rim of the Early Twentieth Century," *International Labor and Working-Class History* 67 (Spring 2005): 148–63; Peter De Shazo, *Urban Workers and Labor Unions in Chile, 1902–1927* (Madison: University of Wisconsin Press, 1983).

23. Stewart Bird, Dan Georgakas, and Deborah Shaffer, comps., *Solidarity Forever: An Oral History of the IWW* (Chicago: Lake View, 1985), 40.

24. Kristine Stilwell, "'If You Don't Slip': The Hobo Life, 1911–1916" (Ph.D. diss., University of Missouri, 2004); Robert Saunders, "The Road," Robert Saunders Papers, Western Historical Manuscripts, University of Missouri–St. Louis.

25. Saunders, "Road," 54.

26. Flynt, *Tramping with Tramps*, 395–96; Anderson, *Hobo*, 147–48.

27. For examples, see McGuckin, *Memoirs of a Wobbly;* and Neufeld, "Portrait of the Labor Historian," 39–71.

28. Nels Anderson, doc. 122, Ernest W. Burgess Papers, University of Chicago Libraries, Department of Special Collections. On the dynamics of urban gay subcultures, see George Chauncy, *Gay New York: Gender, Urban Culture, and the Making of the Gay Male World, 1890–1940* (New York: Basic Books, 1994).

29. Peter Boag, *Same-Sex Affairs: Constructing and Controlling Homosexuality in the Pacific Northwest* (Berkeley: University of California Press, 2003), 18, 46–47.

10

The "Travelling Native"

Vagrancy and Colonial Control in British East Africa

Andrew Burton and Paul Ocobock

BOTH AFRICA AND VAGRANCY have a long history in the British imagination. John Shaw, when writing of vagrants he encountered as a missionary in nineteenth-century London, compared them "to the wildest colony of savages, transplanted by an act of conjuration from the centre of Africa."[1] In 1932 Nairobi, Kenyan African vagabonds were described as "insolent and contemptuous of authority . . . the native counterpart of the 'hooligan,' that objectionable feature of the larger towns of England."[2] To these observers, vagrants of London and Nairobi had been so warped by their environment and economic condition that even European racism failed to distinguish them. Vagrants were a breed all their own. The imagined connection between the English transient and his African counterpart ensured that throughout the colonial period in British Africa, vagrants and others of their ilk—such as beggars, fortunetellers, and urban idlers—would arouse the ire of the colonial state.

In the last two decades, scholars of Africa have turned to the study of urban life, and in particular its outcast populations. Numerous works have explored the lives of prostitutes, vagrants, petty thieves, and street children as well as their relationships with the colonial state.[3] Vagrancy regulations in colonial Africa have provided scholars with a fruitful unit of analysis, an intersection at which diverse socioeconomic and political processes converge, including African migration, employment in European industries, urbanization, and criminality. As Richard Allen has shown (chapter 5), vagrancy had a crucial role in the maintenance of the late-nineteenth-century Mauritian postemancipation economy.[4] Likewise, Paul Lovejoy and Jan Hogendorn have argued that the British used vagrancy policy as a means of restoring freed slaves to their masters without implicating themselves in the ongoing slave trade of northern Nigeria.[5] Robert Gordon and Jeremy Martens have illustrated how the use of vagrancy in southern Africa preserved racial segregation and allayed European settlers' fears of black peril.[6]

Vagrancy law served the colonial regimes of East Africa in their mission to control two critical elements of the colonial rule, specifically in the colonies of Kenya, Uganda, and Tanganyika (known as Tanzania after its amalgamation with Zanzibar in 1964). First, vagrancy legislation was a means to mobilize and discipline migratory African labor and meet the growing demands of the colonial economy. In addition, vagrancy law was a prescription for what officials saw as the disintegration of African social order at the hands of urban life and capitalism, made manifest by increasing levels of urbanization, crime, and unemployment. Beyond the colonial rhetoric of vagrancy's function, the colonial state did interact with migratory and unemployed subjects. Although the colonial regimes of East Africa produced a wide range of vagrancy-related regulations, attempts to put these policies into action were hampered by persistent financial and logistical limitations.

Vagrancy and Compulsory Labor in Early Colonial Kenya

Controlling labor has been one of the hallmarks of vagrancy law since its first incarnation. As A. L. Beier has elegantly shown in chapter 1, vagrancy was one part of a package of laws used to control the movement and behavior of laborers in early modern England. In twentieth-century British East Africa, vagrancy laws were some of the first pieces of legislation gazetted by the colonial administration. Both Uganda and Kenya passed vagrancy ordinances in the early 1900s. However, it was in the European settler colony of Kenya where this legislation was initially most prominent in the local political economy. Here vagrancy became a critical tool in drawing out and directing African workers for a growing number of European settlers requiring labor on their agricultural estates. Kenya's first vagrancy laws came into effect in Mombasa in 1898 and were revised and expanded after the turn of the century. The vagrancy acts gazetted in Mombasa and Nairobi in 1900 and 1902, respectively, were trimmed versions of those operating in Britain and India. According to these laws, a vagrant was anyone found "asking for alms or wandering about without any employment or visible means of subsistence."[7] Those suspected of vagrancy by police could be arrested without a warrant and, if charged, imprisoned for up to three months. While incarcerated, vagrants were put to work until they had earned enough to pay for repatriation.[8]

Kenya proved a special case in East Africa principally because of its labor demands. By 1905 five hundred European settlers had arrived seeking land to establish agricultural estates.[9] The colonial state allocated over sixty thousand acres of land to European setters in Central and Rift Valley provinces removing eleven thousand African people from their farms.[10] To construct their farms and begin sowing their new land, settlers required a large, cheap labor force.[11] However, Africans made few moves to exchange their labor for wages and transfer their efforts from subsistence to commercial production.[12] In response, colonial officials developed the legislation and infrastructure to draw out African labor. This was accomplished in several ways. The introduction of a poll and hut tax forced Africans to find a source of cash. Penalties for tax default ranged from forced labor to forfeiture of home and imprisonment.[13] Furthermore, overcrowding on and degradation of the African reserves, where Kenyans were forced to move after their eviction, were also responsible for the gradual emergence of Africans into the labor market. Yet, as laborers migrated in search of work in larger numbers, colonial officials required new tools to control their movement. The Vagrancy Act of 1902 formed part of a broader package of regulations. The Native Porters and Labour Regulations of 1902, Master and Servants Ordinance of 1906, and Native Registration Ordinance of 1915 were all attempts to manipulate the movement and behavior of African employees.[14] Africans without employment or *kipande* (work passes) were rounded up and arrested in their villages, in labor lines, and in the burgeoning town of Nairobi.[15]

By the 1920s the regime, more confident in its ability to assert authority, gazetted a new range of legislation including, in 1920, a more aggressive vagrancy ordinance. Police now had the ability to arrest anyone wandering about or residing in a space such as a veranda, outhouse, or vehicle without the owner's consent.[16] Adult vagrants were detained until employment could be found. If no work was found, they were repatriated home, but if they refused the work given them by the government, they faced imprisonment.[17] This ordinance was ultimately adopted as a model by other colonies in the region. In 1929 the equivalent legislation in Northern Rhodesia attracted the attention of the International Labour Organization (ILO), which was concerned about the role of the ordinance in mobilizing forced labor.[18] At the 1929 ILO conference, E. L. Poulton, a representative of the British Workers' Delegation, brought to the attention of fellow delegates that those arrested for vagrancy in Northern Rhodesia, after a period of detention, could be compelled to accept work or face three months' imprisonment.[19] Offenders were often put to work on government projects and in private enterprises such as the European mining and agricultural industries. The ILO requested that the Colonial Office look into the matter and reform the legislation. Two years passed with no response, during which two further colonies, Zanzibar and Brunei, passed legislation based on the Kenyan ordinance. In 1931 the ILO threatened to publish a report on vagrancy laws in the empire.[20] This time the Colonial Office quickly responded with an inquiry into which vagrancy policies contained forced labor provisions and how these laws were enforced. As reports from the periphery trickled in, it became clear that many colonies had simply adopted the same vagrancy laws as those found in Kenya.[21] Colonies and territories like Uganda, Zanzibar, Northern Rhodesia, Brunei, Hong Kong, Johore,

Kedah, Sarawak, and the Straits Settlements were all linked to Kenya in this way.[22]

During the Colonial Office inquiry, officials in Kenya explained the 1920 Vagrancy Ordinance in detail to their superiors. They acknowledged that when they gazetted the ordinance they knew full well it would be perceived as a means of "driving to work all natives who were found loose outside the Reserves."[23] In fact, few Africans were actually charged with vagrancy or incarcerated in houses of detention at the time of the ILO investigation. In 1927, two years before the ILO Conference, twenty-three detention camps housed 1,421 people, of which only nine were vagrants. The majority of inmates were detained for other labor regulations or for tax evasion.[24] From 1928 to 1930, 461 people, mostly men, were arrested for vagrancy in the whole of Kenya, most of whom were repatriated home rather than committed to houses of detention and made to work.[25] Yet, the Vagrancy Act of 1902 and ordinance of 1920 were at the administration's disposal for the management of labor. Over time, however, the number of arrests for vagrancy increased in response to other factors such as urbanization and the growth of crime.

The Kenyan ordinance, and those vagrancy laws in other colonies that used it as a model, closely resembled legislation that had operated in Britain and colonial India centuries before, particularly in its provision of compulsory labor for vagrants. There can be no doubt that vagrant Africans were forced to work on government projects and private enterprises, particularly in colonies with large European populations requiring a mobile labor force. In the early colonial period, vagrancy legislation served as part of a much larger package of regulations seeking to manipulate the labor supply. However, as the colonial economies of British East Africa began to develop, as Africans migrated in greater numbers, and as urban African populations increased, vagrancy became a means of social control. From the 1920s onward, vagrancy would be marked by its use to clear East Africa's urban centers of undesirable African populations, to correct perceived African delinquency, and to maintain colonial social order.

The "Travelling Native" and Social Control
in Interwar East Africa

In early colonial East Africa, in the official imagination, nothing posed a greater threat to social order than uncontrolled African mobility. The potential consequences of Africans' detachment from their tribal societies, or of their unmediated exposure to novel foreign influences, were perceived as particularly grave. These concerns found administrative expression in the shape of the governing ideology of indirect rule, which influenced administrative strategies throughout Africa in the period up to World War II.[26] Indirect rule depended on a stratum of African intermediaries, namely chiefs and headmen, who acted as the local arm of the colonial apparatus. They were responsible for collecting taxes, enforcing conscription orders, recruiting labor for government projects and the European agricultural sector, and maintaining basic law and order. Chiefs drew their legitimacy from their tribal affiliations, and the colonial government drew theirs from chiefly rule. Alongside its administrative functions, indirect rule sought to impose tribal order on colonial societies and preserve social cohesion, thereby protecting individual Africans from the corrosive effects of socioeconomic and cultural forces unleashed by colonialism.

Despite the paternalistic instincts of many administrators, fiscal imperatives necessitated the development of a large, mobile, and cheap African labor force, as seen in early colonial Kenya. As the wage labor market drew African workers out of their local communities to find employment, often several hundred miles away from their villages, colonial officials feared, with good reason, that such migration would weaken tribal affiliation and the legitimacy of their intermediaries. Africans leaving in search of work were supposed to retain administrative and social ties with their "Native Areas."[27] Although indirect rule and the personal predispositions of migrants could result in a large degree of tribal cohesion, they failed to prevent the emergence of a class of Africans who, through choice or circumstance, temporarily or permanently, circumvented chiefly authority and colonial supervision. By the interwar period the so-called detribalized African had entered official discourse as a prime colonial bogeyman. A detribalized African represented "incompetence in dealing with the evils of his own society and the potential disruptive influence of Western civilization" and had to be treated with "a blend of moral exhortation and didactic tutelage, backed up by threats of punishment and coercion."[28] Vagrancy legislation in East Africa was adopted to reassert control over such individuals.

The "migrant problem" was particularly associated with emerging urban centers. To many Africans, trying to evade chiefs, elders, parents, and spouses, the relatively large and shifting populations in urban centers offered an unprecedented degree of anonymity. This fostered anxiety in colonial officials—to whom towns represented dens of vice where Africans coming from societies with little or no traditions of urbanism—were exposed to insidious demoralizing influences.[29] In his 1926 report Tanganyikan labor commissioner Maj. G. St. J. Orde Browne gave a classic account of the descent of the African migrant:

> Having left their homes to seek work, in all probability, they remain in some town after they have been paid off at their original place of employment. There they find some casual work, but probably fail to get steady employment; intervals of idleness between jobs tend to increase, until gradually the individual drifts into the class of unemployable loafer, from which stage it is fatally easy to join the definitely criminal class. . . . By this time he is too much addicted to the attractions of the unrestricted town life to be able to return to the village conditions and he finds tribal discipline and custom most irksome. . . . He becomes a unit in the large and growing class of detribalised natives who have fallen away from African social organisation without having qualified themselves to take a place in a Europeanised community.[30]

By the early 1920s, throughout East Africa, British administrators bemoaned the growing presence in towns of such a class of African "undesirables," who, lacking formal employment, were assumed to be up to no good.[31] In Uganda in 1922, attention was drawn to the "hordes of native vagrants and suspects who infest the town[s]—especially Kampala and Jinja," whose numbers were "growing yearly."[32] Dar es Salaam's district commissioner complained "the African community in town must unfortunately be regarded with marked suspicion" composed in part of "a most undesirable floating population of criminals, or quasi-criminals."[33] As a result, varying legislative initiatives were implemented in Kenya, Uganda, and Tanganyika to address the problem, whose character and application were influenced by the differing nature of the three colonies. The improvisation, and increasing implementation, of vagrancy legislation formed part of wider attempts by colonial administrations in the interwar period to assert more effective social controls over African populations.

In Kenya the use of vagrancy law took on added importance in the interwar period as discussion of detribalization reared its ugly head. Nairobi had not been a precolonial settlement, like Dar es Salaam in Tanzania or Mengo in Uganda; rather it was a railway town built to house the African, European, and Asian laborers brought to construct the Uganda railway.[34] From its founding, Nairobi experienced rapid demographic growth, beginning as a humble town of 10,500 people in 1906, growing to 38,224 in 1928, and doubling in size a decade later.[35] As the population of the city swelled, the maintenance of urban order became of great concern for administrators, especially with the emerging European settler presence in Nairobi. Early in its history, Nairobi "looked less to Bombay and more towards South Africa."[36] Europeans, Asians, and Africans were segregated into distinct locations, with Africans left to tend to their own housing on the outskirts of town. The presence of thousands of underemployed African youths scratching out an income through formal and informal subsistence was an offense to non-African sensibilities and security.[37] In 1907 the Nairobi police force was stretched to the limit, as settlers demanded that the force guard their property and persons.[38] While underemployed Africans may have led visible lives on the urban streets, it was their less visible, potentially criminal, dealings that struck so deeply at the colonial consciousness.

Throughout the 1920s the crime rate gradually rose in Kenya, especially in Nairobi, and it became closely associated with migrating, unemployed Africans. When the chief native commissioner noted 1,002 adult and juvenile vagrants had been rounded up in 1932, an increase over previous years, he blamed the rising figures on recidivism and the depressed economic conditions on the European estates.[39] Public and administrative anxieties over rising rates of crime led to the establishment of the Crime Committee in 1932, made up of several branches of the colonial service, such as the Police, Labour, and Native Affairs offices. Committee members believed that among the juveniles, recidivists, and vagrants in Nairobi, juveniles posed the gravest threat.[40] Uncontrolled juvenile migration to Nairobi further fueled fears of detribalization and prompted officials to use vagrancy policy in a new way. In 1931 the chief native commissioner revealed that juveniles arrested for a variety of charges ranging from theft to failure to present a kipande were awarded corporal punishment. Afterward, the police further charged the offenders with vagrancy and repatriated them.[41] In 1931, 268 juveniles were caned. Caning and repatriation became a popular coupling of punishments as magistrates tried to deter recidivism through violence. By the 1930s vagrancy policy was being used to remove criminals from Nairobi, not just the unemployed. Vagrancy policy in Kenya had developed beyond a mechanism to control the labor market; it had become a part of the punishment for African delinquency.

Part of the perceived increase in crime had little to do with the actual number of crimes committed but related more to changes in the effectiveness of the administration. It was during the 1930s, under the leadership of commissioner R. G. B. Spicer, that the Nairobi police force became a more efficient department. Rigorous training and night patrols raised the number of arrests and prosecutions among vagrants and criminals.[42] Numerous bylaws were also used to control African movement and behavior, augmenting vagrancy and pass laws. Bylaw 557 was a vagrancy regulation with a temporal twist in which any African and his family found without residence or remaining within the municipality for longer than thirty-six hours would be guilty of an offense.[43] Other bylaws, such as loitering on traffic islands and the "misuse" of bicycles, increased the number of offenses for which Africans could be hauled into court.[44] As the Kenya administration expanded its powers to control rural to urban migration and Nairobi's transient population, it lost the ability to compel vagrants to work. In 1930, in response to the ILO complaint, Kenya repealed section 6 of the 1920 Vagrancy Ordinance, which granted it the ability to force vagrants to work. Although adult and juvenile vagrants could still be held in houses of detention and prisons, they now had to be repatriated if they refused to work. As a result, the administration began to focus its efforts on roundups and repatriations.

Looking at cases involving Africans under the age of eighteen, the practice of roundups and repatriations can be clearly seen. In 1939 there are about ten roundups identifiable in the record. For example, cases numbering 37 through 46, 264 through 277, and 405 through 434 involve juveniles arrested around the same time and charged with the same crime: vagrancy. During a roundup, the police swept through an African location, arrested between six and thirty young Africans. Juvenile vagrants, and many adults, after a period of detention were then scheduled for repatriation.[45] Yet, repatriation, while not attracting the ire of the ILO, had its own particular constraints. Using roundups required the state to have accommodation available for up to thirty, and perhaps more, Africans at a time. This was unlikely and the courts were compelled to caution and release offenders. Another factor was the cost of the system. Paying for vagrants to take the train or lorry back to their home reserves, while cheaper than incarceration, drained already low Labour Office coffers.[46] Officials gradually realized that repatriation provided no sustainable solution and resulted in recidivism as adults and juveniles removed from the city at the administration's expense returned on foot for free.[47]

In Uganda the issue of controlling such African mobility came to the fore in a 1920s debate over amendments to a preexisting vagrancy Ordinance. Passed into law as Ordinance no. 8 of 1909, the legislation was specifically aimed at controlling European destitution, and at the time of its enactment its use against "natives of the Protectorate was not foreseen." However, by the early 1920s the "advent of the indigenous vagrant" prompted criticism of its inadequacies. Shifts in the character of the Ugandan economy had resulted in a growing migration of labor from remote northern districts to central and southern districts, which included a "class of native . . . which flocks in the town from distant districts . . . and lives from hand to mouth in and about the bazaars, sleeping in odd corners and begging, or possibly earning a few cents from time to time from . . . casual jobs."[48] As in Kenya, both the social order and economic productivity of the African was at issue, though in Uganda it was the national economy rather than the expatriate plantation sector that was to benefit from stricter action against African mobility. "This is essentially a country for encouraging the production of crops etc.," argued a senior police officer advocating amendments to the Vagrancy Ordinance in 1922, "and such people should be sent to their homes and encouraged to grow cotton, sim sim [sesame seed] etc."[49] An amended ordinance was passed in 1925 that placed the onus on the potential offender to provide proof of "gainful" employment. Failure to do so resulted in his prosecution, and upon conviction the offender was committed to the "care" of the labor commissioner, who arranged for suitable employment in public works schemes until the vagrant had earned sufficient money to cover the costs of repatriation. Shortly after its enactment the Colonial Office threatened to rescind the amended ordinance because of its discriminatory nature (proof of being "honestly occupied" fell on Africans only) and its potential use of forced labor.[50] Metropolitan officials were highly sensitive about how legislation designed to restrict African mobility might be interpreted as racially discriminatory or neglectful of basic liberties. The correspondence from Uganda reassured the Colonial Office regarding its racially neutral application and fact that the labor requirement was restricted solely to earning repatriation costs. It also stressed the urgent necessity of reexerting "tribal authority" over a growing class of "wandering natives." Only after this correspondence did officials in Uganda win Colonial Office approval.[51]

As with its northern neighbors, in Tanganyika, a former German colony that came under British control as a League of Nations Mandate Territory after World War I, the perceived dangers of unrestricted African mobility also attracted particular attention in the 1920s. Like Kenya and Uganda, diverse legislation was enacted at this time to deal with the problem. Here, too, the issue was interpreted as an administrative issue in which more effective control had to be asserted over a class of Africans considered subversive of colonial order. In his 1927 annual report on labor, Orde Browne agonized over the emergence of a "type, who . . . divorced from old tribal customs [will] behave decently only because of fear of the police" which "in a country such as Tanganyika is tantamount to saying they will be beyond control."[52] Officials enacted various regulations to address the problem, including a Destitute Persons Ordinance and township regulations aimed at the repatriation of unwanted residents. However, the legislation proved administratively cumbersome and its enforcement was at best erratic.[53] For example, in the 1924 Destitute Persons Ordinance, in contrast to its Ugandan equivalent, onus of proof of lack of a visible means of subsistence rested on the prosecutor and repatriation costs of those convicted under the ordinance were paid by the state, rather than covered by a period of compulsory labor. As a result, the ordinance was rarely enforced. In the late 1920s, to compensate for the inadequacies of the existing legislation, Orde Browne and others, notably administrators responsible for the major urban centers, lobbied for a pass system along the lines of those in place in southern Africa or Kenya. However, local and Colonial Office concerns over international criticism arising from Tanganyika's League of Nations mandate status prevented the introduction of any such system.[54] As a result, despite enduring complaints from officials, Tanganyika diverged from its neighbor to the north, Kenya, and established no thoroughgoing system of checking African mobility. In the interwar period, enforcement of existing legislation remained sporadic, confined mainly to periods of crisis such as the early 1930s, when the Great Depression led to the removal of several hundred jobless Africans from the main towns of Dar es Salaam and Tanga; or to the handful of "hardened" criminals making an appearance in the towns.

The occasionally histrionic nature of commentary on "native loafers" and ne'er-do-wells in interwar East Africa was evidence more of the profound anxiety felt by certain officials over social disruption accompanying heightened African mobility than of any serious urban problem. A growing "criminal class," which administrators viewed as the inevitable consequence of uncontrolled urbanization, remained small.[55] More significantly, although serious urban unemployment had occurred at times of economic crisis, such as after World War I and during the Depression, employers at this time tended to complain of an actual shortage of labor.[56] As we have seen, the legislation aimed at controlling African movement that was enacted in the interwar period often contained practical flaws or was generally neglected in its usage (or both). Occasional resort to mass roundups and the subsequent repatriation or release of vagrants revealed that vagrancy policy did not need to be wholly effective. As long as officials could remove "undesirables" from urban areas, and for a short time city streets appeared clear, a fragile façade hung over the issues of labor crisis and social order. Procedures to remove vagrants provided East African administrations with the ability to circumvent their financial and logistical constraints. Thus, interwar vagrancy policy was a myopic, short-term strategy aimed at relieving the state from costly responsibilities to alleviate underemployment, overcrowding, and crime. However, at the outset of World War II, the social, administrative, and political context was to change dramatically, with significant repercussions for the colonial management of African mobility.

Rapid Urbanization and Social Control in Postwar British East Africa

Accelerating urbanization was the prime factor that influenced the shift in policy after World War II. By the late 1930s, socioeconomic and cultural change that accompanied colonialism had ushered in a substantial upsurge in the numbers of migrants making their way from rural to urban areas.[57] As a result, the economy and infrastructure of East African towns were placed under increasing strain, with overcrowding and ill health increasingly prevalent, alongside an emerging problem of unemployment.[58] Faced with such rapidly growing urban populations, colonial administrators were confronted with the need to devise a comprehensive policy that envisaged a class of Africans as long-term residents of urban areas, albeit one whose size was restricted; in contrast to the temporary sojourners from tribal areas as interwar administrators had tended to view urban Africans. The new urban policy was also shaped by shifts in colonial governance at an empirewide level. Influenced by Lord Hailey's reports on administration in sub-Saharan Africa, from the early 1940s indirect rule as an administrative system was to be replaced by local government structures in which the tribal subject was supposed to give way to the African citizen, enjoying both new freedoms and responsibilities.[59] As a part of this shift, growing attention was paid to the social welfare of urban Africans in formal employment (though it would be some time before the living conditions of most would improve significantly), and to the cultivation of a progressive civic consciousness in place of tribal loyalties. The corollary of this acceptance of a restricted African urban presence, however, was increasing intolerance shown toward the large and growing numbers of Africans entering the towns that were surplus to urban economies.

Like the 1920s, the 1940s was a decade in which a raft of legislation aimed at curbing African mobility was enacted in response to what was viewed as the looming problem of a growing urban class of idle and uncontrolled Africans. In 1940, for example, a special Vagrancy Law was passed in the most populous and developed region in Uganda, the Kingdom of Buganda. The law was a response to the growing numbers of "unemployed and destitute natives . . . collecting at various big centres, particularly Mengo, Mpigi, and Masaka, where they prey upon the local inhabitants and give considerable trouble to the authorities."[60] In Kenya, whose two main towns, Nairobi and Mombasa, grew by over 50 percent in the early 1940s, a number of legislative measures were taken to tackle mounting rural-urban drift and the associated incidence of unemployment and underemployment.[61] Under the 1944 Limitation of Labor Regulations (passed under the wartime Emergency Powers [Defense] Act, which criminalized unregistered inhabitants of urban centers who had resided there for more than forty-eight hours), 2,698 people were rounded up in Nairobi in 1945 and repatriated to their rural homes, conscripted, or directed into approved occupations. The following year, officials arrested and removed as many as 4,390 Africans from Nairobi along with 1,300 from Mombasa.[62] However, the legislation was decreed ultra vires (beyond legal authority) by the Kenyan Supreme Court in 1945, and the Removal of Undesirable Natives Ordinance of 1946 was pushed through the Legislative Council to maintain the controls over urban Africans.[63]

The new ordinance, scheduled to operate only until the end of the year, enabled district officials to remove, among others, Africans lacking either "regular employment" or a "settled urban home." The temporary legislation encountered strong opposition within the Colonial Office because administrators were anxious about its racially discriminatory nature. The Kenyan government was told to prepare "new and less objectionable legislation."[64] This was drafted and subsequently passed in 1949 as the Voluntarily Unemployed Persons Ordinance, which allowed municipal authorities to arrest Africans who had not earned an income within three months of their arrival in the city.[65] Colonial Office opposition to Kenyan legislation was indicative of tensions arising between the drift of metropolitan thinking toward more progressive, developmental policies, and that of East African administrators, whose developmental instincts, such as they were, were constrained by local contingencies taking shape on the ground. Meanwhile, the supreme court's ultra vires judgment on earlier legislation betrayed similar tensions arising from a conflict between administrative expediency and legal principle.[66]

Tensions in East Africa during the 1940s between the metropole and colony, and the judiciary and administration, are best exemplified by parallel debates that occurred over legislation in neighboring Tanganyika. Here the government, despite its politically sensitive status as a United Nations Trust territory after World War II, actually succeeded in promulgating (and maintaining) a similar ordinance to that which had been reversed in Kenya on instruction from Whitehall. The origins of the ordinance lay in an another ultra vires ruling by a Tanganyika magistrate against existing antivagrancy legislation (Township Rule 136) in 1941, of which, in the face of accelerating urbanization and emerging problems of overpopulation and unemployment, officials at this time made increased use. In an unusually frank appraisal of such legislation, Justice McRoberts ruled the bylaw "unjust and oppressive." It rendered "any African . . . subject to expulsion without process of law, without appeal, and without lawful reason" and thereby represented "a gratuitous interference with the rights of the subject who is entitled to travel where he will throughout the country, and to use the public roads for passage wherever they are established."[67] Such concerns about African civil liberties were incomprehensible to most officials, among whom there existed a firm consensus on the urgent need for increasing the powers available to them for dealing with the surplus population. Indeed, the ruling turned out to be an aberration. Less than a month afterwards, a new Removal of Undesirable Natives regulation was passed in Dar es Salaam under the Emergency Powers (Defense) Act. These reinstated a district commissioner's ability to repatriate any African he considered undesirable. The ability to remove unwanted residents was increasingly central to urban governance, and in June 1941 the new legislation was extended to cover all ten major urban centers in Tanganyika.[68]

Despite the reintroduction of repatriation legislation, officials soon complained about its inefficacy. What was required, many argued, was a more comprehensive solution addressing African mobility. Starting in 1943 a vigorous debate was conducted among officials at all levels of the colonial administration, from district officers to Whitehall mandarins, over the best means of controlling accelerated rural-urban migration.[69] In effect, any machinery to restrict African movement within Tanganyika amounted to a pass system. With the situation in the towns rapidly deteriorating, thanks partly to the return of growing numbers of demobilized soldiers, it was argued that such a move should be contemplated. After prolonged discussion about suitable legislation, the Removal of Undesirable Natives Ordinance was introduced in early 1944. According to an accompanying legal memo, the bill was "considered necessary in the interests both of the natives themselves and of orderly life within [the townships]."[70] While the ordinance provided a stricter definition of who may be deemed an undesirable than previous legislation, it remained broad enough to include a good proportion of the urban African population. Any laborer engaged in casual employment could be classed as undesirable, as well as Africans who had arrived in town within the current tax year or who had not paid municipal poll tax the previous year. More-over, the governor indicated to the secretary of state that the bill was just the "first installment of legislation of a more drastic character which will be required to deal with post-war conditions."[71] However, Colonial Office opposition to what one critical official deemed a "walled city policy" prevented the enactment of additional controls.[72] While concern over conditions in Dar es Salaam was widely felt, in the end political considerations arising from Tanganyika's United Nations mandate status ruled out the introduction of any legisla-tion that resembled southern African or Kenyan pass laws.

After the war, in the absence of more comprehensive legislation, urban officials continued to rely on the Removal of Undesirable Na-tives Ordinance. As more and more Africans found their way to the capital, repatriation became increasingly common.[73] Despite its util-ity, the ordinance continued to attract criticism. The chief secretary in 1946 acknowledged that any "severe application of the law or any extension of the control of movement of persons, would be an inva-sion of the liberty of the subject."[74] Officials in Whitehall remained distinctly uneasy. After Kenya was forced to repeal the ordinance in 1946, Creech Jones, the Colonial Secretary, urged the repeal of the equivalent ordinance in Tanganyika.[75] The Tanganyika government was instructed to consult with Kenya over the terms of a new ordi-nance to replace it.[76] In response to these criticisms the application of the ordinance was, in January 1947, restricted to six major townships: Dar es Salaam, Morogoro, Tanga, Korogwe, Moshi, and Arusha. How-ever, this remained the extent of the action taken by officials, who, appearing to stall for time, failed to respond to further Colonial Office correspondence on the issue after a revised ordinance was passed in Kenya in 1949.[77]

If these were indeed delaying tactics, then the motivation be-hind them is readily apparent. Tanganyika's towns were undergoing unprecedented growth at this time, placing serious strains on urban administrations. Between 1940 and 1948, Dar es Salaam's African population increased by 50 percent, and over the following decade the territorial African urban population grew by as much as 83 per-cent.[78] Concern over rural-urban migration reemerged with particular force after a violent strike in 1950 in Dar es Salaam.[79] Heightened public awareness of urban lawlessness also led to growing demands to tackle the "surplus" urban population. "No law-abiding citizen," wrote the editor of the *Tanganyika Standard* in March 1950, "will oppose any step taken to eliminate all doubtful characters from our midst . . . the faster these undesirables of no fixed abode or occupation are sent out of town and back to their own villages, the [better]."[80] Despite Colonial Office anxiety about the ordinance, the Tanganyikan administration refused to concede on the issue. In his eventual reply to correspondence from London, Colonial Secretary Surridge dismissed concerns over the liberty of the colonial subject, because "methods of control which might not be justifiable in normal times should be allowed."[81] In 1952, Governor Twining requested permission from the Colonial Office to extend the application of the ordinance to three more towns: Mwanza, Musoma, and Shinyanga.[82] Faced with persistent defense of the ordinance, the Colonial Office conceded it could remain on the statute books as long as its racially discriminatory nature and unfair appeals structure were amended. A revised ordinance aimed against undesirable "persons" was duly passed in July 1953, though it continued to be applied solely against Africans.

The acceleration of urban migration and the deterioration of housing, health, and living conditions in East Africa's urban centers spurred colonial officials to expand their powers to control African migration. In Tanganyika, having fought for and retained the undesirables ordinance, and in light of increasing African migration, officials implemented it with increasing force and frequency in the course of the 1950s. In Kenya fears of "detribalization," uncontrolled migration, urban criminality, and political unrest were made manifest in the emergence of the violent conflict with Mau Mau. Strengthened with logistical and financial support during the state of emergency declared in 1952, the Kenyan administration used many of the same strategies it had used for vagrants and urban control to manage the conflict with Mau Mau. What East Africans witnessed in the 1950s was removal, repatriation, and detention orchestrated on an unparalleled level.

Spivs and Mau Mau in 1950s East Africa

The labor demands of an expatriate agricultural sector, coupled with uncontrolled urban migration in the interwar and postwar periods, transformed Kenya's use of vagrancy law, and so too did the emergency of the 1950s. To many officials, Mau Mau was proof that poverty, urban life, and migratory labor had corrupted Kenyan society. In fact, the Mau Mau movement was a response, in part, to the growing disenfranchisement among the Kikuyu, the most populous ethnic group in Kenya and the group most entwined in the colonial economy. In the main they labored on the European estates in Rift Valley Province, provided labor for the farms of chiefs and well-to-do Kikuyu on the Central Province reserves, and made up the bulk of Nairobi's African population. The poverty and growing frustration among many Kikuyu compelled them to lash out at their wealthier brethren, European farmers, and the colonial state itself.[83] Organized violence began to take place throughout Central Province and nearby urban centers in the late 1940s, and the colonial government stepped in to quash it. In 1952 the Kenyan administration declared a state of emergency and began a campaign to eradicate the Mau Mau movement. Rift Valley officials, placating European settler anxieties, began rounding up thousands of Kikuyu who had been laboring on European farms. They were placed in transit camps from which twenty-five hundred per week were repatriated.[84] The government also began military operations to eliminate the military arm of Mau Mau. Infused with emergency funding and military support, the colonial regime began a series of military campaigns in the forests of Central Province, where Mau Mau fighters had taken refuge.[85] Furthermore, by 1953 officials had realized that Nairobi was an integral part of the Mau Mau effort, particularly for gathering information and supplies. Indeed, it was within the eastern slums of Nairobi and among outcast Kikuyu that Mau Mau had taken root.[86]

To meet the challenge in the capital city and elsewhere in Kenya, Governor Baring's administration relied on a series of emergency regulations. The Emergency Movement of Kikuyu and Control of Kikuyu Labor Regulations, gazetted in 1952, provided the state with the power to forcibly remove suspected Mau Mau and their sympathizers from Nairobi. Armed with these powers, police and military forces began encircling African townships, rounding up suspect Kikuyu and repatriating them back to their reserves. Many of those arrested were unemployed Africans, of the sort normally arrested for vagrancy and pass law offences. The government repatriated "most of the Kikuyu population living outside the reserves" back to their home areas and confined tens of thousands of suspected Mau Mau operatives in detention camps.[87] The long ineffective policy of repatriation, the primary vehicle to remove vagrants from Nairobi since the city's birth, became the key to rooting out Mau Mau. Operation Anvil took removal and repatriation to an unparalleled level. On April 23, 1954, Nairobi was surrounded by military and police forces and over the course of the next three weeks fifty thousand Africans were interrogated.[88] Anvil cut off Mau Mau operating in the forest from the supplies obtained in Nairobi and severely damaged the group's ability to sustain the conflict. Yet Operation Anvil failed to keep Kikuyu and other ethnic groups out of Nairobi. The massive repatriation scheme caused an extreme labor shortage, which only encouraged African laborers to migrate to the city.[89] Within weeks of the operation, officials had already begun to complain about the rise in crime and vagrancy, particularly among juveniles whose families had been placed in detention or killed.

To manage the problem of juvenile vagrancy, the Kenyan government developed a system known as the juvenile pipeline, the most comprehensive strategy to combat vagrancy in the colony's history. In 1957 the state began to construct juvenile reception centers where repatriated young people could be remanded while officials determined where they were to be sent. Some juveniles were returned immediately to their homes, but recidivist vagrants (those arrested for vagrancy more than once), orphans, and criminals were institutionalized.[90] Many juveniles were sent to youth camps, which had been previously designed to "rehabilitate" hardcore juvenile Mau Mau adherents. Youth camps offered education, but also an intense program of citizenship training to transform Mau Mau fighters into loyal subjects. While hundreds of juvenile vagrants and orphans learned the importance of Empire Day and the glories of British history, other juvenile migrants were returned home and placed in youth clubs.[91] Youth clubs were established as a late addition to the villagization scheme. It was hoped that if some level of education and labor were given to young people in the villages, they would remain there rather than return to Nairobi. Youth clubs initially offered skills-training courses in blacksmithing, husbandry, agriculture, and leatherwork.[92] To officials, the juvenile pipeline became a critical resource in continually rounding up and removing young vagrants from Kenya's cities and trying to secure them in the home areas. The pipeline, which could have been created only under the financial and logistical boom of the emergency, had became so critical to the regime's battle with vagrancy that after the emergency ended in 1960, it was embedded in the amended Vagrancy Ordinance of 1960.

While the Mau Mau emergency meant that conditions in Nairobi of the 1950s were exceptional, accelerating urban growth caused considerable administrative problems to colonial officials in other parts of East Africa. Rising crime rates in Ugandan urban centers led to demands for legislation similar to that enacted in response to urban problems in Kenya and Tanganyika since the war. In a 1950 debate in the Ugandan legislative council, H. R. Fraser, an unofficial member, called for the introduction of an "'anti-spiv' ordinance, similar to that in Kenya [to] clean up some of the notorious areas where these rogues . . . congregate." This he believed would counter the increasing incidence of theft in the territory. However, while the chief secretary considered this ordinance "a pleasant sounding piece of legislation," after consultation with provincial commissioners, the conclusion was reached that the political organization of Uganda complicated a policy of roundups and repatriations, and Fraser's suggestion was rebuffed.[93]

By contrast, in Tanganyika, through application of the Removal of Undesirable Persons Ordinance, roundups and repatriations became a cornerstone of urban policy. The Dar es Salaam–based secretariat received requests from provincial officials throughout the territory, concerned about conditions in urban centers under their watch, for application of the ordinance to be extended to these townships. In

1953 it was applied to Bukoba to control the large numbers of undesirables coming to town from nearby southern Uganda.[94] The following year the commissioner of Eastern Province, in (successfully)
requesting extension of the ordinance to Kilosa, complained of the
"very considerable 'floating population' of undesirables not gain-
fully employed who use the towns as refuges and engage in crime."[95]
By 1955 the ordinance was in force in as many as twenty townships
throughout Tanganyika.[96] Urban officials enthusiastically applied the
legislation to rid their towns of undesirables. Drives in Mwanza on
June 15 and 16, 1954, for example, resulted in the screening of as many
as five hundred suspect individuals, of whom over one hundred were
repatriated.[97] However, it was in the capital where the escalation in
"spiv raids" was most pronounced. By 1955 almost 10 percent of Dar
es Salaam's African population, which then stood at around eighty
thousand, were screened in the course of raids aimed at rounding up
and repatriating undesirables. In both 1957 and 1958, by which time
spiv raids were a daily occurrence, over two thousand Africans were
repatriated from the town. Most of the victims were young Africans
either looking for work or engaged in informal employment. In his
memoir of colonial service, C. C. Harris, the official responsible for
an escalation in raids from the mid-1950s, recognized the injustice of
repatriations, but concluded that public-order imperatives necessitated
such action: "Hard and sometimes unsympathetic—unfair even—
this culling of the wahuni might have seemed. In reality they were
often young pioneers of the African population, leaving home in
their dissatisfaction with the futureless subsistence agricultural economy of the rural areas. However, . . . law and order, as well as internal
security, could only be ensured by controlling the numbers of wahuni
present in the town to indulge in petty theft and similar offences
against property and person."[98]

Action taken by Harris and his successors represented an unprecedented degree of force in Dar es Salaam's administration. It
was sustained up to around 1960, when the raids appear to have
lapsed as a result of political agitation by the Tanganyika African National Union, who were to assume power from the British the following year.[99] In TANU, those on the margins of Dar es Salaam society

saw the hope of release from a colonial regime that had become ever more coercive in the course of the decade. Such hopes were soon dashed. In the case of urban policy the colonial legacy was particularly marked. Faced with ongoing rapid urbanization, the incoming regime soon resorted to a familiar policy of roundups and repatriations.[100]

Just as contemporary observers conflated the images of English and African vagrants, the British government and its imperial appendages used vagrancy regulations in similar ways. One could dismiss as administrative expedience the fact that vagrancy laws in the Great Britain and its empire shared legislative DNA. Yet vagrancy policies had proven long-standing, tried-and-true policies to manage social and economic processes taking place in Europe and elsewhere. Vagrancy laws were part of a package of labor regulations designed either to compel or to curb entrance into the wage labor market as well as restrict human movement. As has been shown in several chapters in this volume, vagrancy took on particular potency in urban settings; this was especially true in British East Africa. As vagrants became associated with urban criminality, moral degeneration, poverty, and squalor, their presence in urban settings unnerved middle and upper classes, and moves were made to cast them out.

Although the case of British East Africa harmonizes with these shared global experiences, there are profound differences. In British East Africa vagrancy regulations were used to preserve colonial notions of African social order. By denying Africans stable and secure urban lives, colonial officials believed they could prevent the disintegration of "traditional" African social structures. Vagrancy laws served to buttress the social and political dimensions of colonialism: the authority of men over households and chiefs over communities pivotal to indirect rule as well as the paramountcy of rural life in an agricultural colonial economy. Another crucial difference is the parsimony of government capacity, which limited the intrusiveness of the colonial state in the lives of the homeless and unemployed. With the exception of Kenya during the emergency of the 1950s, the colonial regimes simply could not cope with the sheer numbers of migratory Africans as well as urban homeless and unemployed. Roundups and repatriations could not circumvent financial and logistical inadequacies and obscure the need for costly urban-housing and welfare programs. Ultimately, the regulation of vagrancy reveals the colonial state's persistent struggle to manage its own incapacities as well as the social and economic forces it had wrought in East Africa.

Notes

CO	Colonial Office
DC	District Commissioner
KNA	Kenya National Archives
PC	Provincial Commissioner
BNA	British National Archives
TNA	Tanzania National Archives
UNA	Uganda National Archives

1. Quoted in Andrew Lees, *Cities Perceived: Urban Society in European and American Thought, 1820–1940* (Manchester, UK: Manchester University Press, 1985), 28.

2. Colony and Protectorate of Kenya, Crime Committee Report (Nairobi: Government Printer, 1932), 2.

3. See, for example, Luise White, *The Comforts of Home: Prostitution in Colonial Nairobi* (Berkeley: University of California Press, 1990); Robert J. Gordon, "Vagrancy, Law and 'Shadow Knowledge': Internal Pacification, 1915–1939," in *Namibia under South African Rule: Mobility and Containment, 1915–46*, ed. Patricia Hayes et al. (London: James Currey, 1998); Simon Heap, "Jaguda Boys: Pickpocketing in Ibadan, 1930–60," *Urban History* 24, no. 3 (1997); Andrew Burton, *African Underclass: Urbanisation, Crime, and Colonial Order in Dar es Salaam* (Athens: Ohio University Press, 2005).

4. See also Richard Allen's previous work on the subject: Allen, "Indian Immigrants and the Legacy of Marronage: Illegal Absence, Desertion and Vagrancy in Mauritius, 1835–1900," *Itinerario* 21, no. 1 (1997): 98–110.

5. Paul Lovejoy and Jan Hogendorn, *Slow Death for Slavery: The Course of Abolition in Northern Nigeria* (Cambridge: Cambridge University Press, 1993), 84–87. For francophone West Africa and the use of vagrancy in a similar way, see Martin Klein, *Slavery and Colonial Rule in French West Africa* (Cambridge: Cambridge University Press, 1998).

6. See Gordon, "Vagrancy, Law"; Jeremy Martens, "Polygamy, Sexual Danger and the Creation of Vagrancy Legislation in Colonial Natal," *Journal of Imperial and Commonwealth History* 31, no. 3 (2003): 24–45. For South Africa more generally, also see B. H. Kinkead-Weekes, *A History of Vagrancy in Cape Town* (Cape Town: SALDRU, School of Economics, University of Cape Town, 1984).

7. East Africa Protectorate, Ordinances and Regulations, vol. 2 (Mombasa: Government Printer, 1900), art. 1.

8. Ibid., arts. 2–4, 6–7.

9. Anthony Clayton and Donald C. Savage, *Government and Labour in Kenya, 1895–1963* (London: Frank Cass, 1974), 21.

10. M. P. K Sorrenson, *Land Reform in the Kikuyu Country* (London: Oxford University Press, 1967), 18.

11. Senior Commissioner of Nyanza to District Commissioner of Central Kavirondo, January 5, 1925, KNA PC/NZA/3/20/17/1.

12. Sharon Stichter, *Migrant Labour in Kenya: Capitalism and African Response* (Harlow, UK: Longman, 1982), 17, 30.

13. R. M. A. Van Zwanenberg with Anne King, *An Economic History of Kenya and Uganda, 1800–1970* (London: Macmillan, 1975), 4–5; Memorandum, Native Taxation—Tax Defaulters and Forced Labour, 1932, BNA CO/795/52.

14. David M. Anderson, "Master and Servant in Colonial Kenya," *Journal of African History* 41, no. 3 (2000): 462–65; and Clayton and Savage, 30.

15. Clayton and Savage, *Government and Labour*, 51.

16. Colony and Protectorate of Kenya, "No. 9 Vagrancy Ordinance, February 11, 1920," Ordinances and Regulations (Nairobi: Government Printer, 1921), sec. 2.

17. Ibid., secs. 4, 6, 9. While adults were imprisoned and forced to work under the Vagrancy Ordinance of 1920, juveniles were immediately repatriated back home, and in cases of recidivism, they would be caned. Ibid., secs. 14, 16. However, magistrates across Kenya had difficulty determining the age of juveniles brought before them. This confusion often resulted in their remand or imprisonment alongside adults, even for crimes such as vagrancy. W. B. Brook, Magistrate, Nyanza, to Senior Commissioner of Nyanza, July 17, 1926, KNA PC/NZA/3/17/15.

18. Antony Alcock, *History of the International Labour Organization* (London: Macmillan, 1971), 89–94.

19. "The Vagrancy Ordinance, 1929," Forced Labour, Report of Colonial Office Committee, May 1929, Twelfth International Labour Conference, Geneva, May 20–June 22, 1929, app. 5, 52, BNA CO 795/29/10.

20. R. G. Somervell at Ministry of Labour to J. J. Paskin at Colonial Office, November 24, 1931, BNA CO 323/1117/11.

21. Uganda, Zanzibar, Northern Rhodesia, Brunei, Hong Kong, Johore, Kedah, Sarawak, and the Straights Settlements were all linked to Kenya in this way. BNA CO 323/1117/11, letters dated November 24–27, 1931; December 11, 1931; January 5, 1932; February 15, 1932.

22. Ibid.

23. Memorandum Regarding Vagrancy Legislation of Kenya, May 1929, BNA CO 533/389/9. Officials from other colonies denied the legislation was used to force Africans to work; they stated it was used principally against European destitutes, who were forced to work or returned to their countries of origin. For Zambia, see, for example, J. C. Maxwell, Governor, to J. F. N. Green, Colonial Office, February 4, 1930, BNA CO 795/29/10; for Zanzibar, see letter dated February 15, 1932, BNA CO 323/1117/11. For information on vagrancy legislation in colonial India, particularly its role in managing European vagrants, see David Arnold, "European Orphans and Vagrants in India in the Nineteenth Century," *Journal of Imperial and Commonwealth History* 7, no. 2 (1979): 104–27; Arnold, "White Colonization and Labor in Nineteenth-Century India," *Journal of Imperial and Commonwealth History* 11, no. 2 (1983): 133–58. We thank Hannah Weiss for this insight.

24. Colony and Protectorate of Kenya, Native Affairs Department, Annual Report, 1927, 57–58.

25. Colony and Protectorate of Kenya, Native Affairs Department, Annual Report, 1930, 74. There is a significant gendered element to vagrancy that must be explored briefly. Vagrancy was the crime of an idle male; very few women or girls arrested for vagrancy emerge from the colonial record. In Kenya the gender divide among visible vagrants was a consequence of both rural and urban lifestyles but also of biases built into the colonial system. The lack of vagrant women cannot be argued exclusively because Kenyan women simply stayed home in the rural areas under the control of male colonial and tribal officials. Many young women, particularly under the age of sixteen, left for Nairobi and found work as domestic servants, prostitutes, beer brewers, and urban wives. In the 1920s some young women were arrested along Nairobi's River Road for prostitution and vagrancy, but as the male population on the street increased, arrests of prostitutes dwindled. An urban girl on the street proved more productive and less dangerous to urban order than her male counterpart. Through the eyes of colonial officials, young men represented a threat to the urban order of Nairobi and the wider stability of colonial

rule. See White, *Comforts of Home*, 158; Bodil Frederiksen, "African Women and Their Colonisation of Nairobi: Representation and Realities," in *The Urban Experience in Eastern Africa, c. 1750–2000*, ed. Andrew Burton (Nairobi: British Institute in Eastern Africa, 2002).

26. For an excellent case study of British indirect rule, see Karen E. Fields, *Revival and Rebellion in Colonial Africa* (Princeton, NJ: Princeton University Press, 1985).

27. Most notably in the shape of colonial taxes, which were levied at rates for the rural areas from which workers originated rather than those for the areas in which they resided while in employment; in addition, registration legislation bound employees to their home areas. For comparisons between nineteenth-century Britain and colonial East Africa, see Burton, *African Underclass*, 17–20.

28. Bruce Berman and John Lonsdale, *Unhappy Valley: Conflict in Kenya and Africa* (Oxford: James Currey, 1992), 238.

29. It is remarkable how similar the perceptions among many British colonial officials to urban life in Africa resembled discussion in late nineteenth-century Britain. There is certainly an influence of urban degeneration theory operating in the conversations colonial officials were having about African urban life. To writers like Charles Masterman, the theater of the street and its multitudinous characters bred generations of young Britons unwilling to exercise restraint. The child of the town became as unnatural and uncontrollable as his environment. In short, the urban lifestyle did not have the modernizing impact that many had hoped it would. It did not turn the rural peasant into a respectable entrepreneur; rather, "civilisation works it miracles, and civilised man is turned back almost into a savage," as Alexis de Tocqueville commented during his five-week visit to Britain. For discussions of urban degeneration theory and British anxiety over the effects of urban life on its own rural populations, see Lees, *Cities Perceived;* Charles Masterman, ed., *The Heart of the Empire* (Brighton, UK: Harvester Press, 1973); Gareth Stedman Jones, *Outcast London* (Oxford: Clarendon, 1971). For the quote from Tocqueville, see Asa Briggs, *Victorian Cities* (London: Odhams, 1963), 68.

30. Report by Maj. G. St. J. Orde Browne on Labour in Tanganyika Territory, 56, PRO CO 691/83. For regional expressions of corresponding sentiments, see 1933 Mombasa District AR, 5, KNA DC/MSA/1/4; for Nairobi, *East African Standard (EAS)*, April 16, 1927, 7; for Uganda, Governor W. F. Gowers to S. S. Col, March 27, 1927, UNA A46/2671; for Tanga, Tanganyika Territory, Report by E. C. Baker on Social and Economic Conditions in the Tanga Province (Dar es Salaam, 1934), 16; for

Dar es Salaam, Andrew Burton, *African Underclass: Urbanisation, Crime and Colonial Order in Dar es Salaam* (Athens: Ohio University Press, 2005), 70–72.

31. Official awareness of the income-earning opportunities offered by what later came to be known as the informal sector was at this stage negligible at best, though it apparently offered important sustenance to urban Africans, including many who struggled to survive on generally inadequate formal-sector wages. For the informal sector in colonial Dar es Salaam, see Burton, *African Underclass*, 53–63, 65–71; for Nairobi, Claire Robertson, *Trouble Showed the Way: Women, Men, and Trade in the Nairobi Area, 1890–1990* (Bloomington: Indiana University Press, 1997).

32. Superintendent of Police, Busoga, to Commissioner of Police, Uganda, October 29, 1922; Chief Secretary to Commissioner of Police, October 15, 1924, UNA A46/2671.

33. TNA 54, Dar es Salaam District AR, 1924, 6.

34. Andrew Hake, *African Metropolis: Nairobi's Self-Help City* (London: Chatto and Windus, 1977), 23–26.

35. Mary Parker, *Political and Social Aspects of the Development of Municipal Government in Kenya with Special Reference to Nairobi* (London: Colonial Office, 1947). I have taken the average of four figures that Parker gives for 1906. These are the Bransby Williams report, annual medical report, census, and Fleetham report.

36. Hake, *African Metropolis*, 26.

37. Robert Gordon in his work on vagrancy in Namibia focuses on the role of European settlers regarding government's preoccupation with underemployed Africans. He argues that vagrancy policy and practice served as a "massive local anaesthetic," effectively sedating the colonizer's worst psychological and economic insecurities. Gordon, "Vagrancy, Law," 75.

38. Robert W. Foran, *The Kenya Police, 1887–1960* (London: R. Hale, 1962), 32

39. Colony and Protectorate of Kenya, Native Affairs Department Annual Report, 1920, 1932 (Nairobi 1931, 1933), 83 and 120, respectively.

40. Ibid., 41.

41. Ibid., Native Affairs Department, Annual Report, 1931 (Nairobi, 1932), 82.

42. David M. Anderson, "Policing, Prosecution and the Law in Colonial Kenya," in *Policing and Decolonisation: Politics, Nationalism and the Police, 1917–65*, ed. David M. Anderson and David Killingray (Manchester, UK: Manchester University Press, 1992), 192–93.

43. Colony and Protectorate of Kenya, Crime Committee Report, May 1932 (Nairobi, 1932), 39.

44. Specific bylaws used to this end include 187, 195, and 193, as well as law CAP 82 of 1931.

45. Paul Ocobock, "Joy Rides for Juveniles: Vagrant Youth and Colonial Control in Nairobi, 1901–1952," Social History 31, no. 1 (2006): 52–54; T. C. Carlisle, Native Affairs Officer, to Labour Commissioner, Nairobi, June 4, 1941, KNA ABK/12/68.

46. P. de V. Allen, Labour Commissioner, to Native Affairs Officer, June 5, 1941, KNA ABK/12/68.

47. D. C. Cameron, Superintendent of Approved Schools, to Chief Inspector of Approved Schools, October 27, 1945, KNA AP/1/1700.

48. Quotes from Governor W. F. Gowers to Secretary of State for the Colonies, March 27, 1927, UNA A46/2671.

49. Superintendent of Police, Busoga, to Commissioner of Police, Uganda, October 29, 1922, UNA A46/2671.

50. Amery to Governor, Uganda Protectorate, August 19, 1925, UNA A46/2671.

51. Quotes from Attorney General to CS, October 5, 1925, UNA A46/2671.

52. Labour Annual Report, 1927, para.177, BNA CO 736.

53. For a discussion of this legislation and its application, see Burton, African Underclass, 76–81.

54. Although an identification ordinance was passed in 1935, according to Issa G. Shivji, concerns that it would invite "harsh criticism from abroad" for being racially discriminatory (alongside its potential cost) prevented its implementation. Shivji, Law, State and the Working Class in Tanzania (Dakar, Senegal: CODESRIA, 1986), 99, 105–6.

55. For Dar es Salaam, see Burton, African Underclass, ch. 7.

56. See Andrew Burton, "Raw Youth, School-Leavers and the Emergence of Structural Unemployment in Late-Colonial Urban Tanganyika," Journal of African History 47, no. 3 (2006): 199–216.

57. For a brief discussion of these migrants, see Burton, "Urbanisation in Eastern Africa: An Historical Overview, c. 1750–2000," in The Urban Experience in Eastern Africa, c.1750–2000, ed. Burton (Nairobi: BIEA, 2002), 20–21. Also published as a special edition of Azania 36–37 (2001–2).

58. Burton, African Underclass, 30–31.

59. For a useful discussion, see R. D. Pearce, Turning Point in Africa: British Colonial Policy, 1938–1948 (London: Frank Cass, 1982).

60. Memo by Attorney-General, Uganda, January 4, 1941, BNA CO 859/79/8; for further legal reports on the 1940 law, see BNA CO 859/79.

61. Burton, *African Underclass*, 29.

62. Frederick Cooper, *On the African Waterfront: Urban Disorder and the Transformation of Work in Colonial Mombasa* (New Haven, CT: Yale University Press, 1987), 76–77.

63. David W. Throup, *Economic and Social Origins of Mau Mau, 1945–53* (London: James Currey, 1987), 192.

64. Changes were also made to the Vagrancy Ordinance of 1920, augmenting the powers of the state. The revisions, similar to the amendment passed in Uganda two decades earlier, enabled the state to arrest anyone without proof of employment. As a result, unless Africans had their pass on hand for a police officer to see, they could be arrested. Scott to Rogers, November 30, 1950, BNA CO 691/208/42431.

65. Colony and Protectorate of Kenya, Ordinances, 1940, "No. 7, Amendment, Vagrancy Ordinance, No.7," April 28, 1941, sec. 2.

66. For the often problematic relationship between the judiciary and the administration, see H. F. Morris and James S. Read, *Indirect Rule and the Search for Justice: Essays in East African Legal History* (Oxford: Clarendon, 1972)

67. *Tanganyika Standard*, March 14, 1941, 10.

68. Burton, *African Underclass*, 105.

69. See correspondence in the following files: TNA 28685; TNA 21616; BNA CO 691/184/42431; BNA CO 691/185/42431; BNA CO 691/191/42431; BNA CO 691/208/42431.

70. "Objects and reasons" accompanying draft bill, BNA CO 691/185/42431.

71. Jackson to Secretary of State for the Colonies, November 15, 1943, BNA CO 691/185/42431.

72. Min., October 13, 1944, TNA 28685.

73. See Burton, *African Underclass*, 251, table 12.1.

74. TNA 20887/vol. 2, Legco questions, July 25, 1946.

75. TNA 21616/vol. 3, quoted in memo 68, May 6, 1952.

76. Scott to Rogers, November 30, 1950, BNA CO 691/208/42431.

77. Letters in February and April 1950 from Whitehall were ignored, BNA CO 691/208/42431.

78. Burton, *African Underclass*, 194; C. J. Martin, "Estimates of Population Growth in East Africa, with Special Reference to Tanganyika and Zanzibar," in *Essays on African Population*, ed. K. M. Barbour and R. M. Prothero (London: Routledge, 1961), 56.

79. See Burton, *African Underclass*, 188–89.

80. *Tanganyika Standard*, March 18, 1950, 21.

81. Surridge to Rogers, January 4, 1951, TNA 21616/vol. 3.

82. Twining to Rogers, November 21, 1952, TNA 21616/vol 3.

83. For more general works on Mau Mau, see David M. Anderson, *Histories of the Hanged: The Dirty War in Kenya and the End of Empire* (New York: Norton, 2005); Caroline Elkins, *Imperial Reckoning: The Untold Story of Britain's Gulag in Kenya* (New York: Owl Books, 2005); Tabitha Kanogo, *Squatters and the Roots of Mau Mau* (London: James Currey, 1987); E. S. Atieno Odhiambo and John Lonsdale, eds., *Mau Mau and Nationhood* (Athens: Ohio University Press, 2003).

84. Caroline Elkins, "Detention, Rehabilitation and the Destruction of Kikuyu Society," in Odhiambo and Lonsdale, *Mau Mau*, 196.

85. David M. Anderson, "The Battle of Dandora Swamp," in Odhiambo and Lonsdale, *Mau Mau*, 160.

86. Anderson, *Histories of the Hanged*, ch. 5.

87. Elkins, "Detention, Rehabilitation," 194.

88. Anderson, "Battle of Dandora Swamp," 161.

89. City Council of Nairobi, Annual Report, 1954, 44, KNA RN/13/28.

90. Acting Secretary of Community Development, "Proposed Place of Safety—Nairobi," February 10, 1957, KNA AB/2/70; "Juvenile Reception Centers, Fort Hall," October 1957, KNA AB/2/74; District Commissioner, Kiambu, "Juvenile Remand Home—Kiambu," February 20, 1957, KNA AB/2/77.

91. Officer-in-Charge, Monthly Report, April 4, 1956, KNA AB/1/116; KNA V1/21/3; Wamumu Approved School and Youth Camp, Annual Report for 1956; Colony and Protectorate of Kenya, Annual Report of the Ministry of Community Development, 1956 (Nairobi, 1957), 40–41.

92. C. F. Atkins, Acting Permanent Secretary of Community Development, May 7, 1958, KNA AB/16/13; Colony and Protectorate of Kenya, Ministry of Community Development Annual Report, 1958 (Nairobi, 1959), 9.

93. Legislative Council Minutes (copies in UNA Library), January 5–6, 1950.

94. Provincial Supt., Lake Province to PC, Lake, December 2, 1953, TNA 21616/vol. 3.

95. EP to MLG [Eastern Province to Minister of local Government], January 11, 1955, TNA 225/80070 PC.

96. Dodoma, Morogoro, Kilosa, Arusha, Moshi, Lindi, Mtwara, Mikindani, Nachingwea, Mbeya, Iringa, Korogwe, Tanga, Mwanza, Musoma,

Shinyanga, Bukoba, Tabora, Kigoma, Ujiji, and the Municipality of Dar es Salaam. Government Notice 130 of 1955.

97. Commissioner of Police to Chief Secretary, June 19, 1954, TNA 34184.

98. C. C. Harris, *Donkey's Gratitude: Twenty-two Years in the Growth of a New African Nation, Tanzania* (Edinburgh: Pentland, 1992). *Wahuni* (sing. *mhuni*) derives from the Arabic for outcast. In Tanganyika it came to mean vagabond or, later, hooligan. From the 1940s it was used by officials to refer to the growing numbers of unemployed, underemployed, and nefariously employed young male Africans who, from the colonial point of view, cluttered the streets of Tanganyika's urban centers. See introduction to Burton, *African Underclass.*

99. For a detailed account see Burton, *African Underclass,* ch. 12.

100. See Andrew Burton, "The Haven of Peace Purged: Tackling the Undesirable and Unproductive Poor in Dar es Salaam, 1950s–1960s," *International Journal of African Historical Studies* 40, no. 1 (2007): 119–51.

11

Thought Reform

The Chinese Communists and the Reeducation of Beijing's Beggars, Vagrants, and Petty Thieves

Aminda M. Smith

China's colonial and semi-colonial status created a vast number of unemployed people in both the countryside and in the cities. Having no legitimate way to make a living, they were forced, against their will, to seek a living through illegitimate professions. This is the origin of bandits, hooligans, beggars. . . . We must be adept at reforming them.

—*Mao Zedong, 1939*

WHEN THE CHINESE Communists succeeded in their national revolution in the late 1940s and early 1950s, they launched a series of efforts to transform the "trash" from the "old society" into "useful laborers."[1] Zhao Jinghe, a homeless beggar with tuberculosis, was included among the "trash." In November 1951 the forty-nine-year-old was apprehended in Beijing and sent to a municipal reeducation center to undergo "thought reform." On July 3, 1953, after two and a half years of forcible internment, Zhao cut his own throat in the institution's hospital ward. According to the staff on duty, as the former mendicant drew the knife across his neck he stood on his bed and cried, "Interned comrades! My committing suicide is not for me as an individual. I do it for all of us!" While the orderlies carried him out of the building, transporting him to a larger hospital, the suicidal internee allegedly continued to shout: "Every one of you, heighten your vigilance! I am your example. In the future do not express your opinion!" Zhao survived his self-inflicted knife wound, but he paid a price for what reeducation center staff called his "attempt to punish the cadres" and to "draw attention to himself." On August 15 custody of Zhao Jinghe was transferred to the Beijing Public Security Bureau, who sent him to an undisclosed location to undergo reform through forced labor.[2]

Zhao Jinghe's labor reform sentence was one of the first instances of a major shift in the way the Chinese Communists dealt with a category of individuals they termed beggars, which variously included petty thieves and pickpockets in addition to nonthieving vagrants and mendicants.[3] In 1949 the newly established central government of the People's Republic of China ordered its subordinates across the country to "intern and reform" China's beggars. This work was to occur in "reeducation through production institutes," officially subordinate to the Department of Social Relief of the Ministry of Civil Affairs.[4] In the two years that followed, administrative summaries describing rehabilitation work emphasized the primacy of education as a reform method. Lauding the efficacy of classroom instruction and small-group discussion, reeducators declared their successes in persuading large numbers of internees that begging, theft, and other "nonproductive" activities were shameful. Although the legislated goal of internment was to "ensure that members of the parasitic population engage in productive labor," reports asserted that education alone was able to convince former "parasites" that "labor was glorious" and thus, writers argued, internees were persuaded, not forced, to join work teams and participate in production.

By 1958 the Ministry of Civil Affairs no longer reeducated beggars, vagrants, or thieves. Unlike earlier directives that ordered staff to rehabilitate all individuals who stole or who solicited alms, new legislation warned that such "persons should not be considered targets for internment." According to the new regulations, units subordinate to the ministry might care for wanderers or mendicants briefly, while staff made a determination as to how to proceed, but most were to be repatriated to their hometowns or work units as soon as possible.

Ministry personnel were to transfer custody of thieves, recidivist beggars, or those who "refused to obey discipline," to local public security bureaus to undergo reform through forced labor.[5] The Ministry of Public Security became the sole agency charged with the administration of institution-based thought reform, which was to be carried out in "reeducation through labor centers." These centers were constituent units in the national penal system, and public security directives ordered reeducators to employ "the practice of labor and production" as the principal method of reform. Officially legislated policies mandated that all internees at all institutions engage in productive work and that they be forced to do so if they refused.

The new legislation still dictated that instruction was to be a component of prescribed practice, but the physical act of labor had taken precedence over education as the primary agent of reform. This radical rearticulation of policy indicated a significant and substantive change in the way the Communist government envisioned and dealt with undesirable behavior in Chinese society.

The policy changes introduced between 1949 and 1958 made those first nine years of Communist governance a defining period in the development of social control in the People's Republic. In areas where the Chinese Communists had established revolutionary bases, efforts to reform the "parasitic populations" had been in effect since at least the early 1940s. But the decade after the official takeover marked the Communists' first interaction, on a national scale, with large numbers of interned beggars, vagrants, and petty thieves.[6] Policies that were earlier devised on the basis of Maoist theory and limited rural thought reform efforts had to be frequently rethought and retooled as they were carried out in some of the world's largest metropolises. When combined with the changing demands of postrevolutionary social and economic challenges, the practical experience of scores of government agents and thousands of internees, in hundreds of different institutions across China, forced considerable reevaluations and reformulations of thought reform theory and policy, which in turn motivated substantial changes in the daily practice of reeducation.

The specific nature of this reciprocal relationship between theory, policy, and practice is well documented in administrative records from the 1950s. The records produced in Beijing allow for a particularly fruitful discussion because the capital was one of the first areas to launch these reform efforts and was often cited in national-level documents as a command center and a model for similar projects in other cities.[7] Ordered by their superiors to compile careful records, reeducation center staff submitted daily, weekly, monthly, quarterly, and yearly reports in which they claimed to be recounting all of the details of their rehabilitation work. Superiors in local, regional, and national offices offered written responses that answered questions, reprimanded mistakes, and made suggestions for the future.[8]

Like most Chinese Communist documents from this period, these texts were almost certainly prone to overstate successes and understate problems, as well as manipulate information to reinforce particular viewpoints.[9] Thus, naturally, they cannot be seen as a transparent record of actual practice in Beijing's reeducation centers. However, the surviving pieces of this internal documentation do represent crucial exchanges in a conversation in which individuals at various levels of the new government discussed and debated the elements they believed should constitute well-executed and successful reeducation efforts. The remnants of this conversation provide insights into the changing notions of ideal practice, which between 1949 and 1957 led to important changes in the very real organization and administration of Chinese Communist thought reform. A closer look at discussions about ideal practice, especially as they related to complaints about internee resistance and disobedience, can flesh out an understanding of a shift that the Communist Party's published documents have portrayed as a response to major economic stimuli.[10] I argue that the actions of beggars, vagrants, and thieves shaped one of the major social-policy issues of the modern Chinese state.

Phase One: Education and Persuasion, 1949–51

When the new government launched its thought reform efforts in 1949, it was, in many ways, continuing an effort that began long before Marxist ideology made its way to China. Despite their passionate condemnations of the groups and individuals who governed the country in the nineteenth and early twentieth centuries, the Chinese Communists shared important commonalities with their predecessors, and these commonalities were quite pronounced in the theory and practice related to the treatment of beggars, vagrants, and petty thieves. Centuries before Mao Zedong pontificated about the reasons and remedies for "social problems," other state leaders were struggling to regulate, reform, or eliminate begging, vagrancy, and petty crime. Drives to abolish or control these behaviors took place around the world during the latter centuries of the second millennium, and these efforts reached a fever pitch in the nineteenth and twentieth centuries.[11] In China a diverse cast of European, American, Japanese, and Chinese reformers and modernizers implemented scores of regulations and programs that sought to control, regulate, reform, or eradicate these so-called social problems.

Organizations, state run and otherwise, that provided aid to vagrants or mendicants have existed since at least the fifth century, and government-run shelters for the homeless poor had been established in many counties by the 1600s.[12] Some Chinese cultural traditions encourage the giving of alms to beggars, and over the centuries many people chose to do so, but the relationship of beggars to Chinese society was always a complicated one.[13] Philip Kuhn has shown how, in 1768, during the reign of the Qianlong emperor, a "mass panic" erupted in northern and central China as sorcerers were apparently roving the land, cutting off queues and stealing souls. During the inquisitionlike trials that followed, Kuhn demonstrates that rootless, wandering people, especially beggars, became the foci of social and imperial anxiety.[14]

This anxiety, according to Kuhn, was related, in part, to the growth of a floating underclass. As China's population nearly doubled in the eighteenth century, neither the contemporaneous commercial development nor increased migration could absorb the surplus labor, causing many Chinese to migrate "downward: into an underclass of beggars."[15] Rising concern about these "people without homes," who were seen as "people out of control," probably led to the numerous efforts, under the Qing, to deal with the presence of beggars on Chinese streets.[16] Both Kristin Stapleton and Lu Hanchao have discussed reforms that targeted beggars at the end of the late imperial period. Signaling the importance of attention to local specificity, however, Stapleton detailed a Chengdu project at the turn of the twentieth century that succeeded in removing nearly all mendicants from the city's streets, whereas Lu argued that the most effective measure in controlling beggars was "to endorse a grassroots institution that emerged over the centuries: beggars' self-regulated and guild-like organizations."[17]

After the 1911 revolution, as the drive to create "modern" cities continued in China, the leaders of the new republic launched a number of attempts to deal with beggars and vagrants. Zwia Lipkin has argued that the Nationalist government's concern about panhandling in Chinese cities exemplified a shift in Chinese attitudes from a view that saw mendicancy as a vocation to one that labeled the practice a social problem.[18] Lu Hanchao, on the other hand, has argued that "although begging might have been 'legal' or tolerated in pre-twentieth century China, it was always seen as a threat to orderly society and thus was subjected to official supervision and containment."[19] Despite their difference of opinion on that issue, however, Lipkin and Lu agree that attempts to deal with begging were part of a series of efforts to achieve national strength and regeneration through modernization. As Lipkin explains, the new Nationalist leaders in Nanjing saw "ragged, smelly, and dirty" beggars and vagrants as contradicting "the new image of modernity that officials had in mind,"[20] and thus the early twentieth century witnessed numerous attempts to institutionalize or otherwise deal with the appearance of beggars in Chinese cities.[21]

As many of the founding members of China's revolutionary vanguard, like Li Dazhao and Mao Zedong, were forming their theories on social reform during the first half of the twentieth century, it is not surprising that there were a number of similarities between the Communists and their predecessors in terms of both discursive and administrative approaches to dealing with beggars, vagrants, and petty thieves. While the Communists were thus indebted to other nineteenth- and early-twentieth-century reformers for much of their pre- and post-1949 ideology and policy, however, it is significant that a key element of the party's rhetoric consisted of assertions to the contrary. In 1949 North China's Ministry of Civil Affairs sent a document entitled "Data on the Beggar Problem" to their subordinates in Beijing, in which the compiler described the origin of wandering urban mendicants: "In every large city, under the long period of Japanese and Guomindang control, economic devastation caused a vast number of poor people to fall into begging."[22] The writer might have been unfairly maligning his predecessors, but the Communist penchant for blaming all of China's ills on the "old society" formed a crucial component in the rhetoric of thought reform. Dramatically worded speeches and directives, vowing to undo the damage allegedly wrought by previous regimes, launched the efforts to eradicate panhandling and petty theft across the country. Making a series of these promises in March 1949, the ministry ordered the municipal governments in its region to begin taking over preexisting poorhouses for the large-scale internments that were about to begin.[23]

The instructions from the regional leadership were somewhat unspecific. Regulations issued in March mandated that beggars and thieves, especially those who were homeless or without other means of support, be organized to perform "suitable labor."[24] Significantly, however, the rules also stressed that staff should provide education. With substantial latitude to proceed "according to their local situation," officials in the Beijing Bureau of Civil Affairs selected veteran party member Hou Shufan, a trained educator with a degree from Jianyang Normal University, to be the man in charge of all six of the city's internment institutions. Choosing a pedagogue, rather than a cadre with experience in penal administration, suggests that right from the start municipal officials envisioned education as a principle component of reform practice.

With the administrative structure in place, staff assigned to rehabilitation work spent the month of April conducting surveys of the city's vagrant and mendicant population. The information they collected led them to estimate that the capital had more than five thousand beggars, and on May 2, Beijing's police force began a roundup.[25] Although the accused were forcibly detained, staff inside the newly established reeducation centers followed their superiors' lead and strove to portray the Communist treatment of beggars as social relief, not social control. Report writers asserted that, while the goal of internment was to ensure that former "parasites" became productive laborers, staff fomented this transformation using methods that "consisted principally of education, with policing as a supplementary measure."[26] Rather than forcing internees to work, writers said, staff first gained the trust of their charges and then explained the benefits of engaging in labor, ultimately persuading reeducatees to make voluntary commitments to participate in production.

Significant portions of their reports were thus devoted to descriptions of curriculum and instructional techniques. The staff reportedly relied on a two-step method. In step one, "students" were taught a new version of China's national history. Of course, internees were not the only people relearning the past. The new Communist leadership spent the early 1950s attempting to teach the entire population of China to reinterpret the years before 1949 and to envision the postliberation future, in a manner consistent with the Communist line. When similar efforts were launched in internment institutions, reeducators employed methods that were nearly identical to those used by their comrades working in areas such as land reform, the women's movement, and labor organization.

Reports claimed that staff organized large group meetings and small group discussions where reeducators attempted to "raise consciousness" and to explain the "causes of suffering," to convince internees that life was miserable before the Communists came to power and that the Guomindang, the Japanese, and institutions like capitalism and landlordism were responsible for that misery.[27] Work summaries cited the use of descriptively titled study materials, like *Several Sufferings Caused for Us by Feudal Society and the Period of Guomindang Rule.* These were said to have been read to internees while staff completed the provision of basic literacy education for their mostly illiterate students.[28]

Although these printed materials were deemed very useful, the authors of the internal documentation claimed that their most effective educational technique involved eliciting personal stories from

the internees themselves. Students were encouraged to "speak bitterness," meaning that each was to "recount their own history of suffering
in the old society." Reeducators reportedly used internee complaints
to help "students realize the causes of their suffering" and learn to
identify "who the enemies [were.]"[29] Quotations attributed to reeducatees speaking bitterness were cited by report writers as examples of
this important element of the curriculum. An itinerant beggar named
Sun Xiangrui, for example, recalled, "In 1936, in Zhangjiakou,[30] I had
a cigarette stand. Guomindang troops stole every last bit of my stuff
and forced me to do hard labor. I dug trenches. I regularly suffered
beatings and verbal abuse. I snatched a moment and ran away to
[Beijing]. Since I didn't have any way to make a living, I roamed the
streets, begging in order to survive."[31] Other internees were credited
with similar stories, variously implicating the Nationalists, the Japanese, landlords, and "local tyrants" as their "enemies."

After articulating grievances was said to have "raised internees' consciousness," the second step in the education process pointed out that
"nonproductive" activities like "begging and theft [were] shameful"
and attempted to persuade students that performing "labor was glorious."[32] This phase in internee instruction was aimed at helping
reeducatees envision a Chinese future in which "the people" would
prosper while their "enemies" suffered. Staff again employed preprinted
pamphlets, including, *The Goal of Internment, First Suffering and
Then Happiness,* and *Production, Labor, and Living by One's Own Toil
Are Glorious; Not Laboring Is Shameful.*[33] Arguing that compassionate
care and classroom instruction alone had the power to remold minds,
writers repeatedly asserted that before internees had performed any
actual labor at all, having undergone only "ordinary" education in
the form of the two steps described above, "the mindsets of the petty
thieves and the beggars underwent a major transformation."[34]

According to reeducators, this "transformation" meant that "the
vast majority [of internees] were all willing to engage in labor and
production."[35] Commitments to that effect were often attributed
to particular individuals. Sun Xiangrui allegedly said, "When the
People's Liberation Army liberated [Beijing], the government set up
shelters to take us in, to make sure we had food, clothing, and shoes,

giving [us] new ones if [ours] were really worn out. They even helped us study. I will resolutely engage in labor and production. I will never again be a parasite on society!"[36]

Reports from 1949 and 1950 claimed that large numbers of reeducatees were thus inspired to work for the creation of a new China, and as a result, writers asserted, internees were volunteering to join work teams in droves.[37] As early as June 1949, just one month after the start of the internment efforts, one author declared that two such teams, with 124 and 138 members respectively, had gone to the Yellow River to build levies and to Inner Mongolia to build dams and reclaim wasteland.[38] Even as the report boasted the rapidity with which reeducation centers were achieving their goals, the writer stressed that all the laborers received education before they joined labor brigades: "The necessary education is carried out to ensure that they [the interned beggars] recognize that a parasitic lifestyle is shameful and without any future. After the initial raising of their consciousness, they are collectively organized into labor teams to ensure that they engage in production and live by their own toil."[39]

In addition to explicit claims, other information further helped to construct images of reeducation centers in which students spent their days studying the importance of engaging in production, but did not perform any actual labor. For example, the following timetable, designed in 1949, was reportedly used in all six of Beijing's institutions. It did not indicate that internees spent any part of their day laboring, with the possible exception of the time when they were to "tidy their dormitories."

In the first two years after the revolution, writers did, on occasion, claim that after students voiced a voluntary commitment to production, putting those internees to work could aid in their rehabilitation.[40] However, it is important to distinguish between the designation of physical labor as a secondary method, credited with the ability to further the reeducation process, and the identification of education as the primary agent of reform, or the force that was always acknowledged as the principle motivator behind initial ideological change. In 1949 and 1950 it was education, not labor, that was credited with the power to compel thought reform.

Table 11.1. Daily Schedule for Beijing Work Teams, 1949

5:00 a.m.	wake up	12:00–2:00 p.m.	afternoon nap
5:00–5:30 a.m.	tidy dormitories and bathe	2:00–4:00 p.m.	discussion
5:30–6:30 a.m.	morning exercise drills	4:00–4:30 p.m.	dinner
6:30–8:00 a.m.	study	4:30–7:00 p.m.	recreation time
8:00–9:00 a.m.	discussion meeting	7:00–9:00 p.m.	discussion
9:00–9:30 a.m.	breakfast	9:00 p.m.	roll call
9:30–10:00 a.m.	rest	9:30 p.m.	lights out
10:00 a.m.–12:00 p.m.	class		

Source: Beijing Municipal Bureau of Civil Affairs, Shourong qigai gongzuo baogao, June 1949.

Staff in reeducation centers, and their superiors in the municipal government, had a number of incentives to construct a vision of ideal practice that stressed the primacy of education and emphasized that internees engaged in production only after volunteering to do so. The use of forced labor was often invoked to criticize the way the Japanese and the Guomindang had attempted to deal with beggars and vagrants.[41] As the policies of previous regimes served as a rhetorical foil for the much more compassionate services the Communists claimed to offer, it was crucial that the new government's reform methods appeared to bear no resemblance to those of their predecessors. Furthermore, Communist Party chairman Mao Zedong had long stressed that the éléments déclassés should be "exhorted" and "persuaded" to join the revolution, rather than be compelled to do so.[42]

The fact that most "beggars" did not consent willingly to internment and rehabilitation could certainly be used to interrogate Maoist claims about the appropriate uses of coercion, but if reeducators were concerned about the possible contradictions to party doctrine presented by forcible internment, such concerns were not reflected in this administrative paperwork. Even though the time reportedly devoted to ideological reform was brief and the sincerity behind internees' commitments to labor questionable (if any internees even made such commitments), the discursive emphasis on textual study and on the avoidance of forced labor illustrates the crucial role education played in the construction of an ideal practice of thought reform between 1949 and 1950.

Phase Two: The Turn toward Forced Labor, 1951–52

There were vocal members of the government administration who continued to favor education as the core of reform practice as late as May 1951. When delegates from across the country convened in Beijing for a national conference on social welfare in the cities, Chen Qiyuan, the deputy minister of the interior, gave the opening report. Setting out the parameters for further work in the reeducation centers, Chen warned attendees against putting beggars to work without first providing the necessary instruction: "Paying attention only to production and neglecting education and reform will have a negative result. . . . [Staff must] rely on developing [internees'] enthusiasm to make them gradually arrive at living by their own toil. Otherwise, [they] will not perform well during production and the goal of labor reform will not be reached."[43]

However, while Chen Qiyuan argued forcefully for the efficacy of education, policy decisions made at the same time suggested that others disagreed. One month after Chen's speech, the Beijing municipal government revised their legislation on the treatment of beggars. Whereas the 1949 document simply noted that internees with the ability to labor should be organized into work teams after a period of instruction, the 1951 regulations stated, more strongly, that "those with labor ability must accept reform and education. Disobedience will be punished according to the seriousness of the offense."[44]

In addition to legislative revisions, other changes in the administrative paperwork hinted that at least some people were losing faith in the capacity of education to reform the most resistant "parasites." In 1951 one writer claimed outright that persuasion alone might not be capable of convincing all internees to participate in production, asserting that because the internees in a particular training program had "severely parasitic mindsets . . . forcing them to labor [would be] very necessary."[45] Although this single line was buried in pages of prose extolling the importance of study sessions and discussion, it marked the beginning of an important trend toward the condoning of forced labor as a method to be used on internees who were otherwise unwilling to produce.

As the internal documentation cited more and more examples of internees who were resistant to reform, writers seemed less and less eager to defend current reeducation techniques. A comment dated August 1952 aptly captured the reeducators' growing despair. The report implied that education alone was not proving sufficient as a reform method, stating that of 1,006 cases of theft reported in the city between January and May, a large portion were allegedly committed by petty thieves who had already undergone reeducation. The writer admitted that staff was not sure how to proceed, noting somewhat helplessly, "Although [we] have interned them [beggars and thieves] many times, they continue to appear endlessly."[46]

One senses, in these two years, a creeping frustration on the part of these administrators. Despite highly publicized claims to the contrary, the new government had not managed to rid the capital of the "beggars" it claimed were the products of the "old society." In addition to fears that such a failure might damage Communist credibility, the continued existence of these "nonproductive elements" was probably especially vexing as the Korean War continued to escalate. The Chinese had entered the war in October 1950, and during 1951 and 1952 thousands of "volunteer" troops were enmeshed in brutal battles just north of the thirty-eighth parallel. Domestic mobilization for war included nationwide campaigns encouraging people to make contributions, of both labor and money, to the Resist America and Aid Korea campaign, and the central leadership regularly emphasized the correlation between increased production and success in the war effort. Thus, it is almost certain that increased demand for wartime production played a major role in the shift toward the use of forced labor in the reeducation centers. At the same time, however, the internal records did not cite war mobilization, or weakened credibility, as factors in this decision. When writers proposed that internees should be compelled to engage in production, rather than be persuaded to volunteer, they justified that suggested policy change by arguing that some of these "nonproductive" elements were too persistently disobedient to respond to anything other than force.

Phase Three: The Birth of a Primacy of Labor, 1953–58

By 1953 reeducators were constantly lamenting their inability to manage disobedient internees. One such complaint was recorded in a report describing an effort to send a work team of 150 beggars to northeastern China. The document claimed that before their April departure, all these internees received several months of "ideological education." However, the writer claimed that "because they lived ten or more years" as vagrants, beggars, or thieves, these individuals' "parasitic mindsets [were] severe," and "they [were] not willing to engage in labor and production." Many allegedly ran away while the team was on the road, and when they arrived at their destination, the author complained, staff had to turn around and take a large group of internees back to Beijing. According to the report, the people who went back to the capital had all suddenly claimed they were suffering from tuberculosis, and under the guiding principle that internees not be asked to engage in labor if to do so might endanger their health, cadres claimed that they had no choice but to excuse self-identified consumptives from the work team. The author of this document asserted that the tuberculosis incident was an act of defiance on the part of internees who were unwilling to participate in labor and production and that work team leaders had been powerless to correct the situation.[47]

Also in 1953, as the People's Republic kicked off its first five-year plan, countrywide drives to industrialize, collectivize agriculture, and centralize administrative and political power meant that "rectifications" were carried out in most government ministries and their subordinate units.[48] In May of that year, the Ministry of the Interior issued a directive to the bureaus of civil affairs in all cities, provinces, and regions, calling for the "rectification" of all reeducation centers. Reports summarizing the findings of the nationwide investigations claimed that staff working in reform institutions had only a "vague understanding of reeducation and internment policies," and that staff "lacked suitable methods for dealing with internees." Attributing recent problems with resistant "parasites" to staff error, one rectification report claimed that when "internees made trouble," and "refused to obey discipline," reeducators "instituted crude and simplistic practices to stop [these occurrences]," and as a result "violations of law and discipline occurred."[49] The report further scolded personnel, claiming that staff regularly bound, hung, and beat internees and often incarcerated the wrong people. These and a host of other "mistakes" were allegedly causing "the masses" to say things like, "The People's Government is unreasonable; they randomly capture good people," or, "They don't do things according to Chairman Mao's policies," and even, "Reeducation centers are even worse than jails."[50]

After this national investigation and rectification effort, the Beijing Bureau of Civil Affairs issued a directive that signaled a major change in the way authorities in that bureau envisioned the ideal practice of thought reform. The directive argued that one of the major problems plaguing internment institutions was that staff did not ensure reeducatees were participating in the actual practice of labor. When former "parasites" did engage in labor, said the Bureau of Civil Affairs, it was beneficial to the reform process. "The majority of those [internees] who have gone through labor exercises were able to overcome problems and stick to the labor. Most of those who did physical labor received the work site supervisor's praise and encouragement. Some individuals were even hired on as long-term workers."[51]

In addition to arguing that personnel should "organize [reeducatees] to labor and produce, so that [internees would] receive reform through the actual practice of labor," the report also introduced another strategy that reeducators could use to deal with uncooperative or disobedient charges, noting that "internees who have received education many times but do not reform, or those who refuse to obey discipline, should be sent to the Public Security Bureau to undergo reform through forced labor."[52] The introduction of these two new methods marked a major change in the ideal practice of reeducation. For the first time, having internees engage in actual production activities was cited as an appropriate method for compelling reform. While these new methods did not explicitly permit reeducators subordinate to the Bureau of Civil Affairs to force internees to engage in work, the mandate that disobedient internees be sent to the Public Security Bureau signaled an acknowledgement that if actual labor were to be a component of reform practice, unwilling internees might need to be compelled to participate.

After the rectification, reports from inside reeducation centers reflected these changes. In June 1953 one writer complained for four pages that large numbers of internees were running away. Between February and April of that year alone, fifty-two people had reportedly escaped from a single institution. During the same period, fourteen people even managed to escape from the unit charged with caring for elderly and disabled internees.[53] While still emphasizing the importance of education as one solution to the problem, the writer also stressed that "all internees with the ability to labor" should "engage in labor and production" because "when internees do not have anything to do, they create things to do." Although the report offered confident-sounding assurances about the efficacy of actual labor, the author also noted that "those vagrants who are idlers by nature who repeatedly run away and are repeatedly interned, who will not accept labor reform can, after petitioning the Public Security Bureau, be sent to the Public Security Bureau for combined education and reform through forced labor."[54]

By the fall of 1953, most of the reports from inside the reeducation centers were dominated by discussions about the benefits of putting internees to work. One author cited the formerly homeless beggar Li Lin as an example of "a great number of internees," who "having gone through the practice of actual labor and production . . . gradually transformed past bad mindsets or bad habits and recognized the gloriousness of labor."[55] According to this report, when Li was first interned, he always "caused trouble" and "was famous for refusing to obey discipline." After joining a work team, however, Li Lin's "mindset underwent a transformation," and he reportedly became a hard worker who often "provided information to the leadership." Li himself was quoted as saying, "inside the [reeducation] center, there was no way out. I was miserable and bored, so I made trouble. Now, engaging in labor and production, I have a future. Relying on yourself is a good thing to do."[56] Citing this and similar examples, the author of the report argued that "education through the actual practice of labor gradually fosters a habit of loving labor."[57]

Even as reeducators increasingly extolled the virtues of using work as a reform method, other reports also claimed with more and more frequency, that many internees were simply refusing to labor. According to a document from December 1953, of the 334 internees in one reeducation institution, only 255 were engaging in production. The other 79 had allegedly "long refused to participate." The author claimed that "cadres in the [reeducation] center [had] criticized and educated them many times, all to no avail."[58] According to the report, the unwilling internees "sleep all day [and] read fiction. Cadres are unable to do anything about it. After the Bureau of Civil Affairs conducted this year's investigation and rectification, there have been no instances of [staff] beating or abusing internees . . . but when [internees] cause trouble and foment discord, [staff] do not have suitable methods to control them. A portion of the internees absolutely refuse to obey cadre discipline. There is chaos in the [reeducation] center. . . . There are those [internees] who have the audacity to say: 'The [rectification campaign] brought the cadres down. Now it's my kingdom.'"[59]

In addition to these blatant refusals to participate in production, the "trouble" and "discord" internees were said to be "causing" and "fomenting" included thefts of money and property from the reeducation centers and from each other. Some male "parasites" were accused of raping fellow internees.[60] Cadres were reportedly exhausted and unable to gain control. The report lamented that, "other than asking the Public Security Bureau to arrest those who don't obey discipline, the cadres in the center do not have any other methods to control these people," and, according to the writer, the threat of arrest was not even enough to deter some internees: "They do not care at all about being sent to the Public Security Bureau or to the courts. They say: 'It's the same there, you still eat steamed buns.' Or 'Fine. The eating is better at the courts. The living conditions are better. The labor skills studied there are much better than here. I am perfectly willing to go.'"[61]

By May 1954 writers had lost the optimistic tone they had employed in earlier reports, and their communications to their supervisors became dismal lists of problems and failures: "Between December 25, 1953, and the beginning of May 1954, [the reeducation centers] interned a total of 541 people. A large number of them were beggars and petty thieves, though some were elderly or invalid individuals with nowhere else to go. Many of the beggars and thieves were people who had been interned (for begging and theft) before and had returned to their old habits after their release. Some stayed in reeducation centers, others were sent to the Public Security Bureau to undergo labor reform, and several escaped and ran away."[62]

In 1954, the Bureau of Civil Affairs revised their legislation once again to state, "Each internee must engage in labor and production, live by their own toil, obey discipline and accept reform and education."[63] Although writers did not typically use the term *forced labor* to refer to methods employed in reeducation centers, reserving that term for the practices used in Public Security Bureau labor reform camps, the internal documentation no longer stressed reliance on verbal persuasion alone. Work summaries claimed that staff employed the "guiding principle of living by one's own toil," which was used to justify reported reductions in the amount of food given to internees who "loafed, ran away, or [otherwise] resisted labor."[64] Further citing the complementary guiding principle of "labor more, receive more; labor less, receive less," writers increasingly asserted that graduated reward systems, and the withholding of food or other necessities, were effective means through which staff could "encourage their [internees'] enthusiasm for labor."[65] This discursive development stood in stark contrast to the 1949 and 1950 emphasis on the provision of food and material goods in ample quantities as a useful way to win the trust and cooperation of the newly interned vagrants, beggars, and thieves.[66]

Even as they declared that labor "decreased the chaos in the reeducation work units," report writers increasingly depicted reeducation centers in which internees were completely out of control, and by 1956 the administrative paperwork was no longer a collection of enthusiastic missives, extolling the power of education and persuasion in reforming the least-fortunate members of the Chinese masses.[67] With thousands still forcibly interned, and new offenders arriving every day, a Civil Affairs report from September complained that Beijing's internees were "retaining their old habits." Claiming that reeducatees regularly fought with one another and stole things from inside the internment center, the report ended in defeat as the writer said flatly, "We don't yet have effective methods to stop this."[68]

As of late 1956 reports like this one had been complaining about cadres' "lack of effective methods" for at least four years. The records from the period between 1952 and 1956 reflect numerous attempts by personnel at all levels to diagnose the causes of the problems reported from inside the reeducation centers. Responding to complaints from reeducators and to information provided by investigators, officials in the Bureaus of Civil Affairs repeatedly revised their policies with the stated aim of providing reeducation center staff with the methods they needed to do their jobs effectively. Over the course of this conversation between reeducation center staff and their superiors, the participants went from arguing that education alone could transform the minds of "nonproductive" people to asserting that internees must be strictly disciplined and that some must even be forced to labor if thought reform was to be successful.

In August 1957 and January 1958, the "Decision of the State Council of the PRC Relating to the Problems of Reeducation through Labor," and the "Regulations for the Treatment of Beggars," respectively, codified the dramatic re-articulation of thought reform policy that had evolved over almost a decade of administrative discussion about reeducation practice. Redefining the parameters within which the ideal practice for the management of vagrants, beggars, and petty thieves was to be formulated, these pieces of legislation effectively relieved the Bureau of Civil Affairs of its duty to carry out "thought reform." The new regulations stipulated that Civil Affairs personnel were responsible only for the rapid repatriation of beggars and vagrants who were caught in Beijing. No longer designated as "targets for internment," individuals caught "roaming the streets" were to be immediately transferred to the custody of their work units or hometown local governments. If the new policies were carried out properly, vagrants and beggars might receive a brief lecture about the importance of remaining in one place and engaging in production, but most would never see the inside of a thought reform institution.[69]

For thieves, those beggars who had been caught repeatedly, and all individuals who were otherwise deemed resistant to discipline, thought reform was still an appropriate measure. However, the Bureau of Civil Affairs was no longer authorized to provide that reform. All allegedly resistant or disobedient people were to be sent to the Public Security Bureau to undergo "reeducation through labor."[70] The new guidelines made official the vision of an ideal practice of thought reform that had been developing over the past eight years: "Reeducation through labor is a measure of a coercive nature for carrying out the education and reform of the persons receiving it. . . . The guiding principle of combining labor and production with political education will be adopted. Furthermore, discipline and a system will be instituted to help [reeducatees] establish a mentality of patriotic observance of law and of the gloriousness of labor, learn labor and production skills, and cultivate the habit of loving labor, so that they live by their own toil and participate in socialist construction."[71]

Between 1949 and 1958 a number of factors encouraged the shift from a vision of ideal practice that emphasized education as the primary agent of reform to one that accorded labor that same primacy. The events of the 1950s placed huge demands on the new economy and it would be unsurprising if those in internment centers were asked to contribute by laboring more intensively. Perhaps more prosaically, interning vagrants, beggars, and thieves was expensive. Work reports had complained about financial pressures since 1949 and the situation did not improve as the years went by.[72] As the costs of postrevolutionary national reconstruction were exacerbated by expensive war efforts, disappointing agricultural production, and Soviet demands for rapid repayment of loans, ensuring that internees in reeducation centers worked and "lived by their own toil" likely seemed a useful strategy to combat rising expenses, especially after the rhetoric of the Great Leap Forward (1957–59) began to call for mass mobilization to increase China's domestic production. Work reports from primary schools claimed that even children were required to participate in steel-making efforts. If young students were no longer supposed to be given the luxury of full-time study, reeducators could hardly tell their superiors that beggars and vagrants were allowed to "lounge on [their] beds all day."[73]

All these external factors surely served to motivate the policy shifts that occurred between 1949 and 1958, but—as a close look at the internal documentation has demonstrated—we cannot ignore a crucial additional reason for the drastic rearticulation of reeducation practice. It is significant that the internal records show a persistent absence of discussion about these external causes and an equally persistent evocation of other justificatory strategies—based on the recalcitrance and resistance of an increasingly recidivistic "parasitic population." Perhaps we cannot be sure that in 1953 a rebelliously suicidal beggar named Zhao Jinghe was labeled "resistant to reform," described as an internee who "refused to obey discipline," and sentenced to reform through forced labor. It is in the details that such stories—both of resistance and of reformation—are most unreliable. Yet the sheer volume of documentation attests to a growing sensibility that the reeducation methods cadres were using were not effective. It was as a response to this fact, as much as to external economic pressures, that reeducators came to argue for the necessity of forced labor in reforming individuals like Zhao. In his, as in so many other cases, resistance and recalcitrance were not, in the end, transformed into redemption, but we cannot understand the contours of thought reform policy without them.

Notes

Epigraph by Mao Zedong from "The Chinese Revolution and the Comunist Party," reprinted in Mao Zedong xuanji, (Beijing: Renmin chubanshe, 1977), 1:616–17.

1. See, for example, Chen Qiyuan, Chengshi jiuji fuli gongzuo baogao, May 1951, Beijing Municipal Archives (hereafter BMA), file 2-3-79.

2. Beijing Municipal Bureau of Civil Affairs, Guanyu jiujifenhui suoshu shourong jiaoyang danwei biaoxian ji huai de shourongren, August 1953, BMA, file 14-2-88.

3. Documents about these internment efforts typically used the word qigai (beggar) as the simplified title for this group. In some cases, however, these texts did use more specific terms as well, especially xiaotou (thief), pashou (pickpocket), and youmin or liumin (vagrant). Not all individuals who were accused of begging, stealing, or "roaming the streets"

were interned. Many were simply sent to their hometowns or home neighborhoods to be managed by local governments. Other people, who weren't accused of any of these behaviors, ended up in reeducation centers for various reasons. According to institutional reports, staff error was the most common reason. Another was that some people entered the reeducation centers voluntarily after hearing that internees received free room, board, and vocational training. For a more detailed discussion of these categories and their changing meanings, see Aminda M. Smith, "Reeducating the People: The Chinese Communists and the 'Thought Reform' of Beggars, Prostitutes, and Other 'Parasites'" (Ph.D. diss., Princeton University, 2006), esp. 69–79.

4. Civil Affairs was the principal agency in charge of supervising reeducation efforts, but many government organizations were also ordered to take active roles, especially the Ministry of Public Security and Ministry of Public Hygiene. For a more detailed description of reeducation administration, see ibid., 90–92, 237.

5. Beijing Municipal People's Committee, *Di sanshier ci xingzheng huiyi jilu*, June 1958, BMA, file 2-10-51.

6. Ma Weigang, *Jin chang jin du* (Beijing: Jingguan jiaoyu chubanshe, 1993). See also the brief description of these efforts in Suzanne Pepper, *Civil War in China: The Political Struggle, 1945–1949* (Lanham, MD: Rowman and Littlefield, 1999), 345–46.

7. North China People's Government, *Wei chengshi chuli qigai banfa xian zai Ping Jin jinxing qita gedi zanhuan juxing you tongzhi*, June 1949, BMA, file 196-2-191.

8. Beijing Municipal Public Security Bureau, *Guanyu shourong qigai baogao de yijian*, October 1949, BMA, file 196-2-191.

9. For a detailed discussion of these documents, their authors (who did not typically sign their names), and the problems associated with the use of these texts as historical sources, see Smith, "Reeducating the People," esp. intro., ch. 3.

10. For example, the 1957 "Decision of the State Council of the People's Republic of China Relating to the Problems of Reeducation through Labor," which is discussed in the final section of this chapter, claimed that the purpose of labor reform was to produce self-sufficient laborers who would participate in "socialist construction." See *Zhonghua renmin gongheguo fagui huibian* (Beijing: Fa lu chu ban she, 1956–), 6:243–44. An English translation is available in Jerome A. Cohen, *The Criminal Process in the People's Republic of China, 1949–1963: An Introduction* (Cambridge, MA: Harvard University Press, 1968), 249–50.

11. For the history and theory of punishment and reform in general, see Michel Foucault, *Discipline and Punish: The Birth of the Prison*, trans. Alan Sheridan (New York: Vintage, 1977); Patricia O'Brien, *The Promise of Punishment* (Princeton, NJ: Princeton University Press, 1982); David Garland, *Punishment and Modern Society: A Study in Social Theory* (Chicago: University of Chicago Press, 1990); Norval Morris, ed., *The Oxford History of the Prison: The Practice of Punishment in Western Society* (New York: Oxford University Press, 2000); Rani Shankardass, ed., *Punishment and the Prison: Indian and International Perspectives* (Thousand Oaks, CA: Sage Publications, 2000). For the reform of beggars in particular, see A. L. Beier, *Masterless Men: The Vagrancy Problem in England, 1560–1640* (London: Methuen, 1985); Thomas McStay Adams, *Bureaucrats and Beggars: French Social Policy in the Age of Enlightenment* (New York: Oxford University Press, 1990).

12. Lu Hanchao, *Street Criers: A Cultural History of Chinese Beggars* (Stanford, CA: Stanford University Press, 2005), 5.

13. Ibid., 4–5.

14. Philip A. Kuhn, *Soulstealers: The Chinese Sorcery Scare of 1768* (Cambridge, MA: Harvard University Press, 1990).

15. Ibid., 42.

16. Ibid., 44.

17. Lu, *Street Criers*, 90; Kristin Stapleton, *Civilizing Chengdu: Chinese Urban Reform, 1895–1937* (Cambridge, MA: Harvard University Press, 2000), 126–29.

18. Zwia Lipkin, "Modern Dilemmas: Dealing with Nanjing's Beggars," *Journal of Urban History* 31, no. 5 (2005): 590.

19. Lu, *Street Criers*, 9.

20. Lipkin, "Modern Dilemmas," 590. For more on beggars in the early twentieth century, see Lu Hanchao, "Becoming Urban: Mendicancy and Vagrants in Modern Shanghai," *Journal of Social History* 33, no. 1 (1999): 7–36; Chen Baoliang, *Zhongguo liumang shi* (Beijing: Chinese Social Science Publishing House, 1993); Sidney Gamble, *Peking: A Social Survey* (New York: George H. Doran, 1921).

21. Both Lu and Lipkin have discussed similarities and dissimilarities between the efforts undertaken in China and those undertaken elsewhere in the world. See Lu, *Street Criers*, 8–12; Lipkin, "Modern Dilemmas," 588–89.

22. North China Ministry of Civil Affairs, *Qigai wenti cailiao*, March 1949, BMA, file 196-2-191. For the history of mendicancy in China, as well as for discussions of various state and nonstate efforts to eradicate beg-

ging, see Smith, "Reeducating the People," esp. ch. 1; Lu, *Street Criers;* Michael Dutton, *Policing Chinese Politics: A History* (Durham, NC: Duke University Press, 2005); Lipkin, "Modern Dilemmas"; Stapleton, *Civilizing Chengdu,* 126–29; Lu, "Becoming Urban"; Chen, *Zhongguo liumang shi;* Gamble, *Peking.*

23. North China Ministry of Civil Affairs, *Chuli qigai zanxing banfa,* March 1949, BMA, file 196 2-191.

24. Ibid.

25. Beijing Municipal Bureau of Civil Affairs, *Diaocha qigi gongzuo baogao,* April 1949, BMA, file 196-2-191

26. Beijing Municipal Bureau of Civil Affairs, *Yijiusijiu nian gongzuo baogao,* December 1949, BMA, file 2-1-55.

27. Ibid.

28. Beijing Municipal Bureau of Civil Affairs, *Shourong qigai gongzuo zhoubao,* May 1949, BMA, file 196-2-199.

29. Beijing Municipal Bureau of Civil Affairs, *Shourong qigai gongzuo zongjie,* June 1949, BMA, file 196-2-20; Beijing Municipal Bureau of Civil Affairs, *Yijiuwuling nian jiu yue shourong qigai gongzuo zongjie,* September 1950, BMA, file 196-2-199.

30. Zhangjiakou is a town near Beijing in northern Hebei Province.

31. Beijing Municipal Bureau of Civil Affairs, *Shourong qigai gongzuo zongjie,* June 1949.

32. Ibid.

33. Beijing Municipal Bureau of Civil Affairs, *Shourong qigai zhoubao,* May 1949.

34. Beijing Municipal Bureau of Civil Affairs, *Shourong qigai gongzuo baogao,* June 1949, BMA file 2-1-55; Beijing Municipal Bureau of Civil Affairs, *Yijiusijiu nian gongzuo baogao,* December 1949.

35. Beijing Municipal Bureau of Civil Affairs, *Shourong qigai gongzuo baogao,* June 1949.

36. Ibid.

37. Beijing Bureau of Civil Affairs, *Yijiusijiu nian gongzuo baogao,* December 1949; *Yijiuwuling nian jiu yue shourong qigai gongzuo zongjie,* September 1950, BMA file 2-1-–55.

38. Beijing Bureau of Civil Affairs, *Yijiusijiu nian gongzuo baogao,* December 1949.

39. Ibid.

40. See, for example, Beijing Municipal Bureau of Civil Affairs, *Yijiusijiu nian gongzuo baogao,* December 1949; Bcijing Municipal Bureau

of Civil Affairs, *Yijiuwuling nian jiu yue shourong qigai gongzuo zongjie*, September 1950.

41. See, for example, Beijing Municipal Bureau of Civil Affairs, *Shourong qigai gongzuo zongjie*, June 1949; North China Ministry of Civil Affairs, *Qigai wenti cailiao*. For discussion, see Smith, "Reeducating the People," esp. chs. 1–3.

42. See, for example, Mao Zedong, "An Analysis of the Various Classes of the Chinese Peasantry and their Attitudes toward Revolution," *Zhongguo Nongmin* 1, no. 1 (1926): 13–20.

43. Chen, *Chengshi jiuji fuli gongzuo baogao*.

44. *Beijing Municipality Temporary Regulations for the Management of Beggars*, June 1951, BMA, file 2-3-57.

45. Ibid.

46. Beijing Municipal Bureau of Civil Affairs, *Beijing shi qigai, yeji, liumang, xiaotou qingkuang baogao*, August 1952, BMA, file 196-2-20.

47. Beijing Municipal Bureau of Civil Affairs, *Gongzuo zhoubao*, September 1953, BMA, file 14-2-87.

48. The details of the first five-year plan were sketchy in 1953. Although the plan was to cover the period between 1953 and 1957, it was not published until 1955. However, work toward its ambitious goals began immediately. For general histories of the plan and the corresponding period of "socialist transition" in the PRC, see Jonathan Spence, *The Search for Modern China*, 2nd ed. (New York: Norton, 1999), 514–43; Craig Dietrich, *People's China: A Brief History*, 3rd ed. (New York: Oxford University Press), 83–110.

49. Central People's Government Ministry of the Interior, *Zhishi*, May 1953, BMA, file 196-2-212.

50. Ibid.

51. Ibid.

52. Ibid.

53. Beijing Municipal Department of Social Relief, *Shengchan jiaoyangyuan ge suo shourongren taopao qingkuang ji chuli yijian baogao*, June 1953, BMA, file 14-2-88.

54. Ibid.

55. Ibid.

56. Ibid.

57. Ibid.

58. Beijing Municipal Department of Social Relief, *Laodong jiaoyusuo bufen shourongren jingchang dao luan*, December 1953, BMA, file 14-2-88.

59. Ibid.

60. Beijing Municipal Bureau of Civil Affairs, *Guanyu jiujifenhui suoshu shourong jiaoyang danwei biaoxian ji huai de shourongren,* August 1953, BMA, file 14-2-88.

61. Ibid.

62. Beijing Bureau of Civil Affairs, *Guanyu linshi shourongsuo shourong chuli qingkuang baogao,* June 1954, BMA, file 14-1-51.

63. Beijing Bureau of Civil Affairs, *Laodong jiaoyusuo guanli jiaoyu shixing banfa,* June 1954, BMA, file 14-1-51.

64. Beijing Municipal Department of Social Relief, *Zuzhi youmin canlao canjia laodong shengchan de qingkuang baogao,* December 1954, BMA, file 14-2-48.

65. Ibid.

66. See, for example, Beijing Bureau of Civil Affairs, *Shourong qigai gongzuo zhoubao,* May 1949; *Yijiuwuling nian jiu yue gongzuo zongjie,* September 1950; Beijing Municipal Bureau of Civil Affairs, *Shourong qigai gongzuo zongjie,* June 1949.

67. Beijing Municipal Bureau of Civil Affairs, *Zhengdun shengchan jiaoyang gongzuo zongjie baogao,* September 1954, BMA, file 14-1-51.

68. Beijing Municipal Bureau of Civil Affairs, *Guanyu Beijing shi shehui jiuji fuli gongzuo qingkuang baogao,* 1956, BMA, file 196-1-88.

69. Beijing Municipal People's Committee, *Di sanshier ci xingzheng huiyi jilu,* June 1958, BMA, file 2-10-51.

70. State Council of the People's Republic of China, "Decision of the State Council of the People's Republic of China Relating to the Problems of Reeducation through Labor."

71. Ibid.

72. Beijing Municipal Bureau of Civil Affairs, *Yijiusijiu nian gongzuo baogao,* December 1949, BMA, file 2-1-55.

73. The cadre in charge of one reeducation center allegedly accused a group of internees of doing nothing besides "lounging on their beds all day." See Beijing Municipal People's Investigation Committee, *Yijiuwusan nian Diyi jidu gongzuo baogao,* May 1953, BMA, file 14-2-15. For a discussion of this incident, see Smith, "Reeducating the People," 173–74.

12

Imposing Vagrancy Legislation
in Contemporary Papua New Guinea

Robert Gordon

VAGRANCY IS ONE of a large parcel of laws dating back to the Middle Ages attempting to constrain freedom of movement. Stimulated in large part by globalization, at present it has metamorphosed into other overarching legislative packets and projects like Homeland Security, migrant "illegality," and "deportability."[1] That there are estimated to be over twenty-eight million "illegal" aliens globally attests to the current ubiquity of the "problem." The term *vagrancy*, but not the practice, has however become decidedly passé as other forms of control have replaced it. Thus, it is intriguing that in a seeming effort to turn the clock back, Papua New Guinea has recently attempted to reintroduce the vagrancy act that had been on the books until independence. In 2003, there was such an outcry:

> Papua New Guinea's vagrancy laws should be changed to help police and others tackle the spillover from ethnic violence in cities, police said yesterday. Police Commissioner Sam Inguba said there was an urgent need for law enforcement agencies and governing bodies . . . to co-operate and revamp submissions to parliament to have the Vagrancy Act enacted. In a parliamentary debate, Prime Minister Sir Michael Somare lent his support for the re-introduction of the Va-

grancy Act to control urban drift. Sir Michael slammed politicians as hypocrites. He said MP's are often hypocrites for shying away from passing tough laws. Central Province Governor Alphonse Moroi . . . said there was strong interest in how the problem was resolved. "If justice is not done, there is a very high probability that people will take the law into their own hands," he told Parliament. Mr Moroi urged that the House look at re-introducing the Vagrancy Act and the repatriation of unemployed people to their home provinces. Police Commissioner Inguba meanwhile said police would take immediate steps to pursue the re-introduction of the Vagrancy Act.[2]

This was not an isolated event. The year before, the Honorable Ebia Olewale, the first minister of justice in independent Papua New Guinea, wondered aloud at a Canberra workshop on the relationship between vagrancy laws and the decolonization process:

> I don't know why the vagrancy act was taken out of our law. The Vagrancy Act is a big concern now in Papua New Guinea; people are coming and settling on other people's land. . . . It is becoming a real problem . . . there is no Vagrancy Act so the police cannot chase people who are settling on other people's land where they have had no right to settle. . . . Lately in Papua New Guinea we have been talking about the re-introduction of that Vagrancy Act.[3]

There is a certain irony here, as the scrapping of the Vagrancy Act occurred during Olewale's tenure as minister of justice.[4]

These calls, though, are not concerned with labor regulation but with the protection of property following a pattern first elucidated by William Chambliss.[5] With unemployment hovering around 50 percent in Port Moresby, the capital and largest city in Papua New Guinea, the Vagrancy Act is hardly useful in coercing people into the wage labor system. Despite this high unemployment rate, beggars, or people without visible means of support, are still relatively rare (although now making their presence felt) because they are supported by their *wantoks*, that is, relatives and acquaintances from their *asples,* or natal settlement.[6] These wantoks will typically range over the socioeconomic spectrum from the rural lumpenproletariat to the jet-setting nouveau riche. This form of homelessness is frequently glossed over as a contemporary euphemism for vagrancy but it has not yet made a political mark in Papua New Guinea. Another main aim of the Vagrancy Act is its use to control the problem of *raskals*, gangs of criminals whose acts of armed robbery and rape belie their scampish name. Their name is slightly misplaced, because while unemployment is a powerful stimulus for gang activity, research has shown that raskals are drawn from all segments of society. Rather than having dominant lines of cleavage run along horizontal socioeconomic criteria, Papua New Guinea is doubly bedeviled with vertical, identity-based cleavages; that is, loyalties to clan and lineage will frequently override socioeconomic disparities. This, coupled to a state that is typically labeled as weak, because it is largely incapable of controlling its inhabitants, is part of the context in which vagrancy needs to be considered. Considering vagrancy legislation and its historic place in Papua New Guinea leads one to develop an alternative characterization of the Papua New Guinea state, not as weak, but as ceremonial. Weak states are incapable of providing the basic services associated with states (a decidedly ethnocentric notion), while ceremonial states are characterized by an emphasis on accoutrements, etiquette, and often exaggerated ceremonialism rather than the provision of services. Furthermore, what spectral presence does the Vagrancy Act have among Papua New Guineans that inspires calls for its resurrection? And, despite all the rhetoric, there is lingering uncertainty among scholars and lawyers as to whether Papua New Guinea has a vagrancy law at all.

The History of Vagrancy in Papua New Guinea

With close to eight hundred different languages, Papua New Guinea is one of the most culturally diverse regions on earth. It consists of Papua, originally an Australian colony, and New Guinea, a German colony until World War I, when it was taken over and administered as a Class C mandate by Australia under the auspices of the Permanent Mandates Commission (PMC) of the League of Nations. After World

War II, the two territories were jointly administered as a United Nations trusteeship and finally in 1975 became the independent state of Papua New Guinea. For the longest period of colonization, indigenes were policed by a state that, lacking manpower and money, was forced to resort to legal regulations. In particular, claim David Weisbrot, Abdul Paliwala, and Aki Sawyerr, there were three pillars of social control (more accurately, state control), namely the Native Regulations, Police Offences, and Vagrancy Ordinances.[7] In essence, the regulations were a massive list of dos and don'ts, including significant impediments to movement. They covered offenses from the frivolous to the serious: adultery, wife stealing, and "disobedience" pertaining to the refusal to undertake "any act which [the white official] considered to be for the good government and well-being of the natives."[8] To prevent a landless proletariat and subsidize the wage labor system, "circular migration" was encouraged. Just as Andrew Burton and Paul Ocobock argue for British East Africa (chapter 10, this volume), in Papua New Guinea the threat of "urban drift" was met by discouraging migration and insisting on Australian standards for urban areas that created, in effect, white enclaves. Until the 1980s the rhetoric of the government and various aid agencies was that the vast majority of Papua New Guineans lived traditionally and did not really need cash or a Western, or capitalist, economy. Thus, development efforts had a distinct antiurban bias, except when it concerned the emergent national administrative petite bourgeoisie.[9]

In the years before World War II, urban migration was strongly discouraged. If a Papuan managed to get permission to be in town, made more difficult by the fact that they were forbidden to come within five miles of Port Moresby, they had to provide an acceptable account of their "means of support." In New Guinea it was illegal to remain for more than four days in a town without employment. If employed, Papuans could not wander around townships without the expressed permission of their employer. It was a criminal offense to loiter, cause an obstruction, or use public conveniences. Nor could they carry weapons, gamble, or sing or dance after 9:00 p.m. They had to reside in specially built compounds or barracks or later "boys quarters."[10] It was only after World War II that the curfew regulations were gradually relaxed under United Nations pressure. Police officers, both black and white, had wide discretionary powers. They could arrest anyone without a warrant if it was suspected that a warrant had already been issued or when they believed that an indigene might have committed any crime or simple offense. Villagers (always male) were not allowed to venture more than twenty-five miles from their villages.[11] As late as 1957 government officers, or *kiaps,* were empowered to order any individual to return home if found outside their home area and believed to constitute a threat to law and order.[12] In 1975 one of the first tasks undertaken by the newly established Law Reform Commission was to abolish the Native Regulations because the laws were considered a racist colonial relic and contravened the constitution's guarantee of freedom of movement.

Yet how effective was the enforcement of these regulations? They were not imposed much in practice. Not only were there few government officials to enforce them, but there was also a high turnover in the administration. In this regard they were similar to officials in the British colonial service in Africa.[13] In 1939 there were forty-six European field staff in Papua and less than a hundred in New Guinea. In 1929, of 233 officials in New Guinea's public service, 161 had turned over in the past four years.[14] By 1943, the total number of officials had reached 313.[15] Many Papua New Guineans, at least those in the rural villages, were protected by what Karl Wittvogel calls the "law of diminishing administrative returns."[16] Furthermore, even senior officials were unaware of what the regulations entailed. For example, the commission of inquiry into the 1929 Rabaul strike suggested that the regulations be amended so that no laborer be abroad after "say nine or ten at night, unless in possessions of a pass issued by the police officer," which was six years after a 9:00 p.m. curfew had been introduced and three years after it was extended to 11:00 p.m.[17] While the colonial state lacked the capacity to implement these regulations, they had an important psychological impact on indigenes. What were little wars for colonizers were big ones for the colonized.[18] For intimidation to occur, violence did not have to occur everyday, and an occasional act was enough for a spectral presence to haunt Papua New Guineans.

Labor Indenture

Like their counterparts elsewhere, the Australians, believed that work was essential for "civilizing" their charges. As the administrator of New Guinea explained to the League of Nations, "the native must be induced to work, for unless the native is given both physical and interest in life to replace the occupations and excitements of his former savage life, he will surely die out."[19] The Australians promised a clean start. Their first aim inspired by the mandate was to "stop evils concerned in the past with recruiting; and to encourage recruited men to take their wives with them."[20] Forced labor was banned but men had to pay a head tax of ten shillings, or if they were indentured, their employers had to pay one shilling a month.[21] The dominant form of labor was indentured labor in which workers signed a three-year contract, mostly to work on copra plantations on the coast; in the heyday of this system as many as 20 percent of the population in certain areas worked under such contracts. Throughout the mandate period settlers never claimed that there was any labor shortage. The indenture system was necessary, the Australians argued, because indigenes had yet to reach a level of development that encouraged "free labor." The colonials failed miserably in their goal of recruiting women as indentured laborers. At the same time the administration had to keep a weather eye on how they were perceived at the League of Nations and its associated organizations like the International Labor Organization (ILO). The driving force behind the ILO, Albert Thomas, was haunted by the fear that racial warfare would break out on a world scale; he feared that if the ILO did not act, the communists would.[22] To this end, the ILO's constant monitoring and occasional hectoring resulted in numerous questionnaires and, every once in a while, a forum where some missionaries or local people complained about "irregularities." Understandably the colonial and mandatory authorities were rather hostile to the ILO and one consequence is that mandatories were forced to develop, on paper at least, comprehensive labor policies.

While these native labor ordinances were complexly comprehensive, indicative no doubt of "low trust" relations, they undoubtedly advantaged the literate (i.e., white settlers) but they were also very much part of the operation to impress the Permanent Mandates Commission and the ILO.[23] Indeed, so seriously was this taken that intending settlers were advised in the official handbook to purchase a copy of the Native Labor Ordinance at their earliest convenience and to study the contents most carefully, as the administration "rigidly enforced" them.[24] This was, of course, a myth because, despite district officers making a "fetish of duty," the rules were nearly impossible to enforce. It is "apparent to an observer that the ideals expressed in the mandate document are not always achieved in practice, and that no major changes have been made in the German legacy of native control."[25]

Quantitatively the labor situation showed a slowly increasing number of workers from 1925, with a reasonably low death rate. Most indentured laborers were placed on coastal plantations, with the rest distributed among mining, shipping, domestic, and administrative sectors. The most common indigenes in the criminal category were charged under offenses such as desertion, negligence, disobedience, and theft. The vast majority of cases in the district courts involved laborers charged with desertion or neglect. The large number of charges of negligence arose largely because employers were prevented from punishing laborers except, for example, by withholding their weekly tobacco ration. Few Europeans were charged. However, Stephen Reed notes, "the amount of illegal punishment of natives that goes on is impossible to determine, but it is obvious to all who have been in the Territory that the cases brought to trial represent only a fraction of those which occur. . . . The majority of officials are lenient, even lax, in their attitude towards illegal punishment and cases are only brought when the victims are seriously injured or died."[26] Other observers support Reed's observations. Clive Rowley, the longtime principal of the Australian School of Pacific Administration, felt that the indenture system was simply a technique to bureaucratize blackbirding (trading in slaves) by giving it the appearance of "legal respectability":

> there are many links in the chain of protective provisions where a break renders the whole series useless. . . . [Indeed] there was a time

when employers could force workers to run away towards the end of the term; the "deserter" might forfeit his deferred pay, and the employer save the cost of his return home. Legal protection could often be rendered useless by a breakdown in the system of inspection, by all the evasions open to recruiters and employers where the government was under-staffed . . . likely, as was all too commonly the case, to regard as their duty assistance to employers.[27]

Law and Order after Independence

The 1950s and 1960s were relatively peaceful, at least judging by official reports to the United Nations, whose surveillance included frequent onsite visits; but gradually issues of "law and order" began to surface. In 1974, on the eve of independence, a Peace and Good Order Committee reported on the issue of law and order to the chief minister, and the next year the chief minister asked the United Nations and the Australian Institute of Criminology to advise him on the problem. The result was a seminar and a study, but very little of practical consequence can be traced to these efforts.[28]

The following year the newly formed Law Reform Commission (LRC) published its first working paper, which took aim at the most visible legal symbol of colonialism and proposed abolishing the Native Regulations and replacing them with a Summary Offences Act. The vagrancy sections were to be abolished, since they constituted an unconstitutional infringement on a citizen's freedom of movement. However, Bernard Narakobi, the chairman of the commission recalled,

> The offence of no lawful or visible means of support, were [sic] vigorously opposed by the police and by some vocal members of the public. The government was forced to compromise by those proposing to introduce curfew laws and identity cards. The compromise was that for such an offence, the courts were first to order the offender to leave the urban area. If such an order was disobeyed, then the offender would be imprisoned.[29]

It was not just the police who opposed the removal of the Vagrancy Act. Narakobi recounted,

> Whilst in Mount Hagen [the largest town in the Highlands] . . . I received almost unanimous submissions from the nationals that the vagrancy laws, which make it an offence for anyone to be without lawful or visible means of support, should not be abolished. My reply that vagrancy laws were part of the colonial device to keep towns for whites met with a blank "No!" One elderly lady put it vividly: "In the good old days, we knew who we were. We were natives. We could not come into towns. We clearly knew where we stood. Now you make things difficult. We do not know where we are."[30]

Tales of how the colonials successfully organized and pacified the area, which often bordered on urban legends, are common currency in stories of indigenes, who like ghosts continue to haunt present-day fears concerning law and order.

The problem of law and order continued to paralyze the country, and in 1981 the prime minister created a Port Moresby Committee for the Promotion of Law and Order, consisting of community leaders. The committee's first recommendation was repatriation of unemployed offenders with an appropriate constitutional amendment to facilitate this, plus more employment and low-cost housing. Commentators pointed out the constitutional problems with these recommendations and suggested a system of residence permits and identity cards. Others felt that the repatriation proposal was unrealistic. These suggestions would repeatedly resurface and states of emergency were regularly proclaimed during this period—most significantly in 1979, 1985, and 1991—and were justified as "waging war on hooligans and rascals."[31] In 1985 the cabinet endorsed a new crime bill allowing for castrations and public hangings as well as identity cards and the vagrancy law to be toughened up. It is perhaps significant that events in 1985, including mass protests in Port Moresby, were ignited by the brutal gang rape of an expatriate and her daughter.

Constitutional issues apparently stymied these proposals, so in 1991, the death penalty was reintroduced as part of a larger anticrime package. The package proposal included construction of additional maximum-security prisons, tattooing of convicted offenders, tightened vagrancy laws and the forced repatriation of "unemployed people and troublemakers."[32] A Human Rights Watch report released in September 2005 illustrates extensive police brutality against the local populace. While the police code of ethics is of a "high standard," it is almost universally ignored, as is the Police Force Act. A government commission found that public confidence in the police force had been destroyed and that it was seen as "largely ineffective." The problem was not so much a lack of training, indeed the Royal Papua New Guinea Police Constabulary is probably the best-trained constabulary in the Pacific, but lack of political will to implement disciplinary charges against members has resulted in a force that acts with impunity.[33]

By 2004, Port Moresby was said to be the most dangerous city in the world, and the situation had deteriorated to such a degree that Australia agreed to send in nearly three hundred police and public officials in an ambitious five-year mission to try to ameliorate the law-and-order problem. The Enhanced Cooperation Program was to cost $A800 million, its largesse derived principally from Australia's middle-power ambitions in the aftermath of 9/11 and a concern for security on its northern boundary. The BBC reported that when the Australian police conducted their first foot patrols they were quickly surrounded by dozens of jubilant, welcoming locals. Six months later they started heading home after Papua New Guinea's supreme court had ruled the visitors' immunity from prosecution unlawful.[34]

The Contemporary Context: Failed, Weak, or Ceremonial State?

Measured by the United Nations Human Development Index (HDI), Papua New Guinea has regressed. It ranked 116th in the world in 1992, but by 1999 it had dropped to 129th, and in 2005 was ranked 137th.[35] Since becoming independent in 1975, PNG has had six parliamentary elections with no government ever serving a full term. On the other hand, the country has never had a coup d'etat and has a vibrant independent press, an active NGO sector, and an independent judiciary that regularly rules against the regime. In twenty-seven years Papua New Guinea has had eleven governments, and while they all present broadly similar platforms emphasizing development, good governance, and law and order, they seldom achieve these goals. In the 2002 elections, an average of twenty-eight candidates contested each parliamentary seat.[36] Political parties are weakly developed and frequently a parliamentarian is elected with less than 5 percent of the vote—support largely derived from their clan or *lian* (kin group). Of the 103 seats declared there were eighty-three challenges. In this first-past-the-post model of democracy, most parliamentarians lose their seats in the next election and this results in an extremely high turnover of neophyte politicians. Yet despite these indicators taken by organizations like Freedom House as positive, some feel Papua New Guinea is a collapsing state. The state is slowly becoming incapable of delivering even the most fundamental services, especially guarantees to security and safety. At independence the police were seen as "the most crippled of any government agency." A quarter century later, a government study concluded, "the law and justice system has become less and less capable of arresting and convicting criminals."[37]

Long held up as an exemplar of a weak state at the point of collapsing, Papua New Guinea seems to show a striking ability to muddle through. The perseverance of the Papua New Guinean state lies in its ceremonial nature. While scholars would have to examine the interplay between external global forces like transnational mining and lumber companies and internal factors like "administrative capacity" to determine the nature of the county's supposed weakness, how do ordinary Papua New Guineans see the state, or *gavman* (local perception of government)? This question has been ignored, with the notable exception of Jeffrey Clark.[38] Some of my own research on tribal warfare has touched on this issue, and as far as I know no one has challenged the validity of the description of local-state interaction. On the contrary, several researchers have commented how it parallels their own experience, especially in the Highlands. While mindful of the problem of making generalizations, especially in polyglot situations as Papua New Guinea, my description appears to be representative of much of the ritual interaction that takes place between local people and state officials. A brief consideration of these rituals and the dynamics driving them provide a means to understand the current rhetoric about vagrancy and its ritual or ceremonial aspects.

In Enga Province, an area famous for its tribal fighting in the late 1970s, when asked what is the state, or gavman, Engans would point to the kiap (government officer) and say, "He is the state." The state was embodied in its officials. Thus in order to examine the nature of state-subject relations, one should look at kiap-local interactions. Within such interactions a strong *lo* (local view of what constitutes law) was manifested. Kiaps, especially expatriates, were believed to be strong because they could enforce their decisions. The lo was strong because the comparative horizon of Engans was limited, and each being an organization of one, kiaps could draw on their other duties and roles to enforce decisions. There was also great social distance between colonizer and colonized, ruler and ruled, and many everyday rituals ranging from well-polished shoes to strategic silence served to emphasize that distance. Such everyday rituals took on an added import, given the pervasive wide-ranging insecurity. A climate of suspicion and distrust appears to be a common characteristic of a loosely structured or acephalous society that, like Enga, espouses a fiercely egalitarian, even libertarian ideology. Such a "loose" social system emphasizes "self-help" and also promotes opportunism, an activity solidly lodged in the lingua franca as *traim tasol. Pilai lucki,* or gambling, was ubiquitous. It is no accident that until the 1970s the colonial authorities banned the importation of playing cards. In such situations, social order is achieved largely through exchange relations.[39]

Conformity was the result not of compulsion so much as the manipulation of wealth in exchange relationships. Social relationships had to be constantly validated publicly by material transactions or observable deeds. It was through manipulating these exchange relationships that one became a Big Man. In this scheme of things, "government is seen not as a mechanism for development but as an instrument [or resource] to be used to establish and extend patronage ties [the dominant means of practicing politics]."[40] Indeed, it could be argued that the power of Big Men was created and sustained by the colonial administration, albeit now in a form of cronyism. This was most favorably facilitated by allowing each member of Parliament to disburse discretionary funds of up to 1.5 million kina,[41] which was immediately put to good use in patronage networks at the home base. Such patronage transformed the nature of Big-Manship by linking national and local levels and simultaneously politicizing both levels. It was a politics of spoils rather than of development.

The rituals of elections continue to survive because no Big Man is capable of developing a network of supporters strong enough to expand beyond his immediate asples (ancestral area). At the same time, the "traditional" ceremonial exchange patterns, like the *te* and *moka*, which enraptured anthropologists in the 1960s and 1970s, have slowly run aground and been replaced by other forms of Big-Manship including infusing Christian rituals with Big-Manship elements and, of course, using the political and civil service arenas as resources.[42] It was, and is, widely believed and expected that politicians and civil servants reward their wantoks with services and obtain favors in return.

Rather than see the problems of law and order as a result of the failure of that black box–like entity known as the state to penetrate into Engan local affairs, it might be more useful to see it in terms of a process of the "infiltration of agencies of the State by Enga in a process of upward colonization. Once a successful politician, public servant or entrepreneur establishes such a bridgehead, other members of his clan exploited the entry and inserted themselves in the administrative machinery, defending their positions by bringing accusations of *wantokism* (nepotism) against enemy clans."[43] The results were readily apparent. In 1996, Sir Mekere Morauta, former governor of the Bank of Papua New Guinea and the country's secretary for finance complained, "Despite the five-fold growth in government expenditure and revenue, the country's infrastructure is breaking down. Government services have declined to the point of being non-existent in many areas. . . . Corruption, both petty and profound, permeates society today. Society is ravaged by crime. There is a general inability to enforce or maintain law and order. Social inequity and poverty are rampant."[44] These Big Men can become so entrenched that authorities are reluctant to prosecute them for fear of retribution. In several well-reported cases individuals were assaulted by their wantoks for not engaging in wantokism.[45]

At the same time the civil service continues to expand. In 1995 the government agreed to cut forty-five hundred jobs from the sixty-thousand-strong civil service; yet three years later, it was forced to promise to slash seven thousand jobs from a service that had ballooned to sixty-five thousand employees. Corruption is rampant and runs the gamut from wantokism though nepotism and bribery to misappropriations, skimming, and outright theft. But of course while others are perceived to engage in corrupt practices, one's own activities are always noble.

State efforts at controlling the law-and-order situation have repeatedly failed. The Papua New Guinean state does not have, nor ever had, the capacity or organization to deal with the pressing problems of explosive population growth and mass urbanization, even if it is clear that the vast majority of the population, elites and hoi polloi included, would like action on that front. Instead it has to invoke the ceremonial rhetoric of giving the Vagrancy Act added bite only, for these efforts to inevitably disintegrate, largely through the Supreme Court declaring them unconstitutional. Such invocations have a ritual quality and are part of a parcel of actions that include highly visible public displays of state power by engaging in mass operations, typically under the proclamation of a state of emergency. Such mass operations, usually involving large concentrated numbers of police and defense personnel and characteristically code-named Mekim Save (enough is enough), are invariably aimed at cleaning up informal settlements. This is a social site "that collectivizes such people for the purposes of displays of crime-fighting efficiency."[46] These operations are like King Canute's command for the sea to stop the waves. Within a few weeks the areas are reoccupied a situation strikingly similar to that described by Ocobock and Burton in British East Africa.

The focus of both vagrancy rhetoric and mass police operations are the informal settlements, which are the most rapidly growing segment in Papua New Guinea. Already it is estimated that more than half of Port Moresby's population reside there. These denizens are believed to be the cause of moral decay, crime, and the stealing of jobs from other residents. Today, such increasingly heavyhanded, large-scale evictions are usually orchestrated not by the central government, but by provincial authorities, often in alliance with local landowners. According to Gina Koczberski, George Curry, and John Connell, these evictions serve several purposes: political point scoring, having a demonstration effect, making such settlements uninhabitable, and signifying a lack of compassion.[47] Indeed, they claim, correctly in my opinion, that the "war on crime" rhetoric allows the state to engage in knee-jerk reactions without the need to develop and implement urban-planning policies. Such calls and activities reflect the incapacity of the state to engage in such complex bureaucratic exercises.

As far as could be ascertained, Papua New Guinea still does not have a vagrancy law, despite repeated efforts to reintroduce one, because such legislation would require a constitutional amendment—and that would require a majority vote, an impossibility, given Papua New Guinea's fractured government. Despite this structural issue, the rhetoric of the necessity of a vagrancy law persists. Even though the police force was unsophisticated and lacked training, a charge of vagrancy would be relatively simple to identify and process, but clearly the rhetoric of imposing the Vagrancy Act derives in part from its deeper meaning. There is another more mundane reason for why a vagrancy law would be attractive. The magical symbolism of the colonial state was explicitly tied into its ceremonial practices and the shell of state ceremonialism. As Michael Taussig has argued, the very core of power is secrecy, but it is secrecy of a certain type, namely public secrecy, that which is generally known but cannot be articulated.[48] Such public secrets are typically performed in public ceremonies. It is probably no accident that the one branch of government that enjoys relative respectability is the one most shrouded in ceremony: the judiciary. One of the criticisms of the local village courts made by expatriate researchers was their excessive formalism; but little did those researchers realize that this was a survival mechanism. Courtly pantomimes or burlesques are common enough to attract anthropological attention.[49] State concerns with ceremonies and "invented traditions" remain important.

Papua New Guinea is one of the few Commonwealth countries that still bestow knighthoods on its stalwart citizens. The only branch of the administration that still carries the appellation Royal is the Royal Papua New Guinea Police Constabulary, and the one budget item that has not been cut is the police band, which is used largely for ceremonial purposes. How locals see the police is significant: "Many policemen think they are above the law when in their uniforms." "Because of their uniforms, police can do anything with women."[50] Even expatriate experts agree. UNICEF representative Bruce Grant claimed that the "police really believe in the notion that it is okay to burn down someone's house."[51] The magic lies in the uniform.

The vagrancy legislation is equally important on a symbolic level, more so than a crass instrumentalist interpretation allows. While relatively powerless, the state still remains influential, especially given the transnational core of its economy, in which Australian aid plays a significant part. Law not only regulates sociocultural life, it represents it as well. As an ideology, law contributes to the social construction of the social world by creating images of social relationships as natural and fair to the state benefactors because they are endowed with legality. The audience for this rhetoric is largely elites and potential foreign investors. It pacifies them. Law was a massive local anesthetic that sedated the contradictions and the necessity of thinking. It successfully "fettered the imagination." This type of power called for what James Scott terms "knee-haltered knowledge" and what I have termed shadow knowledge, in which law provides the outline or silhouette of what is considered legal behavior and the complexity is glossed in a unidimensional, monochromatic blank, as epitomized by the Rabaul strike inquiry of 1929.[52] In *Seeing Like a State*, Scott attempts to answer the question of what impels the state to sedate its subjects. He examines social engineering projects and concludes that they failed because they made use of a shallow, simplified knowledge to administratively order society and nature based on a high modernist ideology with authoritarian overtones coupled to a "prostrate civil society," which lacked the capacity to resist these plans. Clearly Papua New Guinea is the antithesis of such a system. Here the denizens simply ignore these plans.

Sexual Insecurity, White Man's Prestige, and the Machinery of Ceremonialism

There is another angle that must be explored: the importance of fantasy and façade. If one cannot control the body, then it is imperative to control the mind. A study of vagrancy should be accompanied by one of the colonial efforts at censorship. In Papua New Guinea such efforts were certainly draconian, and even in the late seventies magazines like *Playboy* were still banned.[53] Contemporary globalization in Papua New Guinea has invoked fantasy in promoting consumerism.[54] Sexual fantasies continue to permeate many segments of the country. In her pioneering study of Papua New Guinean sexual attitudes and experiences, Carol Jenkins reports that a surprisingly large number of Papua New Guinean males claimed to have had their first sexual encounters with white women.[55] It would seem that the Highlands must have been ravaged by a few sexually rapacious expatriate females.

The problem and impact of colonial sexual insecurity needs to be noted. Historically, there is a contradiction of glaring proportion. Despite the rhetorical importance of the Vagrancy Law, a survey of court records and statistics and annual reports, admittedly incomplete, shows that in reality very few people were ever charged with vagrancy, and this pattern apparently has continued up to the present.[56] Ironically—and it is an irony requiring exploration—in the interwar years the only people charged with vagrancy were European males. Symbolism has a lot to do with this. "The white man's most valuable weapon in this country is the prestige of the white race," the *Rabaul Times* asserted shortly after its founding in 1925.[57] Australia's *Official Handbook* advised intending settlers that "the first qualification for practically any work in the Territory is a capacity to handle the native and retain his respect."[58] This was supposedly obtained by maintaining social distance and above all avoiding fraternization. Advice on this front was plentiful from "old hands" and was typically in the mode of, "Never talk to your boys themselves, under any circumstances; always do it through the boss boys. . . . Apart from your house boy and boss boys never allow any native in your employ to approach you, either in the field or on the bungalow verandah."[59]

The Australians emphasized "the white man's prestige," and students at the Australian School for Pacific Administration were constantly importuned to always polish their shoes and be neat. Georg Simmel appreciated the rigorous observance of such rituals because failure to do so would stress the inconsistencies of the "life world" that break in at the very point where norms and actions meet. It is of course when such ceremonies are revealed to be empty or mere show that the social order becomes fragile.[60]

Given this situation of maintaining white prestige, it is not surprising to find that the only cases of vagrancy found during a search of the annual reports submitted to the PMC concerned Europeans.[61] Clearly this was an important issue because in 1938, the Police Offences Ordinance was amended so that it became an offense for "any person, not being a native, or the child of a native . . . [to be] found lodging or wandering in company with any of the natives of the Territory" unless they could give a good account that they had a lawful fixed address and adequate means of support.[62] Later legislation was passed making it illegal for Europeans to enter "native villages" at night without a permit. This was an extension of the laws prohibiting single European males from having indigenous women residing in their houses.

Social distance in Papua New Guinea was, of course, closely connected with intimacy, especially with white women. "The stock defence to justify an act of brutality in New Guinea," Sir Hubert Murray commented in 1922 was made by, "dragging in the question of white women" and was "generally sheer invention."[63] Indeed, many urban regulations, especially those pertaining to curfews and loitering, were clearly aimed at protecting white women. In Papua, the White Women's Protection Ordinance of 1926 (amended in 1934 as a result of a "moral panic") made death the penalty for rape of a white woman. "European women," complained one traveler, "continued to tell 'never ending tales about the danger of being raped by native men' (and) such intercourse would undermine 'the moral fabric of the territory.'"[64] In the late 1930s, Reed found that organized settler opinion was campaigning for the return of flogging and that such appeals "are usually couched in slogans about white prestige and the danger of sexual attacks on white women by natives."[65] So seriously was this taken that in 1937 the administrator of New Guinea offered to install at government expense "boy-proof" sleeping rooms, enclosed by heavy chicken wire, in all houses where European women resided.[66]

Given the general unenforceability of the vagrancy legislation, except as it pertains to Europeans, one must reassess its role. Clearly this legislation was not part of some crude form of "primitive accumulation," forcing reluctant indigenes into the capitalist labor system. On the contrary, it appears to be geared toward upholding that strange edifice called white prestige, which was of course crucial in maintaining that great lucrative con game called the colonial state. These ceremonies—which ranged from knighthoods to medals to the Boy Scouts, royal salutes, and day-to-day rituals—were crucial in inculcating what A. P. Thornton called "the habit of authority," that unquestioning and unquestioned sense of superiority. Could it thus be that these calls for reinstitution of the Vagrancy Act refer in some way to these submerged fantasies and façades?

Notes

Grateful thanks to Sinclair Dinnen, Polly Wiessner, Ned McMahon, and Peter von Doepp for comments and advice. Laura Douglas helped in collecting the data.

1. John Torpey, "Coming and Going: On the State Monopolization of the Legitimate 'Means of Movement,'" *Sociological Theory* 69, no. 3 (1998): 239–59; Nicholas P. De Genova, "Migrant 'Illegality' and Deportability in Everyday Life," *Annual Review of Anthropology* 31 (2002): 419–47.

2. "Papua New Guinea: Vagrants on Hit List," *Post Courier/PINA Nius,* July 4, 2003, http://www.pacificmagazine.net./news/2003/07/04/papua-new-guinea-vagrants-on-hit-list.

3. ANU, *Hindsight: A Workshop for Participants in the Decolonization of Papua New Guinea,* November 3–4, 2002 (draft, April 4, 2003), http://rspas.anu.edu.au/papers/pah/hindsight.pdf.

4. The irony suggests that the original proponents for the abolition of the Vagrancy Act were in all probability not Papua New Guineans but

idealistic expatriate advisers who largely ran the administration. Olewale was of course simply raising issues that are very much part of concerns in Port Moresby and indeed, as this chapter will show, go back many years. For example, the previous year the teachers' association had called on the government to immediately reintroduce the Vagrancy Act and to protect students, teachers, and school properties from increasing lawlessness in the city.

5. William Chambliss, "A Sociological Analysis of the Law of Vagrancy," *Social Problems* 12, no. 1 (1964): 46–67.

6. Wantoks (lit., one talk) refers to people to whom one is related either by kinship or place. Sinclair Dinnen, *Law and Order in a Weak State* (Honolulu: University of Hawaii Press, 2000); Michael Goddard, "From Rolling Thunder to Reggae: Imagining Squatter Settlements in Papua New Guinea," *Contemporary Pacific* 13, no. 7 (2001): 1–32.

7. David Weisbrot, Abdul Paliwala, and Akilagpa Sawyerr, *Law and Social Change in Papua New Guinea* (Sydney: Butterworths, 1982). In the omnibus version, more correctly known as the Native Administration Regulations in New Guinea and the Native Regulations in Papua.

8. Edward P. Wolfers, "Trusteeship without Trust," in *Racism: The Australian Experience,* vol. 3, *Colonialism,* ed. F. S. Stevens (Sydney: Australia and New Zealand Book Company, 1972), 70.

9. Robert J. Gordon, "The Decline of the 'Kiapery' and the Rise of the Administrative Petty Bourgeoisie," in *Decentralization in Papua New Guinea,* ed. R. Premdas (Port Moresby: University of Papua New Guinea Press, 1979), 107–14.

10. Wolfers, "Trusteeship without Trust," 69.

11. August Kituai, *My Gun, My Brother: The World of the Papua New Guinea Colonial Police, 1920–60* (Honolulu: University of Hawaii Press, 1998).

12. Wolfers, "Trusteeship without Trust," 119. Other regulations at this time still allowed the administrator to proclaim that in certain areas absence from tribal area could be a criminal offense. It defined a "foreign native" as a native who is absent from his tribal area and provided that when such a native "cannot give a good account of his means of support" he could be ordered to return to his tribal area. Failure to do so could lead to three months' imprisonment with hard labor. A similar regulation allowed the administrator to proclaim restricted areas in which noninhabitants of that area were barred from residence there. Law Reform Commission of Papua New Guinea, "Abolition of Native Regulations," Working Paper 1 (Port Moresby: Law Reform Commission, 1975).

13. Anthony Kirk-Greene, "The Thin White Line: The Size of the British Colonial Service in Africa," *African Affairs* 79, no. 1 (1980): 25–44.

14. Commonwealth of Australia, (Annual) Report to the League of Nations on the Administration of the Territory of New Guinea, July 1 to June 30, 1929 (Government Printer: Canberra, 1929), para. 8.

15. Australia, Prime Minister's Office, *Official Handbook of the Territory of New Guinea* (Canberra: Government Printer, 1943), 270.

16. Karl A. Wittfogel, *Oriental Despotism: A Comparative Study of Total Power* (New Haven, CT: Yale University Press, 1959).

17. Wolfers, "Trusteeship without Trust," 140.

18. Kituai, *My Gun*, 170.

19. Commonwealth of Australia, (Annual) Report to the League of Nations (1924), 52.

20. Stephen W. Reed, *The Making of Modern New Guinea* (Philadelphia: American Philosophical Society, 1943), 164.

21. Exemptions were issued to police, indentured workers, unfit natives, fathers of more than four children, mission teachers, and "native authorities" like *luluais* and *tultuls*. In 1927 some £22,000 was collected in head tax. Commonwealth of Australia, (Annual) Report to the League of Nations (1928).

22. Anthony Alcock, *History of the International Labor Organization* (New York: Octagon Books, 1971), 85.

23. Peter Fitzpatrick, "Labouring in Legal Mystification: D. W. Smith, Labour and the Law in Papua New Guinea." *Melanesian Law Journal* 4, no. 1 (1976): 137.

24. Australia, *Official Handbook*.

25. Reed, *Modern New Guinea*, 163, 183.

26. Ibid., 177. Indeed after the 1929 Rabaul strike, the *Rabaul Times* reported, if the administrator "attempts to prosecute residents who thrashed their deserters, he may find that he will have to prosecute them in batches of a hundred at a time" (234).

27. Clive Rowley, *The New Guinea Villager* (Sydney: Cheshire, 1965), 104. Similarly, Lucy Mair, the experienced applied anthropologist sent out to assess Australian policy in New Guinea after WWII, pointed out that in practice officials believed that burdens of plantation owners should not be increased "beyond what they could bear." Inspection was in any case inadequate, and officers who were anxious to enforce the prescribed conditions felt that they could not count on support from headquarters. Lucy Mair, *Australia in New Guinea* (Melbourne: Melbourne University Press, 1970), 184.

28. David Biles, ed., *Crime in Papua New Guinea* (Canberra: Australian Institute of Criminology, 1976).

29. Weisbrot, Paliwala, and Sawyerr, *Law and Social Change*, 19.

30. Bernard Narakobi, "Colonial Laws," *Melanesian Law Journal* 4, no. 1 (1976): 132.

31. William Clifford, Louise Morauta, and Barry Stuart, *Law and Order in Papua New Guinea* (Port Moresby: Institute of National Affairs, 1984), 125.

32. Dinnen, *Law and Order*, 70.

33. Human Rights Watch, *Making Their Own Rules: Police Beating, Rape and Torture of Children* (New York: Human Rights Watch, 2005), 83.

34. News items reported on the BBC, December 9, 2004, May 17, 2005, http://www.bbc.co.uk.

35. Data derived from United Nations Development Programme, http://www.undp.org/.

36. More recent elections took place in May 2007, but reportage and analysis on them has been limited thus far.

37. Cited in Human Rights Watch, *Making Their Own Rules*, 79.

38. Jeffrey Clark, "Imagining the State, or Tribalism and the Arts of Memory in the Highlands of Papua New Guinea," in *Narratives of the Nation in the South Pacific*, ed. Ton Otto and Nicholas Thomas (Amsterdam: Harwood, 1997).

39. For an extended discussion of these features, see Robert J. Gordon and Mervyn Meggitt, *Law and Order in the New Guinea Highlands* (Hanover, NH: University Press of New England, 1985).

40. Ibid., 158.

41. Approximately $375,000 (US) at the 2002 rate of exchange.

42. Pamela Stewart and Andrew Strathern, "Mi les long yupela usim flag bilong mi: Symbols and Identity in Papua New Guinea," *Pacific Studies* 23, no. 1 (2000): 21–49.

43. Gordon and Meggitt, *Law and Order*, 181.

44. Morauta, cited in Ray Anere et al., *Security in Melanesia Report Prepared by the Pacific Islands Forum Secretariat for the Forum Regional Security Committee (FRSC) Meeting, 25–26 June 2001*, http://www.scholar.google.com.

45. Gary Trompf, *Payback: The Logic of Retribution in Melanesian Religions* (Cambridge: Cambridge University Press, 1994).

46. Goddard, "Rolling Thunder," 22.

47. Gina Koczberski, George N. Curry, and John Connell, "Full Circle or Spiralling Out of Control? State Violence and the Control of Urbanisation in Papua New Guinea," *Urban Studies* 38 (2001): 2023.

48. Michael Taussig, *Defacement: Public Secrecy and the Labor of the Negative* (Stanford, CA: Stanford University Press, 1999), 5.

49. David Lipset, "'The Trial': A Parody of the Law amid the Mockery of Men in Post-colonial Papua New Guinea," *Journal of the Royal Anthropological Institute* 10, no. 1 (2004): 63–100.

50. Human Rights Watch, *Making Their Own Rules*, 36.

51. Ibid., 90.

52. Robert J. Gordon, "Vagrancy, Law and 'Shadow Knowledge': Internal Pacification, 1915–1939," in *Namibia under South African Rule: Mobility and Containment*, ed. Patricia Hayes et al. (Athens: Ohio University Press, 1998), 51–77.

53. Wolfers, "Trusteeship without Trust."

54. Robert J. Foster, ed., *Nation Making: Emergent Identities in Postcolonial Melanesia* (Ann Arbor: University of Michigan Press, 1997).

55. Carol Jenkins, *National Study of Sexual and Reproductive Knowledge and Behaviour in Papua New Guinea* (Goroka: Papua New Guinea Institute of Medical Research, 1994).

56. Commonwealth of Australia, Report to the League of Nations (1925), para. 70.

57. Reed, *Modern New Guinea*, 248.

58. Australia, *Official Handbook*, 329.

59. Reed, *Modern New Guinea*, 219.

60. Georg Simmel, *The Sociology of Georg Simmel*, trans. and ed. Kurt H. Wolff (New York: Free Press, 1950).

61. Commonwealth of Australia, Report to the League of Nations (1929), para. 14.

62. Wolfers, "Trusteeship without Trust," 106.

63. Edward P. Wolfers, *Race Relations and Colonial Rule in Papua New Guinea* (Sydney: Australia and New Zealand Book Company, 1975), 98.

64. Ibid., 61.

65. Reed, *Modern New Guinea*, 177n.

66. Ibid., 251.

13

Subversive Accommodations

Doing Homeless in Tokyo's Ueno Park

Abby Margolis

I AM FREQUENTLY asked two questions when I introduce the topic of homelessness in Tokyo. The first is, Are there really homeless people in Japan? When I answer in the affirmative, the second question inevitably follows: How did you become involved with *them*? I begin with these questions because, even more than their answers, they re veal much about the popular perception and contemporary context of homelessness in Tokyo. The questions, and the tone of curiosity in which they are asked, demonstrate two sorts of cultural common sense. First, they demonstrate a widespread assumption about Japan that presupposes all Japanese are middle class. Second, they demonstrate a common view of homelessness that assumes homeless people are socially different. I am also frequently asked if the homeless in Japan are even Japanese at all: Aren't they mostly foreigners? Of course, this misconception, like the others, is not true; but it points to the near incapability of imagining a homeless Japanese. Underlying all these questions are ideas that homeless people are somehow cut off from conventional society, do not follow cultural norms of behavior, and therefore live in states of disorientation or disorder.

Opening a discussion of the homeless in Japan, then, necessitates a rethinking of understandings of marginality, and of the behaviors and identities of those who live in the so-called margins of society. The very word *homeless* seems to shove homeless people into the peripheries of society, dislodging them from a broader cultural context. This is especially true in Japan where the home (*ie*) is frequently argued to be central to both self and national identity.[1] Homelessness poses a unique problem for the study of Japan because it challenges well-established notions of Japanese identity, which locate that identity in the sedentary spheres of the home and work. The very existence of homeless people offends official descriptions of Japanese identity.[2] Karen Kelsky recently noted, "The status of the nonnormative is particularly vexed in the context of Japan anthropology, which to a large extent has depended on, and indeed tirelessly reproduced, normative constructs of 'Japanese culture.'"[3] In this normative construction of Japanese identity, an individual's position within the institutions of work and home has been called the zero-point of entry into Japanese society. If home and work are truly the starting points of Japanese social identity, it follows that the homeless, composed mostly of single, unemployed men, have no entryway. Yet, ethnographic research with homeless people in Tokyo, and exploration into the ways in which they construct their own identities, complicates their presumed disaffiliation from and marginality in Japanese culture. The following discussion of homelessness in Tokyo is meant to provoke a reexamination of the categories of Japanese cultural inquiry and to collapse the distinctions between inside and outside (*uchi/soto*), self and other, and home and away that tend to dominate that inquiry. Yet, while the chapter is meant to provoke a challenge to normative ideas of Japanese identity, it is careful not to assume that homeless identities and activities deviate from the norm. That does not mean this chapter should be read as an attempt to normalize homelessness. It makes no suggestion that rather than part of a marginalized culture, homeless people are part of a broader Japanese culture. Instead, this chapter reveals the flexibility and innovative use of cultural ideals by individuals as they live their lives, negotiate their identities, and "do homeless" in Ueno Park. By showing how homeless people in Tokyo do not match the broader image of their otherness, this chapter demonstrates that that thinking in terms of centers and margins ultimately obscures more than it reveals. This is not to deny that structures of power work through such paradigms, but to suggest scholars and others be very careful as to what they think marginality might mean and what kinds of predictive power such a perspective might have. Rather than viewing homeless people as different, the goal of this chapter is to explore how they might help us think differently about marginality, homelessness, and Japan. This is not the first attempt to think differently about this subject matter; but this chapter, too, is critical of some common alternative perspectives on homeless people that view homelessness as either a survival tactic or resistance practice. It argues that survival and resistance are equally insufficient concepts for representing homeless lifestyles. That is, while homeless people do not simply behave unconventionally, neither do they merely adapt to fit their impoverished situations or behave only in ways that demonstrate opposition to conventional ideas of family, work, and gender.

This chapter looks at the representations of homelessness in both popular opinion and in the ethnographic writing of anthropologists, before turning to examine the ways in which homeless people with whom I researched in Tokyo's Ueno Park articulated the meaning of homelessness in their own lives, best expressed in their phrase *doing homeless* (*hoomuresu o suru*). It is this discourse of doing homeless that I suggest offers interesting ground for broadening our understandings of homelessness, marginality, and Japanese identity.

Homelessness in Japan

The first national government survey of Japan's homeless people conducted in 2003 lists about 25,300 homeless persons living in Japan, with approximately six thousand homeless living in Tokyo's twenty-three wards. The majority of Japan's homeless are men over fifty years of age, with an average age of about fifty-six, who have been living in tents, train stations, parks, riversides, and on the streets for an average total of forty-nine months.[4] Women reportedly make up only 3 percent of the national homeless population; but, according to Ueno Park management, 5 percent of the homeless in the park were women (activist groups estimated up to 10 percent). One study points out that while "it is obvious from the data . . . that the vast majority of [homeless people in Japan] are male . . . characterizing the phenomenon as 'male,' has ensured that the number of females recorded as homeless is low or completely absent."[5] Furthermore, by "identifying only those living on the streets as homeless" the census insures that the total number is undercounted. Because the population is mobile, and sometimes hidden in temporary dormitories, on friends' futons, or in cheap motels, it is clear that total numbers cannot be exact. Yet, both government and advocate polls report that the numbers of homeless have been steadily increasing since the early 1990s. Still, activists' estimates were much higher; based on their experiences with "night patrols," many claimed there were ten thousand homeless people in Tokyo alone.

Many of the recently homeless in Tokyo fell out of the informal day labor system that flourished in postwar Japan. These were men who in their youth were tempted from the countryside by job opportunities in the city but who eventually found themselves jobless due to economic decline, the shift to a service economy, new recruiting strategies, and their own advancing age.[6] Still other men are homeless due to failed loans or corporate restructuring. The history of homeless women in Tokyo is much less well documented. Among the women of Ueno Park, most came to the streets from broken marriages and prolonged states of poverty or illness. Since there is little work opportunity without a fixed address, and since most landlords demand six months' rent to be paid in advance for an apartment, once homeless there are very few possibilities for gaining steady employment or obtaining a permanent residence.

In many parks throughout Tokyo, homeless people lived in tents that they constructed out of blue plastic tarps. There were approximately three hundred such tents in Ueno Park when I conducted research in 1998–99. Most homeless people lived alone in their tents but, including the number of persons sleeping on benches, under awnings, and on the surrounding streets, there were approximately one thousand to twelve hundred homeless people in the Ueno area. Homeless people in Ueno Park supported themselves through the activities of doing homeless, which included recycling, scavenging, occasional day labor, resale of found items, and maintaining personal relationships. Homeless persons tented in Ueno Park did not panhandle. Nor did most attend the church-run sermon and food handout that came to the park several times a week and attracted up to one thousand persons from the surrounding areas. These were not simply economic choices; rather they reflect the moral meanings of doing homeless. Homeless people in Ueno Park prided themselves in their self-sufficiency, honor, and perseverance. In other words, doing homeless was not just about pursuing particular types of labor; it included disciplining these jobs, and each other, with broader cultural virtues of hard work, sincerity, and obligation to others.

On mornings when I would arrive in Ueno Park for a day of fieldwork I was often greeted with a mock-scolding *hima da naa,* "you sure have lots of free time." Some wondered out loud if I should not instead be at school or if I would ever complete my "report" with all the time I spent in the park. I was constantly made to pay attention to virtues like hard work, sincerity, and reciprocity as the means of introducing and proving myself, and as the currency through which to meet new people. These virtues served as the grounds on which Tokyo's homeless people articulated their lifestyle (*seikatsu*) of doing homeless and through which I came to understand how it should be properly done (expressed as either *shikkari suru* or *chyanto suru*). It was by appealing to culturally sanctioned ideals that homeless persons would judge each other, and the ethnographer. Does he keep his tent neat? Does he persevere (*gambaru*) at his recycling, scavenging, or other work? Does he properly greet his neighbors? Is he attuned to other's feelings? In other words, is he fit enough to do homeless? The answers to these questions guided their evaluations of who was good at doing homeless and with whom they might establish relationships. The questions I found homeless persons asking themselves were very different from the kinds of questions other researchers were asking. Homeless people in Ueno were concerned with *doing* homeless, while researchers were more concerned with how individuals become homeless and with how they survive in that presumed otherworldly lifestyle. Doing homeless and homeless people's elaborations on how it should be done, then, are grossly at odds with both scholarly approaches and popular representations of homeless people as disaffiliated, lazy, and outside the moral and cultural values of society. Still, an imagery of otherness proliferates in both Japanese and Western popular representations of homeless people. As Kim Hopper has written on homelessness in the United States, "Whether construed as civilization's exile, its nemesis, or as evidence of its failure, [notions of the homeless person are] built on a prior refusal to recognize him as part of the inclusive world of the observer."[7] Let me offer some examples of this exclusion in the Japanese case.

Typical news headlines about the homeless include such titles as "The Other Japan," "The Other Side of the Coin," "Down and Out in Tokyo" (or Osaka, or Kobe), and, perhaps most poignantly, "The Unsalaried Man," which plays on the term *salaryman* as Japan's prototypical (male) worker.[8] These headlines, which invert the symbols of Japaneseness (and Japanese masculinity), serve to reduce homelessness to a negative identity. The homeless are, by popular headline anyway, what Japan and its archetypal salarymen are not. These representations, in turn, have a real effect on the lives of homeless people in Tokyo. Certainly this imagery of otherness helps explain why homeless men are often targets of violence. There are reports of school children and others verbally harassing them, striking them with rocks and firecrackers, knifing them, and setting them on fire. In fact 39 percent of Tokyo's homeless people say they have experienced some kind of discrimination or attack.[9] While there are also reports of homeless people committing abuses against each other, one rarely if ever reads that a homeless person was violent toward a local resident. Still these same residents frequently complain, especially when protesting a shelter rumored to be built in their neighborhood, that the homeless make local areas unsafe for women and children.[10] Such complaints further exemplify the way in which homeless people are popularly viewed as "others" to be feared.

The Japanese government also contributes to this view. It was not until 1995 that the Tokyo metropolitan government issued its first report on homelessness (though it based its findings on what it called "previous research"). The report states, "there are people who have

356 | *Abby Margolis*

homes in their hometowns who live on the street in the city. In these instances, it can be possible that they choose to live on the street."[11] Following this report, Tokyo's then governor, Yukio Aoshima, announced that homeless people, "have particular views of life and philosophy. They want to be left alone."[12] In other words, without any contemporary investigation, the governor declared homeless peoples' "peculiarity" responsible for their living on the street.

The governor's comments quickly became a rallying quote for the homeless social movement. Homeless support groups and activist leaders began to conduct their own surveys and produce knowledge that demonstrated homeless people were still interested in working. More important, they linked the homeless problem with the day labor market and the postbubble economy that not only left the aging itinerant worker population unemployed but also denied their contributions to the previous economic rise of Japan. Supporters of homeless people in Japan began to refer to them as homeless laborers, and to challenge perceptions of the homeless as others, like that by Governor Aoshima, by linking the homeless problem directly to the political economy and current recession that was affecting the whole of Japan.

Until 2000, the government took little more than cosmetic measures to meet the "homeless problem." What limited relevant public policy did exist was aimed at laborers, not the homeless. While there were government-supported welfare, health, and day labor–related policies that applied to some homeless individuals, usually the very sick or the very old, there was almost no policy specific to homelessness in Tokyo. The metropolitan government still persists with a hands-off approach toward the issue of homelessness. Traditionally its policies have been aimed at cosmetically hiding or confining homelessness to day labor communities, while providing limited emergency assistance for unemployed laborers in those communities.[13] Access to dorms, like two temporary structures that were opened in Tokyo only for the three winter months, was reserved for registered laborers who could demonstrate that they were still living in the *yoseba*, or day labor community. Other services, like yearly bonuses and public works, were also reserved strictly for registered "working" laborers. Of course, even laborers who were working in the yoseba often were not officially registered, so the measures reflect the government's effort to define the deserving poor and to control where they should live. Official actions beyond the day labor neighborhoods include nailing wooden blocks in the center of park benches to keep homeless people from sleeping there, and turning off the water at public drinking fountains to discourage homeless people from gathering and bathing in public. The metropolitan administration also, amid much protest, evacuated hundreds of homeless people from one corridor of Shinjuku station, Tokyo's busiest train station, to make room for a moving sidewalk that it claimed would help commuters get to work faster. During these highly contested evictions, administrators framed homeless people as environmental hazards and vagrants and further defended their evacuation as part of an environmental cleanup.

Unlike in the United States or Britain, where the president or members of the royal family may, especially around Christmas time, schedule photo ops to exhibit themselves aiding the homeless and poor, the Japanese government and imperial family members do not even pretend to participate in such activities. The "special cleanups" that the police and park management conducted in Ueno Park exemplify the official Japanese approach. Ueno Park rests on land that is still owned by the imperial family. The former temple grounds were given to the people in the last quarter of the nineteenth century, as a gift from the emperor, and relandscaped as public space in an effort to make Tokyo look more like a Western city. The park is currently the site of several museums, shrines, and temples and is a destination for both national and international tourists. The emperor, as the cultural head of state, comes to Ueno Park to view traveling artworks or for other events, sometimes as frequently as once a month. State and local officials, in preparation for those visits, would remind homeless people squatting in tents that they were living in the park illegally. They would issue a warning: all homeless people must evacuate by a certain date or risk being dispossessed of their belongings. On the assigned day, park management, police, and other local officials would parade through the park, surveying to make sure all the tents had been removed. In fact, they would conduct a rehearsal of the cleanup three days before the imperial visit and then on the assigned day carry out the "real thing." Homeless people living in the park usually followed the instructions to move out on the specified day. This was seen as part of properly doing homeless. While they might not have agreed with the authorities, many homeless persons I met took pride in their ability to complete the cleanup with efficiency and style. Some would even harshly criticize their neighbors during the event: "Look at how much unnecessary stuff he has," one man scornfully pointed out of a neighbor. And his companion went on, "and look at the state of his boxes. What are we to think of his internal state of mind?" These criticisms revealed much about how these men believed homeless should be done. Still, as soon as the officials retreated to their offices, the homeless residents simply returned to their sites and rebuilt their tents. The next month, they would all repeat the performance. This monthly routine demonstrates how officials in Japan treat homeless people as an unsightly problem, certainly not to be seen when the emperor comes to visit his otherwise beautiful park.

The academic literature (even writing that is sympathetic) has also seized upon these notions of fundamental difference. Tom Gill compares entering a Japanese day labor community (*doyagai*), where many homeless people live in Japan, to entering a foreign country.[14] Gill claims residents there "consider themselves 'outside' society . . . [and] place themselves at the center of an alternative moral universe."[15] He goes on to argue that "everyone in the doya-gai was an outsider . . . they presented the doya-gai as a place for 'uncrafted selves,' to modify Kondo (1990)—*unpolished nuggets of selfhood.*"[16] With words like *unpolished nuggets,* Gill seems to suggest that homeless identities are not only unrefined, wild, and untouched by cultural constraints, but partial and incomplete. To understand Gill's perspective some background is necessary about the history of Japanese studies and its tireless pursuit to document enduring patterns and norms of Japanese behavior. In this context, studies of homelessness, along with those of minorities in Japan, have come to hold particular significance for the project of critiquing widely held notions of Japanese uniqueness and homogeneity. That is, studies of homeless people clearly disrupt conventional ideas of what it means to be Japanese. They do not fit the model of vertical society, or the icon of the work-driven salaryman. It is true, as suggested by Gill and others,[17] that day labor communities offer fertile ground for rethinking such notions, but this is not simply because of the communities' inherent foreignness. I argue that it is a mistake to turn a lack of stable employment and family networks into a rendering of homeless people as culturally other and classifiably different. Scholars must take the challenge further and look at how these "different" others take up the more conventional discourses of Japanese identity. Here, anthropology offers crucial insights into Japan studies.

The Anthropology of Homelessness

While anthropologists have in some ways contributed to the concept of homelessness as otherly, anthropology also has a long history of responding to the view of homeless people as deviant and disorderly. Many anthropologists have used the concept of culture as the key means by which to present a more empathetic view of homeless persons. Stemming from Oscar Lewis's concept of the "culture of poverty,"[18] as well as anthropology's functionalist roots, writings on homelessness in American anthropology often attempt to present homelessness as an orderly culture or subculture and, through ethnographic methods, to provide an insider's point of view on that culture. Unfortunately, this approach can distance the homeless even as it attempts to bring them into better focus. For example, James Spradley, in his classic ethnography *You Owe Yourself a Drunk*, argues that "the distance between most Americans and urban nomads cannot be measured in miles; they are separated from us by cultural distance."[19] His book, in an embrace of cultural relativism, attempted to demonstrate that homeless drunks in Seattle, contrary to popular belief, were not unruly and irrational but operated with cultural logic. This perspective was an important response to earlier views of the homeless as lacking in social order and incapable of rational behavior, and certainly it was an improvement on simply dismissing homeless people as beyond culture. Yet, it overlooked homeless people's intimate connections with the mainstream. Instead, Spradley, and others whom we might associate with the culture-of-poverty school, emphasized how the homeless and poor are enculturated into a wholly different, if equally meaningful, system.

One answer to the shortcomings of the culture of poverty studies has been to focus on the structural causes of homelessness, the political economy, and the marginalizing structures of race, class, and gender. These approaches reject a core principle in the culture of poverty concept—that the poor are isolated and engulfed by a wholly separate cultural ethos. A structural perspective focuses alternatively on the history of labor and race relations and other complex structural causes of homelessness. Its usefulness is found in that it keeps us from blaming and isolating the individual. Instead of suggesting that, once homeless, people learn a new set of ideals and behaviors, structural analysis looks at the situations and behaviors of homeless individuals as intimately linked and responsive to broader social institutions and ideologies of race, class, and gender. But, as Philippe Bourgois reminds us, structural "analysis is not a panacea to compensate for individualistic, racist, or otherwise judgmental interpretations of social marginalization. In fact, a focus on structures often obscures the fact that humans are active agents of their own history, rather than passive victims."[20] Contemporary studies of the homeless and the poor are, then, caught up in the debates between structure and agency. Did class, racial, ethnic, and gender discrimination cause their homelessness? Or was it their own failures? Joanne Passaro points out what is missing from research surrounding this debate: "an analysis of the process of remaining homeless, as opposed to becoming houseless."[21]

The ongoing, back-and-forth debate between structure and agency ultimately raises the question, can there be other possibilities for homeless agency? Many researchers see resistance as one such possibility and have turned to the notion of resistance as a remedy for both the failures of the culture concept and the structural approach.[22] The notion of resistance has been taken up as a cure-all to get around the debates between structure and agency, and in many ways it has pushed the conversation further. The idea of resistance turns our attention to the unevenness of culture, to the complexities of power and domination, and to the subtleties of human agency, given structural forms of repression. However, resistance too is a limiting concept. By looking at the way in which marginalized individuals either resist or accommodate dominant values we often fail to recognize that the two might look the same. A focus on resistance runs the risk of overlooking those practices that appear wholly ordinary. Furthermore, perspectives on resistance often limit the expression of resistance to those forms that reject dominant values. Perhaps resistance, at least as it is usually conceived, is not the only possibility for new representations of homeless agency. While it successfully demonstrates that marginalized individuals are not isolated, it limits their dialogue with broader society to an oppositional mode. Is opposition the only form resistance might take? I argue that in a situation of marginalization, where those in the margins are popularly expected to act as deviants, an effective form of resistance may be the embrace of dominant values.

Doing Homeless: A New Perspective

In the phrase *doing homeless,* the verb *do* itself begins to open up new discussions on homelessness; it challenges the association of homelessness with idleness, as expressed in the usual phrasing, *becoming homeless.* More important, homeless people's elaborations on how homeless is properly done challenge scholars, journalists, and activists to examine the limitations of the conceptual frameworks— be it deviance, subculture, survival strategy, or resistance—that reign in the homeless literature. Doing homeless is not doing whatever one can just to get by, but a way of living up to the ideals of reciprocity, discipline, and national identity. Furthermore, as a discourse of hard work, honor, perseverance, and conventional masculinity, doing homeless demonstrates that agency in the margins does not necessarily oppose mainstream values.

The phrase *doing homeless* not only rejects the association of homelessness with idleness, but forces the question, how is homeless done? In some ways this is best answered by starting with how it is not done. Because Ueno Park is up on a hill and was historically called the mountain (*yama*), homeless people living in the park referred to themselves as people of the mountain (*yama no ningen*), and distinguish their identity from other homeless who lived more nomadically, "down there" (*shita no hoo*) in other parts of the park or city where permanent tents were prohibited. As people of the mountain, homeless people in Ueno associated themselves with a romanticized and idealized rice-based diet, work ethic, pride, and livelihood, and contrasted these markers of identity with the homeless from "down there," off the mountain.[23] Often it was pointed out to me the way in which people from *shita no hoo* queue for soup lines, eat bread crusts, do not cook with stoves, have dirty skin, do not do laundry, and make no effort to "properly" do homeless. Their "improper" and "bad" behaviors were then associated with having less pride, determination, and commitment and therefore with being lesser persons, lesser homeless, and lesser Japanese. Of course the homeless down there similarly dismiss the homeless above, claiming that they are the ones who have given up and given in to homelessness. These more nomadic homeless view the tents as a symbol of giving up the job search and of a commitment to remain on the streets. Thus, making others deviant works in both directions: both tented and nomadic homeless projected ideas of difference, deviance, and otherness onto each other in order to demonstrate their own integrity.

Those homeless people from the mountain who went to collect food and recyclables in the nearby shopping arcade at night often complained to me about homeless people from down there passing through, making a mess of the trash that businesses neatly set out on the curb, and jeopardizing the relationships they claimed to respect with shop owners. They viewed these ill-mannered bums (*kojiki*) as undisciplined, unable to properly scavenge, and unconcerned with human relationships. For example, Kokusai, a man in Ueno Park who called himself a tent-lifestyler (*tento seikatsusha*) explained how his lifestyle was different than a lifestyle of sleeping on the streets (*rojoo seikatsu*): "The color of their face is different; it is darker from being in the sun and from not bathing. . . . They don't have a stove, hot food, or a change of clothes. One can tell just by looking who has a tent or not." Kokusai's neighbor added that those without tents were constipated and could not sleep because they had no fixed schedule or place to rest—the very rhythms and appearance of their bodies were seen as unpredictable and disrupted by their nomadism and instability.

By contrast, yama no ningen insisted, whether they labored, recycled, or scavenged, that they do it adamantly and properly (*shikkari suru*), with all their effort (*gambaru*). I spent many hours listening to ways in which one could better tie newspapers, more efficiently crush cans, or perfect the method of sifting through garbage. This is significant because *gambaru* (to persevere) is an activity that the dominant discourse, as in Governor Aoshima's quote earlier, claims that the homeless, in particular, do not do. The governor suggested that it is precisely because homeless people do not persevere that they "become" homeless. Yet, rejecting this sentiment, one man in Ueno argued, "The only reason we are here is because we gambaru. That is the only reason we are alive." Thus, he recast the notion that the tents represented shame or failure and claimed they stood as a testament to an effort and willingness to persevere.

Among the tented homeless in Ueno Park, it was precisely productivity and activity that lent legitimacy to put up a tent in the park's limited space. Oneesan, a rather influential woman in the park, frequently complained of a neighbor who said that his only job was to sleep. "He should lose his homeless rights [*hoomuresu no kenri*]," she said. Almost no homeless person I met believed that they had legal rights to be in the park,[24] so by rights she was referring to the rights that were gained through discipline and perseverance. In fact, just as the general population may view homelessness itself as an illness and the homeless as unfit, the Japanese homeless persons I talked to judged some of those among them as too weak or ill and unfit to properly do homeless in Ueno Park.

Consider the situation of two park residents, whom I call Neko and Kita. Both had tents in Ueno Park during my research. Neko had been living with her "husband" since her arrival six years prior (the husband had been there already for four years), while Kita arrived more recently, a few months into the research. Yet, despite her seniority and growing despair, it was Neko who was losing legitimacy and support from her neighbors in the park. Neko was from a rural hamlet of Aomori Prefecture, in the northernmost part of Honshu. As with many in Ueno, the story of her arrival is unclear; but Neko's was particularly unclear because she spoke with a strong regional dialect, using Tokyo speech only for thank-you and other pleasantries, in an ironic tone that let you know it was merely performance. She was seventy-six years old and just over four feet tall. She was very energetic, kept a cat for a companion, sang folksongs almost constantly, and was well liked by those around her. She was consistently described as cute (*kawaii*). However, Neko had severe arthritis and a bladder control problem that necessitated more and more of her husband's care. After a brief attempt to "pick up" (*hirou*) another woman to care for Neko, the husband left the park without a word. This left Neko to fend for herself. Her husband had made their money by selling frankfurters and snacks at a stall in front of the park shrine on the weekends, but Neko had no income of her own. Nor could she, with her arthritis, easily raise and lower her tent daily as the park management required,[25] not to mention complete the more strenuous special cleanups to which they were subjected, with full rehearsal three days prior, about once a month. Even changing her clothes, doing laundry, and cooking were difficult chores. In other words, she could no longer do for herself. She had no one to take care of her and little money to pay someone else to do it. She was living mostly from church handouts, which marked her desperation. Most yama no ningen refused the church-run soup lines because they felt the church insulted them by making them listen to long sermons, feeding them soup-doused rice (which they called cat food), and, worst of all, giving to everyone and anyone anonymously. In true human relationships, many yama no ningen told me, offerings are mutually exchanged and given with words of acknowledgment, such as, You must have had a hard day (*otsukaresama*). But the church, "makes you sit, orates a long sermon, and gives to anyone who will listen." Those doing homeless on the mountain viewed those who lined up, who "merely received without giving" and who did so in anonymity, as void of humanity, perseverance, and pride.

Lining up for the soup line in front of all the other park residents called out Neko's situation. At first thinking her husband would come back, Neko's neighbors took pity on her, commiserated with her view of her husband's irresponsibility, and helped with her tent and meals. After all, the couple had seniority over other residents due to their age and tenure in Ueno Park. However, when it became clear that Neko's husband was gone for good, the neighbors retreated. They felt it was Neko's responsibility to do for herself. She was seventy-six years old, with illnesses that made her one of the few easy candidates for welfare.[26] Certainly Neko had her pride, but it was time, her neighbors argued for her to do for herself. "One can not presume on others [amaenai],"[27] Pu-chan, Neko's neighbor, complained. "She may be pitiful [kawaisoo], but I have stopped helping her. Her tent smells horrible because she merely drops her clothes in water, without soap, and hangs them to dry. And the tent is full of roaches. I do not know what she is thinking." Neko, in losing her independence and ability to do homeless, had lost her legitimacy and endangered her relationships on the yama, relationships of reciprocity that were judged crucial to properly doing homeless.

Kita, on the other hand, was younger than Neko. He was sixty-two years old and three years away from receiving his work pension.[28] He left his home and job in a northern prefecture after the death of his wife. He took about two thousand U.S. dollars with him. He traveled and stayed in motels but was draining his resources fast. He had been staying in a room in Ueno when he first came to the yama. He saw all the tents, talked to some people, made some friends, and thought he would "give it a try." He did not drink alcohol, or ever scavenge for food, or even do day labor, but he was quick to offer a cigarette and sometimes, or so I heard, even a loan. He did not cause a big nuisance (meiwake o kakenai). Most important, he did everything for himself. He was his own means of financial support and was able to raise and lower his tent and move it out on special cleanup days. Thus, even though he claimed and everyone knew that his plan for the immediate future was to return to his daughter's home in the north, where she ran a country inn,[29] Kita was self-sufficient and committed to his relationships and active on the mountain and, as a result, was seen as legitimate by his neighbors. He was, after all, properly doing homeless.

These cases make clear that among the homeless it was not the most downtrodden, the most down and out, who were seen as legitimate homeless. Rather it was the most productive, disciplined, and active who were judged as fit to do homeless and who therefore gained local legitimacy. The downtrodden were seen as candidates for welfare or other types of outside support. Thus, while most claimed they did not need or want governmental or institutional support, they recognized its importance for individuals for whom doing homeless was no longer a viable option. Yet these choices were seen as less preferable and those who opted for them were called beggars (*kojiki*) because these options reduced one's sense of independence and called into question the ability to do for oneself. Commitment both to doing homeless and to relationships lent legitimacy in Ueno Park. Homeless people in Ueno Park discouraged each from talking about the difficulties and mistakes of their past that are often the key topics of scholars and others who are interested in how individuals "become" homeless. The homeless claimed to treat their current social relationships with utmost care, as a way to express their commitment to the ideals of duty, obligation, and reciprocity. "If I quit [doing homeless and scavenging food]," one man insisted, "others will suffer."[30] Commitment to doing homeless also brought praise. Oneesan described a man who lived near her and with whom she was involved in mutual exchanges: "Yes it is afternoon and he is sleeping. He drank too much sake from the cherry blossom festival. But he still goes out every night. In the rain, wind, or whatever. He goes to his place in Ochanomizu. Even a salaryman might say, not today, but this man, he goes every day."

Rethinking Marginality and Resistance

Given popular, academic, and official notions of the homeless other, homeless people's use of conventional notions of Japanese identity and virtues are challenging on two levels. First, they provide a critical challenge to national and academic discourses that celebrate corporations, home, and marriage as anchors of Japaneseness and as the decisive locations for the production of Japanese ideals. Second, they problematize the easy association of marginality with a "resistance" that is conceived of as nonhegemonic, subversive, and violating of the codes of conduct. Doing homeless proves to be neither a simple hidden transcript[31] nor an unconscious reproduction of nationally sanctioned ideals. Understanding homelessness requires a more complicated view of otherness, marginality, and resistance: one that neither essentializes the homeless as outsiders, nor romanticizes them as treasures in the academic adventure to seek out diversity in Japan.

A discussion of homelessness in Ueno Park necessitates a rethinking of understandings of marginality and resistance. The common sense that led others to ask me questions about my research might predict that homeless persons reject, or are unconcerned with, social norms as they pursue life at the level of naked humanity. I am frequently asked to compare the homeless in Japan to homeless people elsewhere, but I wonder if that is the only or best point of comparison. Is homelessness the only key marker of their personal identity?

The importance that ideologically thick and nationally salient symbols play in yama no ningen's own narratives of doing homeless demonstrates that marginality and resistance are not sufficient concepts for understanding homelessness in Tokyo, as they do not seem to consider homeless people's view of themselves. A focus on homeless deviance, marginality, or resistance ignores the practices of doing homeless, and seems to exclude the possibility for those practices to be rather ordinary.

The conventional wisdom of Japanese identity is that an individual's position within the institutions of work and home is the zero-point of entry into Japanese society. Yet, the previous discussion of how homeless people in Ueno Park construct their own identities complicates the presumed un-Japaneseness of the homeless in Tokyo. Whereas marginality has been called the defining condition[32] of casual laborers and homeless communities, my research clearly shows that central ideologies are an equally strong influence. Despite the "common sense" that views the margins as a space of cultural exclusion, in these sites, where the identity of individuals is challenged and presumed to be deviant, identities may, in fact, be more intensely rooted in the cultural ideals of the center.

Notes

1. The role of the ie has been the concern of many scholars in their examinations of Japanese identity. In particular see Jane Bachnik and Charles Quinn, *Situated Meaning* (Princeton, NJ: Princeton University Press, 1994); Matthews Masayuki Hamabata, *Crested Kimono: Power and Love in the Japanese Business Family* (Ithaca, NY: Cornell University Press, 1990); Dorrine Kondo, *Crafting Selves: Power, Gender, and Discourses of Identity in a Japanese Workplace* (Chicago: University of Chicago Press, 1990); Chie Nakane, *Japanese Society* (Berkeley: University of California Press,1970); Nancy Rosenberger, ed., *Japanese Sense of Self* (Cambridge: Cambridge University Press, 1992).

2. For more on how the margins are offensive to official discourses, see Anna Tsing, *In the Realm of the Diamond Queen: Marginality in an Out-of-the-Way Place* (Princeton, NJ: Princeton University Press, 1993), 41.

3. Karen Kelsky, *Women on the Verge: Japanese Women, Western Dreams* (Durham, NC: Duke University Press, 2001), 28–29.

4. Nojukusha Jinken Shiryoo Sentaa (Resource Center for Homeless Human Rights), *Center News,* Summer 1998.

5. Patricia Kennett and Masami Iwata, "Precariousness in Everyday Life: Homelessness in Japan," *International Journal of Urban and Regional Research* 27, no. 1 (2003): 67.

6. Day labor communities have recently gained attention in the literature and have touched on issues of homelessness, particularly the processes of becoming homeless as it links with the political economy of labor. See Edward Fowler, *Sanya Blues* (Ithaca, NY: Cornell University Press, 1996); Tom Gill, *Men of Uncertainty: The Social Organization of Day Laborers in Contemporary Japan* (Albany: SUNY Press, 2001); Tony Guzewicz, *Tokyo's Homeless: A City in Denial* (Huntington, NY: Kroshka Books, 2000); Kazuaki Kasai "*Iwayuru 'hoomuresu' mondai to wa,*" *Yoseba* 8 (1996): 5–14; Matthew Marr, "Maintaining Autonomy: The Plight of the American Skid Row and Japanese *Yoseba,*" *Journal of Social Distress and the Homeless* 6, no. 3 (1997): 229–50.

7. Kim Hopper, *Reckoning with Homelessness* (Ithaca, NY: Cornell University Press, 2003), 46.

8. The process of making others of the homeless includes emasculating them.

9. Nojukusha Jinken Shiryoo Sentaa, *Center News*, Summer 1998.

10. "Osaka Postpones Shelter after Clash with Residents," *Japan Times*, November 16, 2000; "Residents Oppose Homeless Plan," *Japan Times*, May 11, 1997.

11. Quoted in Guzewicz, *Tokyo's Homeless*, 83.

12. Ibid., 91.

13. Gill, *Men of Uncertainty*; Carolyn Stevens, *On the Margins of Japanese Society: Volunteers and the Welfare of the Urban Underclass* (London: Routledge, 1997).

14. Gill, *Men of Uncertainty*, 172.

15. Ibid., 152.

16. Ibid., 162; emphasis mine.

17. E.g., Fowler, *Sanya Blues*.

18. Oscar Lewis, "The Culture of Poverty," *Scientific American* 215, no. 4 (1966): 19–25.

19. James Spradley, *You Owe Yourself a Drunk: An Ethnography of Urban Nomads* (Boston: Little, Brown, 1970).

20. Philippe Bourgois, *In Search of Respect: Selling Crack in El Barrio* (Cambridge: Cambridge University Press, 1995), 17.

21. Joanne Passaro, *The Unequal Homeless: Men on the Streets, Women in Their Place* (New York: Routledge, 1996), 29.

22. For examples of this use of ideas of resistance, see David Wagner, *Checkerboard Square: Culture and Resistance in a Homeless Community* (Boulder, CO: Westview, 1993); Talmadge Wright, *Out of Place: Homeless Mobilizations, Subcities, and Contested Landscapes* (New York: SUNY Press, 1997).

23. Homeless women, too, are often constructed as "others" by which to measure the masculine heroics of homeless men on the yama. See Abby Margolis, "Samurai beneath Blue Tarps: Doing Homelessness, Rejecting Marginality, and Preserving Nation in Ueno Park" (PhD diss., University of Pittsburgh, 2002), 134–80.

24. Homeless people I met in Ueno typically said that they "really should not be in the park" (*hontoo ni ikenai kedo*), and used this phrase to explain to me why they choose to follow park management rules.

25. On a revisit to Ueno Park in the summer of 2003, I learned that this was no longer required. The management had prohibited and permanently removed all the tents from in front of the national museum and was apparently less insistent about the lowering of tents in other parts of the park during operating hours.

26. During a brief trip to Ueno Park in April 2000, I heard that Neko did in fact get into a welfare care program under the guidance of an official from Soogidan (a labor union). Soogidan came to Ueno Park once a week to take anyone who might be eligible to the ward office to apply for welfare.

27. Cf. Takeo Doi, *The Anatomy of Dependence,* trans. John Bester (Tokyo: Kodansha, 1973).

28. Since Kita was not an ex-laborer, he had a pension that he could start to collect when he turned sixty-five.

29. Scholars have argued that living for the moment, or emphasizing the present rather than past or future, is a common feature in the lives of people of marginalized groups. See Sophie Day, Evthymios Papataxiarchis, and Michael Stewart, eds., *Lilies of the Field: Marginal People Who Live for the Moment* (Boulder, CO: Westview, 1999).

30. This comment alludes to the complicated relationship between autonomy and obligation. Many homeless people in Ueno Park sang the praises of their autonomous lifestyles; they reveled in the fact that they could "eat, sleep, and drink whenever I want." Yet many simultaneously claimed that "relationships were the most important thing on the yama." Homeless people's use of collective values in support of their autonomy challenges conventional thinking about the group-dependent "Japanese self." See Margolis, "Samurai," 105–33.

31. I borrow the term *hidden transcript* from James Scott, *Domination and the Arts of Resistance: Hidden Transcripts* (New Haven, CT: Yale University Press, 1990).

32. Gill, *Men of Uncertainty.*

Select Bibliography

Adler, Jeffrey S. "A Historical Analysis of the Law of Vagrancy." *Criminology* 27, no. 2 (1989): 209–29.

————. "Rejoinder to Chambliss." *Criminology* 27, no. 2 (1989): 239–50.

————. "Vagging the Demons and Scoundrels: Vagrancy and the Growth of St. Louis, 1830–1861." *Journal of Urban History* 13, no. 1 (1986): 3–30.

Ahuja, Ravi. "The Origins of Colonial Labour Policy in Late Eighteenth-Century Madras." *Social History* 44, no. 2 (1999): 159–93.

Alexander, John K. *Render Them Submissive: Responses to Poverty in Philadelphia, 1760–1800.* Amherst: University of Massachusetts Press, 1980.

Allen, Richard. "Indian Immigrants and the Legacy of Marronage: Illegal Absence, Desertion and Vagrancy in Mauritius, 1835–1900." *Itinerario* 21, no. 1 (1997): 98–110.

Allsop, Kenneth. *Hard Travellin': The Hobo and His History.* New York: New American Library, 1967.

Anderson, Nels. *The Hobo: The Sociology of Homeless Man.* Chicago: University of Chicago Press, 1923.

————. *Men on the Move.* Chicago: University of Chicago Press, 1940.

Andrews, Richard Mower. *Law, Magistracy, and Crime in Old Regime Paris, 1735–1789.* Vol. 1: *The System of Criminal Justice.* Cambridge: Cambridge University Press, 1994.

Archard, Peter. *Vagrancy, Alcoholism, and Social Control.* London: Macmillan, 1979.

Arnold, David. "European Orphans and Vagrants in India in the Nineteenth Century." *Journal of Imperial and Commonwealth History* 7, no. 2 (1979): 104–27.

Arrom, Silvia Marina. *Containing the Poor: The Mexico City Poor House, 1774–1875.* Durham, NC: Duke University Press, 2000.

Augustin, Joseph. *The Human Vagabond: Drama, Comedy and Tragedy in the Underworld.* London: Hutchinson, 1933.

Aydelotte, Frank. *Elizabethan Rogues and Vagabonds.* Oxford: Clarendon, 1913.

Bahr, Howard M., ed. *Disaffiliated Man: Essays and Bibliography on Skid Row, Vagrancy, and Outsiders.* Toronto: University of Toronto Press, 1970.

Barak, Gregg. *Gimme Shelter: A Social History of Homelessness in Contemporary America.* New York: Praeger, 1991.

Barbour, Levi L. "Vagrancy." In *Proceedings of the Eighth Annual Conference of Charities and Correction* (1881): 131–38.

Barry, Jonathan, ed. *The Tudor and Stuart Town: A Reader in English Urban History, 1530–1688.* London: Longman, 1990.

Bassett, Lucy A. *Transient and Homeless Persons: A Bibliography.* Jacksonville: Florida Emergency Relief Administration, 1934.

Beard, Rick, ed. *On Being Homeless: Historical Perspectives.* New York: Museum of the City of New York, 1987.

Beattie, J. M. *Crime and the Courts in England, 1660–1800.* Princeton, NJ: Princeton University Press, 1986.

Beck, Frank O. *Hobohemia: Emma Goldman, Lucy Parsons, Ben Reitman and Other Agitators and Outsiders in 1920s/30s Chicago.* Ringe, NH: Richard R. Smith, 1956.

Beier, A. L. *Masterless Men: The Vagrancy Problem in England, 1560–1640.* London: Methuen, 1985.

———. "Social Problems in Elizabethan London." In *The Tudor and Stuart Town: A Reader in English Urban History, 1530–1688,* edited by Jonathan Barry, 121–38. London: Longman, 1990.

———. "Vagrants and the Social Order in Elizabethan England." *Past and Present* 64, no. 1 (1974): 3–29.

Benson, Ben. *Hoboes of America: Sensational Life Story and Epic Life on the Road.* New York: Hobo News, 1942.

Binder, Rudolph M. "The Treatment of Beggars and Vagabonds in Belgium." *Journal of Criminal Law and Criminology* 6 (March 1916): 835–48.

Blau, Joel. *The Visible Poor: Homelessness in the United States.* New York: Oxford University Press, 1992.

Bonner, Michael, Mine Ener, and Amy Singer, eds. *Poverty and Charity in Middle Eastern Contexts.* Albany: State University of New York Press, 2003.

Bosworth, Clifford E. *The Mediaeval Islamic Underworld: The Banū Sāsān in Arabic Life and Lore.* Leiden: Brill, 1976.

Briggs, Asa. *Victorian Cities.* London: Odhams, 1963.

Brown, John. *I Was a Tramp*. London: Selwyn and Blount, 1934.

Brown, Peter. *Poverty and Leadership in the Later Roman Empire*. Hanover, NH: University Press of New England, 2002.

Bruns, Roger A. *Knights of the Road: A Hobo History*. New York: Methuen, 1980.

Burton, Andrew. *African Underclass: Urbanization, Crime, and Colonial Order in Dar es Salaam, 1919–1961*. Athens: Ohio University Press, 2005.

———. "Urchins, Loafers, and the Cult of the Cowboy: Urbanization and Delinquency in Dar es Salaam, 1919–1961." *Journal of African History* 42, no. 2 (2001): 199–218.

Callahan, William J. "The Problem of Confinement: An Aspect of Poor Relief in Eighteenth-Century Spain." *Hispanic American Historical Review* 51, no. 1 (1971): 1–27.

Carew, Bampfylde-Moore. *An Apology for the Life of Bampfylde-Moore Carew, Commonly Known throughout the West of England by the Title of King of the Beggars and Dog-Merchant General*. London: Goadby, 1750.

Carroll, W. C. "'The Nursery of Beggary': Enclosure, Vagrancy, and Sedition in the Tudor-Stuart Period." In *Enclosure Acts: Sexuality, Property, and Culture in Early Modern England*, edited by R. Burt and J. M. Archer, 34–47. Ithaca, NY: Cornell University Press, 1994.

Chambliss, William J. "On Trashing Marxist Criminology." *Criminology* 27, no. 2 (1989): 231–38.

———. "A Sociological Analysis of the Law of Vagrancy." *Social Problems* 12, no. 1 (1965): 67–77.

Chandler, F. W. *The Literature of Roguery*. Boston: Houghton, Mifflin, 1907.

Chesterton, Mrs. Cecil. *In Darkest London*. Rev. ed. London: Stanley Paul, 1926.

Clark, Peter. *The English Alehouse: A Social History, 1200–1830*. London: Longman, 1983.

Coates, Timothy. *Convicts and Orphans: Forced and State-Sponsored Colonizers in the Portuguese Empire, 1550–1755*. Stanford, CA: Stanford University Press, 2001.

Coldham, Peter Wilson. *Emigrants in Chains: A Social History of Forced Emigration to the Americas of Felons, Destitute Children, Political and Religious Non-conformists, Vagabonds, Beggars and other Undesirables, 1607–1776*. Baltimore, MD: Genealogical Publishing, 1992.

———. "The 'Spiriting Away' of London Children to Virginia, 1648–1685." *Virginia Magazine of History and Biography* 83, no. 3 (1975): 280–87.

Coldrey, Barry M. "'. . . A Place to Which Idle Vagrants May Be Sent': The First Phase of Child Migration during the Seventeenth and Eighteenth Centuries." *Children and Society* 13, no. 1 (1999): 32–47.

Cook, Thomas, ed. *Vagrancy: Some New Perspectives.* London: Academic Press, 1979.

Cooke, John. "Vagrants, Beggars and Tramps." *Quarterly Review* 209 (October 1908): 388–408.

Crawford, James H. *The Autobiography of a Tramp.* London: Longmans, Green, 1900.

Cray, Robert E. *Paupers and Poor Relief in New York City and Its Rural Environs, 1700–1830.* Philadelphia: Temple University Press, 1988.

Cresswell, Timothy. *The Tramp in America.* London: Reaktion, 2001.

Crouse, Joan M. *The Homeless Transient in the Great Depression: New York State, 1929–1941.* Albany: State University of New York Press, 1986.

Culver, Benjamin F. "Transient Unemployed Men." *Sociology and Social Research* 17 (July– August 1933): 519–35.

Davis, Natalie Zemon. *Society and Culture in Early Modern France: Eight Essays.* Stanford, CA: Stanford University Press, 1975.

Dawson, William H. *The Vagrancy Problem: The Case for Measures of Restraint for Tramps, Loafers, and Unemployables.* London: P. S. King and Son, 1910.

DePastino, Todd. *Citizen Hobo: How a Century of Homelessness Shaped America.* Chicago: University of Chicago Press, 2005.

Dubin, Gary V., and Richard B. Robinson. "The Vagrancy Concept Reconsidered: Problems and Abuses of Status Criminality." *New York University Law Review* 37 (January 1962): 102–36.

Duchâtel, Charles. *De la charité dans ses rapports avec l'état moral et le bien-être des classes inférieures de la société.* Paris: Guiraudet et Jouaust, 1836.

Elbourne, Elizabeth. "Freedom at Issue: Vagrancy Legislation and the Meaning of Freedom in Britain and Cape Colony in 1799–1842." *Slavery and Abolition* 15, no. 2 (1994): 114–50.

Ener, Mine. *Managing Egypt's Poor and the Politics of Benevolence, 1800–1952.* Princeton, NJ: Princeton University Press, 2003.

Fergusson, Robert M. *The Vagrant: What to Do with Him.* London: James Nisbet, 1911.

Flynn, Maureen. *Sacred Charity: Confraternaties and Social Welfare in Spain, 1400–1700.* Ithaca, NY: Cornell University Press, 1989.

Flynt, Josiah. *Tramping with Tramps: Studies and Sketches of Vagabond Life.* New York: Century, 1899.

Foote, Caleb. "Vagrancy-Type Law and Its Administration." *University of Pennsylvania Law Review* 104, no. 5 (1956): 603–50.

Forrest, Alan I. *The French Revolution and the Poor.* New York: St. Martin's, 1981.

Fumerton, Patricia. "Not Home: Alehouses, Ballads, and the Vagrant Husband in Early Modern England." *Journal of Medieval and Early Modern Studies* 32, no. 3 (2002): 493–518.

Games, Alison. *Migration and the Origins of the English Atlantic World.* Cambridge, MA: Harvard University Press, 1999.

Gillin, John L. "Vagrancy and Begging." *American Journal of Sociology* 35 (November 1929): 424–32.

Gilmore, Harlan W. *The Beggar.* Chapel Hill: University of North Carolina Press, 1940.

Gladfelder, Hal. *Criminality and Narrative in Eighteenth-Century England: Beyond the Law.* Baltimore, MD: Johns Hopkins University Press, 2001.

Golden, Stephanie. *The Women Outside: Meanings and Myths of Homelessness.* Berkeley: University of California Press, 1992.

Gordon, Robert J. "Vagrancy, Law and 'Shadow Knowledge': Internal Pacification, 1915–1939." In *Namibia under South African Rule: Mobility and Containment, 1915–46,* edited by Patricia Hayes, et al. Oxford: James Currey, 1998.

Gray, Frank. *The Tramp: His Meaning and Being.* London: J. M. Dent and Sons, 1931.

Hands, A. R. *Charities and Social Aid in Greece and Rome.* Ithaca, NY: Cornell University Press, 1968.

Harman, Thomas. *A Caveat for Common Cursetors.* London, 1567.

Haslip-Viera, Gabriel. *Crime and Punishment in Late Colonial Mexico City, 1692–1810.* Albuquerque: University of New Mexico Press, 1999.

Hay, Douglas, et al., eds. *Albion's Fatal Tree: Crime and Society in Eighteenth-Century England.* New York: Pantheon, 1975.

Higbie, Frank Tobias. *Indispensable Outcasts: Hobo Workers and Community in the American Midwest, 1880–1930.* Urbana: University of Illinois Press, 2003.

Higgs, Mary. *Glimpses into the Abyss.* London: P. S. King and Son, 1906.

———. *My Brother the Tramp: Studies in the Problem of Vagrancy.* London: Student Christian Movement, 1914.

Hoberman, Louisa Schell, and Susan Migden Socolow, eds. *Cities and Society in Colonial Latin America.* Albuquerque: University of New Mexico Press, 1986.

Holloway, Thomas. *Policing Rio de Janeiro: Repression and Resistance in a Nineteenth-Century City.* Stanford, CA: Stanford University Press, 1993.

Howe, Nicholas. *Home and Homelessness in the Medieval and Renaissance World.* Notre Dame, IN: University of Notre Dame Press, 2004.

Hufton, Olwen. *The Poor of Eighteenth-Century France, 1750–1789.* Oxford: Clarendon, 1974.

Huggins, Martha K. *From Slavery to Vagrancy in Brazil: Crime and Social Control in the Third World.* New Brunswick, NJ: Rutgers University Press, 1985.

Humphries, Robert. *No Fixed Abode: A History of Responses to the Roofless and Rootless in Britain.* London: Macmillan, 1999.

Iliffe, John. *The African Poor: A History.* Cambridge: Cambridge University Press, 1987.

Innes, Joanna. "Prisons for the Poor: English Bridewells, 1555–1800." In *Labor, Law, and Crime. An Historical Perspective,* edited by Francis Snyder and Douglas Hay, 49–50. New York: Tavistock, 1987.

Jackson, Jason. *Overland Slim the Maverick: The Seven Ages of the Eventful Life of a Genuine American Hobo.* New York: Greenwich, 1957.

Jennings, Frank L. *Tramping with Tramps.* London: Hutchinson, 1932.

Johnson, Robert C. "The Transportation of Vagrant Children from London to Virginia, 1618– 1622." In *Early Stuart Studies,* edited by Howard S. Reinmuth, 132–51. Minneapolis: University of Minnesota Press, 1970.

Jones, Gareth Stedman. *Outcast London: A Study in the Relationship between Classes in Victorian Society.* Oxford: Clarendon, 1971.

Jütte, Robert. *Poverty and Deviance in Early Modern Europe.* Cambridge: Cambridge University Press, 1994.

Karamustafa, Ahmet. *God's Unruly Friends: Dervish Groups in the Islamic Later Middle Period, 1200–1550.* Salt Lake City: University of Utah Press, 1994.

Katz, Michael B. *Poverty and Police in American History.* New York: American, 1983.

Kelly, Edmund. *The Elimination of the Tramp.* New York: G. P. Putnam's Sons, 1908.

———. *The Unemployables.* London: P. S. King and Son, 1907.

Kerouac, Jack. *On the Road.* New York: New American Library, 1957.

Kinkead-Weekes, B. H. *A History of Vagrancy in Cape Town.* Cape Town: School of Economics, University of Cape Town, 1984.

Kinney, A. F., ed. *Rogues, Vagabonds and Sturdy Beggars: A New Gallery of Tudor and Early Stuart Rogue Literature.* Amherst: University of Massachusetts Press, 1990.

Kromer, Tom. *Waiting for Nothing*. New York: Knopf, 1935.

Kusmer, Ken. *Down and Out, On the Road: The Homeless in American History*. Oxford: Oxford University Press, 2006.

Lacey, Forrest W. "Vagrancy and Other Crimes of Personal Condition." *Harvard Law Review* 66, no. 7 (1953): 1203–26.

Lees, Andrew. *Cities Perceived: Urban Society in European and American Thought, 1820–1940*. Manchester, UK: Manchester University Press, 1985.

Levinson, Boris M. "The Homeless Man." *Psychological Reports* 17 (October 1965): 391–94.

Lewis, Orlando. "The Tramp Problem." *Annals of the American Academy of Political and Social Science* 40 (March 1912): 217–27.

Library of Congress. Division of Bibliography. *Select List of References: Vagrancy*. Washington, D.C.: Government Printing Office. Nos. 127–59, 1916.

Lindenmeyr, Adele. *Poverty Is Not a Vice: Charity, Society, and the State in Imperial Russia*. Princeton, NJ: Princeton University Press, 1996.

Lis, Catharina. *Social Change and the Laboring Poor: Antwerp, 1770–1860*. New Haven, CT: Yale University Press, 1986.

Lisle, John. "Vagrancy Law: Its Faults and Their Remedy." *Journal of Criminal Law and Criminology* 5, no. 4 (1914): 498–513.

London, Jack. *The Road*. New York: Macmillan, 1903.

Lu, Hanchao. "Becoming Urban: Mendicancy and Vagrants in Modern Shanghai." *Journal of Social History* 33, no. 1 (1999): 7–36.

———. *Street Criers: A Cultural History of Chinese Beggars*. Stanford, CA: Stanford University Press, 2005.

Luther, Martin, ed. *The Book of Vagabonds and Beggars: With a Vocabulary of Their Language (Liber Vagatorum)*, translated by John C. Hotten. 1528. Reprint, London: John Camden Hotten, 1860.

Mandler, Peter, ed. *The Uses of Charity: The Poor on Relief in the Nineteenth-Century Metropolis*. Philadelphia: University of Pennsylvania Press, 1990.

Marsh, Benjamin C. "Causes of Vagrancy and Methods of Eradication." *Annals of the American Academy of Political and Social Science* 23 (May 1904): 445–56.

Martens, Jeremy. "Polygamy, Sexual Danger and the Creation of Vagrancy Legislation in Colonial Natal." *Journal of Imperial and Commonwealth History* 31, no. 3 (2003): 24–45.

Maupassant, Guy de. *Le vagabond*. Paris: P. Ollendorff, 1885.

Mayhew, Henry. *London Labor and the London Poor*. New York: Harper and Brothers, 1851.

McLynn, Frank J. *Crime and Punishment in Eighteenth Century England.* London: Routledge, 1989.

McMullan, John L. *The Canting Crew: London's Criminal Underworld, 1550–1700.* New Brunswick, NJ: Rutgers University Press, 1984.

Michielse, H. C. M. "Policing the Poor: J. L. Vives and the Sixteenth-Century Origins of Modern Social Administration." *Social Service Review* 64 (March 1990): 1–21.

Milburn, George. *The Hobo's Hornbook: A Repertory for a Gutter Jongleur.* New York: Ives Washburn, 1930.

Minehan, Thomas. *Boy and Girl Tramps of America.* New York: Farrar and Rinehart, 1934.

Mollat, Michel. *Les pauvres au moyen âge.* Paris: Hachette, 1978.

Monkkonen, Eric, ed. *Walking to Work: Tramps in America, 1790–1935.* Lincoln: University of Nebraska Press, 1984.

Myers, Garth A. *Verandahs of Power: Colonialism and Space in Urban Africa.* Syracuse, NY: Syracuse University Press, 2003.

Nylander, Towne. "Wandering Youth." *Sociology and Social Research* 17 (July–August 1933): 560–68.

Ocobock, Paul. "'Joy Rides for Juveniles': Vagrant Youth and Colonial Control in Nairobi, Kenya, 1901–52." *Social History* 31, no. 1 (2006): 39–59.

O'Connor, Philip. *Britain in the Sixties: Vagrancy.* Baltimore, MD: Penguin Books, 1963.

Olejniczak, William. "Working on the Body of the Poor: The Ateliers de Charité in Late Eighteenth-Century France." *Journal of Social History* 24, no. 1 (1990): 87–107.

Orwell, George. *Down and Out in Paris and London.* New York: Harper, 1933.

Outland, George E. "Determinants Involved in Boy Transiency." *Journal of Education Sociology* 11 (February 1938): 360–72.

Pagnier, Armand. *Le vagabond: Ses origines, sa psychologie, ses formes, la lutte contre le vagabondage.* Paris: Vignot, 1910.

Pearson, Geoffery. *Hooligan: A History of Respectable Fears.* London: Macmillan, 1983.

Perry, Mary Elizabeth. *Crime and Society in Early Modern Seville.* Hanover, NH: University Press of New England, 1980.

Pike, Ruth. *Penal Servitude in Early Modern Spain.* Madison: University of Wisconsin Press, 1983.

Potter, Ellen C. "The Problem of the Transient." *Annals of the American Academy of Political and Social Science* 176 (November 1934): 66–73.

Pound, John. *Poverty and Vagrancy in Tudor England*. London: Longman, 1971.

Pullan, Brian. *Rich and Poor in Renaissance Venice: The Social Institutions of a Catholic State to 1620*. Cambridge, MA: Harvard University Press, 1971.

Ribton-Turner, Charles J. *A History of Vagrants and Vagrancy and Beggars and Begging*. London: Chapman and Hall, 1887.

Rice, Stuart A. "The Homeless." *Annals of the American Academy of Political and Social Science* 77 (May 1918): 140–53.

Ringenbach, Paul T. *Tramps and Reformers, 1873–1916: The Discovery of Unemployment in New York*. Westport, CT: Greenwood, 1973.

Rivière, Louis. *Mendicants et vagabonds*. Paris: Librarie Victor Lecoffre, 1902.

Rogers, Nicolas. "Policing the Poor in Eighteenth-Century London: The Vagrancy Laws and Their Administration." *Histoire sociale* 24 (May 1991): 127–47.

————. "Vagrancy, Impressment and the Regulation of Labour in Eighteenth-Century Britain." *Slavery and Abolition* 15, no. 2 (1994): 102–13.

Rose, Lionel. *Rogues and Vagabonds: Vagrant Underworld in Britain, 1815–1985*. London: Routledge, 1988.

Rudé, George. *Paris and London in the Eighteenth Century: Studies in Popular Protest*. New York: Viking, 1971.

Sabra, Adam. *Poverty and Charity in Medieval Islam: Mamluk Egypt, 1250–1517*. Cambridge: Cambridge University Press, 2000.

Salvatore, Ricardo. *Wandering Paysanos: State Order and Subaltern Experience in Buenos Aires during the Rosas Era*. Durham, NC: Duke University Press, 2003.

Schwartz, Robert M. *Policing the Poor in Eighteenth-Century France*. Chapel Hill: University of North Carolina Press, 1988.

Shaw, Clifford R. *The Jack-Roller: A Delinquent Boy's Own Story*. Chicago: University of Chicago Press, 1930.

Sherry, Arthur H. "Vagrancy, Rogues, and Vagabonds: Old Concepts in Need of Revision." *California Law Review* 48, no. 2 (1960): 561–62.

Singer, Amy. *Constructing Ottoman Beneficence: An Imperial Soup Kitchen in Jerusalem*. Albany: State University of New York Press, 2002.

Slack, Paul A. *Poverty and Policy in Tudor and Stuart England*. London: Longman, 1988.

————. "Vagrants and Vagrancy in England, 1598–1664." *Economic History Review* 27, no. 3 (1974): 360–79.

Smith, Timothy B. "Assistance and Repression: Rural Exodus, Vagabondage and Social Crisis in France, 1880–1914." *Journal of Social History* 32, no. 4 (1999): 821–46.

Souden, D. "Rogues, Whores, and Vagabonds? Indentured Servant Emigrants to North America." *Social History* 3, no. 1 (1978).

Srivastava, S. S. *Juvenile Vagrancy: A Socio-Ecological Study of Juvenile Vagrants in the Cities of Kanpur and Lucknow.* London: Asia Publishing House, 1963.

Stanley, Amy Dru. *From Bondage to Contract: Wage Labor, Marriage, and the Market in the Age of Slave Emancipation.* Cambridge: Cambridge University Press, 1998.

Steinbicker, Carl R. "Poor-Relief in the Sixteenth Century." STD thesis, Catholic University of America, 1937.

Stephenson, Svetlana. *Crossing the Line: Vagrancy, Homelessness, and Social Displacement in Russia.* Aldershot, UK: Ashgate, 2006.

Stuart, Frank J. *Vagabond.* London: Stanley Paul, 1937.

Thompson, I. "A Map of Crime in Sixteenth-Century Spain." *Economic History Review* 21, no. 2 (1968): 244–67.

Tobias, J. J. *Urban Crime in Victorian England.* New York: Schocken, 1972.

Tully, Jim. *Beggars of Life.* Garden City, NY: Garden City, 1924.

Vexliard, Alexandre. *Introduction à la sociologie du vagabondage.* Paris: Marcel Rivière, 1956.

Viqueira Albán, Juan Pedro. *Propriety and Permissiveness in Bourbon Mexico.* Wilmington, DE: Scholarly Resources, 1999.

Vorspan, Rachel. "Vagrancy and the New Poor Law in Late-Victorian and Edwardian England." *English Historical Review* 92, no. 362 (1977): 59–81.

Warren, Philip A. *Vagrants and Citizens: Politics and the Masses in Mexico City from Colony to Republic.* Wilmington, DE: Scholarly Resources, 2001.

Wightman, Ann M. *Indigenous Migration and Social Change: The Forasteros of Cuzco, 1570– 1720.* Durham, NC: Duke University Press, 1990.

Williams, Alan. *The Police of Paris, 1718–1789.* Baton Rouge: Louisiana State University Press, 1979.

Woodbridge, Linda. *Vagrancy, Homelessness, and English Renaissance Literature.* Urbana: University of Illinois Press, 2001.

Woolf, Stuart. *The Poor in Western Europe in the Eighteenth and Nineteenth Centuries.* London: Methuen, 1986.

Youmans, F. Zeta. "Childhood, Inc.: Child Beggars." *Survey* 52 (April–September 1924): 462–64.

Contributors

Richard B. Allen received his Ph.D. in African history from the University of Illinois at Urbana-Champaign. He is the author of *Slaves, Freedmen, and Indentured Laborers in Colonial Mauritius* and numerous articles on the social and economic history of Mauritius. He is currently exploring the dynamics of the Mascarene slave trade, labor migration in the Indian Ocean and Atlantic worlds, and the development of creole societies in slave plantation systems during the late eighteenth and early nineteenth centuries.

David Arnold is a professor of the history of South Asia at Warwick University. He has written extensively on colonialism in India as well as medical and environmental history. His major works include *Science, Technology, and Medicine in Colonial India* and *The Age of Discovery, 1400–1600*. His most recent work, *The Tropics and the Traveling Gaze: India, Landscape, and Science, 1800–1856*, focuses on travel, landscape, and botany in nineteenth-century India.

A. L. Beier taught at the University of Lancaster from 1967 to 1990, when he was appointed professor of history and department chair at Illinois State University. His books include *Masterless Men: The Vagrancy Problem in England, 1560–1640; London, 1500–1700: The Making of the Metropolis* (as coeditor); and *The First Modern Society: Essays in English History in Honour of Lawrence Stone* (as coeditor). His recent research has been on Henry Mayhew, and he is currently writing a book on early modern English social theories.

Andrew Burton is the assistant director of the British Institute in Eastern Africa. He is an urban historian specializing on East Africa.

His publications include *African Underclass: Urbanisation, Crime and Colonial Order in Dar es Salaam* and the edited collection *The Urban Experience in Eastern Africa, c. 1750–2000*.

Vincent DiGirolamo received his doctorate in history at Princeton University. He now teaches at Baruch College, City University of New York. His book *Crying the News: A Social History of the American Newsboy* is forthcoming from Oxford University Press. He is editing *Voice of the Newsboy*, the 1860 autobiography of a New York City street peddler, and serving as principal historical consultant for the Center for New Media and American Social History Project's online curriculum, "Young America: Experiences of Youth in U.S. History." He created the online teaching module "The Big Strike: Labor Unrest in the Great Depression" for the Investigating U.S. History Project and contributed an essay on commercial amusements for the exhibition catalogue to Life's Pleasures: The Ashcan Artists' Brush with Leisure, 1895–1925.

Andrew A. Gentes received his doctorate at Brown University and is a lecturer in Russian and European history in the School of History, Philosophy, Religion and Classics at the University of Queensland. He has published on tsarist Siberian exile and penal labor and is currently researching and writing on the Sakhalin penal colony.

Robert Gordon is a professor of anthropology at the University of Vermont and is affiliated with Free State University. Among his books are *Mines, Migrants and Masters, Law and Order in the New Guinea Highlands, The Bushman Myth,* and *Picturing Bushmen,* as well as several edited volumes. He is currently working on a number of projects, including a film on civil courage during the Second World War, an anthropological history of dogs and colonialism in Africa, and a book entitled *Going Abroad: An Anthropological Primer to Getting Lost.*

Frank Tobias (Toby) Higbie is an associate professor of history at the University of California, Los Angeles. He is the author *of Indispensable Outcasts: Hobo Workers and Community in the American Mid-*

west, 1880–1930, which won the Philip Taft Labor History Book Award from the Cornell University School of Labor and Industrial Relations and the Allan Sharlin Book Prize from the Social Science History Association. From 2005 to 2007 he taught courses for apprentices and labor union leaders in the University of Illinois Labor Education Program. From 2000 to 2005 he was the director of the Newberry Library's Center for Family and Community History, where he was curator, with Peter Alter, of the exhibition *Outspoken: Chicago's Free Speech Tradition*. Higbie received his Ph.D. in history from the University of Illinois, Urbana-Champaign in 2000.

Thomas H. Holloway is the director of the Hemispheric Institute on the Americas and a professor of Latin American history at the University of California, Davis. From 1974 to 2000, he was a faculty member at Cornell University. He earned his doctorate in Latin American history at the University of Wisconsin–Madison. His publications include *Policing Rio de Janeiro: Repression and Resistance in a Nineteenth-Century City* and *Immigrants on the Land: Coffee and Society in São Paulo, 1886–1934*. He is currently researching the case of an Afro-Brazilian newspaper editor notoriously murdered in Rio de Janeiro in 1883.

Abby Margolis is currently a research analyst at Ziba Design in Portland, Oregon. Prior to joining the company, she was a producer for Chicago Public Radio and a postdoctoral fellow at the Reischauer Institute of Japanese Studies at Harvard University, where she was working on the first ethnography of homelessness in Tokyo. She has taught at Colby College in Waterville, Maine, and at Lewis and Clark College in Portland, Oregon. She holds a Ph.D. in anthropology from the University of Pittsburgh.

Paul Ocobock is currently a Ph.D. student at Princeton University. He earned his bachelor's degree in history at the University of Michigan and an M.Phil in economic and social history at Oxford University. He has worked on vagrancy and juvenile delinquency in colonial Kenya and is currently working on his dissertation, a study of childhood and youth in colonial Africa.

Aminda M. Smith is an assistant professor in the history department at Michigan State University. She recently completed her Ph.D. in the East Asian studies department at Princeton University. Her thesis, researched in Beijing with the support of a Fulbright fellowship in 2003–4, examines Chinese Communist "thought reform" in the 1950s. In addition to social control in the PRC and the Communist Party's relationship to urban society, she has written on Chinese medical practice in the nineteenth-century United States.

Linda Woodbridge is Weiss Chair in the Humanities and a professor of English at Pennsylvania State University. Her books include *Vagrancy, Homelessness and English Renaissance Literature; The Scythe of Saturn: Shakespeare and Magical Thinking; Women and the English Renaissance;* and the coedited volumes *Women, Violence, and the English Renaissance; Money and the Age of Shakespeare;* and *True Rites and Maimed Rites: Ritual and Anti-Ritual in the Age of Shakespeare.*

Index

Page numbers with an *f* indicate figures; those with a *t* indicate tables.

Thompson, Fred, 260–61
Thornton, A. P., 346
timber industry, 252, 257, 259–60, 264
Tinker, Hugh, 154
Tocqueville, Alexis de, 296n29
Tokyo. *See* Ueno Park (Tokyo)
Tolstoi, Lev, 198
trade unions. *See* unions, trade
tramps, 19–21, 226, 228, 250–65; demographics of, 256–57; railroads and, 18, 209–10, 224, 229–41, 250–51, 254, 257–60; types of, 258. *See also* vagrancy
Trautschold, M., 237f
tuberculosis, 302, 315
Tuchthuis, 9
typographers, 226

Ueno Park (Tokyo), 27, 351–69
Uganda, 271–73, 276–80, 283, 290–91
unemployment: forced labor and, 21, 35–56, 167–69, 173, 188–204, 271–74, 280, 313–22; in Japan, 352; in Mexico, 15–16; in Papua New Guinea, 329; in Russia, 200–201; in United States, 19, 214, 250–65
UNICEF, 343
unions, trade, 251, 261; strikes by, 21, 226–27, 240, 253
United Kingdom. *See* England
United States: Civil War of, 222–24, 223f; colonial, 12–13, 15; forced migration to, 12–13, 36, 186; French-Indian War and, 15; G.I. Bill of, 25; homelessness in, 356; independence of, 79; linguistic issues in, 109; migrant workers in, 18–21, 251–65; Reconstruction Era in, 143; vagrancy laws of, 2, 18–19, 25–27, 224–25
vagrancy: categories of, 64, 174, 212, 216, 322n3; definitions of, 36, 46, 244n17, 253, 258; demographics of, 23, 27, 238, 256–57; historiography of, 252–56; indentured servants and, 140–55, 148t; literature about, 7, 64–73, 76, 80–82,

196–204; news peddlers and, 209–41; "sin" of, 10, 18, 53, 175–76; stereotypes of, 1–4, 6–12, 94–97, 163, 185, 200–201, 256–65, 270; women and, 20, 97, 191, 254–55, 295n25. *See also* beggars
vagrancy laws: African, 2, 14–16, 26, 270–93; apprenticeship and, 36, 47, 49; Argentinean, 143; Brazilian, 17, 143, 162–80; Chinese, 302–22; English, 6, 11–14, 22–23, 35–56, 143, 190, 271–74, 292; French, 23–24; Indian, 121–22, 127–28, 133–34; Mauritian, 142–54, 148t; Nigerian, 143, 271; Papua New Guinean, 17–18, 328–46; Russian, 184–204; United States, 2, 18–19, 25–27, 224–25. *See also* labor laws (England)
vengeance, dramas of, 69–71, 81–82
Verne, Jules, 248n76
villeinage, 40, 43–45, 63n104. *See also* serfdom
Virginia, 12–13, 20–21
Vives, J. L., 7
Voltaire, 10
Voluntarily Unemployed Persons Ordinance (Kenya), 284

Walwyn, William, 84n33
*wantok*s, 329–30, 340, 341
Webb, Beatrice, 11
Webb, Sidney, 11
Weber, Max, 163
Webster, John, 66, 69
Weisbrot, David, 331
welfare programs: Brazilian, 178–80; European, 9–12, 21–23, 45, 80; Indian, 117–23, 128–34; Japanese, 366, 367; Muslim, 5; Russian, 204; United States, 21, 25–26
White, George, 46
Wiener, Martin, 91
Willard, Josiah. *See* Flynt, Josiah
Williams, Raymond, 211
Williams, Whiting, 254
Winchester, Statute of, 40
Winstanley, Gerrard, 77–80, 82